Contents

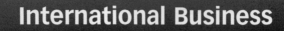

International Business

Frank McDonald and Fred Burton

With contributions from Peter Walton,
Peter Dowling and Helen Decieri

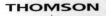

Australia • Canada • Mexico • Singapore • Spain • United Kingdom • United States

International Business

For more information, contact Thomson, Berkshire House, 168–173 High Holborn, London WC1V 7AA or visit us on the World Wide Web at:
http://www.thomsonlearning.co.uk

British Library Cataloguing-in-Publication Data
A catalogue record for this book is available from the British Library

ISBN 1-86152-452-8

First edition 2002

Typeset by LaserScript Limited, Mitcham, Surrey
Printed in Italy by G. Canale & C.

List of figures, tables, exhibits and cases

Preface

The aim of this book is to provide students with a through understanding of the factors that make international business activities different from domestic business transactions. Based on this understanding the book examines the strategic and operational aspects of international business activities. One of the main incentives to write this book was that the authors of the book became convinced that many students are misled by the concepts and arguments used by some of the advocates of the 'globalisation thesis'. In particular, we were concerned about the spread of the idea that national and regional differences that lead to segregated markets are rapidly disappearing leading to the creation of integrated international markets. In these circumstances, managing cultural differences is considered is the major difference between conducting domestic and international transactions. Uncritical acceptance of this view leads to simplistic assessments of international business problems and issues because it downplays the importance of the many legal, political, economic and institutional factors that make the international business environment a complex and rapidly changing system. Thus, in this book we have unpacked the various factors that make up the international business environment. These factors and the main drivers of change to the international business environment are analysed and applied to the experiences of firms to provide a good understanding of the complexities of undertaking international business activities. The authors discovered from their experiences of teaching both in the UK and overseas that many students tend to underplay the dynamic and evolutionary nature of the international business environment because most of the textbooks used static and out dated concepts and frameworks to analyse the international business environment. These deficiencies led the authors of this book to focus on patterns of development and change in the international business environment and the subsequent impact of these changes for international business strategies and operations.

The teaching experience of the authors convinced them that many of the simplistic assessments that students produced stemmed from poor understanding of economic and other types of analysis. However, the authors are aware that many students find analytical concepts difficult and they often seem to the students to have little relevance to the problems and issues that are examined in international business. Consequently, many students rely on basic forms of analysis or sometimes use no analytical frameworks to assess international business activities. This approach normally fails to capture the main forces that drive international business activities and thereby leads to a poor understanding of important problems and issues in international business. In this book, the authors have provided relevant forms of analysis and have taken care to explain them clearly and to apply them to appropriate real world examples. The main analytical frameworks are separated from the general text in exhibits to enable students to quickly understand the techniques and methods used to analyse international business problems and issues. The analytical frameworks in the exhibits are illustrated and expanded upon in the problems and issues raised in the text. Case studies are also used to highlight the relevance of the analysis by providing real world examples of the issues that are being discussed.

Care was taken to provide case studies from a wide range of industries and sectors embracing both large and small firms. The cases include large multinational companies such as, AOL Time Warner, Microsoft and Siemens; and small companies involved in clusters and industrial districts. The case studies are not focussed exclusively on large US companies but include European companies with a few examples from Asia, for example a case study on Korean chaebol and a study on the HRM implications for a Swedish company entering Asian markets. The studies include material on service industries such as media companies – Bertelsmann, News International and Vivendi Universal and financial and business services companies, for example, Accenture, KPMG, PricewaterhouseCoopers and Long-Term Capital Management. The cases consider major European issues, for example, the impact of the euro on UK and Irish companies and the development of European bourses. The cases studies also investigate important US-European issues, for example, DaimlerChrysler merger and the decision by the European Union to prohibit the proposed merger between General Electric and Honeywell. Issues connected to the development of e-business are illustrated with cases on Dell Computers, Napster and General Electric's Global eXchange Services.

Developments in economics and geography theory have significant implications for the study of international business. The combining of new theories of international economics (focussing on economies of scale and imperfect competition) with new economic geography (stressing the importance of physical and human geography factors for business activities) has provided important insights into issues connected to the location of economic activity. These developments have significant implications for theories of trade and investment and provide insights into the development of clusters (geographical concentrations of firms). Many books on international business discuss the importance of clusters such as Silicon Valley and Route 128 but provide little analysis of the process that generates these internationally competitive clusters. This book brings these issues to the fore and provides material on how geographical factors and economies of scale affects location decisions, trade and investment flows and the strategy of multinational enterprises towards their subsidiaries. The book also stresses that these factors can be important for the international competitiveness of small and medium sized enterprises and examines the importance of geographical concentrations of firms for international competitiveness.

The authors also noticed that students of international business were often not exposed to the implications of modern developments in the areas of institutional and organisational theory. Consequently, although research exists on the importance for international business activities of institutional developments such as privatisation, marketisation and reform of economic, political and legal frameworks, few textbooks devote much space to these issues. Moreover, most of the material that exists in textbooks has little or no theoretical underpinning. This book places these issues as a main area of study and uses modern theories such as new institutional economics to analyse their impact on international business activities. Many of the textbooks in international business also neglect developments in organisational theory such as the central role of networks in business transactions and the importance of knowledge, relationship assets and managerial competencies for successful business operations. This book has put these concepts at the heart of the analysis that is used and in the problems and issues that are considered.

The emergence of e-business systems has attracted considerable attention in many areas of business and management including international business. Many textbooks have included material and chapters on the impact of e-business systems for international business. However, few have provided a theoretical analysis of the issues involved or a review of the empirical evidence on the impact of e-business systems. This book devotes a chapter that investigates the implications for international business activities of e-business systems. This chapter assesses the impact of e-business systems for international business activities and likely future developments. This is done by using theoretical frameworks and reviews of the empirical evidence.

The prominence in this book on analytical study combined with extensive application to real world problems of managing international business activities provides a good grounding for undergraduate students of international business. It also will be useful for undergraduate students of accounting, economics, finance, human resource management and marketing who require knowledge of international business. Furthermore, this book provides an excellent primer for students undertaking Master programmes in international business as it supplies an introduction to the background to the research literature in the field. The application to real world problems with extensive discussion of the problems and issues associated with conducting international business makes this book useful for Master students (including MBA) that need to have an understanding of international business as a background to study of management and business issues. The web site that accompanies this book provides guidance on further reading (including the research literature for students on Master programmes), teaching materials (including data on trade and investment flows, material that can be used in seminars and material that can be used in PowerPoint presentations). The authors are confident that this book together with the web site will provide a comprehensive package that will be capable of supporting courses in international business for a wide range of students. This book is suitable for semester teaching as the first eight chapters provide the basis for a one-semester course on the international business environment and chapters nine to fourteen provide the basis for a second semester course on international business management. It is also possible to construct courses that emphasis particular aspects of international business by using a core set of chapters (chapter 1 to 4, 7, 9 and 10) and for example, a focus on the financial aspects of international business using chapters 5, 8 and 12 or a focus on international marketing using the core chapters and chapters 6, 8, 11 and 14.

The structure and plan of the book is provided in chapter 1.

The authors understanding of many of the key issues in international business have been greatly enhanced by conversations with and reading the work of Peter Buckley, John Dunning, Neil Hood, James Taggart and Stephen Young.

We are grateful to our students on whom we piloted most of the content in the chapters in our teaching programmes. The comments and advice from our students on the material was invaluable and helped us to amend and rework the material to make it more comprehensible.

The main authors are grateful to Peter Dowling, Helen Decieri and Peter Walton for their valuable contribution to the book. This book would have never appeared without the constant advice, encouragement not to mention pressure that the authors received from Jennifer Pegg. The help of Sarah McDonald in getting the manuscript in shape and in preparing the index was essential.

Frank McDonald and Fred Burton, March 2002

Acknowledgements

We are grateful to our students on whom we piloted most of the content in the chapters in our teaching programmes. The comments and advice from our students on the material was invaluable and helped us to amend and rework the material to make it more comprehensible.

The main authors are grateful to Peter Dowling, Helen Decieri and Peter Walton for their valuable contributions to the book.

Authors and contributors

Fred Burton researches and lectures in international business at Manchester School of Management at UMIST.

Helen Decieri researches and lectures in international human resource management in Monash University.

Peter Dowling researches and lectures in international human resource management at the University of Tasmania.

Frank McDonald researches and lectures in international business at Manchester Metropolitan University Business School.

Peter Walton researches and lectures in international accounting and financial issues at the Groupe ESSEC in Cergy-Pontoise in France.

1 Introduction

The growth of international trade in goods and services, the large increase in capital flows and the dominance of much of world economic activity by very large multinational companies has focused attention on the so-called process of globalisation. Interest in globalisation is stimulated by a number of developments that appear to be squeezing the world into one large interconnected economic system. Eight major developments are frequently cited as leading to the emergence of a global economic system that is unprecedented in world history (Giddens, 1999; Ohmae, 1990, 1995):

- Trade liberalisation and the removal of capital controls has led to very large increases in trade and capital flows that has generated a process that enables quick and powerful transmission of technological and economic developments across the world.
- The collapse of communism as an economic system and the acceptance of the capitalist economic system by most countries seems to have opened up the world to the ever-expanding operations of market-based international business activities.
- The embrace of market-based reforms by many developing countries, often due to pressure from agencies such as the International Monetary Fund and the World Bank, has encouraged the integration of these economies into the world economy.
- New major trading nations have emerged in China, South-East Asia and in Latin America leading to a new term – emergent economies – to describe countries that are thought to be developing into full blown advanced industrial economies and that are already major players in many international markets.
- Regional integration blocs, most notably the European Union, have made considerable progress in removing the barriers to trade between their members and in creating a single economic space in which the difference between trade in domestic economies and with other members of the bloc are rapidly diminishing.
- Technological developments such as the IT revolution have led to the emergence of large multinational companies, such as Microsoft, that dominate world markets in crucial products.
- New systems of conducting business by using the Internet also hold the prospect of dramatically expanding the potential for international

business transactions by providing a low-cost means of searching for and buying products across national frontiers.

- Developments in government policies in areas such as denationalisation of state-owned industries and the encouragement of market provision of many goods and services that used to be supplied by government agencies has further encouraged the growth of market-based activities and many of these are linked to international business activities.

These developments led to increased interest in the study of international business to increase our understanding of the implications for business of this 'brave new world'. Much of the study of international business assumes that we are in a period of unprecedented internationalisation and that the world has generally become a less difficult place in which to conduct international business. Therefore, many of the books on international business concentrate on strategic planning issues and management techniques that enable firms to develop international business activities in response to the challenges and opportunities arising from a world with increasingly open markets and where technological developments increase the means to capture and develop international markets. Often little attention is paid to political, economic and social factors (other than cultural differences) that affect international business operations. The focus is on strategic and operational policies to create and maintain or develop international competitiveness and on means to manage cross-cultural problems that are normally considered the major obstacle to international business. Indeed, in some quarters the study of international business is regarded as just one of the components in the larger project of understanding how companies can attain and maintain competitiveness in the various areas of business such as organisational design and behaviour, HRM, marketing and operations management. This book is based on the view that differences in political, economic and social conditions in the various parts of the world and the multifaceted interaction between these factors requires a good understanding of the complexity that arises in conducting international business activities. Another reason for a book such as this one is that many of the developments that are said to have led to the globalisation phenomenon are overstated and that these developments are simply another phase in the globalisation process. Therefore, it is necessary to avoid application of simplistic views of the globalisation process to the various areas that are studied by management and business.

The period between 1870 until 1914 was perhaps a time with more pronounced internationalisation of business activities than today. The introduction of new technologies such as electrical goods, the developments of telegraph and later telephone systems (the Internet of its day) and of new production systems based on mass production (perfected into Fordism) led to changes to economic and social life that were perhaps as profound or more profound that those happening today.

Multinational companies also emerged in this period. Companies such as Standard Oil were just as powerful in the heyday of the prior phase of globalisation as Microsoft is today. Furthermore, trade flows and capital flows were less encumbered by restrictions and controls than they are today. A stable international monetary system (the Gold Standard) permitted large-scale capital movements and provided a fixed exchange rate system that eliminated risk in international financial flows.

International labour mobility, particularly to the USA, was considerably higher than it is today. The capitalist economic system held sway over most of the world as the USA and the European powers all had capitalist systems. The control that European countries held over their colonies and dominions meant that most of the countries of the world were open to international trade and capital flows, albeit, for the colonies, in conditions where they had little power or influence on the development of these flows. One country, the USA, is the major economic power in the current phase of globalisation and in the earlier phase of globalisation there was also one country that was the major economic power – Britain. Another similarity between these periods was that just as the economic power of the USA has been weakened by the rise of new economic powers such as Japan and the European Union, the economic power of Britain was reduced by the rise of economies such as Germany and the USA. Nevertheless, there were considerable differences in political, economic and social conditions in this earlier phase of globalisation than in the current phase (Eichengreen, 1998).

This means that it is important to have a good understanding of the contemporary nature of these conditions to enable us accurately to assess the complex environments in which international business activities take place. Consequently, many of the chapters in this book (Chapters 2 to 8) focus on the evolution of political, economic and social conditions and their impact on international business activities.

The global economic system that developed from the 1870s collapsed with the outbreak of World War I. This led, in the inter-war years, to a period of growing protectionism and instability in the international monetary system. Much of the process of trade and capital liberalisation since World War II has been seeking to restore the world to the level of free movement of goods, services and capital that prevailed before World War I. The explosion in the number of independent countries in the post-World War II period also led to the growth of more controls and barriers to trade and capital flows, many of which still exist. Furthermore, international labour mobility is more restricted today than it was in the 1880s. In the post-World War II period developed countries also created new ways to protect their domestic markets by use of non-tariff barriers (NTBs) such as public health and safety rules and controls to protect the environment. In some industries such as agriculture and parts of the manufacturing sector, tariffs and quotas continue to prevent global integration of markets. In the area of services a multitude of NTBs continue to fragment markets even in the European Union which has supposedly established an area of free movement of services (European Commission, 2001).

It is, therefore, incorrect to argue that nothing like the present phenomenon of globalisation has ever been experienced before or to maintain that most of the barriers to the free movement of goods, services and capital have been removed. Indeed, the continuing presence of significant barriers to trade and of political, economic and social differences across the world has led to much of international business being concentrated in particular industries and among a few major countries. The Triad of the USA, the EU and Japan, and countries strongly linked to these three, accounts for the vast bulk of international business activities. These facts have led some to call into question the use of the term globalisation, because clearly the whole world and all sections of business activity are not woven together into one economic system (Rugman, 2000). It is also important to remember that many of the issues that confront firms engaged in international business activities are not new in terms of the basic nature of the problems that they face. In the past, firms struggled to come to terms with the challenges and opportunities presented by the prior phases of the globalisation process and a multitude of 'solutions' arose in line with the conditions faced in different industries and countries and as political, economic and social conditions changed. This book, therefore, seeks to avoid simplistic 'one size fits all' solutions to the challenges and opportunities of inter-nationalisation, but rather explores the many differences as well as similarities in the responses by firms to the internationalisation process.

Changes in approaches to the study of internationalisation are also a strong feature in this book. The orthodox approach to the study of international business was centred on four main areas:

1 The reasons why firms engage in international business activities, which was developed into study of direct foreign investment and other modes of entry into foreign markets by large multinational companies.
2 The stages by which firms developed internationalisation that focuses on a linear evolution of international business activities that progressed from simple to more complex international activities as firms learned how to operate in foreign environments.
3 The problems of managing across cultures that centres on how to cope with different cultural values.
4 Issues connected to organisational design and behaviour to create and sustain competitive advantage with an emphasis on organisational theories often connected to economic imperatives.

This orthodox approach to the study of international business is often reflected in textbooks with some concentrating on the first two areas with a strong focus on economic factors and others centred on the last two areas with an emphasis on social factors. Of course, most books cover all four areas but the focus of attention is often on either the first two or the last two of these main areas of interest. This book seeks to cover all four of these important areas and to integrate them to provide a sound understanding of the complex mix of factors that affect international business activities.

New developments in the study of international business also play an important role in this book. Hence, issues connected to new theories of trade based on economies of scale and the importance of historical, geographical and institutional factors for international business activities are prominently featured in this book. Thus, use is made of new theories such as new trade theory, new economic geography and the new institutional economics to examine international business activities. The importance of networks and relationship between firms, government agencies and individuals for international business activities is also stressed. The importance of information gathering and processing information into useful knowledge on the many and complex factors that influence international business activities is another strong feature of this book. Many international business textbooks focus almost exclusively on large multinational companies with very little attention to the important role of small and medium sized enterprises (SMEs) in international business activities. This book seeks to address some of the key issues for SMEs arising from the process of internationalisation. The implications of new technological developments such as the growth of e-business systems are also a major feature of this book.

Plan of the book

The book consists of 14 chapters with a focus on the many political, economic, geographical and social factors that affect international business activities in Chapters 2 to 8. Chapters 9 to 13 concentrate on strategic and operational aspects of international business that are informed by the assessments of the mainly environmental factors discussed in Chapters 2 to 8. The final chapter considers how developments in e-business systems have and may affect international business activities. All the chapters begin with a set of learning objectives and a list of key terms. Use is made of case studies, exhibits, figures and tables to explore further or to illustrate major issues. Frequent use is made of figures that provide summaries of the major factors involved with particular theories or concepts in international business. This helps students to grasp the main factors and the interconnections between them, which influences international business activities. All the chapters include a summary, review questions and a bibliography. In chapters where useful material to further illustrate or explain issues is available on websites the main sites are listed at the end of the chapter.

The chapters contain few tables of statistics because the data soon become out of date. However, the website that accompanies this book contains tables of data (that are frequently updated), links to websites that contain detailed information on statistics and material on companies, institutions and agencies that are involved with international business activities (www.thomsonlearning.co.uk). The website also includes sources on reports, papers and other sources of information such as political,

economic and social conditions in countries and regional integration
blocs that are valuable to the student of international business. Guidance
on further reading and on where to find research papers on the key issues
in international business are also provided in the accompanying website.
The material provided in the website means that this book is suitable for
use by both undergraduates and postgraduate students of international
business. Students that use the follow-up material in the website will be
able to gather information on the contemporary state of research in the
main areas of international business studies and to access sources that will
further develop knowledge on developments in the subject area.
However, the book together with the website provides material that is
accessible to undergraduates who have a good understanding of the
basics of business studies. Clearly, any textbook cannot cover in depth all
the issues that are important for the study of international business.
Matters connected to the part played by individual entrepreneurs and
companies in shaping international business are not extensively explored
in this book. However, excellent profiles of many of these entrepreneurs
and companies are provided in Tung (1999). This book also provides
summaries of all the major topics in international business. The authors
of this book believe that the combination of this book, the accompanying
website and access to a handbook on international business such as the
one edited by Tung provides the means to develop knowledge of
international business studies up to postgraduate level.

Chapter 2 sets the scene on the debate about the nature of globalisation
and clearly outlines the complexity of the concept of globalisation in
contrast to the often simplistic approach taken by some politicians,
business people and management gurus. This chapter provides the
background for the rest of the book by highlighting the many and various
ways that the growth of international business impacts on and is affected by
political, economic and social differences in countries.

Chapter 3 explores theories of international trade from the early work
in this area by Adam Smith and David Ricardo, that are used to explain
inter-industry trade, to the modern theories involving economies of scale
and overlapping demand patterns, that seek to explain intra-industry
trade. The influence of practical issues on international trade, such as,
transport costs, natural resources and the size of markets are also
considered. The chapter also examines the important topic of countertrade, which plays an important part in many areas of international trade.

Chapter 4 investigates the reasons for and effects of the various
instruments that are used to protect domestic markets from foreign
competition. The role of the major institutions in seeking to remove trade
barriers including non-tariff barriers is explored. The extension of the
move towards free trade in services and investments is also considered
and issues connected to protection of intellectual property and rules for
trade-related investments are discussed.

Chapter 5 examines the history of the evolution of the international
monetary system to highlight the important role that this system plays in

the development of international business. The origins of the present institutional system are traced and the various crises that have led to changes in exchange rate regimes are outlined. This provides the background for a discussion of the effects of fixed versus floating exchange rate regimes on international business activities. The complex nature of the variety of exchange rate regimes that face firms engaged in international business is outlined. A review of the implications of European Monetary Union is also provided. This chapter also provides useful background knowledge for assessment of the strategic and operational aspect of international accounting and finance systems that are discussed in Chapter 12.

Chapter 6 considers the influence of geographical factors on international business. The relative neglect of these factors in international business studies is discussed and the need to incorporate geographical factors into the study of international business is highlighted. The new economic geography is outlined and used to show why geographical concentrations are often important sources of international competitiveness. An application of this to the strategic development of subsidiaries is used which highlights the ways that trade liberalisation can lead to regional specialising via the direct foreign investment strategies of multinational companies. The chapter examines the use of geographical concentrations to help SMEs to attain international competitiveness by forming and developing industrial districts. Famous examples of geographical concentrations such as Silicon Valley and Route 128 are also examined.

Cultural and institutional issues are discussed in Chapter 7. The chapter examines the many and various factors that determine cultural values and the ways that they influence norms of behaviour and thereby business operations. The implications for cross-cultural management and the need for organisational systems that can cope with cultural diversity is assessed by consideration of the Hofstede approach to defining and measuring cultural values. This approach is critiqued and the new institutional economics approach is considered as a method of assessing the institutional obstacles (which includes cultural factors) to effective international business activities.

The importance of regional integration blocs for international business is explored in Chapter 8. In this chapter, the reasons for regional integration and the effects on international trade are considered. The main regional integration blocs are discussed and a taxonomy of regional integration objectives from free trade area to economic and political union is provided. The focus is on the largest and most important of these blocs – the EU. The implications of regional integration for multilateral trade liberalisation and the development of global business operations are examined. The development of single economic spaces (where all barriers to trade in goods, services, capital and labour is achieved) is considered in the light of the progress of the EU towards this objective. The implications of such developments for international business activities are assessed.

Chapter 9 considers the various modes of entry that can be used to operate in foreign markets. The chapter begins with a comprehensive examination of the major aspects of exporting and then moves on to consider other modes of entry. This includes assessments of the motives and outcomes of using DFI, strategic alliances and joint ventures, licensing and franchising to entry markets. The relative merits of the various modes of entry are discussed and the conditions in which one entry mode is preferable to the others are examined.

Chapter 10 considers the issues that are involved in strategic planning for international business. This chapter reveals the complex mix of political economic, cultural, technological and competitive factors that are involved in strategic planning. The rational and methodical approach to strategic planning is outlined. This overview clearly reveals the wide range of factors that must be considered when using such an approach to international strategy. This is contrasted with other views of the strategy process that focus on entrepreneurial behaviour and good fortune as the reasons for successful strategies. The concept of strategic planning as being primarily a learning process is also discussed. This leads into discussion of organisational strategy and the strategic options for the relationships between headquarters and subsidiaries. The final section in this chapter considers international strategic issues for SMEs.

International marketing issues are considered in Chapter 11 (although many of the issues connected to exporting and other means of entering markets are discussed in Chapter 9). The chapter considers the main issues in international strategic marketing – the internationalisation process and international marketing, the use of networks in international marketing and the debate on segmentation versus standardisation. The major types and means of assessing the environments in which international marketing takes place are examined to illustrate the importance of good assessment systems. Some of the practical issues in product, pricing, promotion and place are considered in the light of the strategic plans of firms.

Chapter 12 investigates the accounting and financial aspects of international business. The chapter investigates the relationship between the raising of finance in capital markets and the accounting and financial systems necessary to report to the holders of the equity and debt instruments. The reporting and control problems presented by international business activities are examined as are issues connected to differences in accounting and taxation systems. The practical problems associated with exchange rate risk are considered. Problems raised by differences in auditing and accounting systems are assessed and the moves to harmonise these systems are outlined. The relationship between corporate governance and international auditing, accounting and financial systems are also considered in this chapter.

International human resource issues are examined in Chapter 13. Three major issues are tackled in this chapter – the major difference between domestic and international HRM, assessment of the main approaches to international HRM and the link between the strategic plans of multinational companies and HRM. The most important issues that emerge from this analysis are the problems that are raised by cultural and institutional differences across the various operations of multi-national companies.

The final chapter explores the development of e-business systems in international business. An outline of the various types of e-business systems that are, or can be, used for international business activities is provided and the main benefits of these systems are assessed. The limited empirical evidence on the effects of the use of e-business systems is examined. This evidence suggests that the use of e-business systems has not yet had the radical effect on international business that has been predicted by IT gurus. The chapter examines the main obstacles to the use of e-business systems for international business purposes and finds that, in general, e-business systems do not overcome many of the standard problems of internationalisation. However, the impact of e-business systems is likely to be profound but will mainly benefit large multinational companies or those firms that become large multinationals because of clever utilisation of e-business systems.

Bibliography

Eichengreen, B. (1998) *Globalizing Capital: A History of the International Monetary System,* Princeton, NJ, Princeton University Press.

European Commission (2001) *The Regulation of European Securities Markets: The Lamfalussy Report,* Brussels, European Commission.

Giddens, A. (1999) *Runaway World: How Globalization is Reshaping our Lives,* New York, Routledge.

Ohmae, K. (1995) *The End of the Nation State: The Rise of Regional Economies.* New York, Harper Business.

Ohmae, K. (1990) *The Borderless World,* New York, Harper Business.

Rugman, A. (2000) *The End of Globalisation.* London, Random House Business.

Tung, R. (1999) *The Handbook of International Business,* London, Thomson Learning.

2

Globalisation

Learning objectives

By the end of this chapter, you should be able to:

- discuss the meaning of globalisation and where it can lead
- have an understanding of the processes of globalisation
- appreciate the different perspectives of globalisation: economic, cultural, geographical and political
- recognise the conflict between globalisation and the nation-state
- discuss the interplay between global and local forces
- understand the convergence versus divergence debate
- assess the historical evidence on convergence

Key terms

- globalisation of markets • the drivers of globalisation • the role of the nation-state • globalisation versus national sovereignty • capitalism versus capitalism • global versus local forces • kinds of convergence • convergence versus divergence

Introduction

This chapter looks at the various processes referred to as 'globalisation' in the international political economy and the national business environment and the manner in which these processes are presumed, or expected, to influence the shape of the world economy and national systems in the new millennium. Globalisation is the term used to describe the trends in the world economy that are pulling previously distinct national economies closer together. The notion of globalisation as a catalyst for radical economic, political and social change is a recurring theme in current academic and business literature. However, the lack of general agreement on the strength and likely impact of globalisation is shown in the following scenarios:

1 Globalisation is a totally new phenomenon that will cause organisations, consumers and nation-states to experience radical changes, as typified by the concept of the 'global village'.

2 Globalisation is nothing new, just a current fad indulged in by business leaders and management gurus. This scenario observes little that is new in the framework of the international economy.

3 Countervailing forces will offset any tendencies toward globalisation.

Impact of globalisation

Globalisation as a new phenomenon

The first scenario treats globalisation as a new orthodoxy. Here, its impetus is so overwhelming that traditional patterns of capitalist accumulation and national approaches to political and economic governance cannot prevail but must succumb to 'new realities' and the logic of market forces (Drucker, 1990). Advocates of this scenario, popular with business leaders, management gurus and free market politicians, present a vision of a globalised economy in which increasingly higher international trade flows and the production and marketing activities of multinational firms create tight-knit international economic relationships (Ohmae, 1995). In this vision, global companies continually abandon their original home bases and focus on the 'strategic space' of the global economy. National and regionally rooted multinational companies (MNCs) become disembodied from their origins and transform themselves into footloose multinational companies, uncommitted to any particular nation-state, roaming the globe to achieve the highest returns on their economic activities (Hirst and Thompson, 1996). These developments within the 'real' sectors of the economy are accompanied by corresponding trends in financial sectors, where the ever-increasing volume of highly mobile capital traded on international financial markets take on the characteristic of 'global money' beyond the control of national regulations. The overall long-term consequence of this vision of the 'globalists' is a general shift of power from a system of nationally centred regulatory institutions to an international and deregulated system of *laissez-faire* capitalism encouraging free market power (Boyer, 1996).

Exhibit 2.1 No more government?

In a globalised world there will be a single society and culture occupying the planet. This society and culture will probably not be harmoniously integrated although it might conceivably be. Rather it will probably tend towards high levels of differentiation, multicentricity and chaos. There will be no central organising government and no set of cultural preferences and prescriptions. Insofar as culture is unified it will be extremely abstract, expressing tolerance for diversity and individual choice. Importantly, territoriality will disappear as an organising principle for social and cultural life; it will be a society without borders and spatial boundaries. In a globalised world we will be unable to predict social practices and preferences on the basis of geographical location. Equally, we can expect relationships between people in disparate locations to be formed as easily as relationships between people in proximate ones.

Waters, M. (1995) *Globalisation*, London and New York, Routledge, p. 3

Globalisation as a fad

Advocates of the second scenario, critical of the extreme outlook portrayed in the first scenario and its image of a global village that has already arrived, regard the concept of globalisation as a bandwagon, driven by pressure groups with an interest in promoting new business concepts and prescriptions to enhance competitiveness. The claims of globalisation enthusiasts, it is argued, are often based on simplistic concepts, yet to be substantiated, in which states and firms compete on a deregulated and level global playing field. The proponents of this 'nothing has changed' scenario are led by supporters of Keynesian-style macroeconomic policies and anti-cyclical measures to manage and control national economies. Opponents of the view that globalisation is neither new nor overwhelming claim that this ignores the opening up and deregulation of markets, particularly financial markets – significant indicators of closer economic integration and other major changes in the world economy (Strange, 1997).

A middle-of-the-road scenario

The third scenario is the least satisfying yet perhaps the most appropriate and realistic. This view, aligned against the others, does not accept globalisation as a non-event or, at the other extreme, as a force revolutionising existing policies and practices and leading to a homogenous world society (Palan et al., 1996). This scenario, nevertheless, regards globalisation as a major new phenomenon influencing, and influenced by, changes in the manufacturing and financial sectors and having a bearing on national competitiveness and international economic governance (Strange, 1997). In this scenario, however, globalisation is less dramatic and does not lead to a dominance of the global economy by capitalist market forces, symbolised by *laissez-faire* international markets and multinational companies able to supersede and oust governments and national regulations. Even so, the scenario recognises the growing power of global capitalism, the effects of which differ according to context (Boyer and Drache, 1996). The scenario focuses on the relationship and interplay between 'global' and 'local' forces, such as international competitive pressures (global) and national governance (local), and how global forces are implemented and affect states, societies, geographical areas and industries in different ways.

Analyses of globalisation mostly rely on economic factors and regard globalisation as a market-led process. But since globalisation also affects political and cultural variables in society, it is a phenomenon demanding an interdisciplinary approach. The next section, which summarises the main interdisciplinary elements of the globalisation debate, will show that they share common themes.

Globalisation perspectives

Economic globalisation

The economic debate centres on the decline of national markets and the rise of global markets as the focal points for major players, principally the multinational corporations. This trend is associated with the effects of technological change in reducing temporal and psychic distance between national markets. In addition, in consequence of globalisation, it is generally assumed that the rules of competition are being redefined, to which firms and governments will have to learn how to adapt. The globalisation of finance, as an example, is associated with the ability of unregulated global capital markets to accumulate global economic power and escape the confines of national regulations and controls. The creation of new mechanisms to shift around savings and investment renders ineffective the policy tools used by governments and policy makers to pursue nationally focused macroeconomic policies (Boyer, 1996; Palan et al., 1996). Thus, financial markets are reducing and gradually weakening the nation-state. Further, in the wake of globalisation, the durability of nationally unique banking and regulative systems is called into question, as market forces can be expected to induce 'best practice' models and strategies, which nation-states and firms must strive to accommodate.

Economic globalisation also influences microeconomic phenomena because deregulation and technological developments serve to increase international competition – especially within the triad countries of Western Europe, North America, and Japan and South-East Asia – by creating national 'level playing fields' that offer the same opportunities to domestic and foreign firms alike. These new parameters and a greater homogeneity of consumer tastes and attitudes worldwide are influencing the decision-making processes of multinational firms, which have become committed to global marketing strategies and global manufacturing chains.

With the increasing integration of economic activities, national firms find themselves more exposed to competitive pressures from MNCs (Multinational Corporations) and firms from other countries. Western firms, in particular, experience severe cost pressures from competitors able to source low-wage countries. In consequence, state policies that raise

Exhibit 2.2 Globalisation or regionalisation?

Ohmae's model of a dominant triad – Western Europe, North America and South-East Asia – visualises how competitive, regulatory and market pressures impact on firms in dynamic high technology markets. The high accountability of the triad for international trade and foreign direct investment arose from supposedly changing environmental circumstances. The model was constructed to show how increasing tariff barriers, converging consumer tastes, and the need to achieve economies of scale and cope with ever-increasing fixed costs of investment in technology and research and development, led to the strategic promotion of standardised marketing programmes and a concentration of commercial activity within the triad. This would seem to point to a process of regionalisation rather than globalisation.

Ohmae, K. (1995) *The End of the Nation State: The Rise of Regional Economics*, London, Harper Collins.

firms' costs, such as minimum wages and employment standards, are often condemned by industry for the detrimental effects they have on employment and the ability to compete in the world economy, a view that is held in developed and developing nations alike.

Cultural globalisation

The globalisation debate extends to whether there is a global culture or, at least, a set of universal cultural variables, and how globalisation might overcome and displace embedded national cultures and traditions. Although the onset of a truly homogeneous global culture is fanciful, the intensification of cultural exchanges has, nevertheless, had the effect of challenging the invincibility of traditional, often previously isolated, cultures.

The impact, intensity and receptivity of global cultural flows can be expected to vary from region to region. One view is that cultural globalisation has both homogenising and differentiating effects. This is because features previously unique to a particular locality can become universally dispersed, thereby increasing the impact of a particular culture on a wider scale. A process of hybridisation can occur in which local or regional cultural styles and traditions become detached from their original context to be embraced by other traditions.

Geographical globalisation

Globalisation implies a compression of time and space as a result of rapid electronic exchanges of information and reduced travel times between locations. The consequence is that distance matters to a far lesser extent than hitherto. In addition, due to dramatic advances in the transmission of information, knowledge that was confined to certain geographical areas is now far easier to access and is universally available and, as a consequence, less place bound. Issues within the globalisation debate centre on the potential such a compression of space and time might have on the geographical configuration of the world economy.

A particularly important issue concerns the interplay between space and place, in the sense of cities and regions maintaining or losing significance. Advocates of a neo-liberal persuasion claim the 'end of

Exhibit 2.3 Musical trends

Since the 1950s and the emergence of rock'n'roll as a chartbreaking and lucrative musical force, popular music has been dominated to a large extent by musical trends originating in the USA and Britain. The development of popular music occurs in a series of waves. As examples, hard rock and progressive rock in the early 1970s, punk rock in the late 1970s, rap and heavy metal in the 1980s and Britpop, indie and dance music in the 1990s, all achieved a global reach.

Despite this, local traditional music, unaffected by global trends, has always played an important part in the musical mix of countries. In addition, musical styles have emerged as a mix not only of different waves but also as a mix of global and traditional local music, such as Angora (Latin/heavy metal) and Santana (Latin/pop/rock) and the Japanese heavy metal bands in the 1980s. These styles, while adopting global heavy metal attitudes, attempted to appeal especially to their local audiences. The ultimate eclectic musical style is 'world music' – a hybrid of diverse musical styles, such as African tribal music, Anglo-Saxon pop and Latin rhythm.

geography' (that is, location and place no longer matter) due to recent developments in technology and the ease with which 'footloose' global capital can cross borders. Others, conversely, refer to the importance of the attributes of place in generating the potential for achieving competitive advantages (Porter, 1990; Sassen, 1995). For example, in international finance (banking and securities), arguably the most globalised of industries, there exists a global division and concentration of labour in three global cities, London, New York and Tokyo, and several smaller ones, Chicago, Paris, Hong Kong, Singapore and Frankfurt (Sassen, 1991). This global division is based on the respective strengths, competencies and contribution of these cities to international financial services.

Despite the continuing importance of place and location, there remains a danger that they will succumb to homogenising pressures as a direct result of their efforts to compete for footloose economic resources to secure their place within the world order (Peck and Tickell, 1994: 280–1). Homogeneity can occur because in 'place-marketing' competition, places compete to offer the same kind of services and facilities, such as training and investment grants and a high-quality infrastructure. This uniformity of 'local' strategies, in turn, reopens the debate concerning the significance of place and whether globalisation will bring about an end to geographical and territorial distinctiveness.

Political globalisation

The relationship between the power of markets and the responsibilities of the state has undergone fundamental changes since the end of World War II. The period after the war, the so-called 'golden age of capitalism', was characterised by national demand management and counter-cyclical policies and international cooperation to control economies. The 1970s witnessed the renaissance of a belief in the power of the price mechanism and market forces to allocate resources in an efficient manner and proposals to restrict the influence of governments on market behaviour. The contemporary dominant ideology, linked to the globalisation process, emphasises wealth creation via competitive processes in the private sector, the endorsement of supply-side management and the gradual retreat of the state as an active manager of the economy. Globalisation, however, is not seen to be a deterministic process inherent in the market economy, but a process that is conditioned by market players, particularly MNCs and financial institutions participating in the global economy and having a vested interest in the way it functions. Despite the ability of these players to defend their positions and the trends toward an ever more integrated world economy, questions remain about the durability and irreversibility of globalisation and the direction of the interplay between markets and nation-states.

Political globalisation focuses on the changing role and importance of the nation-state because, through globalisation, political activity and the processes and exercise of political power and authority are no longer primarily defined by national boundaries. The globalisation of politics encompasses old and new debates. An earlier debate was concerned with the power relationships between international markets and the state. A new debate centres on the supposed 'hollowing out of the state' and the consequent 'erosion of sovereignty' (Palan et al., 1996: 1), that is, whether globalisation has actually outflanked and withered away the authority of the nation-state. Globalisation clearly poses some threat to the autonomy of the nation-state and any loss of national authority is unlikely to be substituted by effective control and governance mechanisms on an international or supranational level, with the effect that capitalism will be left without a home, a development that is seen as potentially destabilising (Peck and Tickell, 1994).

Since the march towards globalisation strengthens the case for *laissez-faire* policies, it poses a serious threat to the 'managed economy' and undermines the economic and political foundations of regulation and control. If this is to be the impact of globalisation on the nation-state and national systems, it offers further support to free market propositions that a *laissez-faire* regime is superior to a Keynesian-style welfare state. Free market advocates claim that the state should concentrate on such matters as social stability and military safety but should hesitate to take measures to influence the structure and performance of the economy because they are likely to have harmful effects on the competitiveness of firms and markets. However, although the free market ideology, including deregulation and privatisation, has taken hold around the globe for its promises of economic growth and wealth creation, it is heavily disputed for its lack of mechanisms to deal with unemployment, financial crises, continuing inequalities, and under-investment in education and research (Boyer, 1996).

Globalisation and the nation-state

A number of globalisation themes have already been discerned: the international mobility of capital; cultural hegemony; the declining relevance of places and locations, following advances in information and communication technology; and the durability and viability of the nation-state. A further aspect concerns the interplay between 'local' (that is, national or regional) and global forces, and how national policy makers, corporate decision makers and individual consumers are affected by, and act on globalisation trends. At the national level, governments, industrial associations, individual firms, trade unions, consumers and employees are perceived by some merely to react passively to over-whelming global forces of centralisation and homogenisation over which they are unable to exert much influence. An alternative view is that there is a global–local nexus, an interplay, in which forces on both sides influence and determine each other's actions. But which of the two forces, global or local, is the more dominant and influential? Does the global–local nexus lead to the convergence or divergence of national economic, social and political systems?

Globalisation embraces regimes that encourage unfettered competition and competitiveness. This forces firms and nation-states to conform to globalisation by abandoning deeply rooted cultural traditions, historical homegrown structures and distinctive social infrastructures. Generally, when two forces interact, there are three basic outcomes: one or other of the two forces will dominate or there will be a mixing of the two. The outcome of the global–local nexus, in extreme cases, will be either a clear-cut convergence towards homogenisation, in which event a global logic will have prevailed, or a clear-cut divergence, allowing the localities to remain embedded inside their local identities. The first outcome lends support to the notion of an overwhelming and universally dominant process of globalisation. The second signifies a denial that global forces can overthrow national systems.

It is commonly assumed that the greater power lies with global forces, the dynamics of which will force national economies to converge on one universal economic system and individual firms to adhere to central strategies to enhance and maintain their competitiveness. Local traditions would give way to a predominantly Anglo-Saxon lifestyle, currently the dominant global business culture. Cities that are engaged in a competitive process to attract international capital would have to adopt common characteristics that would meet with the approval of markets and financiers. Nation-states, albeit hesitantly, will surrender parts of their national sovereignty to international organisations. In other words, globalisation implies 'that states and firms have no other choice but to modify their tactical decisions to accommodate such extraordinary environmental change' (Palan et al., 1996: 13).

This inevitability of convergence has been heavily criticised alongside the notion of 'the global village', 'the global factory' and 'the global marketplace'. But the view that there have been no significant trends toward globalisation is a difficult one to sustain. Although there remain a multiplicity of states with different historical developments and diverse cultural backgrounds, there can be no denial that certain groups of countries, as in Western Europe and South-East Asia, have adopted similar policies to tackle economic problems and revive their economies. In addition, the fact that most western countries have abandoned exchange controls and lifted capital restrictions, thereby giving up major independent policy controls, has led to global changes associated with increases in capital mobility. In the manufacturing sector, firms increasingly locate production facilities abroad to limit their dependence on home markets and to benefit from the international division of labour. Tendencies such as these suggest that some degree of global convergence is a reality, although the process of globalisation, rather than being a universal phenomenon, affects nation-states and industries in different ways, which needs to be taken into account.

This analysis of globalisation has pointed the discussion to two issues, namely the role of nation-states and the question of their convergence. Do national governments still have an important role to play or do markets determine economic and corporate governance? Would a decline in the importance of national governments lead to the convergence of nation-states? The answer to these questions may well depend on the ability of the major capitalist systems to respond to and shape the forces of globalisation.

Models of capitalism

The successes of the German and the Japanese economies in the post-World War II era sparked off an interest in the differences between capitalist societies and turned attention away from the American model of capitalist accumulation, often portrayed as a universal best practice model. Following the explicit recognition of national differences in capitalism, a wealth of literature emerged that compared and ranked different types of capitalism systems (for example, Albert, 1993; Dore, 1994; Streeck, 1992).

Differences between capitalist systems have been described in various ways. Keegan (1992) refers to three basic models of capitalism in the developed world. The first is American, democratic or liberal capitalism. The second is continental European capitalism, or social market or corporatist capitalism, which is typified by state intervention and cooperation between institutions and firms (social partners), as exemplified by Germany and Sweden. The third model is Japanese capitalism, sometimes referred to as industrial capitalism due to its focus on manufacturing excellence. Albert (1993) makes a distinction only between a neo-American and a German Rhineland model, while Crouch and Streek (1997) also refer to two basic models: the free market model, symbolised by USA and the UK, and the institutional model, typified by Germany, Sweden and Japan, in which there is a far higher level of government intervention and influence.

A further distinction between economies can be made according to the culture-bound role and management of finance and the dispensation and ownership of capital (Scott, 1997). In the USA and the UK, capital is mobilised by a wide range of financial institutions, but in Germany mainly by the banking sector. In Japan, industrial–commercial networks have bred a complex web of cross-shareholding; in Latin nations, small holding companies and family capital is predominant; in China, the central committee of the party remains in full control of the transfer of capital to the emerging market economy; in post-communist countries, a variety of schemes have been implemented to transfer state-owned enterprises to the private sector.

Boyer (1997: 89) argues that four major capitalist systems have emerged since the break up of the Bretton Woods fixed exchange rate system in the early 1970s. The first model, exemplified by the Anglo-Saxon nations, the USA and the UK in particular, refers to systems in which markets play a major role and market mechanisms take precedence over economic governance and the coordination of market activities. The Anglo-Saxon model is credited with market-led inventiveness and with being able to respond rapidly to environmental changes, but has been criticised for comparatively low levels of investment in education and public services and for promoting social inequality.

The second model is the Rhineland model, represented by Germany and Japan, Germany's functional equivalent. The main characteristic of this model is the network of institutions, such as professional and consumer unions, financial and other pressure groups and large firms, all acting as intermediaries between federal and regional governments. A feature of this system is a focus on education and training, resulting in a highly versatile and qualified workforce. These particular assets are widely regarded to be one of the preconditions for creating and sustaining competitive advantages in industrial sectors, based on quality, innovation, high standards, flexibility and service, rather than cost-based mass production.

The third model is the 'statist' model prevalent in France and Italy. Here, the state has a major role in labour and capital markets and is committed to industrial policy, that is, government intervention to influence the shape and direction of various economic sectors. This model has been credited with a commitment to social welfare and public health provision, but is considered unreliable in its ability to be innovative and technologically competitive. Statist countries have a large state involvement and demonstrate a willingness to protect infant industries and ones in difficulty rather than expose them to competitive market pressures. The fourth model is the social democratic model – a third way between communism and capitalism – associated particularly with Sweden. One of the prime achievements of this system has been the attainment of high levels of both social welfare support and employment. Once praised as a potential best practice model, it has undergone a crisis of confidence due to its inability to adapt to changes in the international economy. Currently, there are pressures on this model to converge to either a Rhineland or even an Anglo-Saxon model (Pontusson, 1997: 68–70).

The main representatives of these respective capitalist systems, however, demonstrate marked differences in their characteristics. In the case of the free market or Anglo-Saxon model, for example, wage negotiations are based on collective agreements in the USA and on fragmented agreements in the UK. The USA has a minimal welfare system compared to a comprehensive package of welfare services in the UK that includes the comprehensive National Health Service. Inside the institutional countries, there is intense competition between major networks in Japan, whereas competition is controlled in Germany by alliances between banks and industry.

A belief in the superiority of Japanese capitalism, specifically its lean management, in comparison to more traditional systems, has many supporters in the west, who argue that the success of Japanese capitalism will lead to attempts to emulate Japanese characteristics and ultimately to hybrid systems (e.g. Campbell, 1994; Dore, 1994). Albert (1993) favourably compares the German Rhineland model of capitalism with the dominant American (Anglo-Saxon) market-based model, although he wonders why the whole world – including the Germans – seems to be

Exhibit 2.4 Anglo-Saxon capitalism

The Anglo-Saxon model emphasises the role of entrepreneurial capital and focuses on the separation of short-term capital from the provision of long-term finance. The role of the City of London is especially important. The City has historically evolved from holding a strategic role in international trade to become the main location for European finance and banking. The organisation and structure of the City, and especially the key role played by the stock exchange, has traditionally been associated with an interest in international investments to gain mainly short-term returns to the detriment of the national economy. Surplus capital is absorbed by investment funds and invested in long-term equity finance and short-term investments – a transfer of funds from personal ownership into impersonal ownership, a particular feature of Anglo-Saxon economies (Scott, 1997). Impersonal ownership refers to shareholding, but far from notions such as a 'property-owning democracy', the majority of shares in the UK is concentrated in the large companies. The constellation of those external shareholders is a major

constraint on management. Shareholders are very often financial institutions, sometimes they are institutional investors, but often they are competing enterprises, who can exert pressure on firms' decision makers.

The shareholder, particularly the institutional investor, is king in the Anglo-Saxon model (Albert, 1993: 74). One view is that this kind of market relationship is the most efficient, because management is forced to achieve the highest returns in their operations to satisfy unbiased and impersonal institutional investors. Contrariwise, critics regard this relationship between finance and industry to be destructive and to impede the long-term development and stability of firms. A further criticism focuses on the often unhealthy relationship between finance and industry, as typified by waves of mergers, acquisitions and (often hostile) takeovers. One strategic defence is for firms to attempt to keep their share prices up, because loyalty, commitment and trust seem to be in vain in an environment emphasising short-termism. This, in turn, reinforces the focus on short-term profitability.

bedazzled by the glamour of American capitalism. 'The neo-American model proudly presents itself as a hard-headed professional, undisguised and untroubled by sentiment or second thoughts. Its main rival comes across as complicated, opaque – if not obscure – and cloaked in too many overlapping folds of social considerations, financial constraints, cherished traditions and good intentions' (Albert, 1993: 207). One of the main differences between the Anglo-Saxon and the German models is the role of high-profile chief executives and entrepreneurs in Anglo-Saxon systems as opposed to their German counterparts. Streeck (1997: 53) claims that there are indications of a cultural internationalisation, which may undermine a society organised and structured like Germany. The self-interest of business leaders, whose behavioural patterns are nationally bound but also subject to other influences, is pertinent to an analysis of convergence, as firms are one of a number of potential change agents.

Different countries have dominated different historical epochs, and certain countries perform substantially better than other countries in a given period, so it is inevitable that perceptions change about whether a particular system represents best practice. More recently, the relatively weak economic performances of Germany, Sweden, Japan, and the Asian 'tigers' since the Asian currency crisis hit hard in 1997, have led to the demise of their systems as best practice models of modern capitalism and are now sometimes seen as examples of antiquated and obsolete systems needful of change.

Exhibit 2.5 The German model

The German model has its roots in an entirely different social structure. Scott (1997) argues that three factors in particular set the German historical experience apart from the Anglo-Saxon one. First was the existence of only a small and weak bourgeoisie, as public life was dominated by the aristocracy's influence in the bureaucracy, the military and the landowners. Second, there was no significantly developed stock exchange. Third, banks, as providers of long-term finance, had a strong influence in the governing of the economy. When the Industrial Revolution finally hit Germany and brought in its wake the emergence of a capitalist class, the absence of stock exchanges meant that profits and investible funds were cycled directly into industry. This specific German banking model is at the heart of the model of social market capitalism because it established strong ties between the political authorities, banks and industry.

The German model of capitalism can be characterised as a system that is governed by national social institutions responsible for creating a competitive high-wage system but low income and standard of living inequalities. The social foundation is one of collectivism and a supportive stakeholder community, rather than Anglo-Saxon individualistic decision making.

Role of the nation-state

There are two dominant views of the role of the nation-state. The first view is that the role of the nation-state is in decline because it is too small to deal with global issues and too big to deal with local matters (Amin and Thrift, 1994: 1). In addition, there is seen to be a conflict between the authority of the nation-state and the manner in which capitalism strives to reorganise along global lines. Neo-liberals argue that national policies are dictated to by the mobility of capital, but associate globalisation with economic benefits. Neo-Marxists, in like vein, argue that the internationalisation of capital leads to international economic monopolisation and the reinforcement of capitalism on a global level, but consider the effects of international capital to be exploitative and regard globalisation as a process that reinforces the dominance of a capitalistic class. If the role of the nation-state is in decline, this is seen as a positive advance by neo-liberals, who argue that intervention by the state impedes efficiency-seeking capital flows and weakens an economy's competitive position in the world economy.

The second view maintains that globalisation does not necessarily weaken the role of the nation-state and that the state still has important functions to fulfil. Palan et al. (1996: 34–5), for example, refer to the fact that in major OECD countries, such as France, Germany and the UK, the state still finances nearly half the research and development expenditures of firms and in addition undertakes major infrastructure investments and subsidises strategic economic activities. Furthermore, markets seem incapable of dealing competently with collective or public goods, such as education and environmental concerns, or able to guarantee long-term innovation-based growth. Consequently, these tasks have to be performed by governments.

One perspective is that the nation-state has changed from a Keynesian welfare state to a 'competition state', a term associated with the importance placed on national competitiveness, industrial policy and interventionist supply-side measures. According to this perspective, the

Exhibit 2.6 The state and deregulation of markets

One reason for decreasing the role of the state, for example by the removal of price controls and the deregulation of markets, is to increase the competitiveness and efficiency of domestic markets, often markets dominated by public utilities. Because state intervention and public utilities are considered to distort competition, the intention was that enterprises should compete on an unregulated but level playing field. The outcome, however, was that instead of creating small, innovative and competitive firms, market forces put pressure on firms' cost structures, which led to the reconfiguration of state-induced competitive markets into oligopolistic structures. One hundred years earlier, Karl Marx had claimed that this would be the logical outcome of market processes. An important function for the state in a globalised economy, therefore, might be to counterbalance the tendency for markets to become increasingly dominated by larger enterprises.

new role of the state is to provide the conditions that allow the private sector to generate growth rather than attempt to control the domestic economy with Keynesian demand-side instruments, which are considered to be no match for global forces.

Conflict between states and markets also has international implications. The pro-globalisation view is that the international activities of the state should be reduced to a bare minimum and economic development should be left to market forces in order that the utilisation of production facilities and international capital can be maximised. The outcome so far, however, seems to depict a different scenario, as the expected benefits of globalisation has yet to come to fruition. For despite the claims of free market advocates that economic benefits will trickle down from the industrial to the developing countries, the gap between the rich and the poor is widening. Yet calls for 'fairer' trade rules and 'fairer' market access for poor countries can only be initiated by political intervention. At present, given the absence of effective international agencies, this implies intervention by individual nation-states, such as the decision in 1999 of the UK to write off its third world debt.

Convergence versus divergence

Will global forces cause nation-states to converge towards a particular global model or will divergent national systems persist? That convergence is inevitable is based on the belief that the dominance of market forces will not only integrate markets and cultures, but will also seriously undermine the power and authority of national policy makers. An opposing view is that globalisation will lead not to a homogenisation of national differences but to a reconfiguration that will feature elements of both convergence and divergence.

In the literature, a conflict is recognised between states and the global market. As discussed earlier, market forces are considered to lead to homogenisation and convergence, whereas nation-states seek to preserve capitalist diversity. Proponents of new institutionalism, for example, argue that nation-states, not globalisation, provide the general framework that determines economic activities, market behaviour and organisational patterns. International political economists, in response, argue that global commonalities in the international economy have an impact on national economies and, subsequently, on international developments. Susan Strange (1997: 184), for example, claims that new institutionalism tends 'to overlook the common problems while concentrating on the individual differences'. Common problems include the rate of technological developments and technical innovation, increasing global competition and the deregulation of markets. In consequence, will global forces allow different historically evolved capitalist systems (with diverse cultures, social structures, state laws and policies) to persist or will the process of globalisation force national systems to evolve towards a common pattern? In other words, will there be divergence or convergence?

Kinds of convergence

Before the fall of the Berlin Wall in 1989 international comparative analyses were dominated by comparisons between capitalism and socialism, rather than by comparisons of differences between capitalist systems. Discussions since then have turned to comparisons of the effects of globalisation on the firm, industries and nation-states.

Convergence can take various forms, including the convergence of:

- capitalistic accumulation and modes of production
- economic organisations
- economic and corporate governance
- market systems
- macroeconomic indicators and policies
- organisational cultures
- organisational behaviour
- organisational performance.

Most studies of convergence are purely conceptual and often rely on anecdotal evidence (for example, using standardised consumer goods such as Swatch watches and Coca-Cola, and the universal appeal of 'pop' groups, such as the Spice Girls), as proof of consumption homogenisation. Studies often single out new and major developments as sufficient evidence of convergence, such as the daily volume of foreign exchange traded in comparison to the annual international trade figures for manufactured goods. They confuse globalisation with the magnitude of trade and investment in the triad, responsible for over 80 per cent of annual trade

Exhibit 2.7 Research and development spending

Intra-state comparisons of R&D spending for 1995 provide some interesting insights. Japan spends most on R&D as a percentage of GDP, namely, 3.05% compared with 2.75% in the USA, 2.66% in Germany, 2.42% in France and 2.08% in the UK. The high percentage in the USA is due to military and defence industry spending. The Japanese government, which is perceived to be far more directive and interventionist than most developed nations (as epitomised by the role of the ministry of industry and international trade) finances far less of national R&D costs, 18.2%, than the so-called *laissez-faire* and free market governments of the UK (34.2%), the USA (46.8%), the USA even surpassing Germany (46.6%).

Palan, R., Abbot, J. and Deans, P. (1996) *State Strategies in the Global Economy*, London and New York, Pinter, pp. 34–5 flows and home to over 80 per cent of the world's 500 largest MNCs. They point to the increasing mobility of labour and, especially, capital as evidence of standardising and deterministic markets forces. Reference is often made to 'universal' pressures that are actually discriminatory in their convergence effects on nation-states, industries and firms.

In the field of international business the convergence–divergence debate is discussed in terms of the effects of globalisation on the organisation and operations of MNCs, and whether their interests are best served by closer integration of their activities or by remaining responsive to governmental and cultural differences, as in the integration–responsiveness model of Prahalad and Doz (1987). In international marketing a major concern is whether increasing consumer homogeneity will enable firms to standardise their international marketing mix (price, product, communication and distribution) or whether continuing legal, economic, technological and cultural differences across markets will force them to adapt to local market conditions. Operations and production management has moved on from analysis of the national location of plants to concerns for global integrated networks. Similar developments can be found in supply management with the emergence and development of global supply chains.

The extensive literature that compares organisational performance and structure in different national contexts not only suggests that firms can learn from managerial practices prevalent in other countries but encourages firms to emulate them. In the 1980s, for example, Japan's organisational and managerial models were widely considered to be representative of 'best practice'. In similar vein, Hutton (1995) argued that it would prove beneficial for the UK to copy Germany's decentralised banking system and have regionally autonomous decision making in the financial sector. But advice of this kind has been severely criticised for ignoring cultural and national differences.

Emulation can occur for reasons unrelated to globalisation. Differences in the economic performance of nation-states can cause weak performing economies to attempt to copy successful ones. The end of a distinct phase of capitalism, namely the era of Fordism (or the golden age of capitalism), ranging from the end of World War II to the middle of the 1970s, was reflected in the emergence of new political forms, new consumption and social patterns and manufacturing processes (flexible

Exhibit 2.8 A view on convergence

Kerr et al. (1973) developed the best-known theory of convergence. Their basic argument is that in the current industrial era societies are more similar than in earlier non-industrial periods and that industrial societies will increasingly converge as societies seek out and adopt the most efficient production technologies. In time, consumption patterns and the division of labour will be influenced by mass production technologies, for which the education system will provide the necessary skills. In the long term, technology will merge into most aspects of social life. As these trends are universal and affect all nation-states equally, industrial societies will ultimately converge.

Exhibit 2.9 Japanisation

Japanese manufacturing processes and management structures – such as lean production and just-in-time inventory systems, lean organisations based on flat hierarchies and the kaizen-style networks of banks, manufacturers, suppliers and trading companies – and Japanese approaches to corporate strategy have often been elevated to the status of universality, despite cultural, historical and institutional obstacles to their widespread adoption.

production being the most prominently debated) and new cultures and lifestyles (Amin, 1994). The collapse of Fordism led to a further re-assessment of the interplay of international relations.

Historical evidence of convergence

Are there historical parallels of convergence? Hirst and Thompson (1996), comparing the extent of internationalisation before 1914 and in the 1990s, rejected globalisation as a late 20th-century novelty, because the pre-World War I economy was more open and international in terms of FDI and financial flows. By the same token, the period between World War I and II, the 1920s and 1930s, were characterised by divergence. Inter-country antagonism, the breakdown of normal trade relationships and the instability of currencies led to isolationist policies aimed at protecting national economies from economic crises abroad. Instead of seeking international solutions to an international problem, nation-states pursued national and parochial beggar-thy-neighbour policies that further diminished the chances of recovery.

The end of World War II and the emergence of the post-war world order, the so-called *Pax Americana*, represented a significant change in economic history. Rather than falling back to the isolationist policies before the war, nation-states, under American leadership, attempted to set up an international economic order based on trade liberalism, the market economy, the sovereignty of nation-states and a fixed exchange rate system, policed by international institutions like the International Monetary Fund and the General Agreement on Tariffs and Trade. The fact that America emerged as the undisputed leader of the western world changed the international focus back from divergence to convergence. America not only became the political and military leader of the 'free world', with considerable influence on international institutions, but also became the host nation of the major international currency. Influenced by this, American, practices and structures came to be seen as superior to those elsewhere, where pressure built up to adopt this America model as the 'best practice' model.

What became apparent during this era, however, was that there were disparate growth rates among the industrialised countries. In particular, Germany and Japan (so-called institutional economies) outperformed other countries. The international system, far from converging on the American model, had to accommodate a situation where certain countries had a persistent competitive advantage over the rest and housed industries that were far more efficient and productive. This led to disparate rates of economic growth, which created tensions between countries' national interests and threatened the stability of the entire system. The Bretton Woods system, on which the post-World War II period managed system was based, had no direct mechanism to force persistent trade surplus countries to adopt corrective monetary policies and the USA, far from being committed to disciplined monetary and fiscal controls, had a chronic balance of payments deficit. These weaknesses in the international system led to its ultimate collapse and the dawn of a new era.

The message from history is that convergence cannot be attributed solely to globalisation or events in the international economy to the neglect of the interplay between national and international pressures. Drawing from new institutionalism, convergence is only likely if the effects of globalisation are more or less the same on all countries and their industries and organisations and if there are no viable options to an ideal model of best practice.

Globalisation and convergence among nation-states

The general conclusion that convergence of productivity is more likely to occur the more similar countries are takes the focus away from economic growth as evidence of convergence towards the capability of political and economic actors to adapt. Boyer, who refers to this as the ability to develop and maintain skills, argues that convergence is not a mechanistic and automatic process, but results from 'deliberate attempts to copy and adapt technologies, organizations, and processes invented elsewhere'

Exhibit 2.10 Fordism and post-Fordism

The Fordist period of capitalism can be described as an industrial paradigm based on mass production and assembly work, scale economies and investment in production technologies, a social organisation based on the family and a mode of regulation based on Keynesian fiscal, monetary and welfare politics. Although the paradigm describes the nation-state, there also exists an international dimension to the era of Fordism, which is generally associated with the *Pax Americana* and the international 'Post War World Order' negotiations at Bretton Woods in 1944.

The focal points of the Bretton Woods agreement were a system of fixed exchange rates to provide stability in international trade and a set of international institutions (the IMF, the World Bank, the IBRD and GATT) to govern the world economy according to free market and liberal policies. At the beginning of the 1970s the previously virtuous cycle of national Keynesian demand management and anti-cyclical policies turned awry, and the western economies could not escape the pincer movement of inflation and high unemployment. The system of Fordism collapsed, mostly symbolised by the breakdown of the Bretton Woods exchange rate mechanism.

The collapse of the Fordist system based on Keynesian policies led to a vacuum as the capacities of governments for market intervention became much reduced, This has led to a re-alignment of global, national, and regional relations which are, according to certain authors, asymmetrical and, therefore, unstable (Peck and Tickell, 1994: 282). One attempt to describe the grand design of post-Fordism in western societies and economies is that it is a shift to the new information technologies; more flexible, decentralised forms of labour process and work organisation; decline of the old manufacturing base and the growth of the sunrise, computer-based industries; the hiving off or contracting out of functions and services; a greater emphasis on choice and product differentiation, on marketing, packaging and design, on the targeting of consumers by lifestyle, taste and culture rather than by categories of social class; a decline in the proportion of the skilled, male, manual working class, the rise of the service and white collar classes and the feminisation of the workforce; an economy dominated by multinationals, with their new globalisation of the new financial markets, linked by the communication revolution.

(Boyer, 1996: 41). Convergence thus arises as a consequence of conscious decisions to absorb international forces within the existing framework of the nation-state, enforcing changes in the behaviour of political and economic actors, which, in turn, lead to convergence.

Convergence has generated interest since the breakdown of the Bretton Woods system and the recognition that the dominant economic leadership of the USA could no longer be assumed but was being challenged first by Germany, then by Japan. Examples of convergence, inspired by German systems and institutions, include the following:

- Attempts by the UK and France to incorporate a German style education system to encourage the kind of vocational skills considered essential to the achievements of a flexible, highly skilled production system (Boyer, 1997: 92).
- Proposals that the UK should introduce a German-inspired decentralised and regional financial system to strengthen the links between finance and industry and so improve the competitiveness of the British economy.
- Attempts by France to achieve macroeconomic stability by replicating Germany's monetary policy.
- Attempts in Western Europe to fight inflation by emulating the rationale, structure and policies of the Bundesbank, Germany's central bank. The Bundesbank is widely regarded as the best role model for the European Central Bank, which is to have the same freedom from political pressure and is expected to operate according to similar monetarist principles and policies.

Convergence is generally associated with under-performing countries' attempts to emulate best practice in successful ones. The last two decades in particular have witnessed remarkable changes in how countries are perceived and evaluated. Throughout most of the 1970s and until the end of the 1980s, the major role models of national systems, rather than American Anglo-Saxon capitalism, were the institutionalised economies of Germany (representing corporatist Rhineland capitalism), Sweden (typifying the third way between capitalism and socialism) and Japan (for the network structures and long-term commitments of its businesses and institutions). Many studies tried to show that institutional, social-market economies were both economically successful and socially just, and did not have to be structured like models of 'Manchester Liberalism', with all its social problems, to be competitive. It was also claimed that the mechanism of resource allocation in institutionalised economies was far superior to the price mechanism of pure market exchanges. The German education system was praised as the foundation of high-quality German production and its social market economy for its contribution to social cohesion. Japan was acknowledged for its manufacturing systems, long-term planning horizons and work ethic. On the basis of the superior performance of the Japanese and the German economies among developed nations, the general conclusion was that economic efficiency depended on a supportive social environment and informal networks rather than market exchanges motivated by neo-classical self-interest and profit maximisation (Crouch and Streeck, 1997: 5).

This emphasis had changed completely by the end of the 1980s. Recession in Germany and Japan undermined the arguments for institutional capitalism, while the expanding and growing market economies of the USA and the UK seemed to confirm economists' prejudices against the uncompetitiveness of institutionalised economies. Now, government intervention was considered to impede market forces and lead to a misallocation of resources.

This change of perception can best be explained by the interplay of international and national pressures. What seems to have happened is that the institutional economies, especially the ones associated with social intervention and high cost structures, have come increasingly under pressure by an international system that rewards countries able to react to price competition. While Germany manufacturers, for example, have rarely attempted to compete in price-sensitive markets, the openings for them in high-quality markets have been much reduced. German car manufacturers, such as BMW and Daimler-Benz, manufacturing and power tool producers, such as Bosch, and many manufacturers in Germany's pharmaceutical and chemical industries, had long pursued strategies to dominate international high-quality, high-price markets in order to accommodate their comparatively high cost structures. As a consequence of globalisation, including market deregulation, market barriers have disappeared and these markets have now become much more price sensitive.

The availability of modern process technologies, allowing low-wage countries to produce to high-quality standards, has further undermined

Exhibit 2.11 Changing economic performance

Germany had the most successful international economy in the 1980s. Although economically far more exposed to world markets than Japan and the USA, Germany, with a far smaller population, had the same market share in visible exports as the USA. In addition, contrary to the deficit-prone Anglo-Saxon economies, Germany had an export surplus that exceeded that of Japan. In contrast to other continental European economies hit by recession in the late 1980s, Germany benefited from the demand-led boom of German reunification. Nevertheless, recession finally caught up with the reunified German economy and the international performance of Germany declined significantly. In contrast, the UK and the USA improved and stabilised their performances, but not in such a dramatic fashion that would justify a complete paradigm change from institutionalised to market economies.

Suddenly, the German model of a social market economy was no longer seen to be exemplary.

Instead, Germany came to be regarded as a country with a 'pampered workforce' and unable to accept the economic realities of a global market and international competition. Sweden, once associated with a middle way between market capitalism and state socialism was forced to reorganise its welfare state. The Swedish car manufacturer, Volvo, which had once attempted to revolutionise car production with new manufacturing processes, was forced by market pressures to close its modern factories and return to conventional production methods. Japan, formerly a 'best practice' model, came under constant American pressure to open up its domestic market and was accused of acting unfairly to the detriment of American industry. Japanese networks, widely praised for their cultural homogeneity and networks of suppliers, original equipment manufactures and financiers that enabled long-term strategies to be pursued, were suddenly labelled corrupt and secretive.

the traditional markets of high wage economies. Crouch and Streeck (1997: 6) conclude: 'The socio-economic model of a high-wage economy with relatively egalitarian wage dispersion and effective democratic participation, in the political system and the workplace, appears to be on the defensive. If advantages lie overwhelmingly with fast moving, low-cost, unregulated market behaviour, then economies of the institutional type that refuse to admit increased inequality, stepped-up pressure on individuals, families and communities, and greater discretion in decision-making by managers and investors may be doomed, and only deregulated, finance-driven capitalism of an Anglo-American kind may stand a chance of meeting the Far Eastern and Eastern European competition.'

In other words convergence is back. What could not be sustained by political hegemony (for example, *Pax American* and *Pax Britannica*), in which one country dominates the global economy, or by a process of technological rationalisation, is being achieved by the process of market globalisation. That is to say, an intensified internationalisation of competition, technological innovation, national deregulation and regional integration is forcing economic actors, national institutions and organisations to converge towards an ideal structures and behavioural patterns.

Globalisation and automatic convergence

The effects of globalisation are likely to differ between countries, as it did under the gold standard, during the inter-war years and in the *Pax Americana*. Globalisation discriminates against institutional economies as opposed to more open economies of the Anglo-American kind 'that have long learned to operate without the succour of an interventionist state and in the absence of strong social cohesion' (Crouch and Streeck, 1997: 14). For example, if, as generally assumed, the effect of globalisation is that national demand management becomes unfeasible, then globalisation will have its greatest impact on institutions and governments in countries where the state is a strong player and has vital resource allocation functions. In other words, globalisation has a subplot: a capitalism versus capitalism debate.

The mechanisms of convergence

The argument so far has linked the ability of countries to maintain diversity and their own unique identity to their economic performance. Successful ones are likely to persist, while those experiencing economic problems will feel the pressures for change. Also, national systems have specific advantages and disadvantages that may prove beneficial in certain situations but not in others. In an international context, there is a preference for the models that appertain in countries that produce superior results. These are then consequently acclaimed as best practice models for less successful nation-states to emulate. In other words, if the conditions in the international political economy favour a particular configuration of nation-states, other nations will feel the pressure to converge on these best practice models.

It is important to reiterate that convergence is unlikely to happen on its own or be an automatic process. There are three mechanisms of globalisation that might bring about convergence among the various capitalist systems. First, convergence could result from the supremacy of the market, whereby intensified international competition leads to the deregulation of markets. Second, convergence could be the result of the strategic choice of decision makers to incorporate best practices found elsewhere to enhance their existing solutions, (so-called 'constructive convergence'). Third, there continues to be political pressures on Japan to eliminate 'structural impediments' (for example, pressure to increase consumer spending, to lower high savings and investment ratios, to reduce huge and persistent trade balances surpluses and to modernise the multitiered distribution system) to bring Japan into line with its major competitors, thus creating a more level playing field in the international economy. However, although all these forces originate from external pressures, it is imperative not to ignore the ability to resist change from domestic pressure groups, such as consumers, producers and political parties, because external pressures have to be absorbed within a national setting.

In other words, convergence is not an automatic and predetermined outcome, as the emulation of best practice and the adoption of particular structures might be prevented because best practice methods and systems cannot easily be detached from their national framework and incorporated in other countries without undergoing some modification. Theoretically, this is referred to as the 'tightness of the institutional fit' or 'institutional interlocking'. This concept rejects a piece-by-piece adoption of variables, such as the concept of the 'Hausbank', the role of the Bundesbank or the German education and training system, as all these features are embedded within a particular context.

Summary

The chapter has argued that convergence only occurs if countries show similar potential in terms of factor endowments and natural resources or if they have the social capabilities required to assimilate the knowledge necessary to built up technological and human potential and to implement decisions geared towards achieving economic growth in a particular way, accepted and sanctioned by the international political economy. Even then, convergence is only an outcome if decision makers respond to and incorporate external forces. Convergence, then, requires an interplay of national and international forces, but also a positive response from national decision makers in government and in public and private sectors.

When emphasising the forces associated with globalisation and their potential to enforce convergence, it is necessary to consider the kinds of change brought about by globalisation. A common argument discussed earlier is that the globalisation of the economy pressurises national economies to deregulate their economies, which will result in a net loss of national control exercised by governments and a surrender of national economic sovereignty by national, democratically elected authorities to global market forces. However, questions remains concerning what the effects of the surrender of national control are likely to be, how the reduction of a government's capacity to regulate and intervene changes the structure of countries' economies, and how firms conduct economic transactions. It is also necessary to question whether changes have equal or discriminatory effects on societies.

Governance mechanisms are significantly different from country to country. The German model, for example, relies on professional associations and on local authorities to a far higher degree than the Anglo-Saxon countries, which follow a far more individualistic firm-specific approach. While professional associations in Germany are highly formalised and rely on state support to facilitate economic decisions or to act as arbitrator in disputes with the unions, the Japanese economy relies far more on informal networks based on mutual commitments and obligations and even family ties. The concept of shareholder value, contrariwise, has a totally different meaning in Anglo-Saxon countries where the maximisation of returns for owners is one of the mandatory principles of management, while the Japanese approach of cross-shareholding has a completely different function and insulates firms against shareholder pressures. Moreover, politically motivated economic governance in a federalist country such as Germany is decentralised and left to the regional authorities, while in France the central government has a key role in committing financial resources, intervening in capital and labour markets and regulating economic activities. Countries such as the USA emphasise flexibility and individualism and consequently retreat from direct intervention, whereas social democratic countries such as Sweden are consensus based and tie firms in to networks of collective social responsibility.

These mechanisms of economic governance are the result of different historical experiences and institutional legacies and are therefore embedded in the respective countries' histories and their existing institutional frameworks. Convergence resulting from increasing economic globalisation is only a likely outcome if global capitalist forces affect all those mechanisms of economic governance in the same way, so that economies have to change and in a similar way. Therefore, it is not sufficient to refer briefly to the undermining of national economic governance following deregulation and governments' inability to intervene, but to examine what effects the general decline of the nation-state has on different national economies. One argument is that globalisation and deregulation are likely to impact more significantly on those nations that require a far higher level of state intervention rather than the market-led economies which have traditionally relied on their individual capabilities and strategies due to a lack of governmental support. According to Streeck (1997: 53), globalisation: 'Discriminates against modes of economic governance that require public intervention associated with a sort of state capacity that is unavailable in the anarchic world of international politics. It favours national systems like those of the USA and Britain that have historically relied less on public-political and more on private-contractual economic governance, making them structurally more compatible with the emerging global system, and in fact enabling them to regard the latter as an extension of themselves.'

A belief that the international political economy sanctions a certain kind of capitalist model, and prefers it to other forms, is the prime reason for convergence claims based on the presumption of market supremacy. However, these claims are facilitated by a narrow and all too simplistic conceptualisation of capitalist countries, proceeding on the assumption of a dualism of market-led and institutional capitalist countries. Consequently, the argument that the globalisation process, when faced with a choice between a free market model and an institutional model, would push institutional economies towards market economies is hardly surprising. The analysis of capitalist diversity in this chapter, however, has shown that variety cannot simply be reduced to a bipolar comparison because a multiplicity of processes, mechanisms and political approaches, let alone the various interest groups, are jointly responsible for governing and structuring a national economy. Therefore, when referring to convergence, it is necessary to consider how global forces change existing patterns, which institutional arrangements they target, and which structures, strategies, transactions and behavioural patterns of firms are most likely to lose out in global competition.

Crouch and Streeck (1997: 14–15), arguing that deregulation only affects those national economies whose governance systems depend on state support, conclude that the demise of state governance will have a severe effect on statist societies, such as France, where the state has a central role in the economy. Moreover, they argue that the German system is vulnerable due to formality of the relationships between institutions and the state and the desire of German firms to gain Anglo-Saxon style flexibility and be rid of the layers of governmental regulations and the constraints imposed by professional associations. By the same token, Japanese and Italian *networks* might be less threatened by governmental deregulation, as their organisation depends less on state support and regulation. These pointers show that global forces can impact differently on various mechanisms in countries, and affect firms in different ways, so that global forces do not necessarily, everywhere and at all times, bring about convergence.

Review questions

1 Summarise the globalisation debate. What are the major interest groups in the world economy? How are they affected by different elements of globalisation?
2 Who benefits and who loses from a shift in jobs to low-wage economies? Consider this question from the perspective of consumers, labour, technological change, firms, nation-states. Are the net benefits likely to be positive?
3 Discuss whether economies are likely to converge towards a 'best' economic system. If not, then why not?
4 Over 80 per cent of international trade and foreign direct investment takes place with the triad of the USA, Western Europe and Japan and over 80 per cent of the largest 500 multinational firms have their home bases inside the triad. What light does this throw on the concept of 'the global village'?
5 Identify and evaluate the sources of conflict between pressures on companies to operate globally and the desire of governments to regulate companies and activities within their borders.
6 Discuss the changes in technology and government policies that have fed the process of globalisation.

Bibliography

Albert, M. (1993) *Capitalism vs. Capitalism*, London, Wharr Publishers.

Amin, A. (1994) 'Post-Fordism: models, fantasies and phantoms of transitions' in A. Amin, (ed.) *Post-Fordism: A Reader*, London, Blackwell.

Amin, A. and Thrift, N. (1994) 'Living in the global economy' in A. Amin and N. Thrift (eds) *Globalization, Institutions and Regional Development in Europe*, Oxford, Oxford University Press.

Boyer, R. (1997) 'French statism at a crossroads' in C. Crouch and W. Streeck (eds) *Political Economy of Modern Capitalism: Mapping Convergence and Diversity*, London, Sage.

Boyer, R. (1996) 'The convergence hypothesis revisited: globalization but still the century of nations?' in S. Berger and R. Dore (eds) *National Diversity and Global Capitalism*, Ithaca and London, Cornell University Press.

Boyer, R. and Drache, D. (1996) 'Introduction' in R. Boyer and D. Drache (eds) *States against Markets: The Limits of Globalization*, London, Routledge.

Campbell, N. (1994) 'Introduction' in N. Campbell and F. Burton (eds) *Japanese Multinationals: Strategies and Management in the Global Kaisha*, London and New York, Routledge.

Crouch, C. and Streeck, W. (1997) 'Introduction' in C. Crouch and W. Streeck (eds) *Political Economy of Modern Capitalism: Mapping Convergence and Diversity*, London, Sage.

Dore, R. (1994) 'Japanese capitalism, Anglo-Saxon capitalism: how will the Darwinian contest turn out?' in N. Campbell and F. Burton (eds) *Japanese Multinationals: Strategies and Management in the Global Kaisha*, London, Routledge.

Drucker, P. (1990) *The New Realities*, New York, Mandarin.

Hamel, G. and Prahalad, C. K. (1985) 'Do you really have a global strategy?', *Harvard Business Review*, 63, 4, pp. 79–91.

Hirst, P. and Thompson, G. (1996) *Globalization in Question: The International Economy and the Possibilities of Governance*, Cambridge, Polity Press.

Hutton, W. (1995) *The State We're In*, London, Vintage.

Keegan, W. (1992) *The Spectre of Capitalism: The Future of the World Economy after the Fall of Communism*, London, Radius.

Kenney, M. and Florida, R. (1993) *Beyond Mass Production: The Japanese System and its Transfer to the US*, Oxford, Oxford University Press.

Kerr. C., Dunlop, J., Harbison, F. and Meyers, C. (1973) *Industrialisation and Industrial Man*, Cambridge, MA, Harvard University Press.

Ohmae, K. (1995) *The End of the Nation State: The Rise of Regional Economies*, London, HarperCollins.

Palan, R. and Abbot, J. with Deans, P. (1996) *State Strategies in the Global Economy*, London and New York, Pinter.

Peck, J. and Tickell, A. (1994) 'Searching for a new institutional fix: the after-Fordist crisis and the global–local disorder' in A. Amin (ed.) *Post-Fordism: A Reader*, Oxford, Blackwell.

Pontusson, J. (1997) 'Between neo-liberalism and the German model: Swedish capitalism in transition' in C. Crouch and W. Streeck (eds) *Political Economy of Modern Capitalism: Mapping Convergence and Diversity*, London, Sage.

Porter, M. E. (1990) *The Competitive Advantage of Nations*, London, Macmillan.

Prahalad, C. K. and Doz, Y. (1987) *The Multinational Mission: Balancing Local Demands and Global Vision*, New York, Free Press.

Sassen, S. (1995) 'The state and the global city: notes towards a conception of place-centered governance', *Competition and Change*, 1, pp. 31–50.

Sassen, S. (1991) *The Global City*, Princeton, NJ, Princeton University Press.

Scott, J. (1997) *Corporate Business and Capitalist Classes*, Oxford, Oxford University Press.

Sorge, A. (1991) 'Strategic fit and the societal effect: interpreting cross-national comparisons of technology, organisation and human resources', *Organisation Studies*, 12, 2, pp. 161–90.

Strange, S. (1997) 'The future of global capitalism, or, will divergence persist forever?' in C. Crouch and W. Streeck (eds) *Political Economy of Modern Capitalism: Mapping Convergence and Diversity*, London, Sage.

Streeck, W. (1997) 'German capitalism: does it exist? Can it survive?' in C. Crouch and W. Streeck (eds) *Political Economy of Modern Capitalism: Mapping Convergence and Diversity*, London, Sage.

Streeck, W. (1992) *Social Institutions and Economic Performance*, London, Sage.

Waters, M. (1995) *Globalization*, London and New York, Routledge.

3 Models of international trade

Introduction

The exchange of goods and services in both domestic and international trade is based on the opportunities it offers individuals and firms, and nations in the case of international trade, to specialise in economic activities that they do best. Specialisation generates the most efficient allocation of economic resources, higher output and incomes and higher standards of living. It is usual, however, to distinguish between domestic trade and international trade because the existence of national borders creates dimensions to international transactions that are not present, at least to the same degree, in domestic ones. The following are some of the more obvious differences.

Differences between domestic and international trade

Relative mobility of factors of production

Through personal choice, and because of language, cultural and immigration barriers, capital and especially labour move much more easily and readily within a country than between countries. To remedy this, one of the purposes of trade blocs is to minimise differences in the mobility of factors of production within and between member countries. This is also happening as part of the process of globalisation, but in recent decades, although the international mobility of capital has greatly increased, the mobility of labour had changed very little. This relative international immobility of factors of production, combined with differences in their quality and abundance, help to explain the kind of goods and services countries specialise in and the pattern of trade between trading partners.

National currencies

In a nation's domestic transactions only the national currency is usually used, whereas most international transactions have to be paid for in the currency of the exporting countries or in readily convertible 'international' currencies. The relative value of national currencies, the exchange rate, constantly changes over time. This gives rise to payments and receivables risks in international transactions, so that the domestic currency value of a contract when a payment or a receipt is due may be more or less than expected when the contract was signed. This exchange risk is not present in domestic trade.

Cultural differences

Differences in language, habits, conventions, standards and tastes commonly give rise to complex interrelationships and impediments and barriers to international trade unlikely to be present in domestic trade. These differences make it much more difficult for firms to penetrate foreign markets compared to their home market.

Sovereign states

The ebb and flow of tension and harmony between sovereign states, the pursuit of national rather than regional or global interests, nationalism in general, also give rise to barriers and impediments to international trade. Thus, as with factors of production, the movement of goods and services across borders is typically less free than within borders. If factors of production were perfectly mobile internationally, there would be no cause for international trade. Thus, international trade is a substitute for factor mobility and, in principle, achieves the same result – the optimal global allocation of economic resources.

National policies

Nation-states have their own objectives and monetary and fiscal policies, albeit closely tied to a common strategy if they are members of a trade bloc, such as the European Union. Different national policies on employment targets, growth rates, inflation, tax and interest rates will affect the cost base of firms and industries and, therefore, the relative international competitiveness of countries. The principle economic role of the nation-state in the global economy is to exert influence on the volume and direction of international trade flows by blocking imports and encouraging exports. In other respects, the nation-state is irrelevant, merely an accident of geography (Krugman, 1993).

Protection

Commercial policy is the term used to describe a nation-state's mix of controls and regulations directed at international trade (and investment) flows. These controls range from tariffs to a wide range of non-tariff barriers imposed on foreign firms to protect the home market and to compensate for the inability of domestic firms to compete successfully in domestic and international markets.

Why trade takes place

Differences between the domestic environment and the international trade environment are perhaps sufficient to explain why international trade is a distinct and traditional field of economics. The differences also have a bearing on the volume of international trade and why countries import and export the goods and services that they do. They also help to explain why many firms choose to invest in import-substituting production facilities in their main markets abroad.

International trade is also influenced by other factors. These include countries' relative endowments of factors of production; the scale of technology and the pace of technological change; innovation; the liberalisation and deregulation of markets; product differentiation; economies of scale; the competitiveness of market structures; political ties and influence; the stage countries have reached in their economic development; and the capacity of countries to respond to the changes brought about by globalisation. With such a range of influences, it would be surprising if any one theory were capable of explaining the pattern of international trade or, for that matter, the flows of foreign direct investment (FDI).

Firms enter into international trade to pursue profit and growth opportunities and to diversify their risks. This basis of all trade theories is that international trade allows countries' firms to maximise their specialisation in the production of goods in which they are best suited to produce. A feature of modern trade theory is that firms can increase their cost competitiveness through trade by enjoying economies of scale when output increases. These two elements, product specialisation and economies of scale, offer some answers to the basic question: how do opportunities to trade arise? However, the basic answer is that international trade is possible and profitable when there are *international price differentials* between similar goods. The act of *arbitrage* (buying in cheap markets and selling in dear ones) exploits the profit opportunities offered up by the existence of these price differences. Trade theories offer explanations why international price differentials exist and what their consequences are for international trade. Almost all trade theories, whether classical, neo-classical or modern, focus on the *principle of comparative cost* (or *comparative advantage*) as the underlying cause of these price differences. Modern theories have led away from the rigid 'classical' assumptions of traditional theory and its static framework of perfect competition and constant returns to scale, but the comparative cost building blocks of traditional theory, although much refined, are still in place.

As with any theory, to isolate fundamental, systematic and predictable influences, trade theories abstract from the many complex and often interrelated factors that influence trade flows. The role of trade theory is to explain how price differentials influence the structure and pattern of the international flow of goods and services: that is, why do countries trade, what goods do they trade, with whom do they trade, and how much do they trade? Theory also attempts to identify the beneficiaries of trade. Only to a certain degree have theories been successful in answering these questions and predicting trends in the structure and pattern of trade. For these reasons the general relevance of traditional theories continue to face serious challenges.

Before considering the major trade theories, it is worthwhile to look at some of the influences on trade that are usually considered to be exogenous.

Natural, artificial and random barriers to trade

Transport costs, learning processes, political ties and country size represent major *natural barriers* or impediments to the ability of trade to flow freely between countries.

The first of these, *transport costs*, are usually assumed to be zero in most theories simply because they are not considered to offer fundamental and predictable explanations of trade flows. However, transport costs cannot be entirely ignored because they generally serve as a natural barrier to market entry, impeding the volume of trade flows and reducing the range of traded goods. If transport costs were zero, most goods would be traded. If transport costs approached infinity, the flow of international trade would reduce to zero. In between these extremes, excluding perishables and other goods and services that need to be consumed immediately, high transport costs relative to their value explain why many goods are non-traded goods, destined only for the home market.

Sometimes, rather than serve as a barrier to trade, transport costs can actually be the cause of trade, for example, between countries sharing a long border. For example, low cross-border transport costs relative to domestic transport costs offer one explanation for intra-industry trade, which can occur when (say) North exports more of a product to South than to other regions in North, and south exports a similar good to North.

Technological changes bringing about big reductions in transport costs have contributed greatly to the growth of world trade by opening up foreign markets to goods for the first time and allowing profitable trade to be conducted over larger distances. In the 1870s an upsurge in world trade occurred following the opening of the Suez Canal in 1869 (which greatly reduced travelling time between Europe and Asia), the creation of nation-wide rail networks in North America and Europe, and the replacement of sail by steam power. A decade later, a further surge in trade in agricultural produce was associated with the refrigeration of ships. The major 20th-century technology-induced productivity increases, bringing down transport costs, was the post-World War II replacement of highly labour-intensive dockside handling of cargo by roll-on roll-off container traffic.

The major influences on transport costs are the weight-to-value ratio of the product being transported and the distance between markets. A high weight-to-value ratio may be sufficient to overprice a product in foreign markets even though its manufacturing costs are low. Transport costs are generally high as a percentage of value for primary products and heavy bulk commodities and low for manufactures. The influence of distance on transport costs partly explains why for most countries their major trade partners are neighbouring countries. However, until recent theoretical advances, it has generally been considered that trade cannot be systematically predicted by transport costs and the distance between markets alone. For example, two countries with close trade ties with the UK – Ireland and New Zealand – are respectively the nearest and furthest away.

Most theoretical analysis of international trade is conducted within a static framework at the country level. For example, it is *countries* that are perceived to have a mutual advantage in trading with each other and, when they do, it is assumed that trade will automatically and instantaneously takes place between them. Unfortunately, this static country level of analysis ignores the major actors in international trade, namely individual firms and organisations in both the private and public sectors. In reality, most trade takes place between firms and their customers and consumers, for whom the establishment of trade links does not happen overnight, but follows a learning process. In essence, *time* is needed for firms to develop knowledge of market opportunities, to establish dealerships and relationships with agencies and distributors and for consumers to become aware of goods and services available from abroad and then become acquainted with their attributes and performance. The learning process and the breaking down of communication barriers between markets constitute a further natural impediment to the growth of international trade. The significance of a learning process is particularly relevant whenever technology and productivity improvements create technological gaps, which can be an important factor in stimulating trade, as in the international product life cycle model (Vernon, 1966) and technology gap models (for example, Posner, 1961).

'Trade follows the flag' is a cliché for military conquest and foreign aid. Certainly, conquest, leading to close political ties, can help explain the origins of trade between particular groups of countries, such as the British Commonwealth and the former Soviet Union. Often trade established through political ties can only be broken by political initiatives and events, such as the UK's decision to join the European Union (which forced former Commonwealth countries to seek new trade partners) and the demise of the Soviet Union and its bilateral east European trading system,

COMECON. Membership of a trade bloc, where the usual mixture is one of freer trade between the members and more protectionism against non-members, can bring about significant changes in a country's trade relationships.

Country size can affect countries' international trade as a proportion of their gross national product (GNP), although the relationship between country size and trade, especially exports, is becoming less strong. Intuitively, it might be expected that the smaller the size of countries measured by land mass the more likely are they to devote resources to external trade and to experience high levels of import penetration. This is because small countries are likely to be seriously short of the level of resources required to approach self-sufficiency and to suffer from resource skewness. Therefore, they would need to export a relatively high proportion of their output to finance essential imports. However, the facts are inconclusive. Ratios of export + imports/gross domestic product (a measure of the propensity to trade) among the high-income OECD countries show that Switzerland and Canada, countries with low and high land mass respectively, each have high trade/GDP ratios, and Japan and the USA, countries also with low and high land mass respectively, each have low trade/GDP ratios. Canada, slightly larger than the USA, has a much higher ratio than the USA. It may be that a country's location has a greater bearing than land mass on its propensity to import and export. For example, Canada's major conurbations are closer to the USA than they are to the rest of Canada, giving rise through trade with the USA to Canada's high trade/GDP ratio. However, there is a closer negative relationship between population as a measure of size and the propensity to trade. Countries with large populations and large domestic markets will have national firms able to exploit economies of scale. Such countries are likely to be less dependent on trade than countries with relatively small populations, which will have the highest trade/GDP ratios.

Artificial barriers to trade are erected by various instruments of state intervention (commercial policy), such as tariffs on imports, subsidies to exporters, quota restrictions, embargoes, 'voluntary' agreements, and controls on the access to foreign currencies to pay for imports. (See Chapter 4 for a detailed discussion of commercial policy.)

Random factors or *unsystematic shocks* can also transform international trade. Examples include the unexpected demise of the Soviet Union, the multiple increase in oil prices in the 1970s and natural disasters. Throughout the late 1990s, for example, the malignant effects of El Niño resulted in crop failure in some regions and bumper harvests in others, distorting market prices, the normal pattern of agricultural supply and demand and the international trade earnings of many countries (see Case 3.1). Political and military disputes can have far-reaching effects on the structure and pattern of trade, simultaneously destroying some trade ties and creating others.

Trade theories

Trade theories ignore many of the obvious and often significant influences on international trade to concentrate on the basic market conditions of supply and demand. But supply conditions are singled out more than demand in most theories because they are considered to have more systematic and therefore predictable effects on the structure and pattern of international trade. We will shortly see that the classical Ricardian explanation of trade emphasises *differences* between countries in the productivity of a factor of production, specifically labour, whereas the neo-classical factor proportions model emphasises *similarities* in the productivity of factors but *differences* in their abundance. The neo-classical assumptions offer an especially plausible explanation of trade between industrial and primary producing countries, which display distinct differences in their factor ratios. However, trade between similarly endowed industrialised countries and between similar industrial sectors (intra-industry trade) has grown steadily as a proportion of world trade. The existence and growth of these types of trade cannot readily be explained by traditional theories. Modern theories, in turn, have challenged the supply-side emphasis of traditional theories and their assumptions of perfect markets, constant returns to scale and zero transport costs, replacing these with models incorporating market imperfections, technology, economies of scale, transport costs and demand side explanations of trade. Before turning to the traditional and modern theories, we will begin with a forerunner, *mercantilism*, which pre-dates modern economics but often continues to inform public and political opinion.

Mercantilism

The mercantilist era in Europe, which lasted from around 1500–1750, established the doctrine that a nation's best interests are served by encouraging exports and discouraging imports. This belief found expression at the time in the trade and industry policies of European nations.

The essence of mercantilism was that national power was dependent on national wealth and that changes in a nation's wealth can be measured by changes in its stock of bullion, that is, precious metals, mostly gold and silver coins. For a country without natural resources of precious metals, the only way they can be acquired is by building up a surplus on the *balance of trade* (a term first used by mercantilists), that is, by an excess of exports over imports, paid for in gold or silver. In a trading world where the natural supply of gold and silver increases slowly, international trade produces winners and losers because one nation's gain in bullion is another's loss. The winners, the surplus countries, accumulate wealth. Deficit countries will experience a fading away of their wealth and, hence, their power.

In the pursuit of national self-interest, mercantilist policies were based around state patronage of commercial and industrial enterprises. Typical mercantilist policies would include the granting of monopolies, patent rights and subsidies to exporters, national laws dictating that goods must be transported in the ships of the home country and tariffs or quotas on imports to encourage and protect home production. Tariffs, effectively a tax on imports, have the added attraction of raising revenues for the state. Mercantilism offered no explanation for trade, but simply argued that it was in a country's interests to export more than it imported.

The quantity theory of money eventually discredited the notion that a country could successfully pursue a strategy of mercantilism to generate a persistent trade surplus. Suppose, in a two-country world represented by country *A* and country *B*, both countries are initially in a position of balanced trade. Let country *A* now experience an excess of exports over imports and move into surplus. By implication, country *B* will now face an excess of imports over exports and move into deficit. The resultant increase in bullion inside country *A* will increase the supply of money in *A*, causing, in turn, an inflationary rise in prices. Abroad, in *B*, a loss of bullion will have the reverse effect; the money supply will decrease, followed by a fall in prices. Back in *A*, the flow of exports to *B*, now dearer, will fall: in *B*, the flow of exports to *A*, now cheaper, will increase. The overall effect, therefore, would be for *A*'s trade *surplus* and *B*'s *deficit* to fall, moving both countries back to balanced trade positions. This tendency for price effects arising from bullion movements to generate an export = import trade balance (*equilibrium*) in each country is referred to as the price-specie-flow mechanism (attributed to David Hume, the 18th-century British economist). Although the relationship between bullion movements, prices and trade flows is more complex than this, the argument effectively destroyed the notion that a country can sustain a persistent trade surplus through the accumulation of bullion and, hence, destroyed the general case for mercantilism.

The birth of modern economics, including the free trade movement led by Adam Smith, David Ricardo, John Stuart Mill, and others and the 'win–win' concept of comparative advantage led to the demise of the mercantilist doctrine, at least in academic circles. Insofar as mercantilism implies the encouragement of exports and the discouragement of imports by the nation-state, a blanket rejection of mercantilism, however, must be resisted. In times of recession and unemployment of resources or international hostilities the protection of strategic industries and inducements to firms to export more cannot be dismissed out of hand. To this day there is a commonly held view, which has its roots in mercantilism, that nation-states, particularly industrialised countries, are locked in a fierce win–lose game of competitive rivalry. It would certainly be foolish to trivialise this view since firms with national identities compete furiously for market share in global markets. But the concept of nations trading as competitors must be qualified by the recognition that they also collaborate by supplying each other with essential goods and services. International trade is a complementary as well as a competitive activity. Moreover, by trading with each other according to comparative advantage each trading country enjoys the benefits of specialisation.

Traditional trade theories

Absolute advantage

In the late 18th century, Adam Smith's book *An Inquiry into the Nature and Causes of the Wealth of Nations* (1776) launched an attack on mercantilism and the belief that trade should be regulated in the pursuit of persistent favourable trade balances. Smith used the concept of absolute advantage to show how international trade can benefit all countries by allowing them to specialise in and export goods made more cheaply at home in exchange for goods made more cheaply elsewhere.

The benefits of trade based on product specialisation can be explained by the concept of *opportunity cost*. In a trading world, the cost of all countries' imports minus what would have been the domestic cost of producing identical goods (the alternative foregone) measures the value of resources saved for their best alternative use. In short, by exporting their least cost goods in return for goods in which they have an absolute disadvantage, trading countries directly benefit and contribute to global efficiency by releasing resources for more productive uses. Absolute advantage also covers the rather obvious case where countries exchange exports for goods they are unable to produce themselves because of a lack of an appropriate or specific resource (perhaps a natural resource, climate or technology) required for their production. The greatest opportunity cost gains are made when countries import goods produced more cheaply than at home or goods they simply cannot produce at all or in any quantity. The principle of absolute advantage indicates that all trading nations can gain from trade (quite literally, they are partners, not competitors, as in the mercantilist doctrine) and the more that countries specialise, the greater the production and consumption gains to be had from trade. On the basis of the doctrine of absolute advantage, Adam Smith argued that minimum interference by governments and *laissez-faire* policies, that is, free trade and markets, would maximise the gains from trade by allowing individuals, firms and nations to concentrate on what they do best.

The concept of absolute advantage, as with all trade theories, offers only a partial explanation of trade. Yet the concept is sufficient to explain a significant proportion of world trade. A more or less permanent trade

Exhibit 3.1 Absolute advantage

It is the maxim of every prudent master of a family, never to make at home what it will cost him more to make than to buy. The taylor does not attempt to make his own shoes, but buys them of the shoemaker. The shoemaker does not attempt to make his own cloaths, but employs a taylor. The farmer attempts to make neither one nor the other, but employs those different artificers. All of them find it for their interest to employ their whole industry in a way which they have some advantage over their neighbours. . . .

What is prudence in the conduct of every private family can scarce be folly in that of a great kingdom. If a foreign country can supply us with a commodity cheaper than we ourselves can make it, better buy it of them with some part of the produce of our own industry. . . .

Smith, Adam (1985) *An Inquiry into the Nature and Causes of the Wealth of Nations*, New York, Modern Library College Edition (Random House), p. 226.

pattern, based on absolute advantage, exists for primary products, such as tea, coffee, sugar, cotton, wool, rubber and various fruits and vegetables. The specific factor creating absolute advantage in these commodities is a natural resource, such as a favourable climate or raw material, which cannot readily transfer from place to place. Where trade is a response to absolute advantage, because there is no direct competition between imports and domestic producers, there are relatively few contentious economic and political disputes between nations (but see the banana war exhibit in Chapter 4). The main threat to exports of this type, the staple exports of poorer primary countries, usually comes from synthetic substitutes. Where the specific factor is technology, the major trade flows tend to be between industrial economies. More so than natural resource-based trade, technology-based trade is subject to shifting patterns over time because technology can be bought, transferred and imitated. Early importers of technological goods often become net exporters, as Japan, Taiwan and South Korea can testify.

A disturbing conclusion of the model of absolute advantage is that there is no basis for trade for a country that can produce no goods in which it has no absolute advantages. As with the mercantilist doctrine of protectionism, the notion that trade *should* be based on absolute advantage is also steeped in the rhetoric of protectionism. The next step forward in the evolution of trade theory replaces the *strong* condition that trade requires countries to establish their own unique absolute advantage with the *weaker* but more complex condition of comparative advantage, which counters some of the arguments of the protectionist school.

Comparative advantage: classical theory

The theory of *comparative advantage*, as laid down by David Ricardo (1817), established that a country could benefit from trade even if it is unable to establish an absolute advantage in any good. The theory offers a supply-side demonstration that it may be advantageous to a country to import goods even if its producers are absolutely more efficient in their production. Ricardo adopted a model of two countries (Portugal and

Exhibit 3.2 Ricardo's example

	Portugal (man days)	England (man days)
Cloth (per unit)	90	100
Wine (per unit)	80	120

All costs are measured in the 'labour days' required to produce the goods in each country. Portugal requires fewer man days than England for the production of both wine and cloth. In England a unit of wine would cost (exchange for) 6/5 of a unit of cloth, and in Portugal a unit of wine would cost 8/9 of a unit of cloth. These ratios measure the opportunity cost of each good in each country. Suppose trade now opened up between the two countries. Ignoring transport and any transaction costs, a trader, exploiting arbitrage opportunities, could buy units of wine for 8/9 of cloth in Portugal, sell the wine in England for 6/5 of cloth and return with the cloth to Portugal to sell for wine, thus reaping a profit through exchange. Trade takes place simply because of price differentials between the two countries.

Exhibit 3.3 Significance of relative price differences

In a two-product model, cars and wheat, and in the absence of money as a means of exchange, the price of cars is the amount of wheat that can be bartered for cars.

In Figure 3.1, assume that two potential trading partners, France and Germany, produce both products. Suppose that if each country allocated all its resources to car production, they would each produce the same volume, OA units (France) and OA^1 units (Germany). However, if both countries devoted all resources to wheat production, allow France, with a more suitable climate, to produce OF units of wheat, twice the volume of wheat as Germany's O^1G units. The lines AF and A^1G define, respectively, the production frontiers for France and Germany.

Any product combination on each country's production frontier represents possible output combinations where resources are fully employed, such as P for France and P^1 for Germany. Any production combinations when each country is in a state of autarky (economic isolation), must, of necessity, be the respective consumption combinations also.

The slope of the production frontiers measures the pre-trade relative price of wheat and cars inside each country. In France the slope of its price ratio indicates that 6-car units exchange for 4 units of wheat. In Germany, 6 car units exchange for 2 units of wheat. If an agreement is reached between the two countries to trade at a price ratio somewhere between the two domestic pre-trade ratios, *some* traders in both countries will recognise that arbitrage opportunities will exist, as in the Ricardian example, if they were to export at this post-trade price (referred to as the terms of trade). Suppose the agreed price is TA (a ratio of 6 car units for 3 units of wheat). French *wheat producers*, who traded 4 units of wheat for 6 car units at home, now need only to trade in the ratio of 3 units of wheat for 6 cars. German *car producers* can now exchange in the ratio of 6 cars for 3, rather than 2, units of wheat. The opening up of trade is explained by the profitable exploitation of arbitrage opportunities. But it should be noted that since the price differentials under autarky are eliminated when trade opens up and a single market is created between the trading countries, the autarkic prices, in reality, cannot be observed.

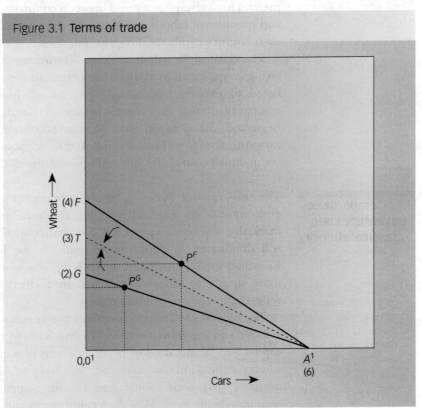

Figure 3.1 **Terms of trade**

England) producing two commodities (wine and cloth) with a *single* factor of production (labour). Portugal is allowed to possess an absolute advantage in the production of both goods. Nevertheless, a mutual basis for trade exists. It will pay Portugal to specialise in and export to England the good (wine) in which its absolute advantage is the greatest, and allow England to specialise in and export to Portugal the good (cloth) in which Portugal's absolute advantage is the least. In other words, comparative advantage, that is, comparative cost (relative productivity), rather than absolute advantage, provides the rationale for trade and the pattern of trade flows.

Comparative cost differences between nations lead to an important proposition: differences in comparative advantage gives rise to pre-trade (*autarkic*) price differences between countries, which allow them to derive mutual benefit if they subsequently trade at some price ratio between the respective pre-trade ratios. Note that at the level of the firm, it is arbitrage, the riskless exploitation of price differences, which drives the desire of firms to trade.

Since comparative advantage is so important in explaining why trade takes place, the basis of comparative advantage requires an explanation. In Ricardo's analysis comparative advantage is derived from differences between Portugal and England, respectively, in the productivity of labour in cloth and wine production (explained by unspecified technological reasons). That is to say, in general terms, the (*technology*) *production function* for a given good varies between countries, so that the same quality and quantity of labour given over to the production of a given good in each country produces different amounts.

The classical Ricardian version of comparative advantage succeeded in giving an explanation of why trade occurs and in what commodities, but it failed to explain convincingly *why* labour productivity, the basis for comparative costs differences between countries, should differ and it neglected the demand side of market transactions. The next stage forward, the neo-classical model offered some explanation of why comparative costs differ but still ignored the demand side of markets.

Comparative advantage: neo-classical theory

The *neo-classical theory of trade*, the factor proportions or factor endowments or Heckscher-Ohlin theorem (Ohlin, 1933) offers a markedly different explanation for comparative cost differences, but is still dominated by supply conditions. As we have seen, the classical Ricardian model attributed these to *differences in production functions* (or, more strictly, to differences in the productivity of labour), which were reflected in relative product prices.

The neo-classical model adopted a two-country, two-product, two-factor (labour and capital) structure. The model held that the combination of capital and labour used to produce a unit of a given good was the same wherever the good was produced (*identical production functions*) and it was assumed that both capital and labour, respectively, were everywhere qualitatively the same. How then could comparative cost differences arise?

Exhibit 3.4 Mutual benefits of trade

When trade opens up between France and Germany, the single market terms of trade (post-trade price ratio) will depend on reciprocal demand, that is, the relative strength of each country's demand for wheat and cars. In the general two country case, the terms of trade will settle closer to the larger country's price ratio under autarky. Suppose country A has a very large population and country B a very small one. When trade opens up, any exports traders from B make to A will hardly disturb the equilibrium balance of supply and demand inside A. Hence, traders from B will have the fullest arbitrage opportunity to trade close to A's pre-trade ratio, where the terms of trade will settle. Conversely, arbitrage opportunities for A's exporters to B will be relatively slight. In other words, the small country will claim most of the arbitrage benefits of trade. This phenomenon is referred to as *the importance of being unimportant*.

Figure 3.2, which demonstrates the benefits of trade, is essentially a portrayal of the gains to be had from trade specialisation. The French and German production frontiers are arranged in a box diagram. The area OGA^1 represents Germany's production possibility frontier, where Germany is shown to produce combination P^G of wheat and cloth. From the north-east corner, the area O^1FA is the production possibility frontier for France, producing combination P^F. The terms of trade, A^1T, for convenience, settle mid-way between the two countries' autarky price ratios, AF for France and A^1G for Germany.

Through increased product specialisation, France in wheat and Germany in cars, which is encouraged by arbitrage possibilities, both countries, through trade, are able to consume a higher combination of both goods (of which S, lying beyond each countries' production frontier, is an indication) compared to their production capabilities before trade. Trade permits the combined production and consumption of trading partners to exceed their pre-trade levels.

The only other means to achieve the same outcome would be through the following:

- increases in the productivity of factors of production
- an increase in the supply of factors of production
- the migration of factors from one country to another where they can be used more efficiently producing the goods they are more suited to produce.

Viewed in this light, international trade has enormous potential to add to global economic welfare.

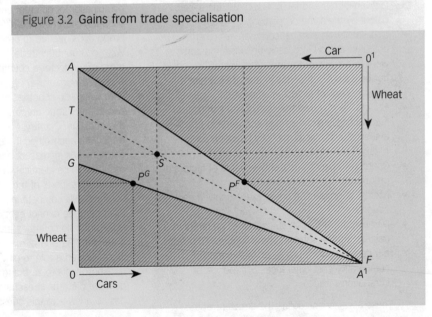

Figure 3.2 **Gains from trade specialisation**

The main feature of the theory explains this, which is that each country is endowed with different *proportions* of factors of production. If the prices of factors reflect their relative scarcity, then abundant factors will be

Exhibit 3.5 Factor proportions theory

Assumptions

- Perfect competition (a large number of buyers and sellers, of goods and factors, so that no individual can influence the market mechanism; the same quality of factors in each country; full employment of factors)
- free trade
- zero transport costs.

(With these assumptions, when trade opens up, a single market is established between the trading partners and domestic and international prices will be the same.)

- There are two goods (which we will refer to as *a* and *b*), two countries (*A* and *B*) and two factors of production (capital, *k*, and labour, *l*).
- There is a common technology (identical production function) for a good wherever it is produced. (This rules out Ricardian differences in relative production efficiency as an explanation of comparative costs.)
- One good (say, good *a*) is always more capital intensive than the other at any factor price ratio (that is, the goods differ in their factor proportions).
- There are constant returns to scale in production (a given increase in factor inputs will increase output by the same proportion).
- Opportunity or marginal cost increases as the output of a good increases (because if factors were to be released from one industry, they could not be used as efficiently in the other where a different ratio of factors is employed).
- Factors are mobile domestically and immobile internationally (so that, in effect, trade in goods is a substitute for factor mobility between countries).
- Countries have different endowments of factors of production.
- Factors of production are in fixed supply in each country.
- Demand patterns, that is, consumer preferences (tastes), are the same in both countries. (This rules out demand conditions as an explanation of comparative cost differences and, hence, of international trade.)

These assumptions define the structure of the model and are made to simplify the analysis, although the neutrality of some of these has been challenged.

Others are considered to have a relatively small part to play and so are held constant, for example, transport costs, economies of scale, and the pattern of demand in each country.

The important elements of the model and its distinctive character, given the various assumptions, are that countries differ in their factor endowments and goods differ in their factor proportions.

Suppose country *A* is well endowed with capital relative to labour and country *B*, therefore, is relatively well endowed with labour. Suppose also that good *a* is produced by a relatively capital intensive process. By virtue of these features, country *A* will have a comparative advantage in the production of the *a* good and country *B* in the *b* good. These comparative *cost* advantages will be reflected in each country's pre-trade price ratios (as in Figure 3.1). Exploiting arbitrage opportunities, producers in country *A* will specialise more in *a* goods and export them to country *B*, and country *B* will specialise more in *b* goods and export them to country *A*.

The factor proportions model seems able to answer the fundamental questions that might be expected of a trade theory:

- *Why* does trade take place? Because of differences in comparative costs brought about by the combination of different endowments of factors between countries and differences in the factor proportions needed to produce different goods.
- *What* do countries trade? The good that requires more of the factor a country is relatively best endowed with.
- *With whom* do countries trade? Because of its two country structure, the theory cannot answer this question. Country *A* and country *B* can only trade with each other. If the number of trading partners was increased, because goods are assumed to be identical wherever they are produced, exports of these goods from all countries will compete in a single global market. Bilateral trade cannot be explained.
- *How much* do countries trade? It would be helpful if the demand side of markets and transport costs were allowed a role to play, but the theory sets transport costs to zero and assumes the same demand patterns in each country and therefore has no answer to this question.

The only convincing explanations are to the questions of *what* and *why*, namely, the structure of trade.

relatively cheap and scarce factors relatively dear. From this, it follows that a country will have a low comparative cost and therefore a comparative advantage in the production of the good requiring relatively more of its abundant (cheap) factor. Conversely, it will have a comparative disadvantage in the production of the good requiring relatively more of its scarce (dear) factor. Thus, the essence of the theory is that a country will have a comparative advantage in, and will export, goods that use relatively intensively its abundant factor, and import goods that use relatively intensely the factor with which it is least endowed.

In the classical and the neo-classical models of comparative advantage, each country increases its production and export of the good in which it has a comparative advantage, in consequence of which global production and consumption will increase. But specialisation will not be complete except in the case of constant opportunity cost. In the Figure 3.1, where this is the case, France will specialise entirely in the production of wheat and Germany in the production of cars. In the more usual case of increasing opportunity cost, which is actually assumed in the factor proportions model, both countries will continue to produce both goods, but with output increasing in the 'advantaged' industry and decreasing in the 'disadvantaged' industry.

After trade opens up the home market, 'disadvantaged' producers will, for the first time, face competition from imports. In the real world, this will present no problem if factors of production released by the 'disadvantaged' industry can be fully absorbed in the expanding 'advantaged' industry (which occurs in the full employment factor proportions model). If not, despite the logical appeal of efficiency gains from trade based on comparative advantage, pressures will be present, yet again, for domestic protection against 'cheap' imports.

Weaknesses of traditional theories

The Ricardian and factor proportions theories both argue that comparative advantage is derived from differences in the supply side of markets – respectively, either differences in factor productivity or differences in factor endowments. Supply conditions were considered to be so much more influential and dominant than demand that demand conditions and consumer tastes are held constant in these models. But, as we have seen, what really matters for trade to take place is the opportunity for arbitrage, which requires there to be price differentials between countries. In addition to differences in supply conditions, differences in demand conditions can also cause this. Suppose productivity is the same in both countries (violating the Ricardian condition) and factor proportions are also the same (violating the factor proportions theory), but demand patterns for the two goods are markedly different. Then, despite the similarities in supply, the price ratios in each country would still be different and arbitrage-based trade would occur, this time driven by differences in conditions of demand.

A further criticism of these traditional trade theories is that they are static models, in which differences in productivity or factor endowments are considered to be immutable and god given. However, a major development since the 1950s has been the use of industrial policies and other forms of government intervention to *shift* comparative advantage from former leading industrial nations, which experienced processes of de-industrialisation as a result. For example, government inspired attempts to 'create' comparative advantage in industrial production has featured in economic development policies in Japan, South Korea, Singapore, Taiwan, Malaysia and Hong Kong, China and India. Japan, for example, began to create its advantage in capital-intensive products in the 1950s and beyond when still a labour-abundant, capital-poor nation. Singapore, through wage inflation, forced domestic and foreign firms alike to switch from labour to capital-intensive and high technology industries.

The traditional theories fail to account for these trends and dynamic shifts in the pattern of world trade. Further refinement to explanations of trade have led analyses beyond the perfectly competitive, static and constant returns to scale framework of the traditional theories. Nevertheless, comparative advantage as the source of international trade continues to provide the foundation for most of the modern reappraisals of the causes and consequences of international trade.

Exhibit 3.6 Vertical specialisation and trade liberalisation

Trade models serve to indicate that a major consequence of trade liberalisation is to increase specialisation and exporting according to whatever explanation is offered for comparative advantage. This kind of specialisation is presumed to be horizontal specialisation, that is, the production and export of final goods from scratch within a country.

Another dimension, however, is provided by vertical trade specialisation, which allows countries to exploit their comparative advantage in particular stages of the production process. This occurs when imported goods are used to produce goods that are exported. This means that the country-specific skills of several countries can be linked sequentially in the supply chain. Whereas this process culminates in the export of finished goods, trade also occurs in inter-mediate goods, therefore vertical specialisation must lead to increased trade.

Vertical trade, which continues to grow, by the early 1990s accounted for 20–25% of total trade, with national variations from as low as 3% in Japan, 12% in the USA, 19% in Germany, 30% in the UK and 47% in the Netherlands. One explanation for this growth is the advances that have been made in communication technology and the persistent downward pressure on communication costs. These have improved the cost efficiency, coordination and monitoring of cross-border production, particularly in diverse locations, facilitating the development of regional production networks incorporating component manufacture and product assembly for multinational firms.

Production networks favour vertical rather than horizontal trade. A second explanation lies in the reduction in tariff barriers, particularly within trade blocs, the effect of which is magnified as reductions are applied to the various production stages of a good.

The growth of vertical specialisation in its modern form was undoubtedly stimulated by the take-off in the 1960s of the *maquiladora*, the non-Mexican production plants located in free trade zones along the US–Mexican border. These plants process and assemble components imported from, and exported back, to foreign firms, of which US firms enjoy tax and tariff exemptions. American firms, seeking ways to source cheap labour, learned how to manage cross-border production in Mexico and other low wage cost locations. In time, multinational competitors from other nations followed their sourcing activities.

**Extensions of
comparative
cost arguments**

Technology

The factor proportions theory concludes that a country's exporting industries will be those which use more of the abundant and, therefore, cheap factor of production. Labour-rich countries, therefore, paying relatively low wages, would be predicted to export labour-intensive products. Kravis (1956) refuted this by showing that exporting industries are usually high-wage industries, explaining this paradox by claiming that technological superiority accounted for the pattern of trade. This observation brought technology to the fore as a new explanation for comparative advantage. Posner (1961), for example, argued that local producers and consumers in a country need time to respond to the challenge imposed by new, innovative imports. This *technology imitation lag*, which has two elements, a consumer demand lag and a producers' reaction lag, will serve to maintain the flow of imports if the consumer demand lag is shorter than the local entrepreneurs' reaction lag.

Learning by doing, the learning curve effect, is another technological influence associated with a decline in producers' unit costs as output increases over time. Unit costs can decline because firms become more familiar with, and develop, manufacturing technology, such as plant design, manufacturing processes and plant layout. In effect, the association between increased productivity and experience creates a technological ascendancy that provides a stimulus to trade. This influence on the pattern of trade could persist through time if the accumulation and diffusion of technological know-how involves costly and specialised training. Technological superiority and *innovation* is also at the heart of the product life cycle, which offers a further dynamic account of how trade occurs in knowledge-intensive products and how comparative advantage in such trade is subject to regional shifts (Vernon, 1966). Exports originate from the innovating country, but in time technological diffusion stimulates production in other industrial countries. Eventually, international technological differences are eroded and wage costs come into play as the knowledge gap is overcome and so production continually migrates from advanced industrial country to newly industrialised countries and on to developing countries. In a scenario where new products are constantly coming on stream, the shifting pattern of trade is one where exporting of *new* innovative products from advanced countries is eventually followed by the production and exporting of these '*old*' products as they reach maturity by imitative developing countries. These are just some of the efforts that have been made to introduce technology and technological differences between countries as explanations for comparative and shifting comparative advantage.

**Increasing returns
to scale**

An assumption of the factor proportions theory is that production functions reveal constant returns to scale, that is a doubling of inputs of factors will double output. However, increasing returns to scale, where a doubling of inputs will more than double output, is a strong possibility, because as output expands factors of production can become more specialised causing their productivity to increase. Also, the cost of raw

Exhibit 3.7 International product life cycle model

The product life cycle hypothesis (PLC) was developed by Vernon to explain how US firms, through sequential stages of domestic expansion, exporting, then overseas production, emerged after World War II as the dominant nation for the export of innovative products and for outward foreign direct investment (Vernon, 1966; Vernon and Wells, 1968). The assumptions of the factor proportions theory, specifically, identical production functions, universally available technology, immobile factors of production between countries, perfect competition, product homogeneity and constant returns to scale, severely constrained his ability to explain the dominance of the USA in technology-driven trade. In the neo-classical tradition, however, he sought to use comparative advantage as the basis for this trade (Dunning, 1999).

The role of technology and innovation is emphasised in the PLC. Technology embodies production know-how and the application of scientific knowledge to machines and processes in the exploitation of market knowledge. Technology is acquired through learning processes and expenditure on research and development and acquiring market information. The technological input in a firm can be recognised by the quality of its blueprints, technical drawings, product and production specifications, the quality and design of its capital equipment, training requirements and dependence on skilled management and labour.

The PLC attempts to explain America's changing trade pattern over time but also why it continues over time to retain ascendancy in the delivery to markets of innovative products. A combination of relatively high income levels, labour scarcity and capital abundance generates a demand in America, much sooner than anywhere else, for sophisticated labour-saving products. In the early stages of the cycle local producers satisfy the domestic US market. As consumer tastes are increasingly identified and shaped by familiarity and usage, markets become more standardised and the surviving firms, emerging from a highly competitive environment, enjoy long production runs and economies of scale. A fall in unit costs and entry to the market of lower income and more discerning consumers push down prices and allow domestic markets to expand. Markets and products stabilise in the next stage of the cycle and firms seek export opportunities in other high-income countries. In the next stage, US firms serve their overseas markets by producing abroad in order to protect their markets and get around trade barriers as similar industries develop overseas. This migration of US firms allows them to enjoy lower labour costs and eventually they may begin to serve their US markets from their overseas subsidiaries.

The model is one of the first to offer an account of trade *and* international investment. The theory has a time dimension lacking in earlier theories and recognises that firms in monopolistic markets constantly strive to protect their markets through innovative product differentiation, technological superiority and the transfer of resources to lower cost markets. In attempting to explain the post-World War II surge in American exports and investment overseas, the model, a creature of its time, has lost its appeal as other countries have shown that technological superiority and the flying geese syndrome is not unique to the USA. The PLC, however, continues to have its place among the modern explanations of international trade in innovative manufacturing products.

materials and components will reduce as larger firms can enforce quantity discounts. Increasing returns to scale offers an additional explanation of comparative advantage (Krugman, 1993). Krugman's *core–periphery* model, which introduces spatial dimensions, offers an account of how one nation or region can emerge as a manufacturing core and another as a periphery. This *new trade theory* relies on a combination of economies of scale and location (and therefore low transport costs), both of which are held constant in traditional models to explain comparative advantage. The new trade theory convincingly demonstrates why countries endowed with similar factors of production, namely, the advanced industrial nations, are just as likely to trade with each other as with dissimilar agricultural countries. The dominance in international trade in manufactures of North America and Western Europe for most of the second half of the 20th century and their continuing close-knit trade relationships can be explained by the tendency for the core to perpetuate itself. This affords further explanation for the desire of Asian countries to create advantages to enable them to overcome their god-given role as members of a peripheral region and join the community of advanced industrial nations.

Intra-industry trade

The traditional models appear best suited to offer an adequate explanation for trade between *dissimilarly endowed* countries, such as industrial and agricultural countries, but trends in the second half of the 20th century cast further doubt on their general relevance. Three trends are particularly apparent since the 1960s. Trade between *similarly endowed* industrial nations has steadily increased to around 60 per cent of world trade; *intra-industry trade* (for example, nations exporting cars to each other's markets) has also increased, and nations increasingly trade with their neighbours whatever their relative factor endowments.

Linder (1961) proposed an *overlapping demand* model to explain trade in manufactures between similarly endowed countries, observing that firms rarely enter export markets before developing their home markets. Demand conditions in the home market, which will be influenced by average incomes, determine the kind of goods a country will specialise in and eventually export. The model specifies the existence of product differentiation by assuming that firms in high-income countries will specialise in 'high-income' goods to satisfy a relatively large demand for luxury goods: firms in low-income countries will specialise in 'low-income' goods to satisfy a relatively large demand for essentials. In common with the product life cycle model, the Linder model argues that high-income countries are likely to find their major markets to be in high-income countries with similar tastes, demand patterns, and factor conditions. Similarly, low-income countries will find their major markets in low-income countries. Trade is still likely between high- and low-income countries, but the extent of this will depend on the degree of overlapping consumption patterns. This can arise because of unequal income distribution – there are rich and poor consumers in rich and poor countries. In general, overlapping demand is the determinant of intra-industry trade in the model a term first used in the 1970s to describe two-way trade within industries.

The more similar the overlap between countries, the greater the trade between them, in relative terms, is likely to be. Thus, income disparities act as barriers to trade. Despite the dominance of demand-side factors in inter-industry trade, comparative cost influences are still present in the shape of economies of scale and industrial concentration. Thus, inter-industry trade is not only greater between high-income countries with similar demand and supply characteristics, but is also most common between industries enjoying economies of scale and dominated by large oligopolists. If economies of scale were not present, all countries with similar consumption patterns and resource endowments would be able to produce efficiently any particular product type, saving on transport costs.

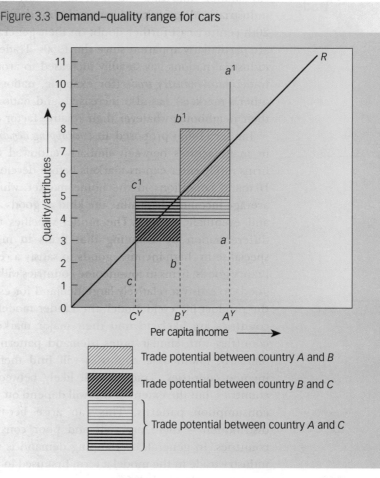

Figure 3.3 Demand–quality range for cars

Counter-trade

Introduction

International trade models purport to describe patterns of trade in a multilateral world, where goods exchange for currency and countries and firms are free to trade with any partner they choose. Trade between any pair of countries need never be in balance. By allowing firms to buy and sell in the most favourable markets in a world free of market barriers, free multilateral trade would maximise global economic efficiency. And yet balanced bilateral trade between pairs of countries and trade arrangements that have more in common with bilateral than multilateral trade is a major feature in the world economy. When trade is locked into bilateral deals, it would appear that economic efficiency is being surrendered in the interest of other goals. This kind of trade of trade, which diminishes the role of currency and introduces payment in kind (that is, goods for goods) is termed *countertrade*.

Countertrade is the term used to describe barter-style exchange transactions in which the seller accepts goods or a combination of goods and services in partial or total settlement. When goods exchange for currency, as in normal trade, all that is required is a single coincidence of wants. Barter trade requires a double coincidence of wants and on these grounds alone is likely to be costly, time consuming and always inefficient and inferior to currency transactions. Yet countertrade, in its various forms, according to various estimates accounts for up to 30 per cent of world trade. Formerly an instrument of bilateral and reciprocal trade and most closely associated with inconvertible currency regimes and state-controlled trading practices in centrally planned economies and LDCs, countertrade nowadays is an indulgence shared by most trading nations. The primary purpose of countertrade is still to impose reciprocity in trading relations in countries with high levels of external debt in order to minimise their dependence on scarce foreign currency. The main forms of countertrade are commercial, industrial and financial countertrade.

Commercial countertrade relates to short-term transactions of under three years and for relatively small amounts. In east–west trade, western firms are often reluctant partners in commercial countertrade, but find that the alternative may be no trade at all. The commonest forms are *barter* and *counterpurchase*. Barter, the simplest and most straightforward form of countertrade, is the exchange of goods for goods of equivalent value between one or more partners under a single contract involving no exchange of currencies. Usually one-off spot transactions between governments, barter involves traders from countries with limited access both to hard (convertible) currencies and outside sources of credit, as in the former Soviet Union, but members of the Organisation of Petroleum Exporting Countries (OPEC), free of foreign currency and trade credit problems, barter oil for military equipment and essential imports. Bilateral clearing accounts, synonymous with centrally planned economies, represent advanced forms of barter.

Counterpurchase (or parallel trade), a post-World War II trading development, involves separate contracts for the exchange of unrelated goods through third parties. For example, counterpurchase occurs when a firm or government agency in country *A* buys goods from country *B* subject to a firm in country *B* agreeing to buy goods from country *A*. The agreement may be less than, equal to or more than the value of the initial export order. Currency payments form a significant element of these transactions and sales of the counterpurchased items are restricted to designated markets. When the value of goods exchanged is not equal, the imbalance is paid for in foreign currency. A high proportion of the foreign sales of military equipment manufacturers consists of counterpurchase transactions.

Industrial countertrade links capital flows and trade flows and offers an alternative to inward FDI. The main characteristic of industrial countertrade is the transfer of technology, plant and equipment to a host nation via *compensation* (buyback) or *offset agreements*. With compensation, an exporter of plant and equipment agrees to buy back part of the output produced with this means of production as full or partial payment, spanning a period up to 25 years. Typically, therefore, compensatory items usually consist of components and finished goods. Offset applies to high technology transfers and is common in aerospace, defence industries, large construction projects, electronics and telecommunications. Here the seller of capital equipment, components and supporting services incorporates into the manufacture of their products materials, components and subassemblies supplied by the buyer or else the seller buys the equivalent value of the contract in goods supplied by the buying country. Many joint ventures and licence agreements between western and developing country partners are countertrade arrangements set up to organise and administer an offset agreement. Western nations also favour offset agreements (disguised as local procurement agreements) as a condition of inward foreign investment. Most offset arrangements are self-liquidating, the plant and equipment becoming the property of the host country at the end of the contract period. In many developing and east European countries, where industrial countertrade is generally preferred to FDI, industrial countertrade is mandated in order to gain access to western technology and to find markets for the product of this acquired technology in western markets.

Financial countertrade, which is necessary to facilitate complex countertrade deals, relates to the financial arrangements that are linked to commercial and industrial countertrade. As examples, with *switch trading* the settlement of accounts between two countries are transferred to one or more third parties. Suppose, for example, country *A* has $10 million of accumulated credits with country *B*. A bank in country *C* may accept the goods at a discount for $7 million, which is used by *A* to buy preferred goods from country *D*. Meanwhile, the bank sells the goods to country *E*. A feature of switch trading, which allows a country to avoid accepting unwanted goods from *B*, is the intervention of third parties to facilitate the movement of goods between source countries and final markets, artificial pricing and heavy discounts to entice buyers and high brokerage costs. *Swap trading* is used to reduce transport and insurance costs on trade in basic commodities such as chemicals, sugar and oil. Suppose Russia has a contract to supply oil to Cuba and Mexico has a contract to supply oil to Greece. In swap trading, by agreement, Russia instead supplies Greece and Mexico supplies Cuba, reducing shipping costs substantially.

Compensation trade was used before World War II between Germany and the Balkan states to neutralise the effects of hyperinflation. Goods exchanged for goods and currency was used only to settle net positions at the end of a financial year. The term countertrade (*Gegengeschäft*) was used to describe these bilateral swaps of goods for goods. During World War II, the UK and her allies used similar bilateral trade to minimise foreign exchange transactions. Similar arrangements quickly followed inside the Soviet Union and between Soviet states and some neighbouring countries, such as Finland. The Soviet system of bilateral countertrade, administered by state (or foreign) trading corporations (STCs), became the cornerstone of COMECON, the international trading network of the centrally planned Soviet system. In the 1950s and 1960s, from a Soviet perspective, trade problems with the west included increasing levels of Soviet trade deficits and external debt, limited trade opportunities because of currency inconvertibility, import controls, a technology gap and the inability of poor-quality Soviet goods to find acceptance in western markets. To overcome these problems and the barriers thrown up by the Cold War between the Soviet Union and the west, the strictly controlled COMECON countertrade system was extended to trade with the west, described as industrial cooperation. At the time of the collapse of the Soviet system in 1989, barter, counterpurchase and buyback accounted for most east–west trade.

In January 1991, the system of planned bilateral trade was formally abandoned between communist states. World market prices were to become the pricing benchmark and it was deemed that goods had to be settled in dollars. But because of inflation, bottlenecks and black markets in eastern states and a continuing scarcity of goods and international currencies, the former system of countertrade was simply modified and continued to dominate ad hoc arrangements between the former communist countries and the west. Firms, not the state, began to conduct countertrade: buyback became linked even more to joint ventures and licence agreements: counterpurchase became preferred to barter and deals became short term, mostly involving small-value transactions. Countertrade, the old and familiar method of trading, is still heavily relied on in Russia in times of financial crisis, as in 1998, and at all times when the rouble is poor value and Russian importers cannot get access to foreign exchange.

The disbanding of the state trading organisations in the former Soviet Union created an unstable vacuum, increasing the financial risks to western firms, because traders in east Europe often lack the authority to make deals. In Poland, Czechoslovakia and Hungary, the countries leading the way towards workable market economies but also strictly monitored by the IMF, which disapproves of countertrade, there is no longer an obligation to countertrade. In the CIS, Romania, Bulgaria and Yugoslavia, because of acute international currency shortages, counter-trade remains an obligation.

The extent to which countertrade is used cannot be measured precisely because its existence is easily hidden and transactions never appear on companies' income statements. Around 20 countries were involved in countertrade in the early 1970s when it was the almost exclusive domain of socialist states. By 1980 fewer than 30 of the 155 member states of the United Nations were free of countertrade and by the late 1980s over 90 countries, featuring the majority of west European states, were formally

involved in countertrade transactions with their trading partners
(Verzariu, 1989).

Explanations for countertrade

A number of attempts have been made to account for the continuing
proliferation of countertrade in an age of increasing globalisation, market
deregulation and the drastically reduced number of centrally planned
economies.

Countertrade as a marketing tool

Firms and governments alike sometimes see countertrade as a strategic
marketing tool to help maintain trade and business links with many
countries and to open up markets that would otherwise remain closed. A
fear of exporters is that any competitive advantage they have will be of no
consequence if they refuse to contemplate countertrade, whereas a
willingness to do so may open up new markets and secure long-term
supply lines and sourcing opportunities for components and subassembly
activities. Firms willing to take a proactive stance towards countertrade
view it as a supplement rather than an alternative to normal, currency-
based trade and as an export opportunity rather than a threat. By
providing a 'service' that others are unwilling to adopt, a firm willing to
countertrade and assist a country to find markets for its goods can
differentiate its products from those of its competitors, establish first
mover advantages, and build up goodwill and establish long-term
relationships with local firms and government officials. In one-off bids
for highly competitive international contracts, ostensibly on the basis of
price, quality and delivery dates, a countertrade proposal may have an
edge.

Countertrade, however, often merely makes the best of a bad situation.
Cash flow problems can arise because of delays in getting delivery of the
countertraded goods, and brokerage fees and commissions have to be
paid.

To overcome their lack of marketing expertise and limited access to
distribution channels an objective of countertrade in east European
countries and LDCs is to get multinational firms to use their market
power and global networks to help these countries' products, especially
non-traditional exports, to penetrate developed countries' markets. Lack
of investment in new technology and product development has often
meant that east European countries made low-quality products which are
ill suited to western tastes. The opportunity to tie in their export trade
with the distribution networks of MNCs requires efforts to be made to
raise quality and product performance standards to those expected in
western markets.

One particular benefit to western firms is that countertrade overcomes
the risk of non-payment by heavily indebted countries, and although
countertrade may be less profitable per capita than traditional trade, it
may enable western firms to increase export volumes. A further attraction
of a willingness to countertrade is that it may give a western firm a
competitive advantage in developing and emerging markets.

Transaction cost explanations of countertrade

The basis of transaction cost analysis, pioneered by Coase (1937) and followed up by Williamson (1975), Buckley and Casson (1976), Hennart (1982) and others is that hierarchies (firms and organisations) substitute for markets when transaction costs in markets are high. (See Chapter 4 for a fuller discussion of transaction costs.) Multinational firms are ones that exploit their ability to reduce transaction costs relative to the costs associated with arms' length market transactions and are able to transfer their 'internal markets' to foreign markets at low marginal cost and retain control of foreign operations. Hennart (1989) regards countertrade as an alternative to foreign direct investment and to normal trading relationships. However, the rationale for countertrade is not to save on foreign exchange or overcome obstacles to trade, but to reduce the transaction costs of conducting international business by making contracts more enforceable (Hennart, 1990). But international institutions such as the IMF, the World Bank, the WTO and OECD, oppose countertrade as being harmful to efficient international trade and to offer an inferior solution to world trade problems.

Hennart argues that compensation (buyback) and counterpurchase are appropriate in circumstances where high transaction costs would otherwise prevent international trade from taking place. There are two circumstances when transaction costs are likely to be high: first, when there is significant information asymmetry between the parties, and, second, when the market is narrow because of scale economies, high transportation costs or the need to make transaction-specific investments. In the case of the sale of technology and the means of production – plant and equipment – a buyback contract will guarantee an efficient transfer of equipment and know-how at a realistic cost by requiring the supplier to purchase some of the plant's output at agreed prices. This observation that the rationale of buyback is to minimise the transaction costs of a long-term relationship ignores the primary feature, namely that the buyback contract allows the host country to exploit the seller's desire to enter the host market by enforcing a reciprocal agreement on the seller to find foreign markets for the resultant output. A similar conclusion can be made about counterpurchase contracts entered into to push non-traditional exports into new markets. The purpose is to surmount trade barriers, not to compensate for an unwillingness to countenance foreign direct investment.

From the perspective of countertrade versus normal trade relations, countertrade in most circumstances is revealed as a high-cost and relatively time-consuming, imperfect and inefficient market transaction. Except in particular circumstances, transaction cost analysis fails to explain either the existence and growth of countertrade or the reasons why firms and trading organisations resort to its use. Western firms accept countertrade as a high transaction cost alternative to no trade at all. Trade partners in LDCs resort to countertrade in order to overcome market failure.

Market failure explanations for countertrade

Market failure occurs when a market for goods or services or factors of production fails to achieve an efficient allocation of resources. A global economic organisation of perfect competition would produce perfectly operating price mechanisms that would yield market clearing prices; hence there would be no motives for countertrade, which would have no role to play. But, if present, countertrade would reduce economic efficiency and the welfare gains to be had from free trade. But international trade, investment and finance mechanisms are far from being efficient due to market failure in various forms, which present obstacles to effective market clearing prices for traded goods.

Market failure can be associated with naturally occurring imperfections in markets, such as transport costs (giving rise to switch trading), and government-imposed market imperfections, which include tariffs and non-tariff barriers, foreign exchange restrictions, and controls and regulations impeding capital mobility and FDI. Major market imperfections include asymmetric information and the absence of forward markets and high levels of risk and uncertainty. Firm-specific market imperfections include proprietary technology, information asymmetry and other elements of market power. Countertrade overcomes the absence of forward markets for many goods and the inability of markets to price uncertainty and risk over long periods, by permitting long-term goods-dominated prices. Information asymmetry introduces the possibility of opportunistic behaviour when contracts are specified by price. The value of technology-based products, for example, are likely to be better known to the supplier than the buyer, inducing the seller to inflate the supply price and the price of management and technical support services. Further, the buyer may not only fear that the technology may be relatively expensive, but also inefficient, outdated and prone to obsolescence. Conversely, the seller may fear for the loss of control over the use made of the technology, perhaps of creating a competitor. Countertrade can circumvent this double informational asymmetry (and any government restrictions on FDI) by a buyback, product-sharing or joint venture agreement. By such means the seller can control the way the technology is applied and be assured of long-term markets. The buyer can bridge concerns about performance characteristics by locking the supplier into a guarantee of quality and gaining unbiased information on market demand, price, cost structures, and the economic viability of the contract.

In effect, countertrade offers a defence against the possibility that the buyer or the seller might under-perform and can secure greater access to protected markets. Although countertrade is a response to such distortions to markets, it can, in turn, lead to further elements of market failure, such as bilateral trade, restricted market access, price distortion and high costs of intermediation. Mandated countertrade, in particular, is both a direct response to, and a creator of, market failure. Since the onset of the sovereign debt crisis in the 1980s, heavily indebted countries find it difficult and costly to borrow and have seen their level of trade credit severely reduced by international financial institutions and western governments. High debt repayments have severely reduced the availability of foreign exchange to pay for essential imports and protectionism denies them opportunities to export. Hence, mandated countertrade reduces the need for foreign exchange but creates further market distortions by bypassing competitive markets for the goods that are involved in mandated exchanges.

Summary

This chapter has outlined the major influences on the pattern and flow of trade between countries. At any one time the free flow of international trade is subjected to natural and man-made barriers of many kinds. Despite this, the growth of world trade continues to outstrip both the growth of global production and growth rates. Adam Smith introduced the concept of absolute advantage to explain how trade between countries, through increased specialisation, would bestow mutual benefit to trading partners. The classical theory advanced the analysis by introducing the notion of comparative advantage to explain price differences between countries for similar products. It is these price differences that drive trade. The aim of all theories is to explain comparative advantage (even though absolute advantage is sufficient to explain much of the trade that occurs, especially between industrial and agricultural economies).

Many trade patterns can be identified, of which the most important are: trade between advanced and developing countries (north–south trade), explained quite adequately by the classical and neo-classical models; trade between advanced industrial countries with similar resources (north–north trade), which requires more complex analysis; and trade in the triad, where around 80 per cent of international trade takes place. Many accounts have been given and theories developed to explain the causes of comparative advantage and international trade: factor productivity, factor endowments, technology, economies of scale, location and transport costs, product differentiation and overlapping consumption patterns. All these explanations, which in their own way have made a contribution, challenge one or more of the assumptions that underpin the factor proportions theory, but the complexity of the arguments and the partiality of their explanations indicate quite clearly that a complete explanation of international trade is beyond the wit of any single theory.

Despite the clear superiority of multilateral trade regimes over bilateral trade in terms of market efficiency, countertrade, in its various guises, continues to have a tenacious hold in the international economy. Some attempts have been made to justify countertrade as a major marketing tool of firms wishing to maintain and expand trade relationships, but it is probably best explained by market failure and some countertrade defies any obvious economic or commercial rationale.

Review questions

1 Show why international price differentials account for most types of international trade. Give examples of trade where price differentials do not seem to be present.
2 Describe the factor proportions theory of international trade and assess its strengths and weaknesses.
3 Try to make sense, if there is any, in the suggestion that national firms are competitors in international trade, whereas countries are trading partners.
4 Examine the assertion that the international product life cycle model has limited relevance in the modern world.
5 Discuss the view that all trade theories are based on one version or another of comparative advantage.
6 Discuss how well trade models explain shifting comparative advantage in the global economy.
7 Account for the existence of countertrade in the world economy and explore the view that its influence will continue as a solution to the problems developing countries face when attempting to export to western markets.
8 Explain the existence of so many varieties of countertrade techniques.

Bibliography

Buckley, P. J. and Casson, M. C. (1976) *The Future of the Multinational Enterprise*, London, Macmillan.

Coase, R. H. (1937) 'The nature of the firm', *Economica*, 4, November, pp. 386–405.

Dunning, J. H. (1999) 'Globalization and the theory of MNE activity' in N. Hood and S. Young (eds) *The Globalization of Multinational Enterpise Activity and Economic Development*, Basingstoke, Macmillan.

Forker, L. (1996) 'Countertrades's impact on the supply function', *International Journal of Purchasing and Materials Management*, 32, 4.

Forker, L. and Pearson, J. N. (1995) 'International countertrade: has purchasing's role really changed?', *International Journal of Purchasing and Materials Management*, 32, 4.

Hennart, J.-F. (1990) 'Some empirical dimensions of countertrade', *Journal of International Business Studies*, 21, 2, pp. 243–70.

Hennart, J.-F. (1989) 'The transaction costs rationale for countertrade', *Journal of Law, Economics and Organization*, 5, 1, pp. 127–53.

Hennart, J.-F. (1982) *A Theory of Multinational Enterprise*, Ann Harbor, University of Michigan Press.

Kravis, I. B. (1956) 'Availability and other influences on the commodity composition of trade', *Journal of Political Economy*, 64, April, pp. 143–55.

Krugman, P. (1993) *Geography and Trade*, Cambridge, MA: MIT Press.

Linder, S. B. (1961) *An Essay in Trade and Transformation*, New York, Wiley.

Leamer, E. E. (1995) *The Heckscher-Ohlin Model in Theory and Practice*, Princeton Studies in International Finance, 77.

Lecraw, D. J. (1989) 'The management of countertrade: factors influencing success', *Journal of International Business Studies*, Spring, pp. 41–59.

Ohlin, B. (1933) *Inter-Regional and International Trade*, Cambridge, MA, Harvard University Press.

Porter, M. E. (1991) *The Competitive Advantage of Nations*, London, Macmillan.

Posner, M. (1961) 'International trade and technical change' *Oxford Economic Papers*, 13, October, pp. 323–41.

Ricardo, D. (1817) *Principles of Political Economy and Taxation*, reprinted in P. Sraffa (ed.) *The Works of David Ricardo*, London, Cambridge University Press.

Smith, Adam (1776), *An Inquiry into the Nature and Causes of the Wealth of Nations*, re-issued, 1937, 1985, New York, Random House.

Vernon, R. (1966) 'International investment and trade in the product cycle', *Quarterly Journal of Economics*, May.

Vernon, R. and Wells, L. (1968) 'A product cycle for international trade?', *Journal of Marketing*, July.

Verzariu, P. (1989) *Barter and Countertrade*, Washington, DC, US Department of Commerce.

Verzariu, P. (1985) *Countertrade, Barter and Offsets – New Strategies for Profit in International Trade*, Boston, MA, McGraw-Hill.

Williamson, O. E. (1975) *Markets and Hierarchies: Analysis and Antitrust Implications*, New York, Free Press.

Case 3.1 Natural disasters: El Niño

El Niño is the name given to unusually warm ocean surface temperatures in the eastern equatorial Pacific. The phenomenon is caused by a reduction in the strength of the trade winds around the equator. Warm waters off the coast of Indonesia flow east towards the Americas. The tendency for this event to occur close to Christmas has led to the name El Niño, the Christ Child in Spanish. El Niño has been the cause of many natural disasters, whether through drought or flooding. The rise in temperature of the ocean increases the moisture content of the air, creating high winds, torrential rain and heavy flooding and, consequently, causing massive damage to the infrastructure and food crops.

El Niño brought the worst drought in 50 years when it hit Indonesia and other countries in March 1997. From being self-sufficient in rice, Indonesia became the world's largest importer and forest fires adversely affected the tourist industry. The effect of widespread torrential rains during the second half of 1998 destroyed the hopes of many countries for a recovery from these severe droughts. From mid-1998 onwards, widespread flooding throughout Asia severely damaged rice production, which accounts for over 90% of world supply.

In the wake of Hurricane Mitch, the child of El Niño, which swept across Central America in October 1998, traditional export crops, vital sources of foreign exchange, were destroyed. In Nicaragua major crops were devastated, including 30% of the coffee crop. In El Salvador 80% of the maize crop and much of the sugar crop was lost and many coffee plantations, major export earners, saw their harvests perish. In Honduras export earning coffee crops were also lost.

In some cases processing plants have been forced to close and production transferred to other countries. The unusually warmer weather in 1998 saw an increase in construction activity in many countries, greatly benefiting exporters of construction industry supplies. Warmer weather also contributed to an increase in the output and exports of some crops, such as palm oil. Fish catches and exports of fishmeal increased in areas affected by El Niño.

Case 3.2 The Al Yamamah paradox

Countertrade formed the basis of the Al Yamamah ('goodwill') agreements in 1985 and 1988. Under these treaties, the UK exported military equipment to Saudi Arabia and established joint ventures there in return for payments of crude oil. Why? Would it not have been easier for payment to be made in currency and the UK, if so desired, to use the currency to buy oil? Why were military exports tied to industrial investment? Can countertrade 'theory' explain this paradox?

Under the 1985 treaty, Saudi Arabia agreed to buy £5 billion worth of equipment, including 72 Tornado aircraft and 30 Hawk and 30 PC9 training aircraft and ongoing maintenance and training services. British Aerospace (BAe) was contracted by the British government to supply and procure all equipment and services. In payment, the Saudis gave the British Ministry of Defence (MoD) a regular supply of crude oil, initially set at 400,000 barrels a day and sold by the MoD on the open market. BAe withdrew funds at predetermined dates and distributed funds to its partners in the agreement, Messerschmitt-Bolkow-Blohm, Aeritalia and Pilatos. BAe typically withdrew £2 billion per year.

Under the agreement, the UK incurred $1.5 billion of offset obligations to Saudi Arabia. To settle these, the UK Offset Committee arranged for UK companies to import from Saudi Arabia and enter into 11 UK–Saudi joint ventures covering food, petrochemicals and pharmaceuticals. In the second, 1988, agreement, Saudi Arabia purchased a further £10 billion of equipment, including 48 Tornados, 60 Hawks, 20 PC9 training aircraft, 6 Sandown class mine hunters, 125 business jets and several 146 airliners (for military use), and 88 Black Hawk helicopters. The agreement also included the construction of two airbases and one naval facility. More offset obligations were incurred. Because of budgetary pressures in Saudi Arabia and sharp falls in the price of oil, Al Yamamah II was not signed until 1993. To compensate for the lower oil value the daily oil delivery was increased to 600,000 barrels, in addition to which Saudi Arabia had to pay additional monies. The value of the deal was £20 billion.

What was the rationale behind the agreement? Barter was not necessary because both the UK and Saudi Arabia had international currencies (sterling and the riyad). Saudi Arabia already had well-established relationships with Exxon, Texaco and Mobil to sell its oil and the UK was a net oil exporter. Perhaps the answer can be found in market failure and transactions cost analysis – imperfect financial markets, lack of forward markets, transaction costs and monopoly power and information asymmetry?

If international capital markets are not operating efficiently, credit may be unavailable to creditworthy borrowers, lending credibility to barter or counterpurchase. Financial markets were certainly under strain in the 1980s, when the rise in oil prices, the fall in commodity prices and interest rate rises greatly increased third world debt. Following the threatened default by Brazil in 1983, banks stopped lending to LDCs, further encouraging countertrade to become a major vehicle for maintaining their trade flows. But none of this would have affected the Saudi government's ability to borrow abroad. As the OPEC leader, it benefited from the oil price rises and was creditworthy. In later years, Saudi Arabia had no difficulty making cash payments to make up for declining oil prices.

Forward markets do not exist for most products, so if traders wish to hedge against price changes they need to do so through barter or counterpurchase. But forward markets do exist for currencies and oil, so if Saudi Arabia wished to hedge, it could have used currency and oil forward markets. The transaction cost argument is that countertrade might lower transaction costs and be cheaper than monetary transactions. A buyback agreement, for example, would make it in the equipment manufacturer's interest to ensure the equipment worked to specification. Yet oil barter certainly increased transaction costs as the Ministry of Defence had no experience of oil sales and had to pay merchant bankers to act on its behalf, and phased in payments created crippling cash flow problems for BAe.

The Al Yamamah agreement could have been an attempt to exchange monopoly output; both sides using countertrade to gain access to each other's products. The Saudi's could achieve monopoly profits by restricting the sale of oil to the UK, an oil-dependent economy. The UK could protect monopoly profits on its advanced technology by retaining proprietary control. But neither country has significant monopoly to exert. Many countries have similar advanced technology as the UK, and many more countries export oil. Further, as a net exporter, the UK had no need for oil and, once UK–Saudi joint ventures were established, Saudi Arabia could respond to monopoly pressures for UK firms by challenging the integrity of the agreement.

Countertrade might arise because one party knows less than the other does about the quality of the traded product or technology and the accessibility of markets. To reassure the buyer that the technology works and that markets are prepared to accept the produce of the technology, the seller, under a buyback agreement, can accept the product in payment. But military aircraft consumes oil – it does not produce it. Yet if military equipment is considered to be a factor of production of oil, in the sense that Saudi Arabia needs to protect itself against its enemies or lose its oil territories, maybe this offers a plausible explanation for Al Yamamah.

A sounder reason might lie inside the OPEC cartel. Under OPEC rules, members' sales of oil were restricted by quota. This control of the supply increased oil prices and generated monopoly profits. A weakness of cartels is the free rider problem: individual members may feel tempted to export more than their quota and gain further revenues, but at the cost of lower prices and damage to the other members. Countertrade allows a cartel member to exceed its quota. In 1985 the OPEC Executive Council, chaired by Saudi Oil minister, Sheikh Yamani, convinced that the cartel could only survive if members stuck to their quota, agreed to ban oil countertrade. Influential members of the Saudi royal family thought otherwise and wanted to sell more oil. Al Yamamah marked the end of Sheikh Yamani's once powerful influence inside OPEC.

4

Protection

Learning objectives

By the end of this chapter, you should be able to:

- understand the main reason why countries should wish to engage in protectionism
- categorise the different forms of protection
- make the distinction between tariff and non-tariff barriers to trade and between 'old' protection and 'new' protection
- appreciate the roles of the major international trade institutions – the General Agreement on Tariffs and Trade (GATT) and its successor, the World Trade Organisation (WTO)
- understand some of the tensions between trade liberalisation and the concept of 'fair trade'
- recognise that the WTO is an enforcer of trade regulations *and* foreign direct investment

Key terms

- trade policy • policy instruments • the costs of protection • the GATT
- the WTO • tariffs • non-tariff barriers • arguments for protection
- market distortions • free trade versus fair trade • intellectual property rights • anti-dumping • trade-related investment measure

Introduction

A basic proposition of international trade theories is that international trade, relative to a state of autarky, increases global efficiency, incomes and output by permitting greater specialisation and a reallocation of resources to more efficient uses. An even stronger proposition is that *free* trade, unfettered by government intervention, will allow the maximum global benefit to be derived from international trade. In similar vein, a more recent neo-classical assertion is that deregulated industrial, financial and services markets, the process of globalisation in general, allowing open-door access in host countries to inward foreign direct investment, will also serve to maximise global wealth and promote economic development. However, in the real world, while the view prevails that some trade is better than no trade, it has never been universally accepted that free trade is the best of international trade regimes and there is also widespread resistance to the merits of unrestricted flows of foreign direct investment. The maxim that free trade maximises global welfare, for example, does not imply that all social groups and all countries will benefit. There will always be losers. In principle, the gains from trade could be used to compensate the losers, but this rarely happens, hence the rationale for protection.

So the flow of goods and services and factors of production between countries, in the tradition of mercantilism, is anything but free. Instead, we live in a protection-ridden global economy, not least among the many trade blocs and regional groupings, which favour relatively free trade among its members and protectionist barriers against non-members. Mostly, protectionism, often referred to as *trade policy* or *commercial* policy, has economic motives, for example, to protect investment in infant and strategic industries, jobs in declining industries and domestic industries when industries abroad, hit by recession, divert supply to foreign markets. Nations employ a wide range of instruments to support their exporters and to protect those of their domestic industries that are losing their comparative advantages in both domestic and foreign markets. In addition to economic motives, countries have always used trade policy to try to bring 'recalcitrant' governments into line, typically through embargoes on trade. In recent years, social motives for protection have begun to surface, such as concerns for health, safety and the environment.

The main objection to home market protection is on economic efficiency grounds: that is, protection causes a redirection of demand from more efficient foreign producers to less efficient domestic producers, which implies a wasteful misallocation of resources. Further, whatever problems protection seeks to solve, there are always more suitable solutions. Consumers meet most of the costs of protection because the effects in the protected home market are always to:

- raise prices to the consumer (the consumption effect)
- restrict the supply of more efficiently produced foreign goods and raise the output of less efficient home-produced goods (production effects)
- reduce the supply of goods to the home market overall (the tariff effect).

These effects generally accompany all protectionist measures, whether or not they are imposed on economic grounds.

This chapter will assess the roles played in the regulation of international trade by the international institutions, the General Agreement on Tariffs and Trade (GATT) and its successor the World Trade Organisation (WTO) and the reaction of countries, particularly the USA and the European Union (EU), to the WTO agenda and the guidelines for the resolution of disputes. The chapter will also introduce the main forms of protection – the classic tariff and the more contemporary non-tariff barriers – and analyse some of the arguments both for and against protection, including the debate on the use of domestic regulations on health, safety and the protection of the environment as a form of trade protection.

In recent years the process of globalisation, the break-up of state industries, and the deregulation of markets have gone hand in hand with increases in the gap between rich and poor nations. In consequence, the fledgling WTO is struggling to assert its authority over the superpowers, anxious to maximise the gains to be had from trade liberalisation, and the many protest groups concerned about the asymmetries associated with the costs and benefits of a liberal-orientated trade regime. In Seattle, in December 1999, for example, protestors, voicing the concerns of developing countries and environmental groups under the slogan 'fair trade not free trade', succeeded in postponing a meeting of the member countries of the WTO convened to set the agenda for the next round of trade talks.

The General Agreement on Tariffs and Trade

After World War II the General Agreement on Tariffs and Trade (GATT), signed in 1947, was set up as an interim and intended short-term agency of the United Nations to enable members to reap the gains from trade according to the principles of comparative advantage. To this end, GATT has administered the guiding principles of reciprocity and treating all member nations the same (through the most favoured nation clause, MFN) and has sought to minimise controls on trade transactions. GATT has consistently favoured the imposition of tariffs (a duty on imports) over non-tariff quantitative barriers such as the quota whenever a country claimed that protection was necessary. Although quotas have generally been prohibited, exceptions include the MFN clause and the use of quotas by trade blocs and countries with temporary balance of payments problems. These exceptions give trade blocs the ability to exercise their power in the trade arena and discriminate between members and non-members.

The major vehicle for GATT to fulfil its role has been successive 'rounds' of multilateral trade talks in which members have traded off tariff concessions, to which the MFN then generally applies. During 1949–1951 the first two rounds of GATT met little resistance from industrial countries to significantly lowered tariffs because asymmetries in trade relationships meant that the dominant member, the USA, had little to fear from freer trade and the major European nations were already heavily protected by quotas and other controls.

In the 1950s GATT, in the next three rounds of negotiations, succeeded in committing members to the elimination of quotas, but made little progress in reducing tariff barriers further because of intransigent national policies. Until 1962, for example, the USA, by Act of Congress, was obliged to raise tariffs or quotas on products if their imports increased at a faster rate than domestic sales. A breakthrough of sorts was achieved in the Kennedy round of GATT trade negotiations, the sixth, from 1963–1967, when the USA, enabled by the Trade Expansion Act, permitted the president to negotiate trade liberalisation with its trading partners by allowing retraining and financial help to be offered to American workers made unemployed by import competition. This change allowed the USA to trade off tariff reductions, but not in agriculture, with the protectionist European Economic Community (Ethier, 1995), with the consequence that tariffs were reduced on two-thirds of manufactures by over 50 per cent. The success of the tariff cuts had two effects. The first effect was to contribute to a doubling of world exports from 1969 to 1973. The second effect was that nations, feeling threatened by this explosion in world trade, began to introduce national competition (industrial) policies and new non-tariff forms of protection to replace the tariff as a protectionist tool.

The seventh GATT round, the Tokyo round, 1973–1979, succeeded in reducing the average-weighted tariff on manufactures to 4.7 per cent, but in other respects, to improve their trade balances, nations hardened their commitment to non-tariff barriers and mercantilist policies. Codes of conduct, introduced to help resolve disputes, covered government procurement policies, the use of customs procedures and technical standards and health, safety and environmental measures as barriers to trade, and the role of anti-dumping duties and subsidies. Nevertheless, non-tariff quantitative barriers continued unabated.

From the mid-1970s and into the 1980s *trade pessimism* – the view that the expansion of world trade could not continue – took hold as sudden sharp increases in oil prices in 1973/4 and 1979 fuelled inflation and recessionary forces already present in the global economy. Trade pessimism was fed further in traditional industrial countries by the world debt crisis, which led to the loss of export markets inside developing countries and by continued shifts in comparative advantage in manufactures from North America and Western Europe to South-East Asia. To dampen imports, western countries began to offer a mix of protectionist threats and financial and fiscal incentives to attract inward foreign direct investment (trade-related investment measures) and the USA renewed its determination to resort to protection to correct its huge bilateral trade balance with Japan, at that time an export-orientated yet closed market economy with respect to imports and inward foreign direct investment.

The eighth trade round, and the last before GATT was absorbed into the WTO, was the Uruguay Round, 1986–1994. Having reduced tariffs to historically low levels the GATT agenda was extended to tackle, among other things, trade in services, agriculture, intellectual property rights (TRIPS), trade-related investment measures (TRIMS), the elimination of 'voluntary' trade agreements and technical standards as trade barriers, and the fair application of anti-dumping duties. The WTO was established from 1 January 1995 as an official international organisation to take over the responsibilities of the extended duties of the GATT (see later section 'The WTO'). The enormous extension to the scope of the guidelines for trade liberation, now incorporating services and foreign direct investment, suggest that whether in periods of trade expansion or decline, increasing world growth or recession, the desire of nations to control trade and movements of factors of production is always present.

Trade policy is not the only government policy relevant to international trade and investment issues. Increasingly, among industrial nations, trade policy measures to *protect* industries from international competition became intertwined with industrial (competition) policy measures to *increase* their international competitiveness. Domestic industrial policies not specifically aimed at international trade but having comparable effects as trade protection include policies to promote national champions, subsidies to home market firms and measures to safeguard health and safety. In recent years, governments have become increasingly active to create competitive advantage in technology-intensive products and to secure a significant share of their home markets for domestic firms in sectors of national importance, such as telecommunications.

The impact of these industrial policies on trade has become a contentious issue affecting relationships between countries, especially the Triad countries – the USA, the EU and Japan. Whereas domestic-focused policies can affect and distort trade relationships, international policies can have similar effects on domestic economies. For example, international agreements to protect the environment use trade measures to achieve their objectives, such as the prohibition of trade in ivory to protect the elephant population in Africa and calls for measures to be taken against the export of timber to protect against the uncontrolled exploitation of rain forests. Such international institutional market intervention, pursued in the interests of the greater good, can have severe consequences on the economies of the countries called upon to cooperate.

The range of trade policy objectives include:

Forms of protection

- tax revenue
- protection of jobs in times of recession or cyclical downswings in activity
- slowing down the pace of decline in industries that have lost their competitive advantage, in effect resisting global shift in comparative advantage
- beggar-thy-neighbour retaliation
- support for infant industries until they grow up (and sometimes beyond)
- strategic protection: that is, protection of new industries seeking, should they survive, to establish an early technological capability and so enjoy the benefits of first mover advantages and economies of scale
- to support industries set up in the cause of nationalism (e.g. airlines)
- support for high-cost 'prestige' industries, which need protection to survive

Exhibit 4.1 Trade embargo on Cuba

The USA and Cuba have been in confrontation since the Cuban revolution in 1959 when the nationalisation of foreign properties in Cuba without compensation led to a ban in the USA on the import of Cuban goods, including sugar, Cuba's largest export earner. Latin America joined the USA in the campaign against Cuba, but swaps of Cuban sugar at inflated prices for Russian oil at deflated prices, which lasted until the Soviet Union disbanded in 1991, considerably wea- kened the impact of the embargo. In 1996, to deter foreign direct investment in Cuba, the USA introduced the Helm-Burton Act, which permitted US citizens to seek damages against any firm using land confiscated from them in Cuba. The USA refused to accede to EU accusations at the WTO that the action was illegal, claiming that it was not a WTO matter since it was a non-trade action undertaken in the interests of national security.

In the past, US embargoes on countries have often created trade opportunities for new suppliers. Brazil replaced the USA when the USA placed an embargo on soybean exports to Japan, and Canada and Australia supplied the Soviet Union when the USA embargoed the sale of natural gas technology to the Soviet Union. USA embargoes on US trade with Cuba have opened up markets for other countries, including the USA's trading partners in NAFTA, Mexico and Canada. Do these countries want the embargo lifted?

- protection of health, safety and environmental standards
- embargoes and boycotts to punish countries guilty of serious human rights violations
- for security, military and political reasons
- import-substituting subsidies to persuade importers to switch to production in the host market.

Arguments for protection

Whatever the reason for protection, the internal weaknesses which protection attempts to compensate for can usually be corrected at lower cost to communities, domestic and foreign, by other means, so that protection, for most purposes, can be described as a policy of second best. Most arguments for protection are false and, even when they have merit, the consequences are distorted markets, higher prices paid by consumers for protected products and a lower utilisation of labour and capital employed in the more efficient foreign industries targeted by protection.

Cheap labour

Perhaps the commonest general argument for protection is that a country's labour-intensive industries are unable to compete against imports produced with cheap labour. But on this basis *all* countries except the one with the lowest wages (net of productivity) would have the same case for protection. But why just labour costs? The same argument must also apply to countries with lower capital or natural resource costs and then the case for almost any kind of trade would disappear. The argument is untenable not just because the cheapness of a factor is relative, but because, as trade theory shows, differences in factor prices give rise to comparative cost differences, which are reflected in difference in product prices, which gives rise to the exploitation of arbitrage opportunities on which most trade is based.

The infant industry argument

One of the oldest and most cherished arguments in favour of protection is the case of infant industries. The basic argument is that the industry needs time to survive, grow and, in time, enjoy economies of scale. The infant industry argument is often confined to a discussion of the merits of protection in developing countries, but the USA, Germany and Japan all began their industrialisation behind infant industry barriers to trade (Krugman and Obstfeld, 1994). Many LDCs, without much success, have used the infant industry argument to encourage import-substituting industrialisation to achieve economic growth. Failure to achieve the desired effects on many occasions suggests that there are practical problems in identifying suitable candidates and estimating trends in costs and market prices in the protected and competing industries. There is also a danger that protection will remain even when it is clear that the policy has spawned inefficient industries that have failed to grow up and instead have become indolent or complacent behind the protectionist barrier. A comparison of successful and unsuccessful outcomes is shown in Figure 4.1.

The tariff $(p_t\text{-}p_f)/Op_f$ allows the industry to survive in the short run and supply q^1 in the face of world price p_f and world supply curve S_f. In time the strength of the case requires that the industry's long-run average cost curve, in effect the industry's learning curve, resembles $LRAC^1$, so that the industry can eventually begin to compete without protection, for example supplying q^2 on world markets. If, however, unit costs follow $LRAC^2$, the industry will always be less efficient, for example, incurring unit costs q^2n rather than q^2m at output q^2.

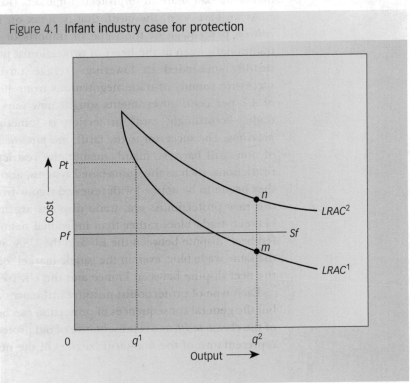

Figure 4.1 Infant industry case for protection

There are also reservations concerning the general merit of the argument. Industries may move down a learning curve or long-run average cost curve as they grow through 'learning by doing', but their competitors, established industries, can become uncompetitive by 'learning by undoing', in which event an infant newcomer might be able to compete with established firms from the onset without protection. In a liberalisation era, it is also pertinent to query why the entrepreneur should not be willing to meet the early risks of potential failure if there is an expectation that net profits will be generated at some future date. Conversely, if this is not the expectation, can there be further justifications for protection? One response is that developing countries often lack adequate capital markets able to mobilise savings and channel them to the private sector, so that entrepreneurial initiative is stifled. Another response is that the infant industry may generate external economies, which will benefit latecomers without incurring the risks of the first movers. These are market failure arguments, which give some theoretical justification to the infant industry case, but the question of making the right selections for infant industry status still remains. The new trade theory (see the trade theories in Chapters 3 and 6) gave rise to models of strategic trade theory, which attempted to give renewed respectability to the infant industry case. The argument here is that the existence of economies of scale, 'learning by doing' and first mover advantages will give domestic producers a position of privilege in the home market that will eventually translate into lower marginal cost and higher market share in unprotected markets (Krugman, 1984: 181).

As we have seen, the tariff, that is, a tax on imports, either as an *ad valorem* percentage of the value of imports or as a specific value, has traditionally been at the heart of protectionist policies. But as the GATT steadily succeeded in lowering average tariff rates through eight successive rounds of trade negotiations from 40 per cent to an average of 4.7 per cent, governments sought new ways to restrict and control trade. Accordingly, tariff protection is sometimes referred to as *old protection*. The successor to the tariff, *new protection*, embraces a wide range of non-tariff barriers, mainly quantitative restrictions. Many quantitative restrictions, such as the quota-based systems, also have a long history, but they began to be applied with renewed vigour from the 1970s onward. In this new protectionist era, trade disputes are increasingly taking place between trade blocs rather than individual nations, as in the 'hormone-fed beef' dispute between the EU and the USA, and between members of the same trade bloc, even in the 'single market' of the EU, as witnessed by the beef dispute between France and the UK (see Case 4.2).

Each type of protectionist measure influences trade in distinctive ways, but the general consequences of protection can be observed from analysis of the classic *tariff*, as a representative of old protection, and the *quota*, as a representative of the non-tariff barriers of the new protection.

By the end of the 1970s, by which time the GATT had succeeded in reducing average tariff levels to less than 5 per cent on manufacturing goods, the tariff, especially on imports, still the dominant protectionist instrument, was being closely matched by non-tariff barriers. The liberalising of the old protectionist regime through the dismantling of tariff barriers offers an opportune moment to analyse the major market distorting effects of the tariff and how its demise, in the absence of non-tariff substitutes, would have truly liberalised international trade.

Figure 4.2 shows the effects of an *ad valorem* tariff on a good. We can see how a tariff increases the output of the protected industry, increases prices in the protected market, decreases the supply of lower cost imports (a prohibitive tariff would reduce imports to zero) and decreases the overall supply to the protected market. The analysis neatly identifies the distortion effects of a tariff in the home market and the cost to consumers in terms of higher prices, reduced supply to the market and an exchange of efficient for inefficiently produced goods. In addition, incomes in the efficient overseas industries will fall and unemployment in the protected market will be transferred abroad.

The free trade price is p_f. If it is assumed that before the tariff the protectionist country is able buy all that it wants of the good from abroad without affecting the price, then the infinitely elastic supply curve S_f can be taken to represent world supply. S_d is the domestic supply of the good:

Figure 4.2 **Effects of a tariff**

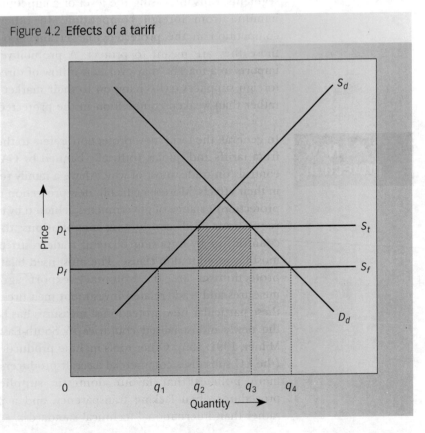

D_d is the domestic demand. At price p_f domestic supply will be q_1 and foreign supply to this market will be $q_1 q_4$.

Suppose that a tariff is imposed which raises the price in the home market to p_t (that is, the tariff rate is $(p_t - p_f) / Op_f$). Domestic supply will rise from q_1 to q_2; domestic demand will fall from q_4 to q_3; and imports will fall from $q_1 q_4$ to $q_2 q_3$. Tax revenue will equate to the shaded area (imports x the tariff), and the price to the consumer will increase.

These static effects of a tariff will be much worse if affected countries impose retaliatory tariffs. In addition, there are likely to be harmful side effects on innocent parties even without retaliation. Foreign producers may be forced to turn their attention to markets elsewhere and in doing so threaten the export markets of exporters in the protected industry. If tariff retaliation does occur, the protected country's exporters, on a comparative cost basis the most efficient producers, and certainly more efficient than the protected industry, will be penalised.

The general effects of protection, retaliation and beggar-thy-neighbour policies are to reduce the volume of world trade and the degree of global specialisation. Where a tariff is targeted at specific countries, the possibility arises that imports will come into the protected market from firms in other countries, attracted by the higher prices, thus thwarting the tariff's intentions. A tariff intended to protect a particular market segment may cause foreign suppliers to switch to other home market segments, thus increasing the level of competition in markets previously immune from foreign competition. In other words, tariffs distort competition in the protected market and also in markets other than those they are meant to protect. A prohibitive tariff, which stifles all imports to a market, may evoke an inflow of direct foreign investment as foreign suppliers try to hang on to their market share, which will stiffen rather than weaken competition in the protected market.

New protection

In general, the term 'new protection' refers to the switch by governments from tariffs and quotas (officially banned by GATT) to non-quantitative controls on trade, most of which have a family resemblance to the quota in their effects. More specifically, new protection refers to the increasingly protectionist stance of governments achieved by evading GATT and WTO regulations and conducting negotiations directly with individual countries or by imposing bilateral trade restrictions in violation of the most favoured nation clause. The most used bilateral instruments of new protectionism are the voluntary export agreement, anti-dumping measures and trade-related investment measures. Much of the weight of these particular new protectionist measures has been aimed at Japan and the newly industrialised countries in South-East Asia (Williamson and Milner, 1991: 353). Other tools include production and export subsidies, (the EU subsidises commercial aircraft producers), government procurement policies that favour domestic suppliers, complex customs procedures often lacking transparency, and a preference for national rather than international technical standards.

The long-banned quota system bestows many of its characteristics onto the voluntary export agreement. A quota, which limits the physical volume of imports, normally through a system of licences, has no direct price implications, but prices are forced up by reducing supply. The effects of a quota demonstrate that quantitative restrictions have a family resemblance to the tariff and create much the same market distortions, the main difference being that the tariff will allow imports to increase if the market expands.

Figure 4.3 shows that the indirect effects of a quota are likely to be similar to the direct effects of the tariff, that is, to raise the price to consumers, raise the supply to the home market of domestic producers, lower the supply of imported goods, and lower the overall supply to the protected market.

The market price before the quota is p_f. S_f is the foreign supply curve and S_d and D_d are the domestic supply and demand curves. At price p_f the supply to the home market is q_1 and the foreign supply is q_1q_5.

Suppose that the quota limits imports to an amount q_1q_3. The supply curve will now combine the domestic supply curve and the quota, following the path $S_d lmS_d$, that is, S_d + the quota. This combined supply curve intersects the supply curve at n to give market price p_q and total supply to the market of q_4. At this quota-ridden price, domestic supply will increase to q_2 and the foreign supply will be q_2q_4 (which equates to the quota q_1q_3).

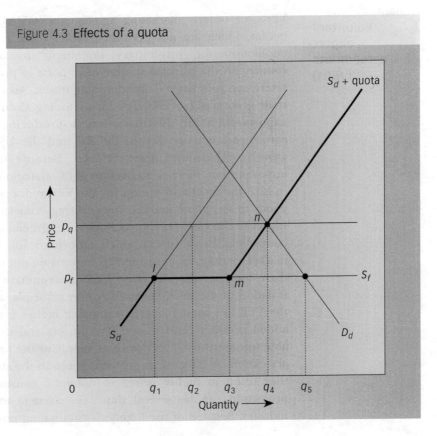

Figure 4.3 Effects of a quota

The quota has reduced the supply to the home market (from q_5 to q_4), raised price (p_f to p_q), increased domestic production (q_1 to q_2) and profits and lowered imports (from q_1q_5 to the amount of the quota, q_2q_4).

Despite the similarity between quotas and tariffs, the tariff raises revenue for the imposing government (equal to the height of the tariff x the volume of imports) and does not discriminate between suppliers, whereas the quota generates profits for the holders of the licences to trade. Also, quotas are insensitive to changes in world and domestic prices and exchange rate movements and so in unstable market conditions their impact is unpredictable.

News of a pending quota system is likely to worsen, at least in the short term, the excess supply of foreign goods in the home market that the quota is meant to correct. For example, if quotas are to be allocated in proportion to the foreign firms' market shares, then suppliers, in anticipation of the quota scheme, may seek to increase their exports to the market to ensure they are allocated the largest possible share of the quota. The allocation of licences to suppliers, whether to domestic or foreign firms, can lend itself to bribery and black markets for licences. Since a quota limits the right of access to a market, the holders of the right have a valued asset. If the government allocates the rights of allotment to foreign governments, as in voluntary marketing agreements, the value of these rights will accrue abroad (Ethier, 1995).

Voluntary export agreements (VERs)

VERs, or orderly marketing agreements (OMAs), are a substitute for quotas, which are not permitted under trade rules. They are often a euphemism for 'involuntary' limitations imposed by the exporting country on the physical volume of imports in preference to even more severe controls, such as anti-dumping duties. About 10 per cent of world trade is covered by VERs. The long-standing Multifibre Agreement limits exports from all the major textile-producing countries and VER agreements between Japan, the EU and the USA control the export growth of Japanese motor vehicles. Because the exporting country imposes them, there is no likelihood of retaliation.

Like the tariff and the quota, the VER reduces the supply of foreign goods to the home market, thus causing domestic prices and domestic supply to increase. One purpose of such agreements is to protect jobs by controlling the speed with which imports are able to penetrate the home market, perhaps by ensuring that imports do not increase at a faster rate than domestic sales. Because VERs discriminate between countries in violation of the most favoured nation principle, exporters subjected to the VER are likely to begin exporting higher grade and higher value-added products, and non-VER exporters and domestic producers are able to raise their prices or their supply to the protected market. VERs are extremely effective at protecting jobs in the short term, but because they result in higher prices to domestic consumers, the cost of job protection can be several times the average wage in the protected industry. Because of the highly discriminating power of VERs and their distorting effects on trade, it is the intention of the WTO to phase out VERs.

Anti-dumping legislation

With the steady and virtual elimination of tariffs and quotas as tools of protection, anti-dumping legislation has emerged as the key instrument of protection used by many countries. The attraction of anti-dumping measures is that countries can apply them without violating GATT or, more recently, WTO agreements, although the practice in the USA of using anti-dumping duties to compensate aggrieved firms is a form of subsidy that is illegal under WTO rules. GATT and the WTO allow duties to be imposed equal to the dumping margin if dumping is deemed to have caused 'injury' to home market producers. Countries apply different interpretations of whether dumping is taking place, but the USA, where the concept of fair trade plays an important role in the formation of trade policy (Pearson and Riedel, 1996), applies the least sympathetic test and pursues anti-dumping claims with more vigour, particularly in the case of steel imports, than its trading partners (McGee, 1996). Thus, in 1999, the USA introduced an action plan for steel imports which included bilateral efforts to counter 'unfair' trade practices, strong enforcement of US laws against 'unfair' trade, tax relief to US steel firms, and financial assistance to steel workers.

The USA's definition of dumping is the benchmark one. Until 1974 US law defined dumping as price discrimination in international markets, that is, the export of goods at prices less than the price in local markets, the so-called normal value. Then the definition was broadened to include exporting at prices below the cost of production. Anti-dumping legislation in the USA was tightened further in 1984 with two new measures. The first measure, to stop the continued export of products from successfully sued firms, was a circumvention provision introduced to allow action to be taken when exporters disguised their export volume by routing their exports through third countries. The second measure was the *de minimus* accumulation rule, which in practice allowed action to be taken against low-volume imports, The basis for this rule was the 'hammering effect', which arises because individual countries' imports may form only a small share of the market but the total volume of imports can cause material injury to domestic producers.

The WTO 1994 Agreement on anti-dumping attempts to slow down and regulate the increasing number of petitions since the 1970s (Boltuck and Litan, 1991) and to counter the small ratio of failed or withdrawn cases. Where cases are withdrawn, this is usually only after an orderly marketing agreement has been negotiated between the parties in dispute (Finger and Murray, 1990). The Agreement, which is mandatory, unlike the earlier 1979 Anti-dumping Code, brought into the net all the member countries that had never used anti-dumping rules, but are now more likely to use them, to be joined also by non-members such as China (Dunn, 1997: 87). In its favour, the Agreement ended the right to take action against low-volume imports and allowed for up to 20 per cent of exports of newly established firms to be sold at less than cost. As things stood formerly, there needed to be only one complainant and duties imposed on guilty firms could remain in force long after the market conditions that gave rise to complaints had changed. Under the new guidelines, complainants must represent a majority of firms in the affected market and all successful actions must be reviewed after five years. The rule changes reflect those of the anti-dumping measures used by the EU (Adamantopoulos, 1997: 41).

A typical accusation of aggrieved firms is that 'unfair' trade practices occur when firms engage in dumping to relieve excess capacity and to maintain sales volumes in foreign markets at the expense of domestic and other foreign competitors. But anti-dumping measures are more commonly applied as a protectionist rather than a fair trade tool, as witnessed by the fact that the number of cases increases in times of depression, as in the 1920s and 1930s and again in the 1970s and 1980s, when unemployment is high, or more generally when markets are shrinking or stagnant and capacity utilisation is low – the classical protectionist motive. The anti-dumping case brought by US steel firms in 1998 is a rare case of a complaint being made when demand was rising in the domestic market and domestic firms were still making profits.

Despite the claims of unfair trade that surround price discrimination, there are a number of reasons to suggest that firms can be expected to charge different prices in different markets for the same good or service. In essence, two conditions are all that is necessary for price discrimination between markets to be possible and profitable for the firm. First, there has to be different price elasticities of demand in different markets. Price elasticity of demand is a measure of the responsiveness of demand to a change in price. Demand is said to be price inelastic if a percentage change in price causes a less than proportional inverse change in demand. Demand is price elastic if the inversely proportional change in demand is greater than the percentage change in price. An indication of elasticity of demand in a market is revealed in the slope of the market demand curve. Generally, if the demand curves in separate markets have different slopes, price discrimination is *possible* (as shown in Figure 4.4). Second, for price discrimination to be *profitable* the firm must be able to keep the markets separate by controlling the channels of distribution between them. If this is not so, arbitrage possibilities will exist which can be exploited by others, effectively destroying the firm's price discrimination strategy. Although price discrimination can occur between different segments of the same market and between markets, the potential is greatest for firms selling in home and foreign markets separated by time and distance.

Assume that a profit-maximising firm, for whom optimum output occurs where marginal cost equates to marginal revenue, operates in both the home and a foreign market. The firm's aggregate demand curve is the lateral sum of each of the respective market demand curves. Suppose that the firm is dominant as the market leader in the home market. This is

Figure 4.4 Price discrimination between home and foreign markets

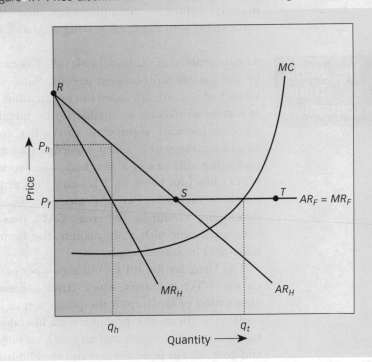

represented by the downward sloping demand curve in the home market, AR_H. In the foreign market assume that the firm faces a competitive market and faces a perfectly elastic demand curve, AR_F.

The aggregate demand curve is made up of RS on AR_H and ST on AR_F (that is, RST). The firm's total output (where marginal cost = marginal revenue) is q_t, of which q_h is sold on the home market at price P_h and the remainder is sold overseas at price P_f. Marginal revenue is the same in both markets, so at these prices there can be no further incentive to transfer goods from one market to the other. Note that if both demand curves had the same slope, and therefore the same price elasticities, prices would be the same in both markets. But if price elasticities are different, price differentiation arises as a natural consequence of different demand characteristic in the two markets.

Usually, the firm is likely to have a competitive advantage in the home market, so that the firm's home market price is likely to be higher than its foreign price. In other words, accusations of deliberate and predatory dumping might well be false and the concept of unfair trade or an unfair price is of dubious merit. As with all forms of protection, the cost of anti-dumping measures is met by consumers. In the case of steel, for example, higher prices are passed down the supply chain to major industries such as automobiles and construction and prices remain high in the long term because of the loss of international competitiveness in the protected firms. Authorities responsible for anti-dumping measures rarely concern themselves with the reasons for price discrimination and lower import prices, but simply investigate whether low-priced imports have caused material injury – unemployment, loss of sales or diminution of profitability – to the firms making allegations.

The World Trade Organisation

As new protectionism took hold, GATT became increasingly constrained by the narrow tariff-focused agenda. Since its inception in 1947, trade issues had not only advanced but negotiations were taking longer to arrive at recommendations acceptable to the members. The Uruguay Round, for example took eight years to reach completion in 1994. However, significant steps were taken towards expanding the coverage of GATT under the auspices of a new body, the World Trade Organisation. The WTO came into being on 1 January 1995 with 81 founder members, the numbers increasing to 134 members by 1999, of which 100 were developing countries. Whereas GATT was a provisional treaty and concerned only with trade matters, the Geneva-based WTO has official status and increased scope.

The Uruguay Round set out a number of WTO Agreements, binding on the WTO members, which cover a continued commitment to the elimination of tariffs, plus the protection of intellectual property rights, trade in services, the promotion of liberalized unfair trade standards, harmonisation of health and an attack on safety standards, rules of origin and government procurement and the elimination of technical standards as barriers to trade. The decision-making process inside the WTO seeks to achieve decision by consensus, but if this fails, a three-quarter majority voting procedure on a one-country, one-vote basis is applied, subject to time limits and the right of appeal (Adamantopoulos, 1997: 36).

Members of the WTO have agreed not to take unilateral action against rule violations. To discourage such action a dispute resolution process, in which a panel of the WTO's Dispute Settlement Body investigates complaints, was designed to settle disputes quickly, that is, within one year. In the event of non-compliance with a panel's decisions, the aggrieved country may apply tariffs on imports from the offending country or region to provide compensation for damages sustained. But the WTO has no power to stop countries procrastinating or taking unilateral action – opportunities that have been exploited to the full by the triad countries.

Opponents of the WTO, who feel that the WTO contributes to the widening gap between developed and developing countries, favour their version of fair trade, which includes improved market access for developing countries, proactive discrimination in favour of female labour, ethical tourism and trade discrimination against abuses of child labour and human rights. But the WTO does not accept this contentious concept of fair trade, which seriously challenges the backbone of the WTO, namely, a commitment to trade liberalisation, reciprocity and the most favoured nation clause as the basis for equitable treatment for all countries, so that the WTO will not even sanction trade discrimination against countries that abuse human rights. For example, the WTO argues

Exhibit 4.2 The banana war

The Lomé Convention of 1948 gave former African, Caribbean and Pacific colonies (APC countries) privileged access to markets for agricultural products on which they were heavily dependent. The agreement, modified in 1993, continued to give APC nations privileged access to EU markets.

Anticipating a lowering of trade barriers in the European Union (EU) after the 1992 single market initiatives, the American banana companies in Latin America invested heavily in modern production facilities. However, instead of opening up its markets, the EU continued to subsidise imports from APC countries. Included among these were bananas from the Caribbean islands. In addition to subsidies, the EU imposed tariffs of up to 170% on 'dollar' bananas from Latin America. Some EU countries, notably Germany, Belgium and Sweden, would prefer to import dollar bananas, the cheapest in the world, but for the sake of EU unity accepted the policy of discrimination.

In Guatemala, Ecuador and Honduras, American multinationals have built railways, introduced modern systems of irrigation and refrigeration, and set high-quality standards to the harvesting of huge tracts of flat and fertile land ideally suited to banana production. More efficient and organised workers earn less than half the income of banana producers in the Caribbean. Banana production in the Caribbean accounts for 60% of export earnings and half the employment and provides a steady income throughout the year. In the Caribbean banana industry there are only basic facilities – water is supplied from standpipes and there is no irrigation – so productivity is lower and costs are much higher. To threaten Caribbean producers with global competition, it is claimed, would tempt them into the profitable production of illegal drugs from the marijuana plant, which is suited to the climate and soil.

The EU argue that protection – a cheaper means of helping these fragile economies than foreign aid – is justified to sustain the livelihood of the Caribbean islands. America argues that discrimination protects efficiency and discourages producers from diversifying or modernising their methods. The consequence of protection is that EU consumers pay 30% more for low-quality bananas than the market price of superior Latin American bananas.

In 1996 the USA, Ecuador, Mexico, Guatemala and Honduras took the EU to the World Trade Organisation, which, in 1998, found against the EU's discrimination and gave the EU until January 1999 to dismantle its policy or face legal trade retaliation by the complainants. In response the EU offered to open its markets slowly but not fully to Latin America, but the proposal failed to satisfy the USA, which was already disillusioned with the ability of the WTO to deal effectively with a host of long-standing USA–EU trade disputes. The WTO, sensitive to the damage that a dismantling of the EU policy would inflict on the Caribbean producers and the economic, political and social consequences this could have for the region, expected the USA to sympathise with the WTO's attempt to arrive at a reconciliation. This would have required the USA to abide by WTO procedures which require dissatisfied parties in a dispute to seek a further ruling from the WTO's disputes tribunal. The USA continued to argue that the EU policy favours one group of poor countries by discriminating against another, the poor Latin American countries. The resort by the EU to repeated WTO dispute procedures was regarded as a tactic to prolong the status quo.

In 1999 the USA decided to take unilateral action that would impose 100% tariffs on strategic targets, mostly small industries with small firms but major employers in their localities and for whom the USA is an important export market. Countries hit hardest were those known to be in favour of EU policy – the UK, France, Portugal, Spain and Italy, but Belgium and Germany, influential sympathisers, were also targeted to encourage them to argue the case for Latin America more forcibly. These industries included cashmere, batteries and biscuits in the UK, cheeses in Italy, handbags in France and coffee makers in Germany. Altogether, 16 industries were chosen to face a 100% tariff, sufficient to cost EU firms as much as the EU's banana policy costs American producers in lost sales to the EU. The main purpose of the strategy was to sow dissent in the EU and force EU states to choose between home and colonial employment.

The dispute, which seriously threatens the integrity, even the survival of the WTO, centres, ironically, around a product which neither the EU nor the USA produces in any quantity. Which side has the better argument, and on what grounds, is worthy of debate.

that countries with high labour standards cannot use these to prevent imports from countries with lower standards, such as the payment of below-subsistence wages and the employment of child labour. The WTO view is that standards will improve with the increases in economic growth and development that will be the consequence of a more liberal international trade and investment regime.

A major advance in the scope of the GATT/WTO agenda has been the introduction of measures to regulate trade-related intellectual property rights (TRIPS), trade-related investment measures (TRIMS) and the General Agreement on Trade in Services (GATS). Despite the emphasis on trade in the descriptors of these agreements, the fact is that foreign direct investment is part and parcel of these agreements because such investment is a primary vehicle through which international trade, via intra-firm trade, and technology transfers (at the heart of intellectual property issues) take place. For example, the opening up and internationalisation of the telecommunications industry owes a debt to the provisions for investment made in the GATS, and motor manufacturers can now source components from abroad without meeting local content requirements as a consequence of TRIMS (Brewer and Young, 1998).

Trade-related intellectual property rights (TRIPS)

Among developed countries a serious issue concerns the rapid growth of parallel imports and the emergence of grey markets. At the centre of the issue is the adoption by firms of price discrimination strategies between cross-border markets to exploit the monopoly power granted to them as owners of branded goods protected by patents or trademarks. Parallel imports occur when retailers of branded goods in high-priced markets are able to buy in the cheap locations and sell at discounted prices in their own outlets. A grey market is said to exist when the proprietors of the branded goods disapproves of parallel imports in their products. Parallel imports and grey markets are particularly prevalent in the EU with its mix of high- and relatively low-priced markets for individual products. Solutions to the problem are typically sought at national and regional level (for example, the EU), but whether parallel imports give expression to free trade or is an example of 'unfair' trade gives some of the flavour of the more general concern for the potential abuse of intellectual property rights.

Issues between developed and developing countries concerning the abuse of intellectual property rights cover a wider range of issues than parallel importing. These include counterfeiting (poor-quality counterfeiting or otherwise) of branded products 'protected' by trademarks, the illegal use of expropriated trade marks, false country of origin claims and the pirating of industrial designs and manufacturing processes. Badly affected sectors in western nations include the arts and entertainment, books, records, CDs, software, pharmaceuticals, perfumery, wines, fashionware, industrial components and industrial goods.

The World Intellectual Property Organisation (WIPO), established in 1967 to adjudicate on multilateral agreements on intellectual property rights, has been recognised as a specialised United Nations agency since 1974. During the Uruguay Round, most members of GATT felt that

Exhibit 4.3 Parallel imports: an abuse of intellectual property rights?

A price discrimination strategy for a firm is possible and profitable if price elasticities of demand differ between markets and if the firm can control the distribution channels. This second condition is often difficult to satisfy. If control is weak and price discrimination strategies are being pursued, arbitrage can occur through parallel markets and grey markets. Parallel importing takes place if a product is imported into a market where the product is already available. A grey market occurs when a market for a product is created seemingly against the wishes of the manufacturer. Arbitrage opportunities have increased as the sale of branded goods at prices well below those in western markets has expanded into lower income countries in Eastern Europe, Latin America and Asia.

Parallel imports are legal in the USA and Japan where the perception is that consumers will benefit from uniform pricing. Until 1998, in the EU, under a ruling termed trademark exhaustion, once goods had been sold, the manufacturer could not restrict their further movement. Now parallel imports are permitted between member states but not from non-members. The European stance stems from late 1995 when an Austrian manufacturer of quality sunglasses, Silouette, sold old stock to a Bulgarian distributor for sale in former Soviet Union states, only to find that that the distributor sold the stock on to Hartlauer, an Austrian discount chain. In July 1998, Silouette argued in the European Court of Justice that they had the right to control where their products were sold under intellectual property rights laws. The Court ruled that EU manufacturers of branded goods had the right to prevent the sale of their products in the EU (and hence control prices) if they were sourced from a non-member country. This ruling, which overrode any contrary legislation by individual member states, supported the stance of the EU, which is against price discrimination in the EU in general, because its existence denies the reality of the 'single European market'.

The ruling upset supermarket chains in the EU, especially in the UK, where parallel importing of branded designer goods at heavily discounted prices had become increasingly common. The owners of branded products, such as Tommy Hilfiger, Calvin Klein and Levi jeans, claim that their intellectual property rights, supposedly protected by trademark, were being abused and their product image tarnished in consequence of the character and ambience of the sales outlets. In an attempt to protect their brand image and profits, the owners of branded goods, such as Tommy Hilfiger and Nike, have made claims that the discounted goods are not strictly parallel imports but counterfeit goods.

The 'free rider' problem is very much in evidence in the debate, because the discounters' actions reduce prices and the profit margins of the brand owners, effectively expropriating some portion of the branded goods' monopoly power, without incurring any of the development and marketing and promotional costs. In the case of large outlay durable goods, such as automobiles, the free rider problem extends to the lack of after-sales service provided by the discounters.

In a wider context, the problem for the WTO is whether to recognise the validity of parallel importing when the contentious issue of the protection of intellectual property rights is on the WTO agenda. For example, the EU ruling that parallel importing is permissible within the EU but not from outside, can be regarded as a protectionist measure, using trademarks as a trade barrier and confining price competition to trade in branded goods within the EU where prices can be up to 50% higher than in the USA and Asia. Thus, similar rulings might be expected from other countries. As things stand, the EU seems set to remain as host to the highest priced markets in the global economy However, in the EU the problems surrounding parallel imports may disappear when prices become denominated in the euro and as e-commerce becomes more widely used by shoppers because cross-border prices are likely to converge. Or are they?

WIPO, not GATT, was the appropriate arbiter of agreements and rules, but the EU, Japan and the USA were keen to have intellectual property issues included in the Uruguay Round and succeeded in doing so. When the TRIPS Agreement was introduced in January 1995, it signified a major, but controversial, addition to the responsibilities of the WTO compared to GATT. The developing countries are concerned that rules to strengthen intellectual property rights serve to perpetuate the technological advantage that developed countries already have. Many developing countries, lacking the innovative and entrepreneurial capacity of the west, regard the stiffer protection of intellectual property as an obstacle to economic development, which is dependent on cheap access to innovations and technology. In western nations, protection of intellectual property, and therefore the creation of temporary monopoly power, is seen as essential to encourage innovation and entrepreneurial risk taking. In time, as the protection runs out, as with patent protection, ownership takes on the characteristics of a universally free good. The issue, therefore, concerns the optimum length of protection and encouragement of commercial innovation versus the socially optimum timing of knowledge diffusion, over which there are serious differences of opinion between developed and developing countries (Bhagwati, 1990: 167).

Whatever the differences, the TRIPS Agreement aims to strengthen, protect and enforce intellectual property rights (UNCTAD, 1996). WTO members are required to treat nationals of other member states no less favourably than their own and, should privileges be granted, treat all nations the same. In other words, the most favoured nation clause is evoked. Members are expected to observe a policy of non-discrimination when granting patents, to protect organisations and individuals against the disclosure of commercial secrets and to offer compensation and legal remedies against abuse. The basic purpose of the TRIPS Agreement is to enhance the flow of technology and proprietary knowledge to the developing world via foreign direct investment. Developing countries are encouraged to participate in technical cooperation and training programmes organised by the WIPO to make their economies more receptive to the inflow of western technology. Nevertheless, many developing countries believe that they are not ready or strong enough to accept the consequences of stronger and effective intellectual property laws.

Trade-related investment measures (TRIMS)

The TRIMS Agreement, by specifically focusing on foreign direct investment for the first time on the WTO agenda, introduced a timescale for the elimination of trade-related investment measures that were already disallowed under the GATT but generally ignored. The Agreement clarifies the investment measures applying to manufacturing enterprises that are inconsistent with the liberalisation of international trade and investment and seeks their removal over two years for developed countries, five years for developing countries and seven years for least developing countries. These include measures by governments to dictate the behaviour of firms with respect to local content requirements and export/output ratios.

The attempt by the WTO, through TRIMS, to seek to free foreign direct investment from controls that are not imposed on domestic firms is another contentious issue between developed and developing countries. Note, for example, how the failure of the Organisation for Economic Cooperation and Development (OECD) to construct a set of guidelines was effectively sidelined by the weight of opposition to the proposals.

Exhibit 4.4 Multilateral agreement on investment: an issue of national sovereignty

In a world stripped of the superpower confrontation, increasingly commercial interactions shape relations among nations. As trade barriers fall away and foreign direct investment increases, the trend of economic interdependence of nations has accelerated at a breathtaking rate.

The Multilateral Agreement on Investment is a glaring example of a particular form of economic integration that benefits the few at the cost of the many.

The Multilateral Agreement on Investment (MAI) was launched by the Organisation for Economic Co-operation and Development (OECD) in 1995 as a blueprint for global economic governance through the lifting of barriers to foreign investment. To accomplish this, the MAI aimed to establish rules to limit the ability of governments to restrict, regulate and control foreign investment. According to an OECD Working Paper (1995), the MAI was designed to impose high standards of liberalisation and protection of foreign investment by providing 'path-breaking disciplines on the areas of major interest'. Membership of the MAI was to be open to all countries.

The main proposals (OECD, 1997b) were as follows:

- *National treatment.* Laws that have a discriminatory effect on foreign firms would be prohibited. (But there is nothing in this provision to prevent a government from treating foreign firms more favourably than domestic firms.)
- *Most favoured nation.* This provision would require governments to treat firms from all countries in the same manner.
- *Performance requirements.* Measures to impose minimum performance conditions, such as local procurement and employment ratios, would be prohibited.
- *Movement of assets.* Host nations would be unable to prevent a foreign firm from repatriating profits or assets. In times of financial crises, host countries would be free to disinvest.
- *Expropriation.* Full and immediate compensation would be required for any action that implied the expropriation of a foreign firm's assets.
- *Market access.* Foreign investors would be granted quicker access to deregulated markets.

The OECD gave reasons why the case for unrestricted foreign investment was too obvious to suffer rejection, namely, positive balance of payments effects, employment and technology transfer effects and the overall effect on economic growth. The aspirations of MAI included the contribution it could make to diverting capital flows to developing markets and integrating them into the global economy – claimed by OECD to be a key aim of any development strategy – by lowering the level of risk and uncertainty surrounding foreign investment.

Short-term balance of payments deficits are likely to arise in a host nation in the early years of foreign investment projects through imports of capital equipment and components, but as local supplier industries develop, it will begin to benefit foreign entrants to source locally. In time, also, their exports can be expected to increase. As older investors begin to repatriate profits, newer arrivals will inject capital into the economy and existing investors will expand operations through retained earnings.

Freedom to expatriate profits will encourage investment in less politically stable regimes and in the most disadvantaged nations, contributing to their economic stability. In economies with unemployed labour, foreign firms are likely to provide employment in non-traditional sectors, pay higher wages than their domestic partners and create through training a new skill base. Indirect employment effects, which can be greater and longer lasting, come through the local sourcing of goods and services (OECD, 1998: 54–6). For every job created directly by foreign investment, it is estimated that another 1.6 are created indirectly. OECD studies have found a significant effect on economic growth through the innovation and diffusion effect of technology (OECD, 1997a). MNEs control most of the world's advanced technologies and are responsible for most technology transfers. Host governments, however, as a condition of investment approval, often require MNEs to enter into joint venture agreements to transfer technology. The OECD sees this as an attack on intellectual property that diminishes the propensity to innovate.

The OECD, architects of the MAI, seem seriously to have underestimated the disquiet that the proposals would provoke in both the developed and the developing world. A particular concern of developing countries was with the ability of MNEs to shift footloose production facilities around the world, hastening a 'race to the bottom' and pressurising countries into lowering living standards in an effort to attract foreign investment. But the perception that there would be a serious loss of national sovereignty became the major issue. To comply with MAI regulations, governments would have to surrender control over environmental protection, regional

Exhibit 4.4 *continued*

development, human rights and the ability to regulate investment in the public interest, transferring sovereignty on such matters to unaccountable MNEs, leaving nation-states with responsibilities but taking away their rights. Without environmental legislation, companies would be able to exploit local environmental resources without this being reflected in market prices. The MAI rules on expropriation and compensation, for example, would allow MNEs to challenge a host government's attempt to recoup the environmental costs they incur, such as the cost of pollution.

The OECD were slow to realise that the MAI would have to be extended to include all nations in the World Trade Organisation, who would receive a free ride into the agreement without having to make any concessions. One way forward would be for the WTO to take responsibility for the MAI. But with the WTO in disarray following the success of protest groups lobbying against neo-colonialist policies of the WTO, causing the WTO to abort the opening of a major round of trade and investment negotiations in Seattle in December 1999, the developing world does not seem ready for a multilateral treaty.

The General Agreement on Trade in Services

Through the GATS, the WTO proposes to match in services the progress made by GATT to eliminate tariff barriers to trade in manufactures and by TRIMS and TRIPS to reduce controls on foreign direct investment in manufacturing. The supply of many services requires the physical presence of the supplier in the market. Indeed, the growth of foreign direct investment is growing more rapidly in services than in other sectors. The purpose of the GATS is to increase the international mobility of services and to remove cross-border obstacles to service providers which international firms depend on to manage their multinational operations. Although not a specific investment agreement, the GATS recognises that foreign investment is one of several ways in which a service can gain access to a market. The services covered in the agreements include communications, professional services, business services such as consulting and advertising, distribution, including franchising, and financial services.

Summary

Trade theories since the mercantilist era all conclude that the most efficient global trading system is free trade. Nevertheless, for many reasons, individual countries resort to protectionism to protect their own interests. Protectionism is not only harmful but also inefficient. Whatever protection tries to do, there are better ways to achieve the same result.

The chapter has outlined the diverse ways in which a nation can influence the composition and flow of international trade to its own advantage. Whatever protectionist instruments are used, trade intervention imposes costs that are usually borne by domestic consumers and the exporters to the home market, but knock-on side effects can spread to groups who are not seeking protection. The classic instrument of trade policy, the tariff, introduces distortions to a market: it reduces the supply to the market of more efficiently produced imports, reduces the overall supply to the market, increases the supply of less efficient home producers and raises the market price to consumers. The tariff is no longer the dominant form of intervention in consequence of the success of GATT, through eight trade rounds, to reduce the level of tariffs on manufactures to less than 5.0 per cent. But in ridding the global economy

Exhibit 4.5 China and the World Trade Organisation

China, with 1.3 billion people, is the largest nation outside the WTO and the tenth largest economy in the world. China's transition to a market economy began in 1979 when economic zones were set up to attract foreign joint venture investment. But China has experienced a weakening economy in recent years, suffering from stagnant exports and falling inward foreign direct investment. China, which failed on three occasions to enter GATT, has committed itself to joining the WTO, under the sponsorship of the USA, by negotiating bilateral trade agreements with individual countries. Following the belated support of the European Union in May 2000, only a few countries remain to conclude agreements.

The USA, by virtue of its first mover and sponsorship status, stands to gain the most among WTO members from China's entry. In negotiations with the USA, China has signified its willingness to open its markets further to western firms, including foreign ownership up to 50% of banking, telecoms, professional services, distribution and Internet business. In a bilateral agreement with the USA in 1999, China agreed to substantial cuts in tariffs on agricultural products and motor vehicles (US–China Business Council: www.uschina.org) and to allow power-gener-

ating systems, aircraft, transport equipment, environmental and telecom networks to be sourced abroad. Employment in China in agriculture and the motor industry can be expected to fall, but employment overall can be expected to rise, alongside rises in gross domestic product, consumption and exports. Consumers in China will gain access to a wider range of higher quality goods at more competitive prices. The USA trade deficit with China will be corrected as American firms gain first mover advantages into all the newly opened markets and labour-intensive US industries set up production in China and establish a gateway to other Asian markets.

Two particular problems are associated with China's application. The first concerns China's cultural attitude to intellectual property, which it regards as a universal free good (the great majority of government offices use pirated computer software!) and is unlikely, therefore, to respect WTO guidelines and rules governing intellectual property rights. The second concerns whether China should be accorded developing country status and enjoy the special privileges in trade that this entails. Can such status be granted to the tenth largest trading nation in the world?

of the pervasive influence of tariffs on international trade, GATT has helped to spawn a more pernicious range of 'new protection' non-tariff instruments (all inferior to the tariff in their effects and less transparent), including voluntary marketing agreements and anti-dumping measures. In terms of the economic effects protectionist measures aim to achieve, the tariff is the least harmful, particularly when the imposing country respects the most favoured nation clause.

GATT was set up after World War II to pursue multilateral trade liberalisation by applying the principles of reciprocity and non-discrimination between its members. Although GATT succeeded in drawing up codes of conduct for the new protectionist measure that took hold in the 1970s, the Uruguay Round created the World Trade Organisation and gave it a new and more sweeping agenda to advance the cause of trade liberalisation. New protectionism, which displays a preference by governments for bilateral agreements and other discriminating measures, poses a formidable challenge to the ability of the WTO to create contestable markets.

In addition to the proliferation of non-tariff barriers and bilateralism, new issues have emerged in recent years. These include attempts by the WTO to impose stricter compliance with guidelines governing intellectual property rights (TRIPS) in developing countries and guidelines for open-door access for foreign direct investment (TRIMS). On this last issue, the

WTO is spreading its net beyond trade matters to becoming a forum for the resolution of foreign direct investment disputes, including cross-border transfers of technology and services. Perhaps the most important challenge to the WTO, a challenge that has already surfaced, is the dissatisfaction of developing countries with the predominantly western view that globalisation and trade and market liberalisation, without adequate safeguards and compensation and pro-discrimination mechanisms, are in the best interests of the majority of its members.

Review questions

1 Discuss the trends in the global economy that influenced GATT and the WTO to change its agenda.
2 Show analytically the distortions in global markets that protectionism can cause. Assess the specific arguments for protection in your own country.
3 Analyse the likely impact on domestic markets of import restrictions via tariffs and quotas respectively. Discuss the dynamic side effects that can arise from import protection.
4 Explain the emergence of non-quantitative trade barriers in recent decades.
5 In the light of the strategic significance of price discrimination between cross-border markets to firms, evaluate the merits of anti-dumping measures.
6 Discuss the sense and nonsense of fair trade in a regime of trade liberalisation.
7 Consider who gains and who loses when anti-dumping duties are imposed on imports of steel when there is a rising demand for steel in the country imposing the duties and excess capacity in the exporters' home industry.
8 Discuss the merits of the developing country argument that without heavy trade discrimination in their favour, the effects of globalisation and trade liberalisation are likely to be harmful to their interests.

Bibliography

Adamantopoulos, K. (1997) 'Legal elements in the WTO structure and operations' in J. Reuvid (ed.) *The Strategic Guide to International Trade*, London, Kogan Page.

Bhagwati, J. (1990) 'Multilateralism at risk: the GATT is dead, long live the GATT', *The World Economy*, 13, 2, pp. 149–69.

Bhagwati, J. (1988) *Protectionism*, Massachusetts: MIT Press.

Boltuck, R. and Litan, R. E. (1991) *Down in the Dumps*, Washington, DC, The Brookings Institute.

Brewer, T. L. and Young, S. (1998) *The Multinational Investment System and Multinational Enterprises*, Oxford, Oxford University Press.

Dunn, A. M. (1997) 'Anti-dumping regulations and practices' in J. Reuvid (ed.) *The Strategic Guide to International Trade*, London, Kogan Page.

Ethier, W. J. (1995) *Modern International Economics*, 3rd edn, New York, Norton.

Finger, J. M. and Murray, T. (1990) 'Policing unfair imports: the United States example', *Journal of World Trade Law*, August, pp. 39–53.

Krugman, P. (1984) 'Import protection as export promotion: international competition in the presence of oligopoly and economies of scale' in H. Kierszkowsci (ed.) *Monopolistic Competition and International Trade*, Oxford, Oxford University Press.

Krugman, P. and Obstfeld, M. (1994) *International Economics: Theory and Policy*, 3rd edition, New York, HarperCollins.

McGee, R. (1996) 'Some thoughts on anti-dumping laws', *European Business Review*, 96, 5.

OECD (1998) *Foreign Direct Investment and Economic Development*, Paris, OECD.

OECD (1997a) *Technology and the Economy*, Paris, OECD.

OECD (1997b) *The Multilateral Agreement on Investment: State of Play as of February 1997*, Paris, OECD.

OECD (1995) *The Multilateral Agreement on Investment*, Working Paper, Paris, OECD.

Pearson, C. and Riedel, J. (1996) 'United States trade policy: from multilateralism to bilateralism' in E. Grilli and E. Jassoon (eds) *The New Protectionist Wave*, London, Macmillan.

United Nations Conference on Trade and Development (1996) *The TRIPS Agreement and Developing Countries*, Geneva, United Nations.

Williamson, J. and Milner, C. (1991) *The World Economy*, London, Harvester Wheatsheaf.

Case 4.1 White gold – international trade in ivory

The Convention on Intenational Trade in Endangered Species (CITES) is a 135-nation treaty that came into force in 1975 under the umbrella of the United Nations Environment Progamme. Its goal is to protect endangered species, such as the African elephant, from commercial exploitation by monitoring and regulating unsustainable international trade. International trade in wildlife was valued at over $4 billion in 1989, of which 47% came from ivory.

The large-scale exploitation of African elephants began in the 1970s by organised gangs of poachers, who laundered thousands of tons of elephant tusks via the African continent to mainly the USA, China, Japan and Taiwan. By the late 1980s Kenya and Uganda had lost 85% of their elephant population and heavy annual declines have been recorded elsewhere, such as Sudan and Tanzania.

Until 1990 CITES allowed for limited trade in ivory, but then listed the animal as an endangered species and introduced a total ban on international trade in ivory. The ban was opposed by Botswana, Namibia and Zimbabwe – countries which relied heavily on foreign currency earnings from the ivory trade – which argued that their elephant populations were not in danger of extinction. An experimental quota was introduced in these three countries and only exports to Japan were permitted. A major problem with Japan, however, is that the registration system fails to distinguish between legal trade and contraband trade because imports of ivory are not closely monitored.

The ban was controversially ended in January 1999. Arguments against the lifting of the ban relate to the decrease in poaching that resulted from it. In the pre-ban 1980s' era the population fell from 1.3 million to 635,000. During the years of the ban the population fell only slightly to 580,000. Environmentalists argue that the ban made a difference and that the elephant is no more an endangered species, heading towards extinction. Before the ban, trade in ivory grew from 240 tons in 1950, 400 tons in 1960, 560 tons in 1970 to 970 tons in 1980. The increases were linked partly to new manufacturing techniques, enabling the mass production of ivory carvings and partly to increased demand from the high-income Asian countries, where ivory is seen as a hedge against inflation and currency devaluation. The majority of revenues earned from the trade went to the professional poaching organisations, not to the countries and communities where the ivory originated.

In some countries elephants play a major role in the maintenance of eco-systems, acting to disperse seeds and clear vegetation, thereby allowing smaller flora access to sunlight. The extermination of the elephant in these countries would have serious ecological consequences. Thus, there are economic, ecological and environmental argument for the lifting of the ban. One economic argument is that an illegal, restricted supply of a commodity forces up prices and profits: in the case of the ivory trade this would fuel even more thriving underground poaching activities. Supply in the source countries was indeed seriously diminished due to the success of anti-poaching units and the commitment to upholding the ban in Kenya, Tanzania and South Africa. But prices did not rise because the USA and the EU shut down the trade in their markets. Ivory prices actually fell sharply after the ban was imposed, from $125 per pound in the late 1980s to $54 per pound in 1993 and remained low throughout the years of the ban.

The ecological role of the elephant population elsewhere in Africa is far from the case in Botswana, Namibia and Zimbabwe. These countries are heavily dependent on the ivory trade and their elephant populations are far in excess of the capabilities of the land to sustain them. In these countries the elephant populations have been steadily increasing and do not appear to be endangered. On the contrary, elephants on their annual migration destroy people's properties and their crops and regularly disturb, even threaten, local communities. Forests have become grasslands and such destruction has increased the extinction rates of some flora and fauna.

The appropriate choice does not appear to be to ban or not to ban, but a system of sustainable trade based on a partial lifting of the ban. This would not necessarily provoke the wholesale slaughter of elephants. Tons of ivory have accumulated over the years from animals that died from natural causes or had been legitimately culled by game wardens. These hoards of 'white gold' in Zimbabwe and Botswana are valued at over $8 billion. To ban the ivory trade in these countries would seem to deny them the opportunity to harvest their comparative advantage to satisfy western environmentalists, who are far removed from African realities. In its time, the cost of the ban ran into many millions of dollars to meet legislation, monitoring and policing costs. Controlled trade in these countries over-populated with elephants, rather than a total ban on the one hand or complete freedom to cull and trade on the other, would create huge foreign exchange earnings, which would generate the funds to police illegal activities, compensate communities for the destruction of their resources by migratory elephant traffic, develop tourism and wildlife parks, create local employment opportunities and secure a balanced environment for elephant and human populations.

African nations are divided over its fairness and environmentalists and economists are split over its costs and benefits. The lifting of the ban in 1999 was so controversial that steps were taken towards its reinstatement in 2000.

References

Barbier, E. (1996) *Elephants, Economics and Ivory.* London, Earthscan Publications. www.cites.org

Genuardi, E. (1999) *The Challenge of African Elephant Conservation.* www.wwf.org/new/issues/feb–99/next.htm

Khanna, J. (1996) 'The ivory trade ban: is it effective?', *Ecological Economics*, 19, 2.

Loomis, J. (1996), 'Economic benefits of rare and endangered species', *Ecological Economics*, 18, 3.

Case 4.2 What's the beef: disputes over trade or health?

The beef dispute between the UK and France is an example of a dispute *within* a trade bloc: a dispute over beef between the EU and the NAFTA is an example of friction *between* trade blocs. The internecine strife within the EU concerns the disease bovine spongiform encephalopathy (BSE), which was first identified in cattle in 1986 and reached a peak in 1992. A link between BSE and Creutzfeld-Jacob disease in humans led to a loss of confidence in markets for UK beef, leading the EU to introduce a total ban in March 1996. The ban affected not only the export of beef but also by-products, such as gelatine and tallow, used in the

cosmetics, pharmaceuticals, soap and animal feed industries.

The EU lifted the ban in August 1999, satisfied that the UK had brought the problem under control. France refused to lift the ban, claiming that health risks remained because the disease was still present in cattle reared in the UK. The European Commission ruled in October 1999 that the French Food Agency had misinterpreted the scientific evidence. The European Court of Justice, which handles intra-EU disputes and is collecting further evidence before giving a decision on France's claims, was expected to report at the end of 2001. In the meantime, the ban remains in France, supported by Germany. Before the EU ban, France, with large trade surpluses with the UK and the second largest market for UK food exports, accounted for over 40% of UK beef exports. In retaliation, British supermarkets began to label French products or banned their sale altogether.

The dispute between the EU and the USA concerns meat treated with chemical hormones. Natural hormones produced by animals and humans coordinate their physiological activities. Chemically synthesised hormones, which mimic natural hormones and acts as an effective growth-promoting agent, is approved in the raising of cattle in the USA and Canada. The US Department of Agriculture claims that every $1 of hormone implant saves $20 in production costs. The dispute between the EU and the USA broke out in January 1989, when the EU banned the production and importation of hormone-treated meat. Exports of hormone-treated beef from the USA are mostly destined for the EU. The USA responded to the EU ban with tariffs on imports of EU agricultural products of like value.

In 1986 the USA sought a ruling from GATT, but the EU exploited the GATT dispute settlement procedure which allows members to block attempts at reconciliation. In 1994 GATT approved the use of hormones, but the ban continued. In 1996 the USA appealed to the WTO, stating that the EU ban violated the WTO agreement on sanitary and phytosanitary standards. On the basis of scientific evidence the WTO ruled that the ban should be lifted, but the EU deepened the dispute by claiming that hygiene measures in meat processing in the USA fell below acceptable standards. The EU introduced a requirement that countries exporting to the EU must comply with EU inspection standards. The EU has lost subsequent appeals but has been given time to make a scientific case. The USA argues that their case has been substantiated, but the EU counter that it has been encouraged by the WTO to seek stiffer safety standards. The WTO again maintained its position in 1998 and supported the imposition in the USA of 100% tariffs on EU food imports. Not surprisingly, in the light of its beef dispute with France, the UK backed the USA and so its food exports are exempt from the tariff.

To date, independent scientific studies sponsored variously by the WTO, the USA and EU have failed to find evidence that synthetic hormones constitute a threat to human health when properly monitored and controlled. But agriculture is highly protected in both trade blocs. The EU gives *export subsidies* to its exporters of farm products, allowing farmers to ignore world prices. The USA applies *import quotas* to counter cheap food imports. Even before the ban, the EU suffered from over-capacity due to the extremely effective Common Agricultural Policy, which compensates farmers when world prices fall below certain levels. The conditions prevail, therefore, for trade protection.

The suspicion exists among aggrieved countries, such as the UK and the USA in these disputes, that health and safety standards are often a blind for a non-tariff barrier to protect producers, not the health of consumers. In the EU–USA dispute the EU argues that the ban is not a trade barrier because it applies equally to EU farmers. Both disputes serve to indicate yet again the ineffectiveness of regulatory bodies, such as the EU, in the case of inter-trade bloc disputes, and the WTO, in resolving inter-regional non-tariff, this time when health and safety standards cloud the issue. In the US–EU hormone dispute, perhaps the USA can afford to wait. If the ban is lifted, the US will have first mover advantages in hormone-treated cattle. Is France, against the UK, and the EU, against the USA, protecting their producers, their consumers, or both?

Case 4.3 Anti-dumping: the case of steel

Industries operating in cyclical markets and with high overhead costs, like steel, are susceptible to allegations of dumping. South-East Asia hosts the largest markets for steel and produces 40% of global output. European and US exports to Asia declined when Asian demand fell following the onset of the Asian economic crisis in 1997 and Asian steel products were heavily diverted to the still buoyant EU and US markets.

In October 1998 US steel firms successfully claimed that Russia, Japan, China and Brazil were dumping rolled carbon steel in the USA causing unemployment and declining profits. The EU made similar claims. Until October of 1998 these countries had doubled their exports to the USA after increasing them threefold in 1995–1997. After duties had been imposed and the exporters had agreed to quotas, exports to the USA fell by one-third. The number of countries accused of dumping grew to include Taiwan, India and Indonesia, even when demand in the USA had returned to normal levels.

In the case of Japan, US producers claimed that excess production was being diverted to the USA at 68% below market prices. The Japanese market is heavily protected, thus allowing low-price exports to be subsidised by high home market profits and preventing foreign competitors gaining access to Japan.

How guilty were the exporters of unfair trade?

5 | The international monetary system

Learning objectives

By the end of this chapter, you should be able to:

- understand the importance of the international monetary system for international business
- outline the main developments in the evolution of the international monetary system
- have knowledge of the stability and adjustment problems that beset fixed exchange regimes
- discuss the pros and cons of fixed versus floating exchange rate regimes
- understand the main theories of exchange rate determination
- describe the various theories of currency crises and identify which crises fit in with these theories
- have knowledge of how firms can reduce the risks associated with floating exchange rate regimes
- assess the main ways that different exchange rate regimes impact on the risk to firms of engaging in international business activities

Key Terms

- the international monetary system • Gold Standard • Bretton Woods • monetary union • currency boards • exchange rate regimes • exchange rate theory • exchange rate fluctuations • currency crises • globalisation and capital flows

Introduction

One of the most fundamental differences between national and international business activities is that the means of payment for international transactions often requires the use of different currencies. In floating exchange rate regimes this leads to risks to firms arising from changes to the value of international transaction as the value of currencies fluctuate. Banks and financial services firms provide mechanisms to reduce currency risks via hedging instruments (for example, forward contracts, options and currency swaps) that reduce the risks associated with fluctuating currencies. Private sector firms such as Reuters and Standard & Poor's provide data and assessments of economic and financial conditions in international money and capital markets to help firms to assess the risks of using these markets. The large accounting and auditing firms such as KPMG, PricewaterhouseCoopers and Ernst & Young also provide help and advice on dealing with the regulations that govern such matters as taxation, financial reporting and the rules for international money and capital flows. Most large multinational corporations have treasury departments that devise and manage policies to reduce the risks associated with currency fluctuations and instability in international money and capital markets. The extensive provision of services to help manage the risks associated with currency fluctuations and to help when using international money and capital illustrates the important influence of the international monetary system on international business activities.

Problems caused by fluctuating currencies and by international financial crises, especially in emerging economies have led to attempts to develop new institutional systems to reduce the risks associated with turbulence in international money and capital markets. These systems include fixed exchange rate systems such as currency boards that fix the currency of a country to a major world currency such as the US dollar and some countries have created monetary unions to reduce financial risk. The development of such systems arises from a desire to reduce the risks and disruption caused to international business transactions by currency fluctuations. Attempts to create more stable financial and monetary conditions often involve considerable political and economic upheaval among the countries that seek to develop such systems. Nevertheless, many countries have decided that stability in the international monetary system is worth the costs associated with surrendering control over national economic policies that accompanies the creation of currency boards and monetary unions.

Chapter 12 provides a detailed investigation on the methods used by firms to deal with the risks and costs associated with using the international monetary system. This chapter focuses on the evolution of the international monetary system that revolves around the long running debate on the virtues of fixed versus floating exchange rate regimes. An overview of the history of the international monetary system provides the background for an analysis of the debate on exchange rate regimes and an assessment of the implications for conducting international business transactions of different regimes. The operations of foreign exchange markets are considered and the impact of fluctuations in these markets on international business transactions is assessed.

The international monetary system

The international monetary system includes the firms (banks and financial services companies) and the governmental and international institutions that enable and govern the exchange of currencies, the settlement of debt and the flow of capital across frontiers. The current international monetary system stems from the creation of a gold-backed international monetary order (the Gold Standard) that emerged from the growth in international business transactions following the Industrial Revolution. This system developed from a series of crises into the current system. The most important stages in the evolution of the current international monetary system were the rise and fall of the Gold Standard and its replacement by the Bretton Woods agreement. This agreement led to a type of fixed exchange rate regime and the development of an institutional system that still provides the basic framework that governs international monetary and capital flows (see Exhibit 5.1). The collapse of the Bretton Woods exchange rate regime led to the emergence of a variety of exchange rate regimes that are still developing and evolving (Bordo, 1993; Williamson, 1995).

These systems have been subject to extensive economic analysis that has provided theoretical frameworks that help us to understand the complex effects that arise from international monetary and capital flows (Daniels and VanHoose, 1999; Krugman and Obstfeld, 2000). None-theless, the periodic emergence of currency and debt crises reveal that the international monetary system is often not stable and that there is much that is not understood about the ways in which the system works (Krugman, 1999a). The frequent outbreaks of currency and debt crises has led a well-known currency speculator to express the opinion that the future of capitalism is under threat because of the inherent instability of the international monetary system (Soros, 1998).

Exhibit 5.1 Major institutions with responsibilities for international monetary and financial matters

International Monetary Fund (IMF)

The IMF was established as part of the Bretton Woods agreement. Members contribute to the reserves of the IMF according to their economic size. This means that the USA, Japan and the large economies of Europe contribute the bulk of assets of the Fund and therefore dominate the policy agenda of the IMF. The Fund was designed to lend to countries experiencing balance of payments problems and to develop rules and codes of practice to facilitate international monetary flows. Its role has evolved since the end of the Bretton Woods system and it now leads the efforts of the international community to combat currency and debt crises. The IMF negotiates rescue packages with countries experiencing monetary in-stability. These packages provide loans to stabilise money and capital markets normally in return for the adoption of stringent controls on budgetary deficits and in some cases the implementation of reforms to economic and financial institutions. The IMF also seeks to provide clear and transparent information on international monetary and capital flows to help reduce the risks associated with these flows. This work is centred on the financial and banking markets in emerging economies. Information on the work of the IMF is available on its website – www.imf.org

International Bank for Reconstruction and Development (IBRD)

The IBRD, known as the World Bank, also emerged from the Bretton Woods agreement. Initially, the World Bank was involved in the provision of capital to help the

Exhibit 5.1 *continued*

reconstruction of the war-ravaged countries of Europe and Japan. This work evolved into organising financial and technical help for the growth programmes of developing countries. The liberalisation of international capital markets led to increasing amounts of development capital being provided from private sector banks. This led to the World Bank reducing its role as a provider of loans. However, it remains one of the main sources of development capital for countries that find it difficult to borrow from private banks and for large investments such as dams. Currently, the main function of the World Bank is to help developing countries to devise and implement policies to deliver sustainable growth and to formulate plans to tackle currency and debt crises. Structural adjustment programmes are negotiated with developing countries that are experiencing monetary instability or that are faced with debt crises. These programmes make loans or the rescheduling of debt dependent on the adoption of reforms to make economies more market based and less reliant on state support and control. This work has led to a degree of overlap with the work of the IMF. Information on the work of the World Bank is available on its website – www.ibrd.org

World Trade Organisation (WTO)

The Bretton Woods agreement envisaged the establishment of the International Trade Organisation (ITO) to oversee a new multinational, liberal world trading regime. The ITO never materialised because Congress decided that it would violate the sovereignty of the USA. The General Agreement on Tariffs and Trade (GATT), negotiated in 1947, became the basis for a multilateral trading regime. GATT remains the basis for world trading rules and dispute settlements. In 1994, the WTO replaced the secretariat of the GATT and it provides the forum for developing trading rules and for the settlement of trade disputes. The work of the WTO influences the development of international money and capital markets because the General Agreement on Trade in Services (GATS) includes banking and other financial services and the agreement on Trade-Related Investment Measures (TRIMs) envisages the development of a regime of rules and codes of practice for international investments. These agreements are seeking to create a set of rules and dispute procedures to enable free trade in financial services and in investments. In these areas, there is a degree of overlap with the work of the IMF and the OECD. Information on the work of the WTO is available on its website – www.wto.org

Organisation for Economic Cooperation and Development (OECD)

The OECD evolved from the Organisation for European Economic Cooperation (OEEC). The OEEC was established in the era of the Bretton Woods agreement to supervise the administration of the reconstruction of Europe after World War II. As this work diminished, it focused on gathering information and producing reports on economic conditions in developed economies and it was renamed the OECD. Membership of the OECD includes all major developed economies and it produces reports and studies on a wide range of matters connected to national and international economic activities. It influences international monetary and capital markets by providing information and data on national and international economic and financial conditions and from the development of codes of practice, for example the 1976 Guidelines for Multinational Enterprises. In 1995, the OECD attempted to negotiate a Multinational Agreement on Investment (MAI) but discussions on the agreement broke down in 1998 and negotiations on this agreement was referred to the WTO. The work of the OECD on matters such as the MAI and in the provision of data and reports on financial and investment conditions overlaps with the work of the IMF, the World Bank and the WTO. Information on the work of the OECD is available on its website – www.oecd.org

The Bank for International Settlements (BIS)

The BIS was founded in 1930 by the central banks of leading economies, but not the US Federal Reserve System. The Federal Reserve did not join until 1994. It provides codes of practice for banks in areas such as capital adequacy and on good practice for the supervision of domestic financial markets by central banks and other authorities. In times of banking and currency crises, it acts as a clearing house for currency swaps and loans between central banks. In 1975, the BIS issued the Basle Concordat, which forms the basis of the procedures used to manage foreign bank failures. The BIS provides a forum for central bankers to discuss and formulate agreements on technical issues connected to international banking. Information on the work of the BIS is available on its website – www.bis.org

Information on these and other international institutions is available in Trebilcock, M. and Howse, R. (1999) *The Regulation of International Trade*, London, Routledge.

Instability in international financial markets leads to significant effects on the growth of world trade and thereby the general macroeconomic environment in which international business activities take place. Moreover, changes in the international monetary system, for example, a move towards new exchange rate regimes such as European Monetary Union or the use of currency boards affect the risks associated with international business operations. Clearly, the evolution of the international monetary system has important implications for international business activities.

The Gold Standard

The Gold Standard emerged in an unplanned manner in the 1870s and provided the basis for the international monetary system until the outbreak of World War I. At the heart of the Gold Standard was the principle of setting the value of national currencies to a fixed amount of gold. National currencies pegged to gold were automatically fixed against each other. In Britain, the price of one ounce of gold was £4.252 and in the USA, the price was $20.646. This meant that the US dollar/British pound exchange rate was determined by the US price of gold divided by the British price of gold, that is $20.646/£4.252 or $4.856 = £1. If the exchange rate changed, it would become profitable to buy gold in the country that had experienced a rise in its exchange rate and sell in the country were the exchange rate had fallen. For example, if the rate became $4.988 = £1, gold could be bought in the USA and sold in Britain at a profit. Arbitrage would force a change in the price of gold or a change in the exchange rate to stop the trade in gold resulting from the 'incorrect' exchange rate. Thus, if the value of national currencies remained fixed in terms of gold this effectively fixed the exchange rate between all countries that adopted the Gold Standard.

This system provided stable monetary conditions in domestic economies because the level of monetary demand in economies was strictly linked to stocks of gold. Consequently, inflation was not a problem in the Gold Standard system. The growth of economic activity depended on investment, technical change and improvements in the quantity and quality of labour. International trade was relatively unhampered by tariffs, quotas and non-tariff barriers and there was no exchange rate risk. The Gold Standard system, backed by institutional systems that led to relatively free trade, provided an environment with stable domestic economic conditions and low risks attached to international business transactions. These were ideal conditions for the growth of international transactions of goods, services and capital (Bordo and Schwartz, 1999). The creation of an international monetary system with the characteristics of the Gold Standard is the 'Holy Grail' for those who seek to create ideal monetary conditions for the growth of international business activities. However, the economic and political conditions that existed in the period 1870–1914 do not and cannot hold in this age. This has led to arguments that the creation of an international monetary system that has the main attributes of the Gold Standard is not possible in our present conditions (Eichengreen, 1998).

In the period 1870–1914 the Bank of England provided an anchor for the Gold Standard system because it rigorously maintained the value of the pound to gold. Britain was also at the heart of the world's financial system that provided ample supplies of capital to finance expansion of international business activities. This gave the Gold Standard credibility and because the link to the supply of gold and the money supply in Britain was enforced, there were no serious problems with inflation in the country that provided the leadership of the system. All countries that were part of the Gold Standard had to follow the lead of Britain otherwise gold would flow out of their country if inflation lowered the value of their currency. New markets were expanding because of the introduction of new technologies and the development of new goods and services produced by the application of capital to plentiful supplies of labour. Demand was increasing for these new products in the industrialising countries and in the countries of the empires of the colonial powers of Europe. These conditions provided fertile ground for the growth of international business activities. Shocks to domestic economies that led to imbalances in trade and financial flows required money wage cuts to induce changes in relative prices and thereby restored equilibrium in labour and goods markets. Conflicts that arose from the need to adjust prices by cutting money wages were dampened by legal restrictions on trade unions. The flow of capital was also largely free from controls and restrictions. Trade disputes were rare because of the power of Britain in the markets for industrial products and her control of the largest empire in the world. The colonial powers also ensured that the markets of their empires were open to industrial products and to secure supplies of raw materials. These were golden days for the internationalisation of business activities.

However, economic and political conditions changed in the early 20th century. The economic dominance of Britain declined as Germany and the USA became major industrial producers, trade unions acquired more power and the colonies of the European powers became less compliant with the restrictions placed on them by the international trade order. The outbreak of World War I led to the suspension of the Gold Standard. In 1925, Britain returned to the Gold Standard at the pre-war parity. This proved to be an unsustainable position, as Britain could not compete on world markets at the pre-war exchange rate. Attempts to achieve competitiveness on world markets by cutting money wages led, in 1929, to a general strike. High interest rates to support the value of the pound by encouraging capital inflows resulted in low investment and consequently to high unemployment. In 1931 the political and economic costs of these policies led Britain to suspend the link of the pound to gold thereby effectively withdrawing from the Gold Standard. Problems in the USA following from economic and financial crises such as the Wall Street crash in 1929 led the USA to withdraw from the Gold Standard in 1933.

By 1936, all the major trading nations had left the Gold Standard and attempted to cure balance of payment problems by erecting trade barriers, implementing capital controls and made frequent recourse to devaluations of their currencies. The collapse of the Gold Standard led to the emergence of an international monetary system that was not conducive to the process of internationalisation because trade barriers were rising, capital flows were restricted and exchange rates were volatile resulting in high risks of engaging in international business activities.

The Gold Standard collapse when problems of adjustment for countries that had fundamental imbalances with their trading partners proved to be intractable. This problem became serious when it became difficult to force labour to adjust money wages to restore balance. The economic and political decline of Britain (the dominant partner in the halcyon days of the system) followed by financial instability in the USA (the rising economic and political superpower) meant that there was no strong leadership of the system that could force the members of the Gold Standard to adopt policies that would restore balance.

The Bretton Woods system

The disintegration of the international monetary system that followed from the collapse of the Gold Standard led to a desire to create a new system to restore stability to the world economy. In the aftermath of World War II, a meeting took place in 1948 in Bretton Woods in New Hampshire to agree a new international monetary system. The agreement made in Bretton Woods laid the foundations of the current international monetary and trading system.

The conditions that prevailed at the end of World War II had a significant influence on the type of agreement made in Bretton Woods. The USA emerged from the war as the only significant economic, political and military power in what became known as the West. Britain was in relative decline and was very much the junior partner to the USA. Japan and Germany were defeated, occupied countries and their economies were in ruins. The Soviet Union was a significant economic, political and military power but the onset of the Cold War effectively shut the Soviet bloc out of the new international monetary system that emerged from the Bretton Woods agreement. The USA assumed the role in the Bretton Woods system that Britain played in the Gold Standard. The objective of the USA was to encourage the rapid recovery of Japan and Western Europe and to create a new international order that would be stable and enable the development of a free trade system. The Cold War meant that the Soviet bloc was not part of this system and it developed its own economic, political and military systems. Competition between the USA and the Soviet Union was strong to recruit the developing countries into the rival camps.

The Bretton Woods system centred on a fixed link between the US dollar and gold with other countries fixing their exchange rate against the dollar. This meant that the currencies of all countries that participated in the Bretton Woods system were fixed to the dollar and therefore against each other. The fixed rate against the dollar could be altered by agreement with the IMF if a case were made that a country could not achieve balance with other countries at the fixed rate. This is an adjustable peg system. An adjustable peg system allows for revaluation or devaluation against the anchor currency, which had fixed value in terms of gold. This fixed relationship between the US dollar and gold provided the stable value for currencies and was the anchor for the expected stability of the new international monetary system. The rationale for the adjustable peg system was to prevent the type of adjustment problems that Britain had experienced when returning to the Gold Standard in 1925. However, countries had to defend their currency's parity against the dollar by adopting domestic economic policies to keep their economies in balance with their trading partners. Countries whose currency was falling in value had to intervene in the markets to defend the parity of their currency against the dollar and could receive loans from the IMF for this purpose.

This required countries to follow the lead of the USA in macro-economic policies so that domestic inflation rates did not diverge from the US rate. If such divergence took place, the currency of the high-inflation country would tend to fall in value against the dollar. Such an outcome led to intervention in currency markets to defend the value of the currency and the adoption of macroeconomic policies to correct the imbalances that were exerting pressure on parity with the US dollar. The Bretton Woods system did not remove the need for countries to adopt polices that led to monetary stability in domestic economies and to international competitiveness. It did, however, remove the need to cut money wages to achieve balance and it provided help via loans from the IMF to defend parities against the US dollar. This allowed economies that needed to adjust their economic conditions time to use the tools of demand management (that emerged from the new Keynesian concept of macroeconomic analysis) to achieve balance. If this were impossible, a country suffering from fundamental imbalance could devalue against the dollar.

The Bretton Woods system was designed to provide the stability that the Gold Standard had delivered but to avoid the problems of adjustment to imbalances between economies that had resulted in the demise of the Gold Standard. The link between the US dollar and gold provided a means to maintain a stable value for all currencies that were pegged to the dollar. The creation of an international institutional system centred on the IMF, together with the tools of demand management and an adjustable peg exchange rate system, were supposed to provide an effective adjustment process to economic imbalances between the countries of the new international economic order. The new international system that developed from the Bretton Woods Agreement appeared to solve the problem of adjustment that led to the collapse of the Gold Standard system while retaining its ability to deliver stability in international transactions.

The growth of income and trade among the members of the Bretton Woods system in the period 1950–1970 was unprecedented in the history of the world. The stability of the international monetary system together with the growth of trade liberalisation has been credited as major reasons for this remarkable period of growth and internationalisation (Solomon, 1982). In the halcyon days of the Bretton Woods system, there were few problems with stability or adjustment. Moreover, the willingness of the USA to supply dollars to international financial markets provided the liquidity necessary to lubricate the large increases in international trade that took place. However, the system ran into a series of crises when the conflict between providing sufficient liquidity to finance the growth in world trade and maintaining the value of the US dollar by keeping parity with gold came into question. A new factor was added to the stability and adjustment problems of the international monetary system. This was the confidence problem, which revolved around the willingness of countries and the international financial markets to believe that the USA could simultaneously provide sufficient liquidity and maintain the value of the dollar against the gold.

In 1960, an analysis of a trinity of problems (liquidity, confidence and adjustment) that could undermine the Bretton Woods system was written (Triffin, 1960). Triffin's analysis proved to be remarkably accurate. Adjustment problems began in the 1960s when Britain found it impossible to solve its fundamental imbalances and in1967 devalued the pound against the dollar. This devaluation led to an increase in the confidence problem and several countries, notably France, began to hoard gold believing that the USA would not be able to supply sufficient liquidity and maintain the value of the dollar against gold. In this period, inflation became a serious problem in the USA further increasing concern about the ability of the USA to maintain the value of the dollar against gold. The attempts by the US government to use macroeconomic policies to curb the imbalances resulting from high inflation led to unemployment. However, there was no significant reduction in inflation and the current account deficit of the USA continued to deteriorate. As the dollar was the anchor currency of the exchange rate regime, the USA could not adjust by devaluation of the dollar other than by reducing the amount of gold that a dollar could buy. This would remove the stability guarantee of the system. It became clear that there was no solution to the imbalances in the system when the dollar became a problem currency. An attempt to curb the problem by reducing the flow of dollars to the world economy would lead to a lack of liquidity but maintaining the flow led to an increase in the confidence problem. Reducing the gold value of the dollar would solve the adjustment problem by effectively devaluing the dollar but would remove the basis for the stable value of currencies. After a series of gold crises the trinity of problems led to the abandonment of the Bretton Woods exchange rate regime when, in 1971, President Nixon announced that the USA was no longer willing to exchange gold for dollars at the fixed rate. This effectively removed at a stroke the foundation of the exchange rate regime of the Bretton Woods system.

The Bretton Woods exchange regime broke down because it proved to be impossible to provide a stable system with sufficient liquidity that also ensured confidence in the value of the anchor currency when the host country of that currency had adjustment problems. By the early1970s, the USA had lost its total dominance of the economic conditions in the western world as Japan and the countries of Western Europe restructured their economies and benefited from the fast growth in income that occurred in the period 1950–1970. Therefore, the USA could not force the leading economies of the west to adopt cooperative and consistent policies to solve the underlying causes of economic imbalances between the USA and the rest of the west. No national economy was large enough to replace the US dollar as the anchor currency of the system. Consequently, the exchange rate regime of the Bretton Woods system came to an abrupt end. Since 1971 no international monetary system has been developed that is capable of delivering the stability provided by the Gold Standard between 1870 and 1914 or the Bretton Woods system in the 1950s and 60s.

Post-Bretton Woods

In the wake of the collapse of the Bretton Woods system, the major economies of the west held a series of summits in 1971–1972 to seek to develop a system of fixed exchange rates not backed by gold or a currency fixed to gold. In 1972, the six members of the European Economic Community (France, West Germany, Italy, Belgium, the Netherlands and Luxembourg) fixed their currencies relative to each other within a 2.25 per cent band. Britain, Ireland and Denmark also joined this system. This basket of currencies floated against the US dollar and the yen within a range of plus or minus 2.25 per cent. This system encountered trouble when Britain, France and Italy had problems maintaining the value of their currencies against the Deutschmark. By 1973, all attempts at operating a fixed exchange rate were abandoned and the era of floating exchange rates began. In the face of the trinity of liquidity, confidence and adjustment problems, no international monetary system could provide fixed exchange rates and therefore this goal was abandoned so that these problems could be avoided.

The risks and costs to international business activities associated with floating exchange rates and the emergence of high inflation in the 1970s stimulated attempts to find partial solutions to inject some stability into exchange rates. The liberalisation of capital markets in the 1980s and the subsequent growth of international capital flows contributed to the volatility of exchange rates because of the large growth in short-run capital flows. These factors increased concern about the effects of floating exchange rates for international business activities. Solutions were sought for three major problems:

- exchange rate risk for firms engaged in international business
- differential inflation rates among major trading partners leading to uncertainty about the level of future revenues and costs from international business transactions
- volatile exchange rates leading to rapid and unpredictable changes to the prices of traded products.

The private sector provided solutions to the first problem by developing hedging instruments to reduce exchange rate risk. Firms also developed techniques to reduce exchange rate risk such as transfer pricing, international cash flow management techniques as well as internal hedging instruments (see Chapter 12 and Moffett and Yeung, 1999). These solutions involve costs in terms of management time and the purchases of hedging instruments. Nevertheless, there is little evidence that the costs of hedging and managing international cash flows significantly reduce international business transactions including direct foreign investment (DFI) (Agarwal and Soenen, 1989), but it is a problem for small and medium sized business that lack the resources to acquire the means to reduce exchange rate risk (Storey, 1994).

The other problems are more serious for the stability and growth of international business activities and affect even large multinational corporations. Differential inflation rates and exchange rate volatility lead to uncertainty about future cash flows because of the distorting effects of inflation and exchange rate changes on prices and therefore on the real value of transactions. These distortions to the price mechanism increase uncertainty about the financial outcomes of engaging in international business transactions and act as a deterrent to the expansion of such activities (Baldwin, 1990). Fluctuating currencies can also lead to problems for exporters that are difficult fully to hedge against because a currency can suddenly become strong and remain so for a long time. The rise of the UK pound against the euro in 1999–2001 illustrates this problem (see Case 5.1). Moreover, the distorting effects of international monetary instability contribute to uncertainty in domestic business transactions that lowers economic activity. The combined effects of these distortions to the price mechanism reduce the potential for economies to grow and thereby diminish the growth of international trade (De Grauwe, 1988).

The harmful effects of floating exchange rates for the smooth growth of international business transactions led to a series of largely unsuccessful attempts to inject more stability into the post-Bretton Woods international monetary system. These attempts are outlined in Exhibit 5.2.

Exhibit 5.2 Attempts to influence floating exchange rates

Plaza Agreement

In 1985 a summit of the governments of France, Germany, Japan, the USA and the UK (G5) held in the Plaza Hotel in New York made an agreement collectively to intervene to drive down the value of the dollar. This was an attempt to manage the floating exchange regime when the leading economies thought the markets were consistently under- and overvaluing currencies. The objective was to take concerted action by central banks by buying and selling currencies thereby nudging the markets in what was considered to be the correct direction.

Louvre Accord

The nations of G5 met with Italy and Canada (G7) in 1986 to assess the Plaza Accord at the Louvre in Paris. At this summit, it was agreed that collective action would be taken by the central banks of the leading economies if the governments of G7 considered that exchange rates were not consistent with economic conditions. However, no clear guidelines were issued as to what constituted inconsistent conditions. The growth of short-run capital flows and the power they exert over exchange rates led to reluctance by G7 countries to try to push the markets in desired directions. Nevertheless, the Plaza Agreement and the Louvre Accord provide the basis for such attempts to manage the floating exchange rate regime.

European Monetary System

In 1979, the member states of the EU formed the European Monetary System (EMS). This system had an exchange rate mechanism (ERM) based on fixing exchange rates against the European currency unit (ECU). The ECU was a basket of the currencies of the member states of the EU. This complex parity system effectively linked the currencies into a fixed exchange rate system. The ERM was an adjustable peg system because it allowed parities to be realigned by agreement of the member states. In many ways the EMS was a version of the Bretton Woods system except it was not backed by gold and it only included the currencies of the member states of the EU. In the period 1979 to 1987, there were frequent realignments to the parity system by devaluing weak currencies against the stronger ones. The strong

currency in the EMS was the Deutschmark and those currencies that were closely link to the German currency (the DM Club). The commitment to establishing European monetary union led to no realignments because fixing exchange rates was part of the process of convergence towards monetary union. There were no realignments in the period 1987 to 1992.

The UK joined the ERM in 1990 but the pound had trouble maintaining parity with the Deutschmark because of different economic conditions from the countries of the DM Club. The Italian, Portuguese and Spanish currencies also had trouble maintaining parity due to fundamental differences in their economic conditions compared to the DM Club. These differences were exploited by currency speculators who became convinced that realignment was inevitable. The very large capital flows that speculators were able to organise defeated the ability of the central banks of the EMS countries to maintain parity to the ECU. In 1992, a currency crisis forced the UK and Italy to suspend their membership of the ERM and to devalue their currencies. The currencies of Spain and Portugal were substantially devalued against the ECU. In 1993, speculators attacked the link of the French franc to the Deutschmark and the pressure exerted led to the effective demise of the ERM.

The end of the ERM clearly illustrated that the ability of currency speculators to organise very large capital flows to buy and sell currencies made it very difficult for central banks to intervene to maintain parities in the face of concerted speculation. Since the crises of 1992 and 1993, there have been few attempts by governments to use the Plaza Agreement and Louvre Accord type of arrangements to try to influence exchange rates. The problems encountered by the ERM were similar to the adjustment problems of the Gold Standard and the Bretton Woods system. Clearly, when economic conditions among the members of the ERM diverged, it became impossible for the weak countries to adjust by using domestic economic policies. This led to speculative attacks that eventually forced the system to collapse.

Further information on these attempts to managing floating exchange rates and the experiences of the ERM is available in Krugman, P. and Obstfeld, M. (2000) *International Economics: Theory and Policy*, New York, Addison-Wesley Longman.

New types of fixed exchange rate regime

The failure of policies to establish fixed exchange rate systems among a subset of countries and the difficulties of intervention by central banks to influence parities (see Exhibit 5.2) led to an emphasis on other methods to reduce international monetary instability. Two major systems have emerged to overcome the problems posed by floating exchange rate regimes:

- crawling peg systems
- currency boards.

These approaches seek to reduce the problems of fixing exchange rates that arise from speculative pressures. The need for such arrangements stems from the power of speculators to organise very large capital flows to attack fixed exchange rate systems. This has forced defenders of fixed exchange rate regimes to devise system that are less vulnerable to speculative attacks. In the case of crawling peg systems there is also an attempt to lessen the problems of adjustment to fundamental imbalances (Williamson, 1999).

Crawling peg systems

Crawling peg systems link a currency to an anchor currency that is strong and will, therefore, enforce monetary discipline on the home country. Normally, the anchor currency is the US dollar. The economic conditions in the USA are likely to be different from those of the home country. Therefore, the trend is for the weaker home currency to depreciate against the dollar. The crawling peg system accommodates this by establishing a band above which the currency cannot appreciate and a crawling peg of deprecation based on the trend of the exchange rate. The crawling peg system alters the exchange rate according to assessments of the divergence between conditions in the economies of the anchor and the home currencies. An alternative to the use of an anchor currency such as the dollar is to use a basket of currencies as the anchor. The advantage of this is that home currency is fixed to a group of countries and is therefore less likely to be caught up in changing economic conditions that mainly affect the country of a single anchor currency.

Crawling peg systems seek to achieve stable parities that adjust slowly and in a predictable manner and therefore reduce the costs associated with floating exchange rate regimes. They also impose a degree of domestic monetary stability by linking the home country to an economy with a good anti-inflationary stance. The crawling peg permits slow adjustment to the divergent conditions between the anchor (or basket currency group of countries) and the home country. It is conceivable that discipline of the crawling peg system will lead to convergence between the home and anchor countries and thereby lead to a fixed exchange rate system. The attraction of the crawling peg system is that it should prevent speculative attacks because divergence between the two economies is slowly reflected in the exchange rate. Crawling peg systems do not eliminate exchange rate risk but they make exchange rate changes more predictable and therefore lessen the need for hedging instruments and other means of managing the risks. They also reduce the likelihood of the emergence of significantly different rates of inflation between the anchor and home countries.

However, if significant differences emerge between the economic conditions of the anchor and home countries speculators will spot the opportunity to profit from the devaluation necessary to restore balance. This happened to the crawling peg system that Mexico established in1991 using the dollar as the anchor currency. Speculative pressures on the peso emerged due to a financial crisis that highlighted economic differences between Mexico and the USA and this led to the abandonment of the system in 1994.

The problem of periodic need to adjust to fundamental imbalance indicates that crawling peg systems are susceptible to speculate attacks if economic conditions between the anchor and home countries become large. Clearly, the problem of adjustment that afflicted the Gold Standard and the Bretton Woods system can also strike crawling peg systems.

Currency boards

Establishment of a currency board leads to a rigid fixed exchange rate system. The currency board is required by law to link the growth of domestic money supply to its holdings of a given currency, usually the US dollar. This system works on similar lines to the Gold Standard except that the source of stable value is the dollar and the home currency floats against all other currencies in line with movements of the dollar to those other currencies. The attraction of currency boards is that they provide strong curbs to the growth of domestic money supply and thereby deliver a very creditable anti-inflationary policy. If currency fluctuations are largely determined by differences in inflation, as is indicated by the purchasing power parity theorem (see later), currency boards should be able to maintain the conditions for a fixed exchange rate regime because inflation rates will be very similar between the two countries. However, if the dollar rises against most currencies because of economic conditions in the USA the countries that fixed their currency to the dollar will also rise in value. Unfortunately, this may lead to a serious loss of competitiveness for countries that fixed their currency against the dollar.

The most famous case of this problem is the recession that afflicted Argentina when its main trading partner, Brazil, devalued against the dollar. In 1991 Argentina established a currency board to provide a creditable anti-inflationary policy to escape a long history of hyperinflation. The currency board was very successful in providing stable domestic monetary conditions in Argentina. However, the devaluation in 1999 of the Brazilian currency against the US dollar significantly reduced the competitiveness of Argentina. The sudden loss of competitiveness following from the devaluation led to reduced exports and disinvestments by multinational companies that had used Argentina as a base to supply the Brazilian market. These problems led to the onset of a severe recession in Argentina. In contrast, Brazil experienced increased growth because of its increased competitiveness. Moreover, Brazil did not suffer from high inflation because of the devaluation and financial markets did not enter into a period of chaos. Indeed, financial markets in Argentina have been more volatile than those in Brazil. The conflicting experiences of Argentina and Brazil illustrate the problems of using currency boards to reduce monetary instability (Krugman, 1999b). It appears that currency boards are susceptible to severe adjustment problems like all other types of fixed exchange rate systems.

Monetary union

The ultimate protection against speculative attacks on fixed exchange rate systems is to form a monetary union. This requires the irrevocable fixing of exchange rates and in some cases, replacement of the currencies of the members with a new currency. In monetary unions with a single currency, a central bank becomes responsible for monetary policy and the exchange rate. The prime example of such a monetary union is European Monetary Union (EMU). The members of EMU (Euroland – Austria, Belgium, Finland, France, Germany, Greece, Ireland, Italy, Luxembourg, the Netherlands, Portugal and Spain) have irrevocably fixed their exchange rates and will replace their national currencies with the euro in 2002 (Gros and Thygesen, 2000). The members of the EU that are not part of Euroland (Denmark, Sweden and the UK) are facing strong pressure to join Euroland. All future members of the EU will be committed to joining EMU when they have satisfied a set of convergence criteria set out in the Maastricht Treaty and the condition that will be included in the treaties that will establish the rules for full membership. The emergence of Euroland has created a large economic area with a rigidly fixed exchange rate regime and it is likely to become bigger. If the UK joins, Euroland will include four of the largest economies in the world and will rival the USA in terms of output and the size of capital and money markets. An overview and assessment of the main implications of European monetary union for firms is provided in Chapter 8.

EMU removes exchange rate risk and currency-conversion costs by replacing different currencies with a single currency. The adoption of a common monetary policy by the European Central Bank (ECB) ensures that inflation rates in the members of Euroland do not significantly diverge, other than in the short term. EMU therefore provides a solution to exchange rate risk for intra-Union trade and to distortions to the price mechanism that arise from floating exchange rate regimes, but only within Euroland. If the monetary policy of the ECB delivers low and stable inflation, the value of the euro within Euroland will be stable. However, the euro floats against the other major currencies of the world and its value on a global scale is not necessarily stable. The rapid decline of the euro against the US dollar in the aftermath of its introduction in 1999 indicates that monetary unions do not necessarily deliver a currency with a stable international value. EMU has removed the problems of floating exchange rates for its members but it has not eliminated these problems for international business activities conducted outside Euroland.

Monetary union and domestic adjustment policies

Monetary unions do not remove the need to make adjustments between the members if economic imbalances exist. Unexpected economic changes that lead to different affects across countries (asymmetric shocks) leads to imbalances between the economies of a monetary union (see Case 5.2). To restore balance it is necessary to adopt domestic policies to adjust labour costs and thereby to alter relative prices to restore balance. In EMU, exchange rates are irrevocably fixed and there is a common monetary policy. Therefore, countries with imbalances cannot use changes in monetary conditions or exchange rates to restore balance. In Euroland, a stability pack constrains the use of domestic fiscal policy thereby further constraining the tools available to curb imbalances. This means that the main adjustment process to asymmetric shocks is 'supply-side' policies that encourage changes to labour costs and thereby adjustments to prices to restore balance (De Grauwe, 1997). Adjustment within EMU requires similar processes to those used in the Gold Standard. Cutting money wages is not a feasible option within Euroland. Consequently, adjustment is likely to require use of labour flexibility and other policies that reduce unit labour costs allowing productivity to increase and thereby permitting relative prices to alter (McDonald, 1997).

If economic conditions vary significantly between the members of Euroland, asymmetric shocks are likely to be common. The more countries that join Euroland, the more likely it is that economic conditions will diverge and that the adjustment problem will assume growing importance. EMU abolishes exchange risk and distortions to the price mechanism for intra-Euroland transactions. However, it moves the prime adjustment problem within Euroland from exchange rate changes to 'supply-side' policies and to firms that must adjust to a lack of competitiveness caused by asymmetric shocks by controlling unit labour costs.

Political and economic union

If Euroland develops into some type of political union with the ability directly to levy taxes and with public expenditure powers the adjustment problem will become mainly a challenge for regional development. The example of the USA illustrates how adjustment takes place in an economic and political union. If some states in the USA suffer a decline in economic activity relative to other states, federal tax revenue will fall in those states that suffer decline and expenditure will rise. This reduces the adjustment problem because federal taxes/expenditure systems redistribute income to those states that are suffering from reduced economic activity. Labour will also move from the states with problems to the more economically active states. In the USA differences in the income levels of the states vary considerably indicating that it is not always possible for states to adjust to the competitive position with an economic and political union. This is the regional development problem.

If the states in the USA had their own currencies those states that could not achieve the same level of competitiveness as the more successful states would see their currency depreciate to achieve balance. As they do not have their own currencies balance is maintained by net transfers via the federal tax/expenditure system, labour leaving the poorer states and lower income levels in the poorer states. However, the federal tax/expenditure system provides some compensation for the absence of state currencies. This, together with the desire to be a political union and to avoid the costs to intra-state trade that would follow from state currencies, provides the rationale for a federal currency and for redistributive tax/expenditure systems. The case of the USA illustrates that existing monetary unions normally have a strong political union underpinning.

Euroland does not currently have such a political underpinning, although monetary union is likely to lead to increased pressures to develop some kind of political union. The ability of Euroland to adjust to imbalances is not as great as the USA because not only does it not have an effective redistributive tax/expenditure system, it also lacks the level of labour mobility that exists in the USA. These factors suggest that the regional adjustment problem in Euroland will be considerably more difficult than is the case in the USA. The lack of political underpinning for Euroland means that the adjustment problem centres on 'supply-side' policies taken by the governments of the members of Euroland and the ability of firms to adjust unit labour costs to maintain competitiveness. This may have implications for the geographical location of firms within Euroland. This issue is explored in Case 5.1 and in Chapter 6.

The euro and the international monetary system

The creation of the euro introduces a major currency that could rival the US dollar as a world currency. The successful establishment and development of EMU could lead to significant changes to the international monetary system by transforming it from a dollar-based system to a dual euro and dollar regime. The development of large capital and money markets denominated in euro will provide an alternative to the current dominance of the dollar in these markets. The euro may become a major reserve currency used by central banks to settle debt and to intervene to defend exchange rates. The euro could also displace the dollar as the major vehicle currency and as the main currency for invoicing and as a means of payment in international business transactions (McDonald, 1999). These developments would lead to the emergence of a bipolar international monetary system dominated by the USA and Euroland with Japan playing a minor role. It is not clear if this would lead to a more stable international monetary system.

New institutional systems are likely to be required to deal with the emergence of the euro as a major world currency (Henning, 1997). The introduction of the euro backed by the large economy of Euroland means that for the first time since the early part of the 20th century there exists a potential rival to the US dollar as a world currency. However, it will take time for euro money and capital markets to develop to be feasible rivals to dollar markets. Moreover, Euroland currently lacks the type of political union that would allow it to rival the USA as a political force in international monetary matters. Nevertheless, EMU has the potential radically to change the international monetary system. Whether this will increase the stability of the system or lead to crises and instability is not, at this stage, known. It has been argued that history suggests that stable international monetary systems depend on the existence of a hegemonic power – Britain in the Gold Standard and the USA in the Bretton Woods system (Eichengreen, 1998). If this is true the growth of the use of the euro as an international currency will have serious implications for the stability of the international monetary system unless new institutional systems can be developed to secure effective cooperation between the USA and Euroland.

Firms face choices as to whether to move from the use of the dollar to the euro for international business purposes. Given the large fixed costs in moving from the use of the dollar, because of the need to alter accounting, payment and treasury management systems, it is unlikely that this will happen quickly. However, as euro markets develop it may become attractive to use the euro instead of the dollar or as a complement to the dollar. The possibility of the development of a new international monetary system based on the twin pillars of the dollar and the euro holds the prospects for the emergence of a different system with unknown characteristics. Such a development could be as profound as the introduction of the Bretton Woods system.

Exchange rates

Currency markets have a major influence on international business activities because changes in exchange rates lead to risks for firms that conduct international business activities. There are three main types of risk associated with fluctuations in the value of currencies – translation, transaction and economic exposure:

- Translation exposure results when converting assets and liabilities denominated in different currencies into a common currency to construct consolidated accounts. It occurs because exchange rate changes alter the value of assets and liabilities and leads to variations in accounting values. Hedging against translation exposure requires the use of forward currency contracts or options that fix the value of assets and liabilities in the desired currency at the time of translation. It is also possible to reduce translation exposure by using the same currency (for example, the US dollar) to denominate assets and liabilities.
- Transaction exposure arises when buying and selling activities are completed but before payment has been settled. It emerges as the price to buy or sell a good, service or asset denominated in a foreign currency depends on the exchange rate that prevails when the transaction is settled. Hedging against the risk that a currency will fall in value can be done by using forward and options contracts or by using the same currency for invoicing and settlement.
- Economic exposure is due to change in exchange rates altering the volume of sales as foreign trade prices change. This changes the value

Exhibit 5.3 Foreign currency markets

Definitions of exchange rates

Nominal exchange rate
The nominal exchange rate is the price paid for one currency in terms of another currency.

Real exchange rate
Real exchange rates are bilateral rates that have been adjusted for price changes in two countries. Real exchange rates can alter even in fixed exchange rate regimes if rates of inflation differ between the two countries.

Effective exchange rate
Effective exchange rates are a measure of the weighted average value of a currency relative to the currencies of main trading partners. Changes in the effective exchange rates reflect the average change in the competitiveness of a country as measured by nominal exchange rates. Real effective exchange rates are a measure of the average change in competitiveness of a country in real terms.

Main actors in exchange markets

Interbank actors trade in wholesale markets. They are normally large commercial banks that conduct very large transactions with a minimum over $1m. The largest interbank market is located in London.

Retail actors engage in small-scale selling to firms and to individuals. They are normally retail banks and financial services firms that buy on interbank markets and sell on, at a margin, to small buyers that wish to make deals that are too small for interbank markets.

Central banks enter the markets to smooth out dramatic fluctuations and to try to influence changes in exchange rates. In times of currency crises central banks can play an important role in the currency markets by cooperating with each other to buy currencies that are subject to rapid decline.

Types of contract to purchase foreign currencies

Spot rate
The exchange rate on the interbank markets – the current nominal exchange rate.

Forward rate
This is the nominal exchange rate in 30 days, 60 days, 90 days etc.

Future contract
These are contracts to buy a foreign currency at a specified delivery date at a fixed price. These futures can be sold at a discount before the maturity date.

Currency options
Currency options are contracts that enable an agent to buy or sell a currency on a certain date at an agreed price. The contract need not be exercised. Options are a type of insurance that is taken up if spot rates move in an adverse direction.

Quotation of exchange rates

Direct quote	Indirect quote
€1.12/$	$0.89/€
(i.e. $1 = €1.12)	(i.e. €1 = $0.89)

In the UK banks tend to use indirect quotes, the rest of Europe uses direct quotes and the USA uses both (direct quotes for home customers and indirect for overseas customers).

Bid and offer rates and spread

Dealers offer two rates:

- offer or ask rate is the price that they are prepared to accept when selling a currency
- bid rate is the price that they are prepared to offer when buying a currency.

The difference is the spread:

$0.80 – 0.93/€

| bid rate of $0.80 | offer rate of $0.93 |

The size of the spread depends on the depth of markets. Deep markets have a large volume of trade and there is good information on trading conditions for currencies. Deep markets tend to have small spreads because there are many traders and they have good knowledge of prices. This encourages competition between traders that reduces spreads. In a shallow market, there is a small amount of trade and limited knowledge of prices. This tends to discourage competition. The pressure for low spreads tends to lead to concentration of currency markets to provide large markets with many traders.

Vehicle currencies

To reduce the costs of trading in currencies where there is a small amount of trade, use is made of vehicle currencies such as the US dollar. Vehicle currencies reduce the costs of trading currencies that have shallow markets. For example, trade in Mexican pesos for South Korean won and for Australian dollars is small. The deepest markets for these currencies are with the US dollar. Therefore, if Mexican pesos are exchanged for US dollars and these dollars are used to buy South Korean won and Australian dollars the spread of buying these currencies will be lower than using the peso directly to buy these currencies.

of revenues and costs and thus influences the overall value of the firm by changing the profits that emerges from buying and selling on foreign markets. Economic exposure is reduced by diversifying buying and selling and production activities across a number of countries. This averages out adverse exchange rate movements and permits adjustment of buying, selling and production to those countries whose currency has moved in a beneficial direction.

Exchange rates are determined in currency markets that are influenced by a wide variety of factors. Exhibit 5.3 provides an outline of the main definitions and concepts used in currency markets.

Models of exchange rate determination

The orthodox view on the major factors that determine exchange rates are based on models that assume that exchange rates emerge from interaction between rational agents operating in efficient markets. Models based on these assumptions are the basis for the most widely held view on the main determinants of exchange rates (Baker, 1998; Daniels and VanHoose, 1999). However, the growth of currency and debt crises has led to criticism on the over-reliance on rational behaviour and efficient markets to explain the determinants of exchange rates. Orthodox models of exchange rate determination appear to provide good explanations for long-run outcomes in stable conditions but they do not provide good explanations for financial crises. In times of crises markets seem to be dominated by a 'herd' instinct that appears to conflict with the rational and efficient view of the operations of financial markets (Shiller, 1989). The financial crisis in Latin America in 1994–1995 and in Asia in 1997–1998 provoked increased interest in the role of herd behaviour as an explanation of currency crises (Krugman, 1999a).

Orthodox model of exchange rate determination

Orthodox models of exchange rates are based on two theorems and two effects:

1 purchasing power parity theorem
2 interest rate parity theorem
3 Fisher effect
4 international Fisher effect.

Purchasing power parity theorem

The purchasing power parity (PPP) theorem is related to the law of one price. This 'law' states that in competitive markets with no restrictions to trade and when there are no transport and transaction costs, the price of products will be equal in all markets. If the law of one price does not prevail, arbitrage will take place. Arbitrage will continue until the price differential is eliminated. For example, if the exchange rate between the UK pound and the US dollar is £1 = $1.5 and a CD costs $1.50 in the USA it will sell for £1 in the UK otherwise arbitrage activities will take place. The PPP theorem holds if the exchange rate is at a level that permits the law of one price to operate. An exchange rate of £1 = $1.5 allows the PPP theorem conditions to be fulfilled. However, if inflation in the UK is 10 per cent per annum and in the USA it is 5 per cent the price of CDs in the UK will rise to £1.10, while in the USA they will cost $1.57. At the exchange rate £1 = $1.50 it is cheaper for UK citizens to buy CDs from the USA. The exchange rate will alter if the law of one price is to hold. If the exchange rate does not alter, arbitrage will force the price of CDs up in the USA and down in the UK until the law of one price prevails. If there where no intervention in the exchange markets and CDs were the only traded item, the increased demand for dollars to buy CDs in the USA would lead to a depreciation of the pound against the dollar. The required change to the exchange rate is given in Equation 5.1:

change in UK pound and USA dollar
rate = difference in inflation rate between UK and USA

$$e£/\$ = (i_{uk} - i_{usa}) \div (1 + i_{usa}) \qquad \text{(Eq 5.1)}$$

$e£/\$$ = expected change to exchange rate
i_{uk} = inflation rate in the UK
i_{usa} = inflation rate in the USA

Thus if the rate of inflation in the UK is 10 per cent and in the USA it is 5 per cent the required change in the £/$ rate:

$$e£/\$ = (0.1 - 0.05) \div (1 + 0.05) = 0.0476 \text{ or } 4.76 \text{ per cent}$$

The PPP theorem states that exchange rates will adjust in proportion to the difference in the inflation rates that prevail between countries. The PPP theorem implies that differential inflation rates determine exchange rate changes. If all products where traded across national frontiers, there were no restrictions to international trade and there were no transport and transaction costs for such trade, it is possible that the PPP theorem would hold. However, these conditions do not normally hold. Nevertheless, differential inflation rates exert pressure for changes in exchange rates but in the long term. These pressures will be stronger for nations with a large proportion of the GDP devoted to traded goods and services.

Interest rate parity theorem

The interest rate parity (IRP) theorem defines the condition under which arbitrage in interest-bearing assets will take place. The theorem predicts that the rate of return to assets (the interest rate) between countries will be equal after allowance for expected exchange rate changes. This relationship is expressed in Equation 5.2:

rate of return in £ = rate of return in $ + forward premium

$$r£ = r\$ + \frac{(f£/\$ - s£/\$)}{s£/\$} \qquad \text{(Eq 5.2)}$$

or

difference in nominal interest rates = forward premium

$$r£ - r\$ = (f£/\$ - s£/\$) \div s£/\$$$

r£ = interest rate on £ assets
r$ = interest rate on $ assets
f£/$ = forward exchange rate £/$
s£/$ = spot rate £/$

Equation 5.2 states that rates of return on financial assets are at parity when the interest rate differential between the countries is equal to the expected change in the exchange rate. The IRP theorem implies that the forward premium is an unbiased predictor of the expected change in the spot rate. A numerical example helps to explain the IRP theorem:

	[1]	[2]	[3]	[1] − [2] − [3]
Case	r£	r$	$\dfrac{(f£/\$ - s£/\$)}{s£/\$}$	Rate of return difference between £ and $ assets
			[expected change in £/$ rate]	
1	0.10	0.06	0.00	0.04
2	0.10	0.06	0.04	0.00
3	0.10	0.06	0.08	−0.04
4	0.10	0.12	−0.04	0.02

In case 1, there is no expected change to the £/$ rate. Therefore, the interest rate differential would induce capital to move from the USA to the UK to take advantage of the 4 per cent interest rate differential. Eventually, these arbitrage activities would eliminate the difference in the interest rates. In case 2, the 4 per cent interest rate differential is exactly offset by an expected 4 per cent depreciation of the £/$ rate. The IRP theorem predicts that in these circumstances there would be no capital flows between the USA and the UK. In case 3, the 4 per cent interest rate differential is more than offset by an expected 8 per cent depreciation of the £/$ rate. Therefore, arbitrage activities would lead to capital flows from the UK to the USA, until the IRP theorem conditions are fulfilled. In case 4, the 2 per cent interest differential is not enough to offset the expected 4 per cent appreciation of the £/$ rate. Arbitrage activities will therefore result in capital flows from the USA to the UK.

The capital flows arising from arbitrage activities generated by these differences in interest rates and by expected exchange rate changes will alter interest rates and exchange rates until the conditions of the IRP theorem are fulfilled. Therefore, the IRP theorem predicts the conditions under which capital flows will take place and also highlights how short-run arbitrage activities lead to changes to exchange rates. The IRP theorem is normally a good predictor of short-run exchange rates.

Fisher effect   The Fisher effect holds that nominal interest rates reflect the real rate of return on assets and the expected rate of inflation. According to this theorem, the difference between the real and the nominal rate of interest is determined by the expected rate of inflation. This shown in Equation 5.3:

$$\text{nominal rate of return} = \frac{\text{real rate}}{\text{of return}} \times \text{expected inflation}$$

$$1 + r^* = (1 + r)(1 + i)$$
$$r^* = r + i + ri \qquad \text{(Eq 5.3)}$$

r* = required nominal rate of return
r = real rate of return
i = expected rate of inflation

Thus, if current real rate of return is 3.5 per cent and expected inflation is 5.4 per cent the required nominal rate of return is:

$$r^* = 0.035 + 0.054 + (0.035 \times 0.054)$$
$$= 0.091 \text{ or } 9.1 \text{ per cent}$$

The Fisher effect implies that the real rate of interest is equalised across frontiers. Thus, countries with high rates of inflation will have higher nominal interest rates than those countries with low rates of inflation. If this is not true, arbitrage will take place to take advantage of higher real rates of interest. These arbitrage activities result in equality of real rates of return across countries.

International Fisher effect

The international Fisher effect states that the rate of appreciation and depreciation of currencies are related to the differences in nominal rate of interest. If the law of one price holds for real rates of return as implied by the Fisher effect, then nominal interest rate differentials will reflect differences in inflation. According to the PPP theorem differences in inflation rates will lead to changes in exchange rates. The combination of the Fisher effect and the PPP theorem leads to the international Fisher effect. This is illustrated in Equation 5.4:

Expected exchange rate £/$/ = (1 + UK interest rate)/(1 + USA interest rate)

$$e£/\$ \div s£/\$ = (1 + ruk)/(1 + rusa) \qquad \text{(Eq 5.4)}$$

ruk = home interest rate
rusa = foreign interest rate
e£/$ = expected exchange rate £/$
s£/$ = spot rate £/$

If the rate of inflation in the UK is 10 per cent and 3 per cent in the USA and the spot rate is £1 = $1.4 the expected rate between the pound and the dollar is £1 = $1.5:

$$e£/\$/ 1.4 = (1 + 0.1) / (1 + 0.03)$$
$$e£/\$ = 1.5$$

The international Fisher effect links the economic fundamentals of changes in inflation and nominal interest rates to the expected future exchange rate.

Integrated model of exchange rate determination

The main elements in the orthodox model can be combined into a system where exchange rates are determined by the economic fundamentals of inflation rates and nominal interest rates. This is illustrated in Figure 5.1. This model indicates the general direction of exchange rate movements. At any particular point in time changes in inflation rates and nominal interest rates will exert influences that move exchange rates in particular directions. However, transaction costs in financial markets, government intervention in these markets and other obstacles to the working of efficient markets prevents the achieving of simultaneous equilibrium in all these relationships as economic fundamentals change. Therefore, the orthodox model only provides an indication of the overall effect on exchange rates as the economic fundamentals change. Consequently, these models do not provide an accurate means of forecasting short-term movements in exchange rates. Indeed, the assumption of rational expectations and the efficient markets hypothesis imply that accurately forecasting short-term exchange rate movements is impossible (see Exhibit 5.4). Nevertheless, agents in financial markets make frequent use of forecasting models based on economic fundamentals, statistical extrapolation techniques and modern mathematical theories such as chaos theory (Walmsley, 1998).

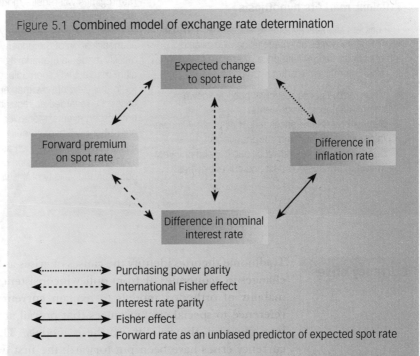

Figure 5.1 Combined model of exchange rate determination

(For a detailed exposition of the combined model of exchange rate determination see Baker, J. (1998) *International France: Management, Markets and Institutions*, London, Prentice Hall International.

Exhibit 5.4 Rational expectation and efficient markets hypotheses

Rational expectation hypothesis

The rational expectation hypothesis postulates that agents seek to maximise the benefits from their economic activities and that they do this by assessing all possible information to select the optimal choice for all transactions. The hypothesis assumes that agents use all available past and current information when forming their expectations on future market prices. They are further assumed to draw on the best possible understanding on how the various factors that determine economic outcomes interact thereby enabling them to accurately predict the outcome of changes to the underlying economic determinants on market prices. If mistakes are repeated, the underlying model of economic interaction will be amended so that the new model provides the best possible understanding on how the world works. Consequently, mistakes will occur only when the underlying conditions that determine interaction between economic factors change. When this happens agents will quickly amend their view on how the world works. Under these conditions systematic mistakes do not occur.

Efficient markets hypothesis

The efficient markets hypothesis states that a market is efficient if choices are made using all available information in determining price. There are three forms of the efficient market hypothesis.

1 *Weak form* – prices reflect all publicly known information about past events.
2 *Semi-strong form* – prices reflect all publicly known information on past and current events.
3 *Strong form* – prices reflect all publicly and privately known information on past and current events.

The hypotheses and currency market

If currency markets are efficient (in the semi-strong or strong form) and traders follow the rules of the rational expectations hypothesis no systematic mistakes will be made. In these conditions, changes in short-run market prices for currencies will be random, that is, just as likely to rise as fall. These prices changes are random because all the factors that systematically determine market prices have been taken into account in setting the price. Therefore, it is impossible for traders systematically to 'beat' the market by predicting short-run market prices that turn out to be different from the actual market price. This is because it is impossible to predict short-run change in price as these changes are random. Forecasting models are of no use in these conditions.

If the underlying factors that determine exchange rates change because, for example, large increases in short-run capital flows, this will alter information flows and will lead to mistakes until the new data are incorporated into current information. This should happen very quickly if agents act in a rational manner and markets are efficient. Fundamental changes to the way that the world works such as new exchange rate regimes will require modification to the models that explain the way that the world works. However, this will cause only temporary instability to markets as modification of the underlying model will be quickly made and rational agents operating in efficient markets will soon adjust to the new conditions.

In this view of how markets operate, currency crises are regarded as requiring adjustments to unforeseen events. Moreover, this view implies that adjustment will happen quickly. The persistence of many currency crises such as the Asian crisis in 1997–1998 and the Russian crisis in 1998, has cast doubt on the validity of this view.

Currency crises

Traditional theories identify the causes of crises as fundamental structural changes in economies or from policy inconsistency by governments. The inability of orthodox models to explain currency crises other than by reference to special circumstances that prevail at the time of crises calls into question the validity of these models. Three main theories of currency crises have been put forward: the first two are compatible with the orthodox model of exchange rate determination, but the third casts doubt on the validity of this model (Krugman, 1998):

1 *Canonical or classical models.* In fixed exchange rates regimes currencies are supported by buying and selling currencies in excess demand and supply. However, reserves to defend parities are finite, therefore continuing attempts to defend exchange rates will eventually deplete reserves unless adjustment policies to solve imbalances can be successfully made. The expectation that imbalances are due to fundamental structural differences between economies reinforces the view that a change in the exchange rate is inevitable thereby stimulating capital flight and thus ensuring the depletion of reserves. The gold crises that emerged in the end days of the Bretton Woods system had many of the conditions specified in canonical models.

2 *Second generation models.* Canonical models assume that governments cannot or will not adopt domestic policies to cure fundamental economic imbalances. However, governments normally respond to divergent economic conditions by using macroeconomic policies that seek to tackle the sources of imbalances. For example, raising interest rates to support a beleaguered currency and in the longer term to solve the differential inflation rates that cause difficulties in maintaining exchange rate parities. However, if the markets expect that the required macroeconomic changes are not feasible for political reasons or that they will further worsen the underlying economic imbalances, the markets will expect that the trade-off between conflicting economic policies (fixed exchange rate and required macroeconomic policies) will break down and the currency will have to devalue. This expectation generates capital flight that leads to a currency crisis. The crises that afflicted the EMS in 1992–1993 have many of the hallmarks outlined in second generation models.

3 *Contagion and herding models.* If investors suspect that major economic imbalances exist due to, for example, financial crises from asset price bubbles, some investors will withdraw short-term capital to reduce exposure to debt default. This will lead to capital flight if other investors join the herd and withdraw short-run capital. Concern may spread to other similar countries. This contagion effect strengthens the herd instinct and spreads capital flight to other countries. This may happen even if the direct economic and financial links between these countries are small because the herd instinct leads investors to fear for the safety of their investments in what they regard as similar countries. The dramatic growth in short-run capital flows to emerging economies are thought to encourage herding and contagion because investors often have poor information about conditions in these economies. This leads to large-scale and rapid capital flight when information becomes available that indicates that economic and financial conditions in emerging economies are deteriorating. The crises in Latin American in 1994–1995 and in Asia in 1997–1998 have been linked to the herding and contagion view of crisis.

The herding and contagion theses on the origins and development of currency crises suggest that financial markets do not operate with agents with rational expectations and in accordance with the efficient markets hypothesis. This implies that where herding and contagion is prevalent it may be possible to use new models based on economic fundamentals or that use statistical extrapolation techniques and modern mathematical theories to forecast exchange rate changes. Such models are based on psychological theories that analyse human behaviour in response to changing economic conditions rather than on rational economic calculation in efficient markets. Statistical extrapolation models and modern mathematical theory models are based on data mining that hopes to find statistically significant patterns from past behaviour. The ability to forecast exchange rate movements is valuable for firms conducting international business activities because accurate forecasts indicate the need for hedging and other techniques to reduce risk when exchange rates regimes are volatile.

The crises caused by herding and contagion behaviour suggest that modification to the international institutional system are necessary to help prevent crises and to reduce the likelihood of these crises spreading from financial markets to the real economy and causing high economic, political and social costs (Dornbusch, 2001; Eichengreen, 1999; Radelet and Sachs, 1998; Stiglitz, 2000). In this view the international monetary system has become very unstable and a threat to the well being of the world economy.

The international monetary system and international business

The evolution of the international monetary system since the middle of the 19th century has provided the monetary and financial conditions that have enabled a large-scale increase in international business activities. The period between the world wars saw a set-back to the growth of internationalisation because of the emergence of competitive devaluations and protectionism. The post-World War II period has seen a remarkable growth of internationalisation not only of trade in goods and services but also of capital flows. The post-World War II international monetary system has been able to generate very large flows of capital for portfolio and direct foreign investments. Indeed, international capital markets are among the largest and most global markets in the world and they are at the heart of the globalisation process (see Chapter 2). However, the growth of international capital flows, particularly short-run flows to emerging markets, appears to have created the conditions for instability in currency and capital markets that has frequently surfaced in currency and debt crises. These crises have added to the risks associated with the current nature of the international monetary system.

The collapse of the Bretton Woods system introduced exchange rate risk that has induced firms to develop treasury control processes and the use of hedging instruments to manage these risks. These add to the costs of conducting international business, especially for small and medium sized firms. Floating exchange rates also lead to economic risk that affects the value of international business transactions as exchange rate changes alter prices and thereby the magnitude of the revenues and costs connected to international trading. Moreover, floating exchange rates allow countries to have different rates of inflation because exchange rates alter to take account of inflation differentials. This adds to the uncertainty of conducting international business activities as differential inflation distorts the price mechanism.

The costs of the risks that emerged from floating exchange rate regimes have led, since the collapse of the Gold Standard, to many attempts to establish fixed exchange rate regimes. Most of these have failed due to the problems of maintaining stability when economic conditions between economies require extensive adjustment policies to cure persistent imbalances. In cases where countries maintain fixed exchange rate regimes in the face of inadequate adjustment policies, the result is often deep recession such as happened when Britain returned to the Gold Standard in 1925 or in the EMS crises of 1992–1993. The cost of removing exchange rate risk appears to be severe adjustment problems that can lead to deep recessions. Monetary unions, currency boards and crawling peg systems all have the potential to suffer from adjustment problems if persistent imbalances emerged among the members of a fixed exchange rate regime. In these cases, the choice is between reduced exchange rate risk and recession connected to adjustment problems. Moreover, fixed exchange rate regimes that include only a subset of major trading partners do not remove exchange rate risk from all international business activities. This can lead to major adjustment problems when currencies that are fixed to a currency such as the US dollar rise against other currencies, for example the problems that afflicted Argentina when the Brazilian currency devalued against the US dollar.

Although the international monetary system is based on floating exchange rates, there is a wide variety of fixed exchange rate regimes among subsets of countries (see Figure 5.2). The heart of the floating exchange rate regime is the trade in the currencies of the USA, Euroland and Japan. Many countries operate some kind of fixed or quasi-fixed exchange rate system (currency boards, crawling peg systems) with the US dollar or the euro. Consequently, the current international monetary system is a mixture of fixed, quasi-fixed and floating exchange rate regimes. Furthermore, these fixed and quasi-fixed regimes often break down or are subject to crises. Therefore, the nature and extent of exchange rate risk faced by firms conducting international business activities depends on which countries they trade with and on the fluid state of many fixed and quasi-fixed exchange rate systems.

The fluidity of the international monetary system is also increasing due to the emergence of the euro, which could become a major currency to complement or even largely replace the dollar, at least in some parts of the world. The frequent occurrence of currency and debt crises in emerging economies also influences the stability of the international monetary system. New institutional system may be necessary to try to

Figure 5.2 Floating exchange rate regimes and with fixed exchange rate blocs

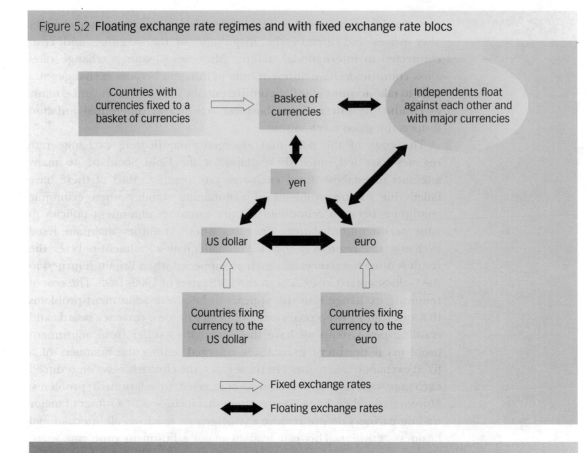

The core of this system is the floating relationship between the major currencies – US dollar, euro and the yen. The dollar–euro relationship is the most important as these are the two major world currencies.

Independents include countries such as Australia, Canada, Switzerland and the UK. These currencies float against each other and against the major currencies.

Currencies that are fixed to a basket of currencies float against those currencies not included in the basket. Therefore, these currencies are fixed against those of the major currencies that compose the basket and float against the others.

The currencies of many developing countries are not fully convertible into major currencies and many have capital controls. These countries include much of sub-Saharan Africa, Russia, China and India. The exchange rates of these currencies are often fixed or quasi-fixed to the US dollar.

prevent these developments from undermining the international monetary system. The experiences of the collapse of the Gold Standard indicated that chaos in international monetary systems has very serious implications for international business activities and for the well-being of the world economy. The growth of international trade and capital flows in the post-World War II period means that chaos in the international monetary system would have very serious implications for international business and therefore for the world economy. An outline of the various types of exchange rate regimes and the main implications for firms is given in Table 5.1.

The industries that suffered most from the rise in the pound were in price sensitive markets and where there was over-capacity in the EU. UK production of standard saloon-type cars and white goods such as washing machines, refrigerators and dishwashers was reduced because of the decline in price competitiveness due to the rise of the pound. Over-capacity and successful policies by the commission of the EU to reduce anti-competitive practices that had artificially boosted the price of cars added to the woes of the car manufacturers. The steel industry, which supplied one of the key inputs to these industries, suffered because of these conditions. The problems that the high pound caused to the industries were centred on those that produced price-sensitive products and where there was over-capacity in the EU.

The long-term effects on DFI inflows into the UK are not known. Japanese car companies appear to believe that the UK will join and have therefore maintained and even increased their investments in the UK. It is possible that Japanese car companies will disinvest if the UK does not join Euroland. However, Japanese DFI is only a small part of the DFI inflows into the UK (about 8% in 2000). DFI in high tech industries and the service sector account for the largest part of DFI inflows into the UK. It remains to be seen if the disadvantages of the UK not being in Euroland in terms of exchange rate risk will be stronger than advantages such as a large domestic market, flexible labour markets and access to technology and important sources of information that appear to attract large volumes of DFI inflows to Britain. It is possible that multinational corporations have assumed that the UK will join Euroland and that DFI inflows will be reduced and disinvestments take place if this assumption proves to be false.

The experience of NAFTA may shed light on this issue. Floating exchange rates between the countries of NAFTA (USA, Canada and Mexico) has not prevented significant and growing DFI flows between these countries. However, if the UK were to remain outside Euroland, firms would face choices that do not exist in NAFTA trade. In the EU, firms face the choice of supplying the European market from a variety of developed economies, the majority of which are members of · Euroland. Selection of an EU country not in Euroland means that they are subjected to exchange rate risk. In the case of NAFTA, there is currently no prospect of a fixed exchange rate regime such as monetary union. There is also not a variety of countries from which it is possible to supply the NAFTA market that are free from tariffs. Therefore, firms face choices in the EU that they do not in NAFTA. In those areas where exchange rate risk is important or where the other factors influencing DFI flows are equal it is likely that DFI connected to supplying EU markets will flock to Euroland.

Economist (2000) 'Still coming in', 20 January 2000; 'Hard pounding', 13 April; 'Sunshine, with a chance of showers', 6 July; and 'Micra economics', 19 October. *Financial Times* (2001) *Corus Group: AGM Statement*, 27 April.

Case 5.2 Ireland and the euro

Since Ireland joined what became the EU in 1973, it has moved from one of the lowest GDP per head in Western Europe to fifth position and, in the 1990s, growth rates have been the highest in the EU. Much of this success has been due to large DFI inflows, particularly from the USA, to supply the markets of the EU.

In 1979, Ireland joined the Exchange Rate Mechanism of the European Monetary System (see Exhibit 5.2). Before this time it had been in a type of a monetary union with the UK. When the UK did not join the ERM the monetary union was broken. Ireland remained in the Exchange Rate Mechanism during the crises of 1992 and 1993 and joined European Monetary Union when it began in 1999. Therefore, Ireland has decoupled its monetary links with the UK and established new links to the continental economies of the EU. This has led to stronger integration with these economies, although the UK is still a major destination for Irish exports.

The high growth rates in Ireland compared to most of the rest of Euroland led to higher inflation in Ireland than the average in Euroland. If Ireland was not part of Euroland and floated its currency, the inflation conditions in Ireland would have required tighter monetary policy and an appreciation of the Irish currency. These macroeconomic conditions would have damped demand in Ireland and lessened inflationary pressure.

In the period 1999 to 2001, the Irish economy continued to boom despite higher inflation and a rising current account deficit. DFI inflows remained high, as did growth rates. The continuation of these problems would require domestic policies by the Irish government to prevent a serious loss of competitiveness and an unsustainable current account deficit. However, the boom conditions in Ireland were sustainable because DFI inflows had made Ireland more productive and thus able to remain competitive despite higher inflation. Ireland also benefited from the appreciation of the pound against the euro because this made Irish goods more competitive in one of Ireland's largest export markets. In the long run, continuation of the differences in inflation rates with the rest of Euroland is only sustainable if productivity growth outweighs the loss of competitiveness due to higher inflation. When productivity growth reaches the point where differences in inflation cannot be compensated, Ireland will have to adjust by adopting policies to reduce unit labour costs. The need for Ireland to take domestic measures to curb imbalances would also increase if the UK joined Euroland and thereby removed the competitive advantage that Ireland enjoys due to the strength of the pound. Domestic adjustment policies include measures to induce greater flexibility in labour markets, reductions in non-wage costs and other 'supply-side' measures. Fiscal policy could also be used to raise taxes and/or cutting public expenditure to reduce domestic demand. None of these policies is likely to be popular. However, as the history of fixed exchange rate systems clearly illustrates if economic imbalances exist domestic policies must be employed to restore balance.

The Irish government saw no need to take these actions because the increase in productivity and increased competitiveness with non-Euroland countries compensated for the higher rates of inflation.

However, Ireland attracted criticism from the European Commission for failure to take action to curb a rise in the deficit in the government's budget. This criticism stems from the 'stability pack', which places restrictions on budget deficits to prevent uncoordinated fiscal policies by the governments of Euroland undermining the monetary policy of the European Central Bank (ECB). The small size of the Irish economy means that it has very little impact on economic conditions within Euroland. Nevertheless, the European Commission sought to force the Irish government to take action to curb its imbalances although they did not undermine either Irish competitiveness or the monetary policy of the ECB.

The action by the European Commission appeared to be stimulated by the need to enforce its right to put pressure on governments under the rules of the 'stability pack'. The reason for this is that imbalance in a large economy such as France or Italy could have strong destabilising effects on Euroland. The Irish case underlines the problems of the need for effective domestic adjustment policies to economic imbalances in fixed exchange rate regimes. This problem may prove to be a serious dilemma for the countries of Euroland as countries with different economic conditions join Euroland or if such differences emerge within the existing members.

Economist (2001) 'Ireland's euro sins', 15 February; www.europa.eu.int – website of the European Commission (details on the operations of the stability pack)

6 Geographical factors

Learning objectives

By the end of this chapter, you should be able to:

- understand the limited role given to geographical factors in traditional theories of trade and DFI flows
- have knowledge about the 'new economic geography' and the main implications of this for trade and DFI flows
- outline the main incentives for economic activities to concentrate in particular geographical areas
- understand why there are forces at work for dispersal from geographical concentrations of firms
- assess the role of the development strategies for subsidiaries in the process of the geographical concentration of firms
- outline the underlying forces at work in the formation and development of clusters and industrial districts
- have knowledge on the roles of business and social networks in the development of industrial districts
- understand the main links between geographical concentrations of firms and competitiveness

Key terms

• new economic geography • clusters • industrial districts • trade flows and geography • DFI flows and geography • regional specialisation

Introduction

The implications for international business activities of geographical factors have become subject to considerable research because of the rise of international trade theories that place geographical factors at the heart of the development of trade flows (Helpman and Krugman, 1985; Krugman, 1991). The work of economists and economic geographers has also focused attention on the importance of place in influencing regional economic development (Amin and Thrift, 1994; Krugman, 1995). Writers on competitiveness have further increased awareness on the benefits that the geographical proximity of firms facilitates (Dunning, 1996; Porter,

1990, 1994; Porter and Solvell, 1998; Scott, 1995). This work has often centred on the benefits of clusters and industrial districts (Krugman and Venables, 1994; Pyke et al., 1990; Saxenian, 1994; Schmitz, 1992). The impact of geographical factors on the location decisions of direct foreign investment (DFI) and subsidiary development strategies of multinational corporations has also been subject to investigation (Dunning, 1999; Dunning and McKaig-Berliner, 2001; Rugman and Verbeke, 2001). Clearly, geographical factors affect trade and DFI flows, competitiveness and subsidiary development. Consequently, investigation of the impact of geographical factors on trade, DFI flows and subsidiary development is important to help to understand the development of international business.

This chapter begins with a review of the very limited role that geographical factors play in traditional trade and DFI theory. An examination is then conducted on new types of economic analysis that have emerged that place geographical factors at the heart of the determinants of trade and DFI flows. This analysis is used to examine developments in trade and DFI flows and for subsidiary development. The chapter concludes by considering the role of geographical concentrations (clusters and industrial districts) for international competitiveness.

Trade and geographical factors

The role of geographical factors in economic theories on the determinants of trade flows and non-export-based entry methods such as licensing, franchising and direct foreign investment (DFI) varies significantly depending on the importance attached to economies of scale and the emphasis placed on understanding the evolution of international business activities. Traditional economic theories that are based on constant returns to scale tend to regard geographical factors as a set of exogenous factors that influence trade flows but which are not central to the analytical thrust of trade theories. These theories, especially theories of trade, tend not to examine the evolution of geographical concentration but to focus on the effects of price changes on economic welfare resulting from trade liberalisation. However, trade theories based on economies of scale place geographical factors at the heart of the analysis of trade and DFI flows and the evolution of geographical concentrations is often central to the investigation of the effects of trade liberalisation.

Traditional theories

Traditional economic theories, including the main trade theories (absolute and comparative advantage and the Hecksher-Ohlin model – see Chapter 3), are based on constant returns to scale. This means that there are no benefits from concentrating economic activity to reap economies of scale. Thus, if economic activity is concentrated it is because of the transport cost advantages of being close to large markets as this minimises the costs of supplying markets. Barriers to trade also influence location because firms locate within countries or regional integration blocs to avoid the cost disadvantages (arising from tariffs, quotas and non-tariff barriers) of supplying markets by exporting from sites located close to large markets. In these circumstances, firms locate near to their large markets when transport costs are high. If transport costs are very low or zero, location is assumed to be the result of historical developments that encouraged firms to locate in particular areas. According to traditional theories the prime determinants of location and patterns of trade are transport costs, the size of markets and trade barriers.

In traditional trade theories, geographical factors affect trade patterns because physical geographical factors such as climate, rivers, mountains and oceans have an impact on the development of transport systems and the type of economic activities that develop. Human geography factors such as population movements and settlements influence the development of cities and other densely populated areas and the types of economic activities that evolve, thereby affecting the location of firms. However, these factors are assumed to be exogenous in traditional economic theories and are not central to the analysis of trade flows. The evolution of geographical concentration of firms is not, therefore, considered by traditional theories. The reasons why a country or a region has developed a comparative advantage are largely taken to be given and the focus of analysis is on the effects of trade flows on prices and welfare. The use of non-export-based trade by licensing, franchising and direct foreign investment (DFI) is thought to arise from market failures, trade barriers and high transaction costs that lead to lower costs by use of these non-export-based modes of entry (see Chapter 9). It is recognised that market failure and transaction costs can be influenced by geographical factors because population movements and settlements affect the evolution of institutional arrangements in particular geographical areas.

Traditional theories indicate that core–periphery development is likely to arise because of the benefits of locating near large markets if transport costs are positive. Trade liberalisation is likely to reinforce the core–periphery nature of economic activity because firms will take advantage of the ability to supply markets by relocating close to their large markets and exporting to their smaller markets. Traditional theories predict development of the periphery if input prices, land and other factors are cheaper in the outlying regions. However, even in these cases the advantages of being close to large markets arising from transport costs will mitigate against the development of the periphery unless input prices and other factors are considerably cheaper than at the core. The role of geographical factors in traditional theories is illustrated in Figure 6.1.

New theories

The new international economics argues that trade between countries with similar economic structures is largely based on the ability to reap increasing returns to scale in the design, production and distribution of goods and services (Helpman and Krugman, 1985). The new international economics predicts that DFI flows are partly a consequence of the attempts to secure the advantages from locating in different regions. Models using this approach are focused on the benefits of geographical

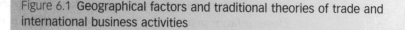

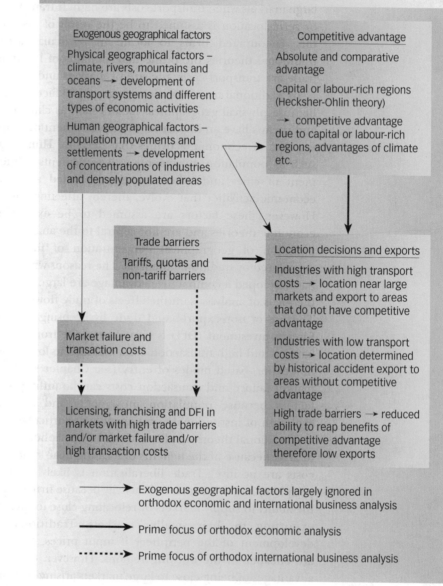

Figure 6.1 Geographical factors and traditional theories of trade and international business activities

concentration (clustering) to reap internal and external economies of scale and to achieve low-cost access to large markets (Krugman, 1991; Krugman and Venables, 1994). These models suggest that as trade costs are reduced, firms will cluster near their large markets and supply other markets by exporting. Clustering leads to benefits from market linkages (backwards – good access to supplier and forwards – closeness to large markets), pools of desirable labour and knowledge spillovers from other firms, R&D agencies and government bodies.

The insights into the importance of geographical factors that arose from the new international economics led to an increased focus on what has became known as the new economic geography (Ottaviano and Puga, 1998). Models based on the new economic geography focus on the importance of the elasticity of supply of inputs, the mobility of inputs and congestion costs as limiting factors in the incentives to cluster (Helpman, 1997). In these models the process of clustering initially leads to cost advantages from internal and external economies of scale and from the expansion of the size of the market as concentration raises the income of factors of production within the cluster. The advantage of clustering induces inputs to migrate to clusters thereby creating a virtuous cycle of success breeding further success. However, as clusters develop, incentives to disperse operations increase because factor prices rise for those inputs that are immobile or that have inelastic supply. Congestion costs also increase as clusters develop and grow.

In these circumstances DFI decisions are influenced by the desire to find locations that confer the best possible supply of those factors of production that are immobile and that provide more elastic supply of the factors that are experiencing large price increases in existing clusters. A trade-off emerges between economies of scale and scope and the advantages of proximity to large markets that clusters obtain compared to rising production costs associated with input supply and congestion. Therefore, a differentiation of operations emerges with core activities that benefit from geographical proximity being located in clusters while operations that have low proximity benefits are consigned to peripheral locations. In some cases the immobility of key resources can induce relocation of core activities to an area that has adequate supply of such resources, even when these areas are congested and have high input prices. The continuing extensive migration of investment banking firms to the City of London and of IT firms to Silicon Valley illustrates the importance of key, but immobile resources, in location decisions. The incentives to cluster and disperse are illustrated in Figure 6.2.

The limited empirical evidence available on the new economic geography tends to support the view that reduction in trade costs stimulates agglomeration. A study found that 14 out of 18 industries in the EU had increased geographical concentration and that those industries with strong economies of scale had the highest levels of concentration (Brülhart, 1998). Concentrations in these industries tend to be strongest close to their largest markets (Amiti, 1998). DFI flows also tend to be concentrating within the EU but that there was also DFI flows to the periphery as a result of trade liberalisation (Dunning, 1997a and b). Further evidence on the dispersal effect has been found in a study on geographical concentration that found that the bulk of DFI flows where to the core regions but that there had been significant dispersal to the periphery since 1980 (Brülhart and Torstensson, 1996).

The new theories, like the traditional theories, imply a core–periphery type of development because on top of the transport cost advantages of locating near large markets there are also economies of scale benefits from geographical concentration of firms. These advantages expand as

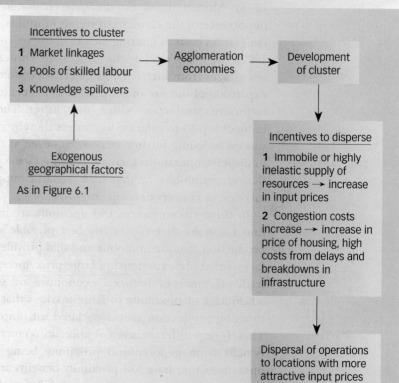

Figure 6.2 Geographical concentration and dispersal

concentration leads to increased agglomeration benefits that further stimulates the geographical concentration of firms. Development of the periphery arises from dispersal activities as firms in clusters search for lower input prices and congestion costs. However, the proximity benefits of concentration tends to limit dispersal to low-level operations. Trade liberalisation further reinforces the tendency towards concentration because it permits firms to congregate in favourable locations and to supply other markets from clusters. According to these modern theories the development of the periphery depends on the creation and development of clusters within peripheral regions that confer competitive advantages arising from proximity benefits that are not available in the core. This will normally require more than lower input prices and congestion costs in the periphery because these are unlikely to outweigh the proximity benefits of being in a cluster that is located in a region rich in terms of demand and in the quantity and quality of desirable resources.

However, this type of analysis still treats geographical factors (such as why cities and densely populated areas develop or why specific types of firms concentrate in particular areas) as exogenous. This is partly because many economists and modellers seek to construct theories that are capable of determining equilibrium outcomes and that can be compared and constrasted to more orthodox general equilibrium economic models (Fujita el al., 2000; Krugman, 1998). Moreover, the reasons why proximity benefits arise from market linkages, knowledge spillovers and pools of skilled labour are not explained by many of these models. These models also neglect the role that the strategic objectives of multinational corporations play in the development of geographical concentrations. An understanding of how proximity benefits arise from clustering and the affect of the strategic objectives of multinationals on geographical concentration provides useful insights into the role of geographical factors for the development of international business activities.

Strategic development of subsidiaries and regional specialisation

Traditional theories of DFI such as the eclectic or OLI paradigm suggest that DFI flows arise from the desire to develop international markets and sources of supply while retaining control over ownership rights using the least transaction costs methods of securing these objectives. Location specific advantages such as labour costs, taxation and subsidies also influence DFI flows (Dunning, 1992). Stage theories of internationalisation indicate that the evolution of DFI flows moves from simply international operations such as exporting to more complex (and higher valued-added) operations that can include product development and R&D activities (Johanson and Vahlne, 1977). However, these models are rather mechanistic and suggest that multinational corporations follow a rigid linear development of internationalisation that is not verified by empirical evidence (Andersen, 1993). Theories based on the development of networks (Nordstrom, 1990) and contingency theories (Reid, 1983) have sought to clarify the complex factors that appear to determine the internationalisation path of multinational corporations. Most of these theories and empirical evidence provide support for the view that DFI flows follow an evolutionary process, but that the time path and major characteristics of this evolutionary process seems to be influenced by a variety of complex factors (Young, 1987). However, these modified traditional theories do not provide insights as to why some host regions become specialised in high or low value-added operations other than due to location specific advantages/disadvantages such as low-/high-cost access to desired resources or proximity to large/small markets.

Modern theories that focus on spillover effects, technological and geographical factors provide a clearer understanding of some of the reasons for regional specialisation. Spillover benefits to domestic firms and industries from DFI activities arise from demonstration effects and the transfer of knowledge to suppliers and other supporting firms and organisations connected to foreign subsidiaries. Some studies suggest that DFI leads to spillover benefits that improve the general level of productivity in host countries (Blomstrom and Kokko, 1998). Such spillover effects are most pronounced in regions that have a high capacity to assimilate technology transfer embodied in DFI flows. Beneficial spillover effects generate desirable conditions in regions that may encourage more investments to take advantage of the enhanced productivity potential thereby creating a virtuous cycle of DFI inflows begetting more investments both foreign and domestic. Thus, the process of clustering once begun, becomes a self-generating engine for regional specialisation as investment leads to spillovers that lead to improvements in regional productivity that encourage further investments.

Models based on the new economic geography focus on the importance of factor mobility and availability and congestion costs as limiting factors in the incentives to cluster. In these models, the process of clustering initially leads to cost advantages from internal and external economies of scale, benefits from low-cost access to essential resources that lower costs and/or increased quality and from the expansion of the size of the market as concentration raises the income of the population within the cluster. Spillover effects further stimulate costs and quality advantages. Consequently, the advantages of clustering induce inputs and investment to migrate to clusters thereby creating a cycle of success breeding further success. However, as clusters develop, incentives to disperse operations increase because factor prices rise for those inputs that are immobile or that have inelastic supply. Congestion costs also increase as clusters develop and grow. In these circumstances, DFI decisions are influenced by the desire to find locations that confer the best possible supply of those factors of production that are immobile and that provide more elastic supply of the factors that are experiencing large price increases in existing clusters. A trade-off emerges between the economies of scale and scope and the market size advantages of clusters compared to rising production costs associated with input supply and congestion. A differentiation of operations emerges with core activities that benefit from geographical proximity being located in clusters while operations that have low-proximity benefits are consigned to peripheral locations.

These factors can explain the development of regional specialisation in response to reductions in trade costs that lead to high-level subsidiary development in those regions that provide a pool of desirable resources. Subsidiaries located in regions with such desirable resources will tend to source a large part of their operations in the host region and will supply a large part of the operations of the MNC as a whole from its key subsidiaries. However, regions that do not possess such benefits are likely to attract subsidiaries with low-level mandates such as sales and distribution and some low value-added manufacturing mainly for the domestic market. The main factors that influence regional specialisation with Europe are illustrated in Figure 6.3.

The factors that influence regional specialisation outlined in Figure 6.3 do not take into account the strategic objectives of multinational corporations. Clearly, the strategic objectives of multinational corporations is important for the development of their subsidiaries and therefore for the development of regional specialisation in which subsidiaries operate. Resource-based theories of multinational corporations provide a means of analysing the possible role of the strategic development of subsidiaries on regional specialisation.

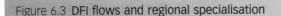

Figure 6.3 DFI flows and regional specialisation

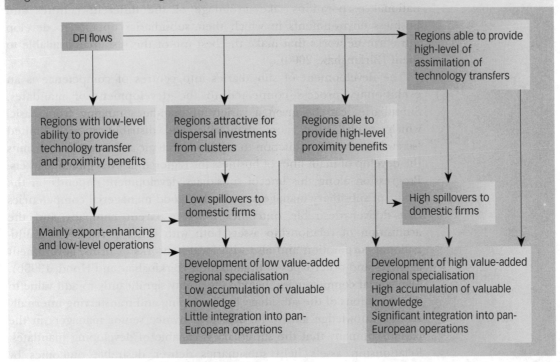

Resource-based theories regard differentiated networks of subsidiaries as a major method of developing competitive advantages (Bartlett and Ghoshal, 1989). Multinational corporations that develop differentiated networks transform some of their subsidiaries into centres of competence. These centres are subsidiaries that develop core activities that play an important role in the operations in all, or significant parts, of the multinational corporations. Therefore, subsidiaries located in areas capable of development into centres of competence become central to the overall objectives of multinational corporations (Birkinshaw and Hood, 1998a).

Subsidiaries selected to be centres of competence have desirable resources based on local networks that are founded on trust and access to inputs that are useful in achieving the goals of multinational corporations. Pools of skilled labour, access to high-quality products, membership of local networks that include organisations and agencies that help to achieve the strategic objectives of the parent company provide attractive locations for multinational corporations. If these desirable resources cannot readily be transferred to other parts of the firm it is beneficial to develop subsidiaries into centres of competence and to use output from these centres to satisfy demands over all, or large parts, of the operations of the firm. Contrariwise, if desirable resources can be easily transferred to other parts of firms they can be moved to those locations that grant the greatest benefits to firms. The goal of the resource-based strategy of multinational corporations is to blend their network of subsidiaries into a more effective unit. Therefore, multi-national corporations take advantage of the different cultures and business environments in which their subsidiaries operate to develop intra-firm networks that make the best use of the resources available to them (Birkinshaw, 2000).

The development of subsidiaries into centres of competence is an evolutionary process connected to the development of mandates. Subsidiaries can be given a variety of mandates ranging from basic, which involve little more than sales and distribution with limited 'screwdriver' type production to top level strategic autonomy that permits the develop of main lines of business for regional or even global markets. Progression along this line of subsidiary development depends on the ability of subsidiary managers to develop good managerial competencies that deliver desirable outcomes for the parent company and the acquisition of relationship assets both with other parts of the multi-national corporation and also with local networks of firms, government agencies and other types of organisation (Birkinshaw and Hood, 1998b). Managerial competencies include the ability significantly to add value to the operations of the subsidiary by developing and transferring internally created knowledge and to be able to convince senior managers in the parent company that the subsidiary is capable of developing mandates. Relationship assets help subsidiaries deliver desirable outcomes by granting access to resources and information that is not available (or can only be secured at high cost) to the parent company. Relationship assets include memberships of local networks that permit high-level performance and good contacts with useful information sources such as R&D centres, governmental agencies etc. (Zander and Kogut, 1996). Accumulation of relationship assets together with the development of managerial competencies permits subsidiaries to develop mandates. This process is illustrated in Figure 6.4.

If there is no significant accumulation of managerial competence and relationship assets, subsidiary development will stop at a mandate level appropriate to the accumulated management competencies and relation-ship assets. In cases where there is deterioration in managerial competencies or accumulated relationship assets or where they fail to 'keep up' with developments elsewhere, mandates may be withdrawn from subsidiaries leading to a move down the line.

The initial point of entry to this line need not be at a basic mandate level. For example, an international financial services firm entering a well-established cluster may well enter at a mid- or even top-level mandate by acquiring a firm that already has high-level relationship assets and managerial competencies (Anderson et al., 1997; Mattson, 1998).

The analysis of the development of mandates centres on the internal resources of subsidiaries, but indicates that the types of factors relevant to regional specialisation (ability to assimilate technology transfers, proximity benefits and spillovers) are important for the development of subsidiaries because they influence the ability of subsidiaries to

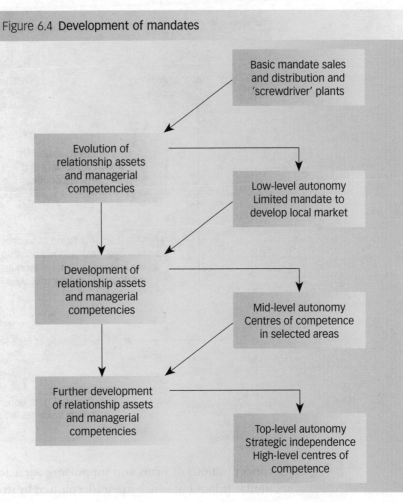

Figure 6.4 **Development of mandates**

accumulate and develop relationship assets. Moreover, the labour market conditions in host regions affects the development of managerial competencies because regions that have developed high value-added specialisation are more likely to have access to a pool of labour with the attributes and skills necessary for the effective management of subsidiaries that have high-level mandates. The main factors that affect the development of high-level mandates thereby contributing to regional specialisation are illustrated in Figure 6.5.

Clusters and industrial districts

The relationship between clusters and industrial districts and how they can confer competitiveness illustrates many of the benefits that arise from proximity benefits and also highlights the many and various forces that are at work in the creation and development of such concentrations (McNaughton and Green, 2002). Although the terms cluster and industrial districts are often used interchangeable, they cover two distinct concepts. Clusters can be defined as 'a group of producers making the same or similar things in close vicinity to each other' (Schmitz, 1992: 65). Whereas industrial districts are geographical

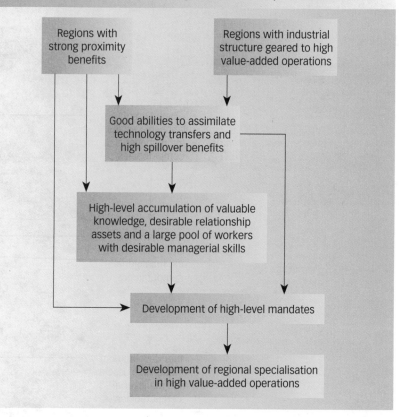

Figure 6.5 Characteristics of host regions and development of mandates

concentrations of firms and supporting agencies producing the same or similar things but which are underpinned by strong networks that confer benefits to the participants in the district (McDonald and Vertova, 2002). Thus, all industrial districts are clusters, but in principle, not all clusters are industrial districts.

Clusters

Clusters have two defining characteristics, geographical concentration and sectoral specialisation. Three specific factors provide the main influences on the development of clusters.

1 geographical factors
2 historical events
3 institutional factors.

Geographical factors lead to a trade-off between transport costs, size of the market and trade barriers as discussed earlier. These geographical factors lead to the generation of proximity benefits but also incentives to disperse. However, the existence of favourable geographical conditions that are conducive to good transport systems and densely populated areas are not sufficient to generate clustering of firms. Historical events and institutional factors that are conducive to concentration provide the setting in which it is possible to reap proximity benefits.

Historical events strongly influence the clustering process. The attraction of a particular location today often has its origins in historical accidents that occurred a long time ago. There are many examples of historical accidents leading to the development of clusters. Silicon Valley, perhaps the best-known example of a cluster, grew out of the few electronic companies gathered in that area in order to take advantage of the proximity of the aerospace industry and from a concentration of computer scientists in Stamford University (Saxenian, 1994). (See also Case 6.1.) There are many other less famous examples of the importance of historical events in the development of clusters (Porter, 1990). Historical accidents that place people and events in geographical locations at particular points of time often lead to the beginnings of economic activity that develop because the geographical conditions favour the creation and evolution of clusters.

Institutional factors are another important determinant of cluster formation and development. Institutions are the rules of the game in a society and, therefore, they shape human interaction (see Chapter 7). There are formal institutions, such as constitutions, laws, bills of rights, courts, regulations and standards, which form legal and political frameworks for social interactions. In addition, there are informal institutions, such as cultural norms, conventions, codes of conduct, norms of behavior, traditions, habits, attitudes and generally accepted, but informal, procedures for governing social interactions. Institutions carry out three basic functions for any economy to work, they reduce uncertainty, they manage cooperation and conflicts and they provide incentives that influence behavior in human interaction. Institutional frameworks affect the transaction costs of doing business by influencing the time, effort and, especially, uncertainty associated with business activities. Institutional frameworks can be effective in reducing transaction costs because they affect levels of uncertainty in transactions and provide incentive systems for finding solutions to conflicts (North, 1990). Moreover, some institutional systems have high levels of 'adaptive efficiency' that permits quick and effective adjustment to new economic, political, market and technical conditions. Countries, and some regions within countries, can develop institutional frameworks that are more capable of reducing uncertainty and transaction costs and have better 'adaptive efficiency' than other countries or regions. In these cases, the decision to locate in such countries and regions will bring benefits in terms of lower transaction costs and will therefore encourage the growth of clusters in these areas.

The characteristics of industries and markets also influence the formation and development of clusters. Clearly, geographical concentration is only beneficial for firms in industries that are capable of reaping proximity benefits. Moreover, firms in industries where labour costs are a low portion of total costs are likely to cluster because the harmful effects of increasing labour costs, resulting from geographical concentration, will be small. Firms in markets that have strong elements of non-price competition may also be more willing to cluster because the resources available to obtain quality advantages resulting from geographical concentration will help to offset the increase in labour costs arising from clustering. The ideal industry for clustering would have low transport costs, low labour costs relative to total costs, benefits from internal and external economies of scale and strong non-price competition. The main factors that influence the formation and development of clusters are illustrated in Figure 6.6.

Some clusters may not deliver significant proximity benefits. For example, retail outlets of a particular type such as restaurants often cluster because of the benefits of reducing search costs for customers who may walk around a small area to select their preferred place to eat. This type of cluster can emerge through a process of a few restaurants initially finding themselves in close proximity and discovering the benefits of the low search costs for customers. This success leads to other restaurants locating in the same district. The competitive nature of these types of markets means that cooperation between firms is minimal, but some proximity benefits can arise from improved connections to supplier networks and other types of logistical and distribution issues. However, the main benefits of clustering arise from cutting down the search costs for customers and/or improvements in logistical and distribution operations.

The process of self-organising clusters arising from historical accidents that leads to firms locating in close proximity discovering that this delivers benefits can lead to the quick growth of clusters. This type of evolution appears to be prevalent in many cities where the existence of factors such as a natural harbour or navigable river leads to geographical concentra-

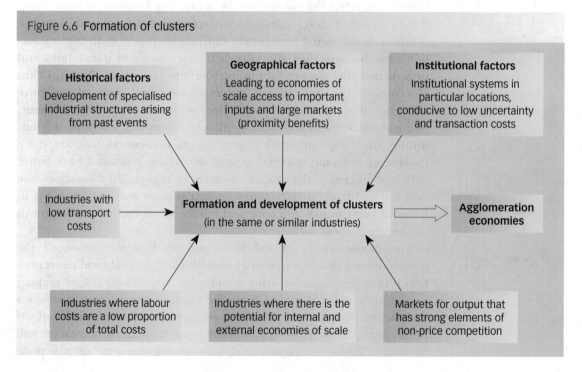

Figure 6.6 Formation of clusters

Historical factors
Development of specialised industrial structures arising from past events

Geographical factors
Leading to economies of scale access to important inputs and large markets (proximity benefits)

Institutional factors
Institutional systems in particular locations, conducive to low uncertainty and transaction costs

Industries with low transport costs

Formation and development of clusters
(in the same or similar industries)

Agglomeration economies

Industries where labour costs are a low proportion of total costs

Industries where there is the potential for internal and external economies of scale

Markets for output that has strong elements of non-price competition

tion of firms engaged in activities that require low-cost transport systems. These firms discover, by accident, the benefits of locating close to firms engaged in similar types of operations and a process of clustering spontaneously emerges (Fujita et al., 1999; Krugman, 1996). This analysis suggests that clusters are not planned rather they emerge from the uncoordinated and self-interested actions of agents responding to historical accidents and geographical and institutional conditions.

Industrial districts

Networks are the means by which clustered firms develop into industrial districts. Networks involve relationship, which are neither purely market transactions nor hierarchies and are embedded in social and cultural conditions (Powell and Smith-Doerr, 1994). Networks are, therefore based on different institutional arrangements from the market or the internalised firm. Network linkages rely on trust between the parties, sustained by moral incentives, such as respect, reputation and sense of loyalty. Morality creates a climate of trust, thus avoiding opportunistic behavior. Face-to-face communications and contacts encourage information to be shared in a more cooperative and less competitive way, thus reinforcing the sense of mutual obligation. Moreover, the embedded argument shows the importance of networks in generating trust and discouraging malfeasance, by recognising that human behaviour is embedded in the structure of social relations, which are crucial for the production of trust in economic life (Granovetter, 1985). Furthermore, continuous and repeated relationships have a tendency to build trust among parties.

Two different kinds of networks can be identified, business and social networks, leading to the creation of different kinds of industrial districts. Business networks are inter-firm relationships involving all firms within a district. The main task of these networks is the gathering, processing and diffusion of information that helps in the operation of the system. Such networks require communication and coordination systems that have low transaction costs and that deliver the required quality of outputs. Entrepreneurs need to make decisions in a volatile environment and these networks help to obtain (at low cost) useful information on which to base the decisions.

The balance between cooperation and competition within business networks must also be determined. In literature based on an analysis of competitiveness in geographical concentrations, a judicious mix of cooperation and competition is deemed essential to generate advantages (Porter, 1994). Cooperation helps firms and organisations to solve common technical and economic problems. However, too much cooperation, especially among final firms can lead to high levels of x-inefficiency and slow responses to changing conditions. Much of the literature based on Italian industrial districts places considerable less emphasis on competition even among final firms (Becattini, 1990). Here the beneficial aspects of cooperation are deemed to outweigh any harmful outcomes arising from low competition within the industrial district. Italian industrial districts are often involved in highly competitive international markets where competition comes from firms located in other countries. Italian industrial districts are also underpinned by strong social networks that may militate against internal competition. It seems that the balance between competition and cooperation is influenced by the market conditions and the nature of the networks that sustain geographical concentrations.

Social networks are interpersonal relationships deriving from social factors and cultural characteristics, involving all the geographically concentrated firms and the local community. The literature about industrial districts refers to the importance of these kinds of networks (Becattini, 1990; Pyke et al., 1990). Therefore, sociological as well as economic features are important in some industrial districts. Extended families, churches, educational organisations, local government authorities, local political parties and trade unions, professional associations and local banks can be involved in these networks. Since local actors share a strong homogeneous system of values, a sense of belonging encompasses the entire industrial community, thus giving the base for these social networks. The creation of trust-based networks provides the basis for these social networks to reduce the time, effort and uncertainty associated with gathering and processing information, thus reducing transaction costs. Furthermore, these kinds of networks are more likely to be important in societies where the institutional structures have difficulties in institutionalising trust across a wide band of society. Therefore, people may be encouraged to form local social networks to compensate for the inadequacies of their national institutional frameworks. Moreover, some regions within nations may be more able to develop more effective social networks than other regions. These differences are likely to be rooted in the historical development of regions. However, social networks may become an obstacle to economic growth. These kinds of networks may change only gradually and incrementally over time because of the commitment to a shared system of values, consequently, they may adapt slowly to new economic and social conditions.

Links between business and social networks

There are differences between business and social networks. Business networks are *inter-firm relationships*, which can occur over long distances, especially with the increasing possibilities of using information and communication technologies to create and develop virtual business networks (see Chapter 14). However, geographical concentration is important for business networks when it is possible to acquire the benefits of external economies of scale based on proximity, such as access to a pool of skilled labour and to technical expertise that are largely based on tacit knowledge. Transactions in business networks that are largely market based are governed by laws and institutional systems. These kinds of networks discourage the incentive to cheat because of the legal and institutional frameworks that govern market transactions. Although there may be problems with opportunistic behaviour in transactions covered by contracts, efficient organisational and institutional systems mitigate against these problems (Williamson, 1979). However, institutional systems that generate high uncertainty and transaction costs exchange may make greater use of non-market exchanges within business networks. These networks would have characteristics similar to 'clans' (Ouchi, 1981).

Social networks are *interpersonal relationships*, which normally need short distances to work, because they are based on face-to-face communications and contacts. Consequently, social networks require proximity between the actors that compose the network. In social networks, there are no laws against opportunistic behaviour. Moral incentives are the strongest defence mechanisms. In this case, self-imposed moral and emotional sanctions discourage cheating because of the possibility of acquiring a negative reputation among the community and a sense of guilt and shame. The necessity of short distances for effective social networks is enhanced by the fact that moral mechanisms work better in small groups.

Clustered firms primarily based on business networks lead to the creation of what may be term industrial district type 1 (ID1), which is very similar to the Marshallian district, described as a concentration of small businesses in the same or similar industries in a particular geographical area (Marshall, 1890). Geographical concentrations that have extensive social networks, together with business networks, lead to the creation of what we call industrial district type 2 (ID2). Italian industrial districts epitomise the main characteristics of ID2 districts (Becattini, 1990). All industrial districts have elements of both business and social networks (see Case 6.1) but social networks appear to be central to the effective operation of some industrial districts, for example Italian districts, compared to Silicon Valley or Silicon Fen (see Case 6.2).

The majority of clusters are likely to evolve into ID1, where business networks are predominant. After all, the primary characteristic of industrial districts is business activity. However, some clusters may develop only very limited business networks, such as geographical concentrations of retail outlets selling the same or similar products. In these cases, the limited business network connections would hardly warrant the title of an industrial district. Some clusters, especially those located in areas where institutional frameworks are not conducive to low transaction costs may develop important social networks to lower these costs. This would lead to the development of ID2.

The existence of industrial districts does not per se guarantee that proximity benefits will be reaped. Networks may be ineffective because the firms, organisations, agencies and social groups that compose the networks are not optimal in terms of the size of the network and/or the required range of participants is not created and developed. Further-more, networks that have achieved optimal size and composition may not have appropriate communication and coordination systems. Additionally, geographical concentrations that have had effective networks may be unable to respond to changing conditions and thereby find that their proximity benefits begin to disappear. Indeed, the decline of Sheffield in the UK as an industrial district based on steel products (identified by Marshall) resulted from technological and economic changes that made the location advantages of Sheffield obsolete. The balance between competition and cooperation is also likely to influence the continuing effectiveness of geographical concentrations. Networks that lack competitive pressures may rapidly lose effectiveness in the face of unexpected changes if they have become locked into obsolete methods that cannot be quickly changed because of long experience of operating in an environment with few challenges.

Clusters and industrial districts: a source of competitiveness

Firms within geographical concentrations may obtain competitive advantages that could not be achieved outside of a cluster. The importance of geographical proximity for international competitiveness is witnessed by the fact that regions with successful industrial districts performed particularly well in the global economic crisis of the 1970s and 1980s (Harrison, 1992). The possibility to reap proximity benefits can be due to the presence of two different kinds of networks, business and social networks. Both these kinds of networks can lead to a reduction in production costs and improvements in quality of outputs via two main benefits:

1 reductions in transaction costs
2 reductions in learning costs.

Transaction costs derive from three different factors – bounded rationality, opportunism behaviour and uncertainty (Williamson, 1979). Bounded rationality is the result of human limitations to gather and process information; opportunism is the result of guile and self-interest behaviour; and uncertainty is the result of unforeseen difficulties embedded in every transactions. Under these circumstances, prices do not provide sufficient information to make decisions. Therefore, additional information is required to help make decisions that produce desirable outcomes. Reductions in transaction costs between cooperating agents enhance the possibilities of increasing the amount and level of beneficial exchanges. External economies of scale and quality improvements depend on the level and extent of exchanges between partners. Therefore, reducing transaction costs by forming appropriate networks provides opportunities to widen and deepen external economies of scale and enhances abilities to improve quality. When contract negotiation, monitoring and enforcement are expensive, exchange will be concentrated within groups that trust the members of the collective. By contrast, when information, measurement and enforcement costs are low, exchange can take place over greater distance and longer periods. Moreover, cultural, legal, political and institutional factors affect transaction costs by influencing levels on uncertainty in transactions. Therefore, some institutional frameworks are better than others in reducing transaction costs are. Hence, firms located in areas with institutional frameworks conducing to reduce transactions costs, will reap advantages that are not available for those firms that do not or cannot locate in areas with such a favourable institutional conditions. Moreover, the concentration of business activities in these regions encourages the evolution of institutional frameworks, which help to maintain a low transaction costs environment, thus beginning a path-dependent trend.

Firms are learning organisations and the capacity for learning is related to individual skills as well as the organisation of the firm and the institutional set-up of the economy. However, knowledge can be difficult to transfer if it embodies a large amount of tacit knowledge. Personal contacts and interpersonal relationship may enhance the diffusion of tacit knowledge among people sharing the same culture, traditions and history. Industrial districts meet these requirements, because they are geographically concentrated firms in an area where people share the same culture and the same economic and organisational systems. Consequently, geographically concentrated firms support and enhance the feasibility of transmitting tacit knowledge. As it is often easier to develop business activities among people who belong to the same group, as they are more likely to trust each other, learning that embodies tacit knowledge may be more effectively achieved within industrial districts than within geographically dispersed networks.

Two other factors enable the acquisition of competitive advantages by the development of cluster and industrial districts – first mover and quality advantages.

- First mover advantage leads to cost advantage to producers and enables them to retain competitive advantage even if some other producer could potentially supply the same goods or services more cheaply. Since these potential competitors are not first movers, it is difficult for them to compete because they cannot gain the agglomeration economies which are typical within clusters and industrial districts. Thus, a pattern of specialisation established by, for example, historical accident might persist even when new producers could have lower costs if they could form geographical concentrations and thereby reap external economies of scale. These advantages explain many examples of national export success as the result of self-reinforcing clusters or industrial districts, where first mover advantage of firms in some particular industries has led to continuing international competitiveness (Porter, 1990).
- Quality advantages can arise in markets where non-price competition is a crucial element. In these markets, firms must provide the quality of products and services that the markets demand. Firms are, therefore, obliged to obtain suitable factors of production in order to supply what the markets requires. In this case, proximity plays a crucial role because firms, organisations and people can more easily procure suitable factors of production that convey advantages more readily than firms that are not geographically concentrated.

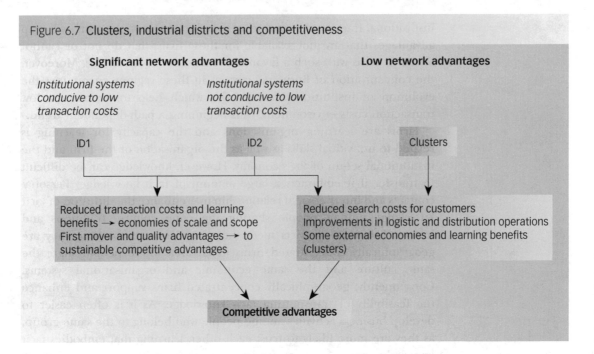

Figure 6.7 Clusters, industrial districts and competitiveness

Figure 6.7 provides an outline of the links between the various types of geographical concentrations and competitive advantages.

In areas where significant network benefits exist that are based largely on geographical proximity, the development of industrial districts will generate competitive advantages by reducing uncertainty and transaction costs leading to external economies of scale, learning benefits, first mover advantages and quality improvements. In areas where institutional systems are not conducive to low uncertainty and transaction cost market-based exchanges these benefits are more likely to arise from ID2. However, in areas where institutional systems are conducive to low uncertainty and transaction costs market-based exchanges, ID1 are likely to be sufficient to generate competitive advantages. Where low network benefits exist, but when proximity advantages are available from low search costs for customers and from improvements in logistics and distribution operations, clusters that involve only limited network connections will deliver competitive advantages.

Policy implications

The increased focus on the geographical concentrations of firms as a means to attain competitiveness has led to interest in the possibilities of government policy to encourage the development of clusters and industrial districts (OECD, 1999). Government policy in this area is normally focused on providing a facilitating role that permits the creation and development of effective networks between firms, R&D agencies, universities and training organisations and government bodies. These types of networks are indeed at the heart of many of the most famous industrial districts (Porter, 1990). Attracting and retaining DFI inflows are also considered crucial for the successful creation and development of industrial districts

(Enright, 2000). However, the path-determined nature of the historical, geographical and institutional determinants of clusters and their development into industrial districts implies that it is easy to make mistakes in government policy towards clusters. In particular, attempts to replicate models of successful clusters in other parts of the world are unlikely to succeed unless the conditions in the host region are similar to the region that is used as the basis for replication. Identifying clusters that are already developing and seeking to help them develop may be a more fruitful policy approach. This requires a carefully constructed and implemented policy involving complex public–private partnerships (Raines, 2002). Successful clusters such as Silicon Valley and Route 128 in Boston have been connected to government policies but these have been to support programmes to overcome difficulties and obstacles to further development (such as congestion costs) rather than as a catalyst for the creation and development of the clusters. Indeed, in these clusters the main help from government has been from government procurement contracts and technical help from universities and R&D agencies (see Case 6.1).

Summary

This chapter has examined the role of geographical factors in the evolution of trade and DFI flows. Traditional theories have tended to relegate geographical factors to the sidelines and to concentrate on economic variables such as prices, trade barriers, market failure and transaction costs to explain trade and DFI flows. Location decisions in traditional theories are largely determined by transport costs, size of markets and trade barriers. In cases where transport costs are low and the sizes of markets are fairly evenly distributed, location is decided by historical accidents that locate economic activities in particular places. In any event these factors are not explicitly considered in traditional theories as they are assumed to be exogenous to the models used.

Increasing attention on the role of economies of scale as a main reason for trade and DFI flows has focused attention on geographical factors. The incentive for firms to concentrate in particular geographical areas is a complex relationship between historical events, physical and human geographical factors and institutional developments. The development of networks both business and social is at the heart of successful clusters. These networks lead to the ability to reap economies of scale and other proximity benefits that grant competitive advantage to firms that locate in geographical concentrations. These theories place geographical factors at the heart of the analysis of trade and DFI flows. Moreover, these theories focus on the evolution of clusters and industrial districts and they provide a means to investigate the dynamics of geographical concentrations in the light of such changes as trade liberalisation. These theories provide a framework to investigate the relationships between the strategic development of subsidiaries and regional development.

Investigation of the advantages of clusters and industrial districts highlights the complex relationships between historical, geographical and institutional developments and the evolution of business and social networks that lead to competitiveness. These factors open up the possibility of government policies to develop clusters and industrial districts that often involve attempts to attract particular types of DFI inflows.

Review questions

1 Outline the limitations that arise from the relative neglect of geographical factors by traditional theories of trade and DFI flows.
2 Explain why a core–periphery type of development is likely to arise from trade liberalisation between high income and lower income countries using both traditional and new theories of location.
3 How is the strategic development of subsidiaries influenced by geographical concentrations?
4 What are the main reasons for dispersal from geographical concentrations of firms and indicate which type of operations are likely to be dispersed.
5 Outline the main competitive advantages that arise from successful clusters and industrial districts.

Bibliography

Amin, A. and Thrift, N. (eds) (1994), *Globalization, Institutions, and Regional Development in Europe*, Oxford, Oxford University Press.

Amiti, M. (1998) 'New trade theories and industrial location in the EU: a survey of the evidence', *Oxford Review of Economic Policy*, 14, 2, pp. 45–53.

Andersen, O. (1993) 'On the internationalization process of firms: a critical analysis', *Journal of International Business Studies*, 24, pp. 209–32.

Andersson, U., Johanson, J. and Vahlne, J. (1997) 'Organic acquisitions in the internationization process of the business firm', *Management International Review*, 37, 2, pp. 67–84.

Bartlett, C. and Ghoshal, S. (1989) *Managing Across Borders: The Transnational Solution*, Boston, MA, Harvard University Press.

Becattini, G. (1990), 'The Marshallian industrial districts as a socio-economic notion' in F. Pyke, G. Becattini and W. Sengenberger (eds) *Industrial Districts and Inter-firm Co-operation in Italy*, Geneva, International Institute for Labour Studies.

Birkinshaw, J. (2000) *Entrepreneurship in the Global Firm*, London, Sage.

Birkinshaw, J. and Hood, N. (eds) (1998a) *Multinational Corporate Evolution and Subsidiary Development*, London, Macmillan.

Birkinshaw, J. and Hood, S. (1998b) 'Multinational subsidiary evolution: capability and charter change in foreign-owned subsidiary companies', *Academy of Management Review*, 23, pp. 773–95.

Blomstrom, M. and Kokko, A. (1998) 'Multinational corporations and spillovers', *Journal of Economic Surveys*, 12, pp. 247–8.

Brülhart, M. (1998) 'Economic geography, industry location and trade: the evidence, *World Economy*, 21, 6, pp. 775–801.

Brülhart, M. and Torstensson, J. (1996) 'Regional integration, scale economies and industry location', Discussion Paper No. 1435, London, Centre for Economic Policy Research.

Dunning, J. (1999) 'Location and the multinational enterprise: a neglected factor', *Journal of International Business Studies*, 29, 1, pp. 45–66.

Dunning, J. (1997a) 'The European internal market programme and inbound foreign direct investment – part I', *Journal of Common Market Studies*, 35, 1, pp. 1–30.

Dunning, J. (1997b) 'The European internal market programme and inbound foreign direct investment – part II', *Journal of Common Market Studies*, 35, 2, pp. 189–223.

Dunning, J. (1996) 'The geographical sources of competitiveness of firms: some results of a new survey', *Transnational Corporations*, 5, 3, pp. 1–30.

Dunning, J. (1992) 'The competitive advantages of nations and the activities of transnational corporations', *Transnational Corporations*, 1, pp. 135–68.

Dunning, J. and McKaig-Berliner, A. (2001) 'The geographical sources of competitiveness of professional business firms', *Transnational Corporations*, 10, 1, pp. 45–60.

Enright, M. (2000) 'The globalization of competition and the localization of competitive advantage: policies towards regional clustering' in N. Hood and S. Young (eds) *Globalization of Multinational Enterprise Activity and Economic Development*, London, Palgrave.

Fujita, M., Krugman, P. and Mori, T. (1999) 'On the evolution of hierarchical urban systems' *European Economic Review*, 43, pp. 209–51.

Fujita, M., Krugman, P. and Venables, A. (2000) *The Spatial Economy: Cities, Regions, and International Trade*, Cambridge, MA, MIT Press.

Granovetter, M. (1985) 'Economic action and social structure: the problem of embeddedness', *American Journal of Sociology*, 19, pp. 481–510.

Harrison, B. (1992) 'Industrial districts: old wine in new bottles', *Regional Studies*, 26, 469–83.

Helpman, E. (1997) 'The size of regions' in D. Pines, E. Sadka and I. Zilcha (eds) *Topics in Public Economics, Theoretical and Applied Analysis*, Cambridge, Cambridge University Press.

Helpman, E. and Krugman, P. (1985) *Market Structure and Foreign Trade: Increasing Returns, Imperfect Competition and International Economics*, Cambridge, MA, MIT Press.

Johanson, J. and Vahlne, J. (1977) 'The internationalisation process of the firm – a model of knowledge development and increasing foreign market developments', *Journal of International Business Studies*, 8, pp. 23–32.

Krugman, P. (1998) 'What's new about the new economic geography?', *Oxford Review of Economic Policy*, 14, pp. 7–17.

Krugman, P. (1996) *The Self-Organizing Economy*, Blackwell, Oxford.

Krugman, P. (1991) *Geography and Trade*, Cambridge, MA, MIT Press.

Krugman, P. and Venables, A. (1994) *The Location of Economic Activity: New Theories and Evidence*, London, Centre of Economic Policy Research.

Marshall, A. (1890) *Principles of Economics*, London, Macmillan.

Mattson, L. (1998) 'Dynamic of overlapping networks and strategic actions by the international firms' in A. Chandler, P. Hagstrom and O. Sölvell (eds) *The Dynamic Firm: The Role of Technology, Strategy, Organisation and Regions*, Oxford, Oxford University Press.

McDonald, F. and Vertova, G. (2002) 'Clusters, industrial districts and competitiveness' in R. McNaughton and M. Green (eds) *Global Competition and Local Networks*, London, Gower.

McNaughton, R. and Green, M. (eds) (2002) *Global Competition and Local Networks*, London, Gower.

Nordstrom, K. (1990) *The Internationalisation Process of the Firm: Searching for New Patterns and Explanations*, Stockholm, Stockholm School of Economics.

North, D. (1990) *Institutions, Institutional Change and Economic Development*, Cambridge, Cambridge University Press.

OECD (1999) *Boosting Innovation: The Cluster Approach*, Paris, OECD.

Ottaviano, G. and Puga, D. (1998) 'Agglomeration in the global economy: a survey of the new economic geography', *World Economy*, 21, 2, pp. 707–31.

Ouchi, W. (1981) *Theory Z*, Reading, MA. Addison-Wesley.

Porter, M. (1994) 'The role of location in competition', *Journal of the Economics of Business*, 1, 1, pp. 35–9.

Porter, M. (1990) *The Competitive Advantage of Nations*, London, Macmillan.

Porter, M. and Solvell, O. (1998) 'The role of geography in the process of innovation and the sustainable competitive advantage of firms' in A. Chandler, P. Hagstrom and O. Solvell (eds) *The Dynamic Firm: The Role of Technology, Strategy and Regions*, Oxford, Oxford University Press.

Powell, W. and Smith-Doerr, L. (1994) 'Networks and economic life' in N. Smelser and R. Swedberg (eds) *The Handbook of Economic Sociology*, Princeton, Princeton University Press.

Pyke, F., Becattini, G. and Sengenberger, W. (eds) (1990) *Industrial Districts and Inter-firm Co-operation in Italy*. Geneva, International Institute for Labour Studies.

Raines, P. (2002) 'Cluster development policy and new forms of public–private partnership' in F. McDonald, H. J. Tüselmann and C. Wheeler (eds) *International Business: Adjusting to New Challenges and Opportunities*, London, Palgrave.

Reid, S. (1983) 'Firm internationalisation transaction costs and strategic choice', *International Marketing Review*, 1, pp. 45–55.

Rugman, A. and Verbeke, A. (2001) 'Location and the multinational enterprise' in A. Rugman and T. Brewer (eds) *Handbook of International Business*, Oxford, Oxford University Press.

Saxenian, A. (1994), *Regional Advantage. Culture and Competition in Silicon Valley and Route 128*, Cambridge, MA, Harvard University Press.

Schmitz, H. (1992), 'On the clustering of small firms', *IDS Bulletin*, 23, 1, pp. 64–9.

Scott, A. (1995) 'The geography foundations of industrial performance', *Competition and Change*, 1, 1, pp. 51–66.

Williamson, O. (1979), 'Transaction-cost economics: the governance of contractual relations', *Journal of Law and Economics*, 22, 233–261.

Young, S. (1987) 'Business strategy and the internationalization business: recent approaches', *Managerial and Decision Economics*, 8, pp. 31–40.

Zander, U. and Kogut, B. (1996) 'Knowledge and the speed of transfer and imitation of organization capabilities', *Organizational Science*, 6, 2, pp. 76–92.

Case 6.1 Silicon Valley, Silicon Fen and Route 128

Silicon Valley in the San Francisco and San José area of California and Route 128 in the Boston area of Massachusetts are two of the most famous clusters in the world. These clusters developed in the early 1950s and came to prominence, first, with the development of semiconductors (the transistor was the first of these semiconductors that revolutionised electronics and thereby the computer industry), then with the subsequent development of the computer industry. The basic raw material for semiconductors is silicon, hence the name Silicon Valley. Both these clusters are focused on high technology semiconductor-based products. Silicon Valley is centred on computer equipment with companies such as Cisco Systems, Sun Microsystems and the founding high tech company of Silicon Valley, Hewlett-Packard, all having a major presence in the Valley. Route 128 is also based on semi-conductor-based products but with a focus on avionics for defence equipment and other types of electronic control equipment. Companies such as Digital Equipment Corporation (DEC), Raytheon and Lotus Development have major R&D and high technology production plants located in the Route 128 area. However, the focus of the work in both of these clusters is in R&D with the development of new products and the application of new computer-based technologies to an expanding array of business, defence and public services operations. These two clusters are at the heart of nearly all the major developments in computer-based technologies in the world. Their prominence and success in capturing and developing global markets has been one of the prime reasons for the increasing interest in clusters as sources of global competitive advantages.

Both Silicon Valley and Route 128 have their origins in the decision by leading universities (Stanford University in Silicon Valley and the Massachusetts Institute of Technology in Route 128) to disseminate scientific and engineering knowledge to the local business community. Indeed, these universities became involved in helping to create new and entrepreneurial business communities that had strong links to the universities. The presence of leading scientists in the new field of computing science also encouraged young, bright students to congregate near these universities. In the case of Silicon Valley, some of these students went on to found some of the most famous companies in the world, for example, David Hewlett and William Packard who established Hewlett-Packard. In both clusters, the universities provided a good supply of entrepreneurial computer scientists and engineers who were trained in leading edge technologies. The growing demand for high tech electronic equipment by the defence industries and the space industry also help in the development of these clusters by providing markets for new computer-based technologies.

Silicon Fen, located in the area near Cambridge in the UK, is an example of an attempt to replicate US high tech clusters such as Silicon Valley and Route 128. Silicon Fen is a cluster of high tech companies including R&D facilities of IBM and Microsoft. Silicon Fen appears to have a less well-defined sphere of operations than Silicon Valley and Route 128 as it includes both hard and software computer companies as well as pharmaceutical companies such as Glaxo SmithKline Beecham. Silicon Fen has its origins in the setting up of Cambridge Science Park in early 1970s as a result of the Mot Report. Another study published in 1985 on links between the University of Cambridge and the business community promoted the idea of developing small high tech companies to take advantage of the cooperation that developed between the university and businesses. By the late 1990s there were over 1000 high-tech companies in Silicon Fen with a turnover of $3 billion. Venture capitalists based in the City of London have made Silicon Fen the second largest venture capitalist-funded cluster after Silicon Valley.

Silicon Valley developed with considerable co-operation between the computer scientists and engineers who frequently moved between companies and established their own companies. Informal discussions and 'brainstorming' events often took place with people from different firms to find solutions to common problems and to assess how to commercialise new discoveries. Small companies were rapidly formed to solve particular problems and they were dissolved once solutions had been found. The rapid growth in demand for specialist R&D services meant that labour released by the dissolution of companies was soon redeployed within the valley. Thus a dynamic and fast pace of technical change was sustained. Moving between companies was frequent, which was made easier because of the large pool of entrepreneurial and talented people in the valley which attracted companies that wished to enter the new computer-based industries. The culture that developed in Silicon Valley permitted a cooperative, but highly competitive industry to be built. This was helped by high and rising demand, initially from the defence and space industries, but increasingly from companies as scientists and engineers developed commercial applications for the new technologies. This demand spread to global markets leading to Silicon Valley becoming the world centre for computer-based technologies.

In Route 128, a rather different culture emerged. The East Coast cultural tradition is different from the more freewheeling culture of California. Labour is less likely to move between firms and the rate of start-ups and dissolutions of firms is lower. Cooperation between companies is less pronounced and scientists and engineers are less likely to discuss common problems and opportunities in informal gatherings. Geography plays a role in the lower incidence of informal meetings between scientists and engineers because Route 128 is more of a linear development than Silicon Valley thus making face-to-face meetings more difficult because of the distance between companies and R&D agencies. The concentrations of high tech companies in the area led to the establishment of a pool of skilled labour that attracted many firms to establish in the Route 128 cluster. Many of the leading companies in Route 128 are old established firms such as DEC and Lotus Development that have operated in the area for many years. This has contributed to a less entrepreneurial and more conservative culture than in Silicon Valley. The sources of demand for the output of these companies was and remains strongly connected to government orders from the defence and space industries. This also contributes to a less entrepreneurial culture than Silicon Valley. Route 128 is also less of a global influence than Silicon Valley, which may be explained by the stronger reliance on government contracts and the less dynamic and entrepreneurial culture in the Boston area as a whole.

In both Silicon Valley and Route 128 universities and local and national government agencies continue to be important players in the success of these regions. Demand for output, especially in Route 128, is strongly influenced by government contracts. Government agencies also help to overcome problems with overcrowded infrastructures and labour shortages especially for public services such as education of children. Planning laws are also very relaxed and permit rapid construction of new buildings with the required transport links and other services. The universities continue to be crucial providers of talented labour and new cutting edge technical developments.

Conditions in Silicon Fen are less favourable in terms of entrepreneurial dynamism with a more staid 'British' attitude to job shifting and company start-ups and dissolutions. Many of the companies at the heart of the area are subsidiaries of large US multinationals such as IBM and Microsoft, which tends to limit entrepreneurial activity as permission needs to be sought from headquarters. Government agencies are also less helpful with a number of problems in obtaining planning permission for new buildings and more constraints in pulling down old properties to make way for new developments. Government procurement contracts for R&D for the defence industry and from equipment play an important role in stimulating demand for the output of companies located in the area. Cambridge university also plays an important role by providing access to world-class scientists and engineers. The university has entered into a partnership with MIT to develop technologies that emerge in Boston. This has proved to be necessary because the top US universities tend to attract the leading scientists and become the centres for new technologies. Therefore, participation in the leading edge technologies requires partnerships with these US universities.

This highlights perhaps the key difference between Silicon Fen and Route 128, in that Silicon Fen is more dependent on external help in technology and has a larger foreign-owned presence among leading companies in the area. Silicon Fen is an important area of competitive advantage in Britain and is also one of the most dynamic and entrepreneurial clusters in the UK. It attracts many companies and is one of the fastest growing areas in the UK. However, it has many of the attributes of a subsidiary of a larger and more powerful parent. It has less of a global reach than Silicon Valley and is in many ways dependent on support from US companies and universities.

Saxenian, A. (1994) *Regional Advantage: Culture and Competition in Silicon Valley and Route 128*, Cambridge, MA, University Press, Harvard; *Economist* (2001) 'Silicon Fen strains to grow', 14 April; 'The Silicon Fen story, www.siliconfen.com

Case 6.2 Sassuolo and the ceramic tile industry

Most of the interest in geographical concentrations of firms is centred on high tech clusters such as Silicon Valley (see Case 6.1). However, geographical concentrations of small firms producing low tech products can also achieve competitive advantages in global markets. Italian industrial districts are excellent examples of such competitive geographical concentrations of small firms. The centre of many of these industrial districts is the Emilia–Romagna region in northern Italy. Sassuolo is a town of 165,000 inhabitants in the Modena province in this region. A flourishing industrial district based on the production of ceramic tiles has developed in Sassuolo. There are approximately 400 firms in the Sassuolo area engaged in the production of ceramic tiles, employing about 20,000 people. Most of the firms are small, employing fewer than 50 workers. The majority of these firms are privately owned and have developed from people starting their own business. The level of education of owners and workers is low with very few having a university education. However, this industrial district is responsible for 7% of Italian exports in the ceramic tile industry.

Industrial districts in Modena province are strongly linked to universities in the Emilia–Romagna region such as the Università di Bologna and the *università popolari* (teaching centres for working class people). These links provide technical help and the provision of skilled artisans. These links do not provide leading edge technologies but rather the provision of effective solutions for practical problems. The *università popolari* play an important role in the dissemination of technical knowledge by training artisans in the latest technologies including the business use of computers as well as matters connected to the manufacture and distribution of products such as ceramic tiles. Local government also provide help and advice to firms and have well-established informal networks with small firms, trade unions and educational establishments to help promote the interests of small business. These networks originated from the socialist tradition of local politics in Modena province that has existed since the early part of the 20th century.

Ceramic tile production has been taking place in Sassuolo since the Middle Ages when production was centred on master craftsmen who obtained charters from the powerful city-states of medieval Italy to pursue their craft. These master craftsmen obtained rights to do business and this was developed into a 'guild'-type system that restricted membership to family and those with close personal connections to master craftsmen. The importance of such social networks has been carried forward into the modern industrial district where membership of social networks is important for the working of the district. Cooperation between firms is very strong with sharing of labour and capital equipment to ease bottlenecks. Production lines are often integrated across a number of small firms and self-employed labour move between firms and processes in line with current demand patterns. Firms also cooperate to complete export contracts. Such cooperation requires strong levels of trust that is provided by strong social networks based on extended family connections and other social groupings such as church attendance. The geographical concentration of firms and labour in the town of Sassuolo means that face-to-face contact is inevitable, therefore breaking trust leads to considerable loss of face and potential exclusion from the cooperative processes. The guild system that developed in the Middle Ages in Modena province continues to have an influence in the modern industrial district in Sassuolo.

In the post-World War II period a construction boom in Italy led to a large increase in demand for building materials. Sassuolo was in a good position to benefit from the expansion of demand for ceramic tiles because it had a tradition of ceramic tile manufacture, a pool of skilled artisans and a concentration of firms producing the inputs for the tiles including moulds, glazes, packaging materials and transport systems. Assopiastrelle, the ceramic tile industry association, whose members are concentrated in Sassuolo, provided help with bulk purchases of materials, foreign market research and technical help with tax and legal issues. Help with tax and legal matters are important given the complex bureaucracy of the Italian state. In 1979, the Università di Bologna, together with the Assopiastrelle established the Centro Ceramico di Bologna to help develop solutions to technical problems in the manufacture of ceramic products. Much of the research of the centre is connected to improving the quality of products and in reducing costs of production.

The industrial district in Sassuolo highlights many of the characteristics of successful geographical concentrations, including the importance of geographical, historical and institutional factors. Moreover, the role of social networks can be seen to be very important in the context of the history and institutional setting of Italy and the Modena province. The role of universities in helping the industrial district in Sassuolo indicates that assistance with technical issues from universities is not restricted to high tech clusters such as Silicon Valley. The Sassuolo case also illustrates the path-determined nature of industrial districts. Therefore, replication of the Sassuolo pattern for an industrial district in another cultural and institutional system is unlikely to work. The differences in the high tech clusters outlined in Case 6.1 also highlight that successful industrial districts have to be developed in line with their history, institutional frameworks and cultural characteristics.

Vertova, G. (2002) 'Sassuolo and the ceramic tile industry' in P. Harris and F. McDonald, *European Business and Marketing*, London, Sage.

7

Cultural and institutional factors

Learning objectives

By the end of this chapter, you should be able to:

- outline the main determinants of cultural values
- understand how cultural values influence the development of moral codes, attitudes and norms of behaviour
- have knowledge on how historical experiences affect the development of cultural values
- discuss and assess the main approaches to the definitions of cultural dimensions
- understand how different cultural values affect the management of international business activities
- outline the main features of new institutional economics
- discuss and assess how institutional frameworks are influenced by cultural values
- understand why different institutional frameworks can limit the development of cross-cultural business activities

Key terms

• definitions of culture • cultural values • culture and international business • cultural dimensions • managing cultural differences • new institutional economics • formal and informal institutional constraints • adaptive efficiency • transaction costs and institutional constraints

Introduction

For many international business academics, the study of cultural differences and the implications of these differences for international strategies and business operations are at the heart of the subject matter of international business. Many international management textbooks are largely devoted to the affects of cultural differences on the management process (Hodgetts and Luthans, 1994; Lane et al., 1997). The development of conceptual frameworks that identify key cultural dimensions provides the basis for most of the analysis of cultural differences (Hampton-Turner and Trompenaars, 1994; Hofstede, 1980,

1991; Trompenaars, 1993). These frameworks provide the basis for examining the effects of cultural differences across the whole range of international business operations (Hofstede, 1994). Agendas based on these types of cultural analysis form one of the largest areas of contemporary research in international business. Most of this research focuses on measuring cultural differences using variations of Hofstede and Trompenaars' types of frameworks and on methods of assessing how firms manage the complex issues that arise from these cultural differences. Applications of this type of work include such issues as strategy formation (Harris and Ghauri, 2000), financial management issues (Carr and Tomkins, 1998), organisational behaviour (Tayeb, 1988) and international human resource management (see Chapter 13).

Clearly, cultural differences play an important role in the development of international business activities and in the problems of managing these activities. However, the ways in which the cultural characteristics of countries or regions affect the process of human interaction (including ways of doing business) are influenced by more than the sociological and psychological factors that determine many of the well-known cultural frameworks used in the majority of culturally based international business research. A complex mix of cultural attitudes working within political, legal and economic institutions governs human interaction. These institutional frameworks are both influenced by and influence culturally determined norms of behaviour and thereby affect the way in which businesses operate. Thus, the impact of cultural differences on business operations is affected by the institutional setting in which these cultural groups operate. The new institutional economics provides a means of analysing the complex interactions between cultural attitudes, institutional frameworks and the costs of conducting business operations (Matthews, 1986; North, 1990). This work has not been subject to the scale of research that has been applied to the cultural models of Hofstede and Trompenaars, but the World Bank has carried out studies on the importance of 'good' institutional frameworks for the process of development including the attraction and retention of direct foreign investment flows (World Bank, 1997a and b).

The chapter defines culture and assesses the main factors that determine values and attitudes that lead to cultural differences. The conceptual framework of Hofstede on cultural dimensions is considered and the main implications of this type of work is examined. A critique of this type of approach to the importance of cultural differences leads to an outline of the new institutional economics and an examination of how this approach leads to a richer understanding of the reasons for significant differences in ways of conducting business across cultures. This analysis also indicates that cultural differences that lead to institutional systems with high transaction costs for foreign firms are likely to lead to powerful economic and strategic reasons to restrict international business activities between radically different cultural groups.

Defining culture and its main determinants

The word culture stems from the Latin *cultura* which is linked to the concept of *cultus* or cultic worship. This Latin meaning of culture implies the existence of a set of belief systems and ways of worship that identify the members of the cult. Most definitions of culture are centred on the identification of values systems and ways of behaviour that define a group with similar characteristics. This leads to problems when attempts are made to dissaggregate national or regional or even local cultural groups because it is possible to redefine cultural similarities such that people become members of a host of cultural groupings that are often overlapping. It is also possible to dissaggregate the members of countries and regions into very small coherent cultural groups. However, economic interaction requires people to cross over from their small cultural group to deal with other cultural groups. The process of internationalisation extends this interaction to cover a wide variety of cultural groups. However, cross-cultural interaction is not restricted to international business activities but occurs within countries, regions and even local districts when people with different cultural characteristics conduct business with each other. This problem is considered in the critique of the Hofstede approach to the study of cross cultural interaction.

The main components of a cultural group are similar values and the attitudes that emerge from these values. Values influence the development of moral codes on how to behave and these in turn affect attitudes, which form the basis for norms of behaviour. These norms influence the ways in which people interact with each other, including interaction involving business activities.

Values and attitudes

Values are sets of beliefs about what actions and ways of life are considered good or bad and acceptable or unacceptable. These values form the basis for standards that establish moral codes on how people ought to behave. Standards are influenced by such factors as religious belief systems, education and family circumstances. Values can also emerge from philosophical systems such as libertarian utilitarianism (individual actions that do not harm other people should be permitted even if some people object to the actions) or communalism (individual actions must conform to rules and principles as decided by the community to which a person belongs). Libertarian utilitarianism and communalism are important sources of values in many societies. For example, libertarian utilitarianism influences the acceptance of homosexual behaviour in many western countries and communalism thinking underpins the respect afforded to older male family members in many developing countries.

Probably the strongest influence on values comes from religious systems. Indeed, many philosophical systems have their origins in religious systems. For example, libertarian utilitarianism exercises its strongest influence in countries with Protestant traditions that emphasis individualism and the rights of man. Although libertarian utilitarianism is in direct opposition to many of the central beliefs of Christianity, the links between this and other western philosophical views and the historical development of Christianity in Europe and the USA are very strong. It is no coincidence that libertarian utilitarianism has its most powerful influence in countries with a Protestant tradition but where the authority of the teaching of the church is in decline. Similarly, male-dominated communalism is most pronounced in countries that have had religious systems that have strong paternalistic or stratification overtones such as Roman Catholicism or Hinduism.

Many of the country classifications of cultural groups are closely connected to the religious history of countries. European and North American cultural groups display many similarities compared to Asian, Middle Eastern or Russian groups (Hofstede, 1983; Ronen and Shenkar, 1985). Within Europe, countries that have large Protestant populations (for example, Britain, the Netherlands and Scandinavian countries) tend to have more cultural similarities with each other compared to those with large Roman Catholic populations (for example, France, Italy and Spain). Perhaps the greatest divide within European cultural groups is between those with Protestant and Roman Catholic populations (most of Europe) and those with Orthodox (much of the Bulkans and Russia). India and China have many similarities in terms of level of economic development, demography and development objectives. However, they are culturally very different, reflecting, in part, the influence of Hinduism in India and Buddhism and Confucianism in China. The long-lasting influence of religious beliefs systems on values, including the development of secular philosophies, illustrate that the determinants of culture are deeply rooted in historical developments and change only slowly.

Cultural characteristics are in a state of flux resulting from the evolution of values as new forces of change emerge from the rise and decline of religious belief systems, economic, political and technical changes and the process of internationalisation. These changes lead to the gradual evolution of new values that eventually alter norms of behaviour thereby changing the process of human interaction, including business interactions. However, values and attitudes are strongly linked to historical developments and they evolve along path-determined routes. This means that convergence of cultural characteristics need not follow from the same or similar developments such as internationalisation and the adoption of capitalism by most countries in the world. Values stemming from religious belief systems and their philosophical offshoots place cultural groups in very different starting points that result from different historical experiences that continue to affect the values and attitudes of modern cultural groups.

Many of the most significant changes in values have arisen from very radical and comprehensive changes such as the split into a western and eastern church in the end days of the Roman Empire, the Reformation leading to division of the western church and the spread of Islam in the Middle East and North Africa. The effects of such dramatic events in the mists of history can still be seen in the contemporary problems of many countries. For example, in the Balkans, past clashes between the Orthodox and the Roman Catholic church and the deeper divide with Islam continue to exercise a powerful influence on values and attitudes that still affect the process of human interaction in many Balkan countries. Northern Ireland is another example where past events, the history of the fierce disputes between Protestants and Roman Catholics in the period of the Reformation, continue to exert a very powerful influence on contemporary cultural values.

It is doubtful if the growth of the internationalisation of business activities in the 20th century has exercised anything like the same influence on the evolution of values and attitudes as these great events. Indeed, the period of internationalisation connected to the development of the Atlantic slave trade and development of the colonies of the European powers had a much larger affect on the evolution of values and attitudes than 20th-century developments. This early period of internationalisation stimulated large increases in world trade and transported elements of African culture to the New World and European culture to most of Africa and Asia.

Clearly, the evolution of values and attitudes is complex and has its roots in distant historical events. Care must be taken not to place too much emphasis on contemporary events which are often trivial in comparison to the great religious, political and economic movements of the past that continue largely to determine the values and attitudes of many cultural groups. Cultural characteristics evolve as economic, political, technical and social changes exert pressure for values to alter to new conditions. Nevertheless, the process of cultural evolution is affected by great economic and political events of the past.

Managing across cultural differences

The internationalisation of business has exposed firms to a large range of norms for 'doing' business. The more firms move away from business transactions with similar cultural groups the more difficult it is to use home-based norms for conducting business activities. This is one of the explanations for the large amount of trade and DFI flows between countries with similar cultural characteristics. However, there are also powerful economic and strategic reasons that are important determinants of such flows (see Chapters 3, 6 and 8). These forces can lead to substantial trade and DFI flows between countries with very different cultural characteristics, for example, trade and DFI flows between Japan and the USA and Europe. Cross-cultural problems emerge not only due to differences in national cultures between home and host country but also from clashes of corporate cultures (see Case 7.1).

In some cases, cultural diversity is beneficial for firms if some types of operations can be more effectively done in subsidiaries due to cultural differences in the host country. For example, a subsidiary located in a culture that values creativity and the challenging of accepted ways of doing things may provide a good location for product development; whereas a culture that considers adherence to rules and strict implementation of instructions will be an ideal site for the assembling of products. However, the headquaters of such differentiated networks have to overcome the problems that arise in meshing together the network of subsidiaries into a well-functioning whole. This will often lead to locating the various activities of the firm in similar but slightly different cultural setting because of the problems of coordinating disparate cultures. Therefore, although cultural differences can lead to opportunities for more effective international operations these differences nearly always require the development of policies to reduce the problems of coordinating dissimilar cultures. The issues connected to developing an effective differentiated network of subsidiaries is examined in Chapters 6 and 10.

Managing the problems created by cross-cultural differences increases the transaction costs of conducting international business activities (see later section 'New institutional economics'). Consequently, if cultural differences between potential trading partners are large, the economic and/or strategic benefits of engaging in business activities most be large enough to offset the extra costs of 'doing' business with different cultures. Various management systems have been advocated to reduce these costs by using policies such as education, training and a careful use of national and expatriate managers (see Chapter 13). The effectiveness of these systems depends to a large extent on whether managers and workers suffer from ethnocentrism (the belief that your culture is superior to others because it is regarded as morally superior) or parochialism (the believe that your culture is superior to others because knowledge about other cultures is limited). The use of education, training and a well-thought out mix of national and expatriate managers is more likely to work if the problem is mainly one of parochialism. Even if the problem is mainly one of parochialism, the costs of dealing with this could be greater than the economic and strategic benefits of engaging in large-scale interaction between countries with substantially different cultures. In these circumstances, business interaction between such countries will be restricted.

The many forces at work in the formation and evolution of cultural characteristics and the impact of these on international business management are illustrated in Figure 7.1.

Cultural dimensions

Anthropologists have sought to identify the main dimensions of cultural groups by reference to basic value systems on issues such as views on the characterisitcs of human nature and attitudes towards the nature world, for example, dominate or cooperate with nature to deliver desired results (Kluckhohn and Strodtbeck, 1961). This type of an approach permits a board classification of cultural types and can be used to assess good locations for international business activities by reference to the type of cultural systems that can deliver desirable outcomes (see Exhibit 7.1). These types of anthropological approaches have been very influencial in those areas of study where the focus is on managing people and devising

Figure 7.1 Determinants of culture and managing international business activities

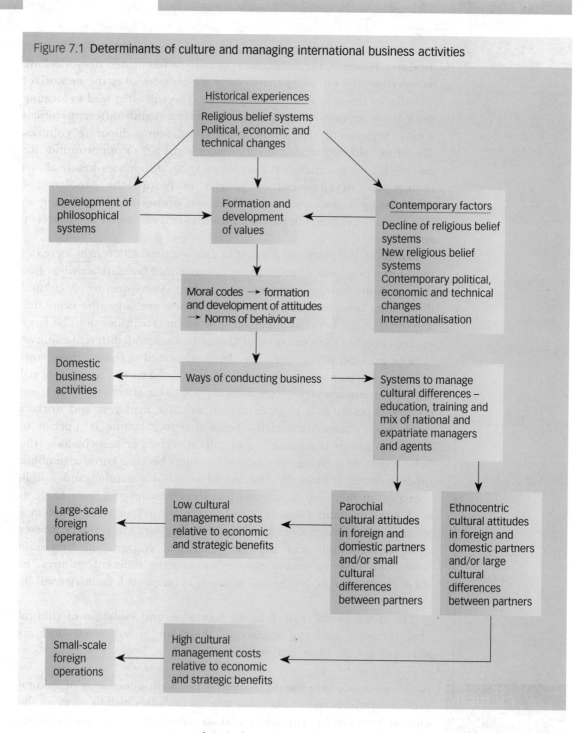

systems that induce managers and workers to deliver the strategic and operational objectives of firms. Indeed, large areas of the study of management are devoted to these type of issues.

Anthropological approaches to the study of the impact of culture on business activities provide important insights into the types of values that different cultures possess. However, many of the dimensions of values are rather vague. For example, many societies place high value on consensus

Exhibit 7.1 Anthropological models of cultural dimensions and international business management

Key cultural dimensions	Implications for management
Relationship to nature	
1 Societies that view nature as a resource to be dominated to fulfil human needs	1 Use of technology to fulfil human needs will be valued, as will specific goals and means to achieve targets
2 Societies that think human needs must be compatible with a moral imperative to conserve nature as it is, rather than use nature, as a resource for human wants	2 Technology may be accepted but reluctance to pursue goals and means that are considered to harm the order of the natural world
3 Societies that see human needs as being largely determined by natural conditions over which human beings have little power	3 Technology will be viewed with suspicion and is regarded to be largely self-defeating against the order of the natural world.
Time orientation	
1 Societies that are past orientated – the past is the best guide to how to satisfy present and future needs	1 Economic and business activities dominated by past ways of doing things reluctance to adopt new technologies and products
2 Societies that are present orientated – actions are largely governed by present needs and wants	2 Economic and business activities geared to current needs with little focus on likely future conditions
3 Societies that are future orientated – concern about present actions on future outcomes	3 Economic and business activities focused on expected future developments new technologies and products at the forefront of current decisions
Human nature	
1 Human nature is basically evil and needs to be controlled	1 Strong emphasis on rules to stop or limited bad behaviour with a strong focus on limiting human endeavours that departs from accepted ways
2 Human nature is basically good and if people are treated well an ordered and effective society based on trust and goodwill will emerge	2 Focus on education and training to induce appropriate responses to working together and efforts to build trust and goodwill
3 Human nature is a mix of good and evil hence, norms of behaviour should reward good actions and penalise bad actions	3 Incentive systems in workplace that reward good acts and penalise bad acts selection of people that respond well to good actions
Activity orientation	
1 Emotion-based societies organise actions on feelings and intuition	1 Management systems need to be adaptable to emotional needs of workers to engender good results and that allow people to satisfy their emotional needs in the workplace
2 Task-orientated societies take actions on perceived need to get things done based on rational calculation	2 Rational and scientific management systems to clearly define tasks and desired outcomes
3 Mixed societies that seek a balance between feelings and rational calculation to order activities	3 Mixture of rational and emotion satisfying policies leading to a strong emphasis on pragmatic management systems
Social interaction	
1 Individualistic societies place most emphasis on satisfying personal needs and wants	1 Strong emphasis on individual rewards, penalties, and career development
2 Hierarchy societies seek to preserve power structures based on families or social classes and castes	2 Management systems that are hierarchical with clear chain of command
3 Cooperative societies emphasise group needs and wants and focus on social interaction and consensus to meet needs and wants	3 Group and teamwork encouraged with emphasis on reaching consensus

Lane, H., DiStefano, J. and Maznevski, M. (1997) *International Management*, Oxford, Blackwell Business and Kluckhohn, A. and Strodtbeck, F. (1961) *Variations in Value Orientations*, Westport, CT, Greenwood Press.

and on group work and achievement, but most societies also have a role for consensual and cooperative values. Equally most societies place some emphasis on the needs and wants of the individual. Clearly, to make these anthropological values useful it is necessary to identify and measure values and to assess how these values impact on the process of the management of business activities. The approach of Hofstede to this problem dominates research in this area. Trompenaars has also developed a set of cultural dimensions that are similar to those of Hofstede (Hampden-Turner and Trompenaars, 1994; Trompenaars, 1993).

Hofstede's cultural dimensions

Hofstede conducted two surveys of the cultural attitudes of the employees of IBM in 40 countries, involving over 116,000 completed questionnaires. Based on these responses Hofstede used anthropological classification systems to define four major cultural dimensions (Hofstede, 1980).

1 individualism
2 uncertainty avoidance
3 power distance
4 masculinity.

Individualism is the degree to which individual decision making and action is encouraged and supported. Hofstede found that some countries placed high emphasis on individualism while in others it was viewed with suspicion and disapproval. Uncertainty avoidance is a measure of the willingness of society to take risks. The survey discovered that countries varied from high uncertainty avoidance where risk taking was discouraged to countries where taking risks was regarded as an important and valued action. Power distance is connected to the willingness of a society to accept hierarchical power systems. Countries with high power distance believe that established power hierarchies are necessary for the smooth operation of society. Other societies, however, distrust power hierarchies and view power as something that needs to be curbed and controlled by the members of society. The masculinity measure is related to the importance attached to male values such as competitiveness, performance and assertiveness as compared to feminine values such as nurturing, concern for others and the quality of life. Values for this measure also varied across countries from high regard for masculine values to a more pronounced value placed on more feminine values. Hofstede added a fifth dimension – time orientation – after comparing western attitudes to time compared to Asian, especially Chinese (Hofstede and Bond, 1998).

The approach used by Hofstede has proved very useful for research into the role of cultural differences for international business management because it provides a measurable way of identifying and clustering cultural groups by surveying the attitudes of people and using the results to construct indices of values. This process can also be used to cluster according to all four dimensions by use of diagrams (see Figure 7.2). These clusters can then be used to match desirable cultural characteristics to international business operations.

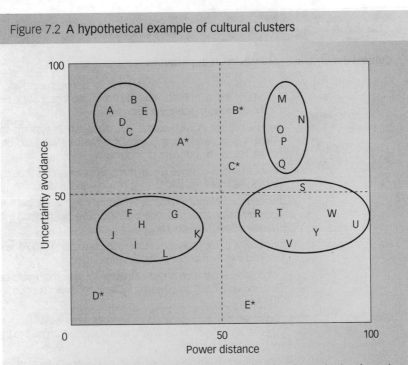

Figure 7.2 A hypothetical example of cultural clusters

Source: Based on Hofstede, G. (1983) 'The cultural relativity of organizational practices and theories', *Journal of International Business Studies*, 14, 2, pp. 234–58 and Ronen, S. and Shenkar, O. (1985) 'Clustering countries on attitudinal dimensions: a review and synthesis', *Academy of Management Review*, 10, 3, pp. 435–54.

The figure reveals that in the relationship between uncertainty avoidance and power distance, four clusters exist. For example, the cluster in the north-west quadrant is composed of five countries with high uncertainty avoidance and low power distance. Five countries are not clustered – A*, B*, C*, D* and E*. This type of analysis can be carried for all the possible combinations of the cultural dimensions to cluster countries according to the data revealed from studies of cultural dimensions. This analysis can then be used to identify appropriate management systems for clusters and for outlier countries (see Exhibit 7.2).

Some of the main implications for international business management of cultural dimension models are illustrated in Exhibit 7.2.

Critique of the Hofstede approach to cultural values

The cultural dimensions approach to the study of problems of cross-cultural business activities has been subject to criticism (Punnett and Withane, 1990; Tayeb, 1988; Yeh and Lawrence, 1995). Some of the criticisms are fairly trivial, such as many of the cultural dimensions appear little different from national sterotypes. For example, most studies find that the USA has high values for individualism and low for uncertainty avoidance and power distance, while Japan scores high for uncertainty avoidance and low for power distance and for individualism. These kinds of result conform to national sterotypes about the USA and Japan. This may mean little more than that in some areas national stereotypes reflect

Exhibit 7.2 Management implications of cultural dimensions

Cultural dimension	Management implications
Individualism	Countries with high individualism require management systems that reward individual effort and that permit individuals to have a significant say in defining the goals of the firm and the means to achieve these goals
	In cases where individualism is low, management systems should provide strong leadership to develop group goals and means and should develop policies to relieve stress caused by pressure on individuals
Uncertainty avoidance	If uncertainty avoidance is high management systems should reduce anxiety about risks by detailed planning and sharing of goals and means
	Whereas in countries with low uncertainty avoidance, planning and sharing of information on goals and means can be more informal and there is less need to cater for anxiety among workers about taking risks
Power distance	In cases with high power distance, decision making should be top down with strong well-defined hierarchical command systems
	When power distance is low, management systems should be decentralised with encompassing and empowering systems to attract support for the goals and means of the firm
Masculinity	Countries with strong masculine features require management systems that are goal specific and performance related with little attention paid to the wider social implications of business activities
	Where a more female culture exists management systems need to take account of the wider implications of business activities including the environment, the impact on families and the general well-being of the workforce

underlying realities. Another fairly trivial criticism is that Hofstede's original study was limited to one large American multinational company that tended to employ a certain class of people in most of its subsidiaries (well educated, middle class) and at one point in time. This, it is argued, undermines the value of the study. However, since Hofstede's original study there have been many studies covering a multitude of companies and countries over a large number of time periods. There are, however, three non-trivial problems connected to the Hofstede approach:

1 Cultural clusters are not homogenous over all parts of a country as there can be signficantly different subcultural groups within a country.
2 Some subcultural groups cross national boundaries.
3 The definitions of cultural dimensions used in Hofstede-type approaches reflect a particular sociological and anthropological view of the world.

The existence of subcultures within national cultures has been recognised and subjected to study (Lenartowicz and Roth, 2001). This study found that distinct subcultures exist within the Brazilian national culture and that these subcultures record different levels of performance in business operations. Indeed, Hofstede has recognised the potential signficance of subcultural groups within national cultures, but maintains that they are mainly a stratification of the national cultures into layers of different values within the same grouping (Hofstede et al., 1990). Hence, national cultural characteristics are still held to be valid, but they need to be broken down into subcultures to obtain clearer guidance to help to develop appropriate management systems.

In many countries subcultures have more in common with subcultures in other countries than those within their own country. For example, the subculture of south France is in many respects more closely connected to the subcultures of northern Spain than to northern France and the Flemish-speaking part of Belgium is culturally closer to the Netherlands than to French-speaking Belgium (Vandermerwe and L'Huillier, 1989). A country such as Indonesia is composed of a large number of subcultures, some of which have very different characteristics. Consequently, to speak of an Indonesia culture is nearly without meaning. To rescue the Hofstede approach from this problem it is necessary to identify these subcultures as layers within the national culture or to regard these cases as special and to separate out some national cultures into distinct subcultures, for example, northern and southern Italy. This approach has the danger of arbitary classifications to permit the retention of the concept of a cultural cluster.

This problem is further complicated by the way in which cultural dimensions are classified. Anthropologists and sociologists are influenced by their socialisation and cultural training as much as anyone else, therefore their views on cultural classificiations are, at least to some extent, affected by their own cultural perceptions. Concepts such as masculinity and power distance perhaps reflect a modern western view of the world. The values ascribed to cultural classifications may be differently described by people with a different set of values. This introduces yet another degree of arbitariness into Hofstede-type approaches. The reliance on the Hofstede or Trompenaars approaches in much of the research in the area has led to a remarkable degree of consistency in the definitions of cultural dimensions. However, this does not mean that the Hofstede and Trompenaars approaches are consistent with the *underlying cultural dimensions.* Neither does empirical support for these approaches undermine these criticisms because alternative models based on different definitions of cultural dimensions may also be supported by empirical evidence.

It is possible to conceive of a variety of cultural clusters if they are dissaggregated within national boundaries into subcultures, allowed to cross national boundaries and where different classifications of cultural values are used. The international marketing literature suggests that subcultural groups within and across countries have a significant affect on buying behaviour. Moreover, many of these studies use different and simpler concepts of cultural values than those used in Hofstede-type approaches (Domzal and Unger, 1987; Whitelock, 1987). It appears that attempts to take into account some of the problems with the Hofstede approach by considering layering of subcultures within national cultural blocks, creating special cases for some countries to permit distinct subcultural blocs and using different definitions of cultural values could lead to a host of diverse and perhaps conflicting cultural clusters. This may be a better expression of the complexity of real world cultural clusters but it reduces the usefulness of this concept as a management tool because the number and variety of possible cultural clusters grows. This makes it difficult to determine appropriate management policies unless the clusters are robust and do not alter significantly as more realistic forms of analysis are used. If more realistic forms of analysis are not used, identified cultural clusters may be poor representations of underlying conditions and therefore prove to be of limited value for devising policies to manage cross-cultural problems.

Adjusting national cultural values

The value of Hofstede types of approach to cultural dimensions for management depend on the assumption that cultural differences either confer advantages for foreign firms or the costs of managing these differences are less than the economic and strategic benefits of engaging in business activities with countries with different cultural values. However, there are two major forces at work that undermine these conditions, especially for developing and emerging countries.

- External factors are forcing some countries to adopt management systems that run counter to many of their cultural values.
- Some firms have to adopt particular types of management systems to be able to compete in international markets, which leads to firm-specific cultures that, at least to some extent, transcend national cultures.

The Asian crisis has led to pressure from the International Monetary Fund (IMF) and the World Bank for change to the systems of corporate government in Asian countries (Brealey, 1999). These changes are altering financial and corporate governance systems that have developed from norms of behaviour that are deeply embedded in national cultures (see Case 7.2). Many developing and transition countries are also being pressured by the IMF and the World Bank to adopt market-based reforms such as privatisation, reduction in subsidies and the adoption of transparent and arms' length financial systems. In many cases these reforms run counter to the cultural values in the countries that are reforming (or are being pressured to reform) their economic systems (World Bank, 1997a and b). Many central and east European countries are also changing their economic and business sytstems in preparation for membership of the European Union (EU). For those countries that have little tradition of market-based systems for conducting business and where cultural values are very different from those in the core countries of the EU (for example, Bulgaria and Romania) the challenge to traditional cultural values of adjustment are large (EBRD, 1999)

In many markets firms have to adopt particular types of management systems to meet the competitive challenges that they face. Requirements to meet quality standards and to adopt production systems such as just-in-time and total quality management mean that management systems have to conform to certain conditions regardless of cultural settings. There is room for adjustment at the margin to cater for cultural differences but on the whole workers have to adapt to company cultural norms rather than the company adjusting to national cultural values. This process was evident in the adoption in the USA and Europe of Japanese management systems in car production (Womack et al., 1990). There were adjustments to the different cultural conditions into which Japanese systems were introduced but, on the whole, the workers adjusted to the new systems rather than the systems being adjusted to the norms of behaviour in host countries.

These problems suggest that, in many cases, national or subnational cultural systems must adjust to the requirements of modern capitalism and if these systems cannot adequately adjust that will lead to limitations to the growth of international business activities with such cultural systems. The new institutional economic methods of analysis provide a powerful tool to investigate the nature of this problem.

New institutional economics

New institutional economics is based on a synthesis of institutional theory and transaction cost economics. The essence of new institutional economics is the examination of institutional frameworks as the setting in which human interactions take place. The operation of cultural values within the setting of institutional frameworks is central to new institutional economics. By linking institutional theory to transaction cost economics, new institutional economics provides an explanation as to how different institutional frameworks (that are underpinned by different cultural values) affect the costs of doing business.

Institutional constraints

Institutional frameworks are defined as the rules that govern human interactions between individuals in, and between, the various organisations to which people belong (Matthews, 1986; North, 1983). The ability to adjust institutional constraints in response to economic, political, social and technological change is called the adaptive efficiency of institutional systems (North, 1999). Institutional frameworks are considered to be affected by two main constraints (North, 1990):

- Formal institutional constraints, which define and limit the rules of human interaction. These include constitutions, laws, property rights and agencies such as courts, governmental agencies and regulatory bodies that monitor and enforce formal constraints.
- Informal institutional constraints, which define and limit how formal institutional constraints actually operate. These constraints are such things as moral codes, norms of behaviour and conventions.

Formal institutional constraints are determined by historical experiences that forge values and ideologies on how human beings should interact. These formal institutional constraints can change as values and power structures alter. They are, however, path determined by historical experience and rarely radically change other than by revolutionary economic or political or technical change. Nevertheless, changing constitutions, laws and the agencies that monitor and enforce the rules of human interaction can be easily achieved if those who wield power in societies wish to alter them. Countries with good adaptive efficiency are able to change institutional frameworks more readily than those that are unable to muster sufficient support for change. In the past 20 years or so most countries have adopted pro-market institutional frameworks with a strong focus on privatisation and market-orientated institutional systems. However, there are differences between these new pro-market institutional frameworks among the countries that have adopted them, reflecting the path-determined nature of formal institutional developments and the adaptive efficiency of the countries.

Historical experiences influence the development of informal institutional constraints because of the effect on cultural values of past events. Cultural values lead to the development of moral codes, attitudes and the emergence of norms of behaviour and conventions. The complex interaction between historical experience and the evolution of norms of behavior and conventions mean that informal constraints change very slowly. Indeed, many of the main determinants of cultural values such as religious and philosophical belief systems rise and fall over long periods in response to changing historical experiences. Many of the determinants of cultural value such as religious belief systems retain their major characteristics over hundreds of years and even when they decline, exercise long-lasting influence on moral codes and views on how people should interact with each other and with the natural world. Consequently, changing informal institutional constraints happens very slowly as compared to the quick changes to formal institutional constraints that arise from new laws or reform of governmental agencies. The speed of change to informal institutional constraints is connected to the adaptive efficiency of societies, which is influenced by cultural values. Thus, societies that place a strong emphasis on stability in social interaction and the dominance of traditional values are likely to have low adaptive efficiency compared to those societies whose values are more linked to individualism and that relish the challenges of dealing with new issues.

The importance of informal constraints is at the heart of the analytical process in new institutional economics. The disparity in outcomes between societies with the same or similar formal institutional constraints is attributed to differences in informal constraints because the effectiveness of formal institutional frameworks depends on how people work these systems and this is largely determined by informal constraints such as norms of behaviour and conventions.

Transaction costs and institutional frameworks

Transaction costs economics focuses on the costs associated with exchanges between individuals and organisations. Transaction cost economics indicates that institutional frameworks can increase opportunities for mutually beneficial exchange by facilitating low-cost exchange by reducing the uncertainty and transaction costs associated with exchange (Williamson, 1985). Some countries have institutional systems that facilitate large volumes of potential exchanges between economic actors because they provide low uncertainty and transaction costs. This permits extensive opportunities to trade leading to economies of scale and scope, the development of new market opportunities and effective response to changing economic conditions. However, some countries have institutional structures that are less able to facilitate such effective exchange. The new institutional economics considers that the characteristics of institutional systems, path determined by historical factors, are the major determinant of economic development. Societies with institutional frameworks that are ineffective at reducing transaction and uncertainty costs are hampered in the search for enhanced economic performance because of the high uncertainty and transaction costs that arise from ineffective institutional frameworks. The linking of institutional theory to transaction costs by new institutional economics leads to a very functional view of institutional systems. Effective institutional systems are deemed 'good' if they lead to low uncertainty and transaction costs and are therefore helpful to the conducting of economic exchanges that promote widespread and effective development of business operations.

Institutional frameworks and types of exchange

The analysis of the importance of institutional framework for the level of transaction costs is focused on the types of exchange that is possible with given institutional frameworks. Three main types of exchange are considered in the new institutional economics (North, 1990):

1 personalised exchange systems
2 impersonal exchange without third-party enforcement
3 impersonal exchange with third-party enforcement.

Personalised exchange systems are based on repeated dealings within culturally homogenous blocs, or groups with common set of values (families or primitive tribal groups). These systems are based on high levels of trust and/or hostage mechanisms that ensure that implicit contracts are honoured. These types of arrangements eliminate the need for third-party enforcement. They have low transaction costs providing that exchange is restricted to the homogenous bloc. However, this reduces specialisation and provides only a small number of agents with whom it is possible to exchange. It is difficult for such systems to take advantage of even the main benefits of wider trading opportunities. These systems normally have poor adaptive efficiency and they often disintegrate when confronted by minor economic, social or technical change.

Impersonal exchange without third-party enforcement is predicated on groups that have shared values and/or informal enforcement process (tribes, guilds, informal networks). They have problems in establishing trust or hostage mechanisms that ensure that implicit contracts are fulfilled. This type of exchange has low transaction costs providing that enforcement procedures are effective. To achieve this most exchanges are

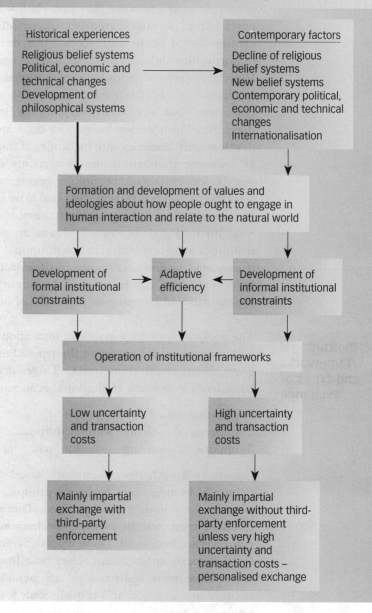

Figure 7.3 Institutional systems and types of exchange

limited to members of the tribe, guild or informal networks. If these
groups lack a strong force that binds them together, they are prone to
break up. These types of systems find it difficult to take advantage of the
benefits of wider trading opportunities and to reap economies of scale
and of scope and they tend to have poor adaptive efficiency and often
find it difficult to adjust to economic, social and technical change.

Impersonal exchange with third-party enforcement may make use of
trust and/or hostage mechanisms by business arrangements based on
tribal or guild or informal networks arrangements, but they also have
formal systems based on laws, courts and regulatory agencies that act as

third-party enforcers of explicit contracts and provide incentives to keep implicit contracts. Systems of this type require institutions that are able to create, maintain and develop the conditions that permit low transaction cost exchange. Informal constraints are important in this type of exchange because they reduce the need to use expensive legal procedures since agents tend to play by the rules of the game. Moreover, informal constraints provide incentives to play by the rules of the game, even in the case of implicit contracts. This type of exchange has low uncertainty and transaction costs that permits substantial levels of specialisation and a large pool of potential traders with whom it is considered safe to do business. The problem with this type of exchange is to construct and develop institutional structures (with effective formal and informal constraints) that can enforce implicit and explicit contracts at low cost. Moreover, these types of institutional structures must have high levels of adaptive efficiency that allows them to adjust quickly to new conditions that arise from economic, political, social and technical change. Such systems can acquire the main benefits that arise from wider trading opportunities and can successfully adjust to changes in economic, social and technological conditions.

The main institutional factors and the impact on uncertainty and transaction costs are illustrated in Figure 7.3.

Exchange systems and mode of entry

Institutional structures that have effective formal and informal constraints and a high level of adaptive efficiency are conducive to efficient impersonal exchange with third-party enforcement. Institutional systems that have poor third-party enforcement and/or poor adaptive efficiency will not be able to sustain efficient impersonal exchange with third-party enforcement and will therefore have high uncertainty and transaction costs, unless agents operate within tribes or guild types of arrangements. When agents from institutional systems that have effective impersonal exchange with third-party enforcement interact with agents in systems that do not have such effective institutional systems, high uncertainty and transaction costs are likely to arise. The links between institutional systems and types of exchange are illustrated in Figure 7.4.

As it is not possible to reform formal and especially informal institutional constraints quickly a solution to the problem is to engineer a synthesis between different institutional systems. This can be done by forming collaborative arrangements such as international joint ventures that incorporate the parties from the different institutional systems into one organisation that conducts trade in the institutional system that does not have efficient impersonal exchange with third-party enforcement. This enables multinational companies to reduce the uncertainty and transaction costs that arise from the nature of institutional systems in host countries.

However, international joint ventures are often suboptimal because they restrict the benefits that could be obtained from trade between the two systems. They tend to be unstable and liable to disputes and to

Figure 7.4 Exchange systems and institutional constraints

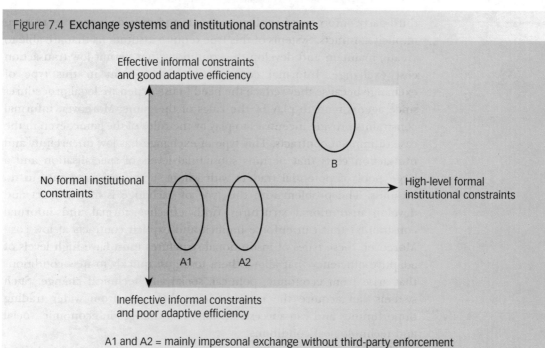

A1 and A2 = mainly impersonal exchange without third-party enforcement
B = mainly impersonal exchange with third-party enforcement

Reforms that move a country along the horizontal axis may not lead to the development of impersonal exchange with third-party enforcement unless the reforms also alter informal constraints and develop good adaptive efficiency. A country that is located in a space such as A1 that reforms its institutional system may move to an area such as A2. However, a multinational company that normally conducts business within an area such as B will face problems when operating in a country with an institutional framework such as A even after reforms move the country from A1 to A2. The problem is that the modifications to institutional frameworks have not improved the informal constraints and adaptive efficiency in reforming countries. Moreover, reform or formal institutional constraints that lack legitimacy may worsen informal constraints and adaptive efficiency by generating resentment among some members of the society who do not agree to the changes. This can lead to the growth of tribal or guild-type economic activity as alienated members of the society disassociate from formal institutional structures and create and develop their own institutional frameworks based on impersonal exchange without third-party enforcement. In these circumstances, A2 could move downwards indicating that institutional reform has led to an increase in transaction costs for 'outsiders' who will find it difficult to penetrate the tribal or guild or informal network structures that will characterise many business operations.

breaking up. Moreover, because of the lack of control and trust that frequently exists between partners in international joint ventures high-level transfer of technology can be restricted (Inkpen and Beamish, 1997). The development of specialisation and the evolution of new trading opportunities that could be possible will be limited by the need to operate in an institutional system that is not conducive to such improvements. Therefore, reforming institutional systems that permit the development of low transaction cost impersonal exchange with third-party enforcement would promote specialisation and wider trading opportunities and would probably bring benefits to multinational companies and host countries.

The privatisation programmes and reforming of government policies and agencies that are common in many countries may fail in many cases because they are often based on off-the-shelf blueprints for institutional systems that come from developed countries. Moreover, these programmes focus on changes to the formal constraints on institutional systems, but informal constraints are perhaps more important in developing an effective exchange with third-party enforcement. Many developing and transition countries have engineered substantial changes to the formal constraints in their institutional systems, but this has not led to significant improvements in economic development. The problem is that informal constraints have not been sufficiently adjusted and in many cases the reform to formal constraints are not accepted by the people that have to operate within the new institutional systems. Therefore, these countries continue to operate on a tribal, guild, or informal network basis, thereby making it difficult for multinational companies to move away from the use of international joint ventures. Consequently, multinational companies are unable to take full advantage of the potential to develop their business in host countries and have to continue to use suboptimal international joint ventures.

The solution to this problem requires countries to transform the informal constraints on their institutional systems and develop good adaptive efficiency. Furthermore, the reforms to formal constraints must be made legitimate and acceptable to the people. Societies that are unable or unwilling to induce such changes to their formal and informal constraints are likely to face the use of suboptimal international joint ventures as multinational companies use this method to reduce the high uncertainty and transaction costs of conducting business in such host countries.

Reforming institutional frameworks

If developing and transition countries wish to promote economic development it is clear that they need to reform *both* formal and informal constraints to their institutional systems such that the evolution of extensive impersonal exchange with third-party enforcement becomes possible. This raises a question as to why many countries appear to be failing to achieve such an outcome. The answer to this conundrum, according to North, is that the creation of institutional structures involves large sunk costs arising from negotiating to create and implement new institutional frameworks (North, 1990). Therefore, there are strong vested interests that seek to retain the status quo unless there are powerful reasons to change these frameworks. Furthermore, the feedback on outcomes from existing institutional structures (to the various actors involved) is incomplete and slowly disseminated. In these circumstances changes to the formal and informal constraints on human interaction, that are the essence of the evolution of institutional frameworks, normally change slowly. They change in response to feedback that indicates persistently unacceptable outcomes. Institutional evolution is largely the result of the realisation by actors that a new round of institutional building, or modification, is necessary and that sunk costs must be incurred in this process. Incurring such costs is justifiable if the cost of existing outcomes exceeds the sunk costs necessary to build new institutions, or to modify existing institutional frameworks. In most cases, change will be incremental because the various actors are likely to have different ideas and information about the size of the sunk costs and the costs associated with existing outcomes. If actors have very different estimates of these costs it will be difficult to agree on significant change to institutional structures because actors will have different perceptions on the magnitude of the problems connected to existing outcomes.

In these circumstances institutional frameworks that are inefficient can be constructed and maintained because the actors involved in setting up institutional structures have been unable to resolve the different perceptions on the costs involved in establishing or modifying institutional frameworks. Therefore, societies inherit institutional structures based on a set of beliefs, resources and power bases from their history that can persist even if they lead to high uncertainty and transaction costs that hamper economic development (Akerlof, 1976). Institutional change is path determined not only by the nature of inherited institutional frameworks, but also by the perceptions and beliefs of actors that are determined largely by the experiences of these actors. Therefore, unless detailed information is available on the perceptions and views of actors on the relative costs of institutional change it is very difficult to predict the direction or pace of institutional change. However, it is unlikely that actors will make dramatic changes from the path they have been following (Zucker, 1986).

Altering formal constraints involves changes to such things as constitutions, law, regulations and procedural conditions in courts and governmental agencies. Changing informal constraints requires changes to the perceptions of actors. North regards the altering of informal constraints as most important because the perceptions of actors determine their views on the costs associated with institutional change. Societies that have good adaptive efficiency have cultural values that are conducive to searching for and finding acceptable solutions to the problems of human interaction. These cultural values are determined by the interaction between historical experience and current and expected changes to the environment in which human interaction takes place. In these circumstances radical change to institutional frameworks are likely to be rare and to arise in periods of significant change in current and expected conditions that influence human interactions. Revolutions or crises that fundamentally alter the costs of human interaction can make radical change necessary and possible, but there is no guarantee that such dramatic changes will result in efficient institutional frameworks. History plays an important part in the effect of revolutions or crises on institutional change, for historical experiences influence the views of the actors which undertake radical reforms.

In societies with good 'adaptive efficiency' institutional frameworks are built and evolve in an effective manner in response to changes in the conditions that influence human interaction. This implies that the actors involved in building and modifying institutional frameworks have a high level of awareness about the existing and likely future costs of engaging in human interactions and this stimulates actions to create and maintain efficient institutional structures. The key to such a desirable outcome is that the behaviour of actors (largely determined by historical experiences) leads to the creation and development of informal constraints that are conducive to the search for effective institutional structures. Nevertheless, before institutional change can take place the sunk costs involved in creating and maintaining effective institutional structures must be lower than the benefits that arise from creating and/or developing institutional structures.

New institutional economics indicates that institutional change is largely path determined and is strongly influenced by the 'adaptive efficiency' of societies. Moreover, when actors have different perceptions on the magnitude of the costs associated with institutional change the prospect of creating efficient institutional structures diminishes. This suggests that institution building and modification in the face of differing historical experiences and perceptions of actors is a difficult task and is likely to lead to inefficient institutional structures that can persist for long periods. Countries with cultural values that are uncomfortable with the dynamics of modern capitalism are likely to have informal constraints that are not conducive to low uncertainty and transaction costs. Such countries may be successful in reforming their formal institutional constraints but this will not be sufficient to effectively embrace modern capitalist ways of doing business. In these circumstances, multinational companies will face high costs of managing the effects of the institutional framework differences between home and host locations.

Problems with the new institutional economics approach

The new institutional economics provides a rich understanding of the complex links between cultural values and institutional frameworks and explains how many countries find it difficult to adjust to the ways of modern capitalism even if they reform their formal institutional systems. It also indicates the deep nature of the problems that are caused to multinational companies when they interact with very different institutional systems. The focus on uncertainty and transaction costs also centres attention on some of the hard facts of business life that indicate that failure to adjust cultural values may lead to limited exposure to international business activities with consequent harmful effects for economic development.

However, new institutional economics adopts a very functional and 'business' view of effective institutional frameworks. Indeed, it has elements of western or even American views on the purpose of institutions. Moreover, societies with 'good' adaptive efficiency may prosper in the modern capitalist world but they also tend to lead to segregation of society into small heterogeneous groups that have very little sense of solidarity with other groups in their society. The decline of religious belief systems has contributed to the decline in solidarity with other members of society. This leads to problems with excluded groups in society that find it difficult to prosper in finding jobs or at least well-paid jobs. This group suffer from social disintegration as they often lack family and community support. This can lead to high crime rates, health problems and the exclusion of a significant part of the potential labour force from productive work. The inequality of income and opportunity that follows from this type of social distintegration was identified by Schumpeter as the most likely factor that would undermine capitalism success in promoting economic development (Schumpeter, 1961). The growth of national and global inequality has led to heated debate about the ability of western-type institutional systems to continue to provide the setting for the growth and expansion of business activities (*Economist*, 2001). New institutional economics has thus far tended to ignore this problem with institutional systems that have good adaptive efficiency but which leads to poor levels of solidarity.

The most serious problem that faces the practical application of new institutional economics to international business issues is the lack of a coherent system to identify and measure the factors that influence uncertainty and transaction costs. Such a system would allow for a systematic approach to the design and implementation of policies to manage the problems caused by different institutional systems. There is a dearth of empirical studies on these issues mainly because there is no equivalent of the consistent and well-defined Hofstede and Trompenaar's approach for the investigation of institutional differences. A range of ad hoc studies based on studies of corruption, the opacity and number of bureaucratic rules and subjective measures of how difficult it is to 'do business' in various countries are available (see, for example, the opacity index published by PricewaterhouseCoopers – www.PriceWaterhouseCoopers.com/). However, these types of study lack a coherent and consistent approach to the empirical study of the impact of institutional differences.

Summary

This chapter has examined the influence of cultural differences on international business activities. The determinants of cultural values and the ways in which these values lead to moral codes, attitudes and norms of behaviour results from complex interaction between historical experiences and contemporary events. However, major historical experiences such as the rise and fall of religious belief systems and large-scale economic, political and technical changes form the backbone of the evolution of cultural values. Thus, cultural values are largely path determined and change slowly unless there are revolutionary changes that involve the overthrow of traditional values. Even in these cases the influence of religious belief systems and other major determinants of cultural values often continues to affect moral codes and thereby norms of behaviour.

An understanding of cultural differences provides the starting point for the design of policies to manage cross-cultural business activities. The use of concepts of cultural dimensions such as those of Hofstede and Trompenaars provides the means to construct cultural clusters of countries or subcultures within and across countries. These clusters can be used to identify areas where different management systems need to be developed to reduce the problems caused by cultural differences. Indeed, this type of approach dominates much of the research and policy planning in international business management. However, this approach is leading to the development of ever more complex layers of subcultures both within and across national boundaries. Different classifications of cultural characteristics (such as those used by marketers) leads to the identification of even more complex cultural clusters that makes the process of developing appropriate management systems more difficult.

These approaches to cultural differences assume that they either lead to advantages to firms that locate in different cultural clusters or that the costs of managing the cultural differences are less than the economic and strategic benefits of operating in different cultural settings. However, the demands of modern capitalism often require national cultural values to be modified to meet the needs of competitive environments. External factors such as IMF and World Bank programmes and the desire of former communist countries to integrate into the world economy also put pressure for cultural change. The new institutional economics provides an approach to the investigation of cultural values in their institutional setting that indicates the uncertainty and transaction costs disadvantages that result from some cultural systems. The path-determined nature of cultural values affects institutional development because of the impact of values on informal institutional constraints. This implies that international business activities between countries with very different cultural values will be limited by these cost disadvantages. However, the implications of new institutional economics for the management of international business are underdeveloped. Nevertheless, new institutional economics offers a rich and business-orientated way of investigating the implications of cultural differences.

Review questions

1 Outline the major determinants of cultural values and discuss how these give rise to norms of behaviour that affect business activities.
2 Assess the usefulness of Hofstede-type approaches to developing management systems to manage cultural differences.
3 What are the major problems associated with Hofstede-type approaches for the identification of cultural clusters?
4 Outline the main features of new institutional economics and explain the role of cultural values for the effectiveness of institutional frameworks.
5 Explain why the reform of formal institutional constraints is not sufficient to lower uncertainty and transaction costs.

Bibliography

Akerlof, G. (1976) 'The economics of caste and of the rat race and other woeful tales', *Quarterly Journal of Economics*, 90, pp. 599–617.

Brealey, R. (1999) 'The Asian crisis: lessons for crisis management and prevention', *International Finance*, 2, 2, pp. 249–72.

Carr, C. and Tomkins, C. (1998) 'Context, culture and the role of the finance function in strategic decisions: a comparative analysis of Britain, Germany, the USA and Japan', *Management Accounting Research*, 9, 1, pp. 213–39.

Domzal, T. and Unger, L. (1987) 'Emerging positioning strategies in global marketing', *Journal of Consumer Marketing*, 4, 4, pp. 23–40.

Economist (2001) 'Does inequality matter?', pp. 11–12 and 'Survey – the new wealth of nations', 16 June.

European Bank for Reconstruction and Development (EBRD) (1999) *Transition Report, 1999*, London, EBRD.

Harris, S. and Ghauri, P. (2000) 'Strategy formation by business leaders: exploring the influence of national values', *European Journal of Marketing*, 5, 1, pp. 126–41.

Hodgetts, R. and Luthans, F. (1994) *International Management*, London, McGraw-Hill.

Hampden-Turner, C. and Trompenaars, F. (1994) *The Seven Cultures of Capitalism*, London, Piatkus.

Hofstede, G. (1994) 'The business of international business is culture', *International Business Review*, 3, pp. 1–14.

Hofstede, G. (1991) *Cultures and Organizations: Software of the Mind*, London, McGraw-Hill.

Hofstede, G. (1983) 'The cultural relativity of organizational practices and theories', *Journal of International Business Studies*, 14, 2, pp. 234–58

Hofstede G. (1980) *Culture's Consequences: International Differences in Work-Related Values*, London, Sage.

Hofstede, G. and Bond, M. (1998) 'Confucius and economic growth: new trends in culture's consequences', *Organizational Dynamics*, 16, 1, pp. 4–21.

Hofstede, G., Neiujen, B., Ohayu, D. and Sanders, G. (1990) 'Measuring organizational cultures: a qualitative and quantitative study across twenty cases', *Administrative Science Quarterly*, 35, 2, pp. 286–313.

Holt, D. (1998) *International Management*, New York, Dryden Press.

Inkpen, A. and Beamish, P. (1997) 'Knowledge, bargaining power, and the instability of international joint ventures', *Academy of Management Review*, 27, pp. 177–202.

Kluckhohn, A. and Strodtbeck, F. (1961) *Variations in Value Orientations*, Westport, CT, Greenwood Press.

Lane, H., DiStefano, J. and Maznevski, M. (1997) *International Management*, Oxford, Blackwell Business.

Lenartowicz, T. and Roth, K. (2001) 'Does subculture within a country matter? A cross cultural study of motivational domains and business performance', *Journal of International Business Studies*, 32, 2, pp. 156–73.

Matthews, R. (1986) 'The economics of institutions and sources of growth', *Economic Journal*, 96, 2, pp. 903–18.

North, D. (1999) *Understanding the Process of Economic Change*, Occasional Paper No. 106, London, Institute of Economic Affairs.

North, D. (1990) *Institutions, Institutional Change and Economic Performance*, Cambridge, Cambridge University Press.

North, D. (1983) 'A theory of institutional change and the economic history of the western world' in M. Hechter (ed.) *The Mircofoundations of Macrosociology*, Philadelphia, PA, Temple University Press.

Punnett, B. and Withane, S. (1990) 'Hofstede's value survey model: to embrace or abandon?', *Advances in International Comparative Management*, 5, 1, pp. 69–90.

Ronen, S. and Shenkar, O. (1985) 'Clustering countries on attitudinal dimensions: a review and synthesis', *Academy of Management Review*, 10, 3, pp. 435–54.

Schumpeter, J. (1961) *The Theory of Economic Development*, Oxford, Oxford University Press.

Tayeb, M. (1988) *Organizations and National Culture: A Comparative Analysis*, London, Sage.

Trompenaars, F. (1993) *Riding the Wave of Culture*, London, Economists Books.

Whitelock, J. (1987) 'Global marketing and the case for international product standardization', *European Journal of Marketing*, 21, 1, pp. 32–44.

Williamson, O. (1985) *The Economic Institutions of Capitalism: Firms, Markets, Relational Contracting*, London, Macmillan.

Womack, J., Jones, D. and Roos, D. (1990) *The Machine that Changed the World*, New York, Rawson Associates.

World Bank (1997a) *World Development Report 1997*, Oxford, Oxford University Press.

World Bank (1997b) *Promoting Foreign Direct Investment in Jordan: Policy, Strategy and Institutions*, Washington, World Bank.

Vandermerwe, S. and L'Huillier, M. (1989) 'Euroconsumers in 1992', *Business Horizons*, January/February, pp. 34–40.

Yeh, R. and Lawrence, J. (1995) 'Individualism and Confucian dynamism: a note on Hofstede's cultural route to economic growth', *Journal of International Business Studies*, 26, 3, pp. 655–70.

Zucker, L. (1986) 'Production of trust: institutional sources of economic structure, 1840–1920', *Research in Organizational Behavior*, 8, pp. 53–111.

Case 7.1 Daimler-Chrysler: a marriage between disparate national and company cultures

In 1998 Daimler-Benz, owner of the high-quality Mercedes marque announced a merger with the America car company Chrysler, whose marque is rather more down market than Mercedes? Although the deal was announced as a merger, it was, in fact, a takeover by Daimler-Benz. The public relations efforts by Daimler-Benz to classify the deal as a merger reflected a fear that US customers would react badly to a German takeover of a leading American firm. This indicated a concern with cultural values, that is, a perception by Daimler-Benz of ethnocentric values in the USA. The concerns over ethnocentric values in the USA initially led to a plan to maintain two headquarters, one in the USA and the other in Germany. This plan was not put into effect, but office space (ironically, in the famous Chrysler Building in New York) was rented to provide space for meetings of American and German managers. The concerns about national cultural clashes were amplified by American managers who expressed fears that they would be forced to adopt Germanic engineering-based management systems instead of the more freewheeling and entrepreneurial American approach. Attempts by Daimler-Benz to reassure American managers notwithstanding, a number of senior staff left Chrysler.

Company cultures also clashed when poor performance by DaimlerChrysler required the adoption of cost-cutting measures and attempts to improve the Chrysler marque. The Daimler approach was based on engineering solutions to share technical information and achieve synergy by sharing components and engines. The Chrysler approach was focused more on marketing tactics such as price discounts and promotion that had flourished in the 1980s when Chrysler was led by Lee Iacocca. The attempts to achieve synergy were hampered by the different traditions of the companies, with Daimler focused on high-quality products with highly engineered components with final products that sold at premium prices. Chrysler had adopted policies with less emphasis on quality competition and more on price competition and niche marketing of products such as Jeeps. The differences in company cultures was reflected in the predominance of middle-ranking German managers with a training in engineering while American managers were more likely to be trained in accounting and finance or marketing. This also reflects national cultural differences in what is regarded as the best way to train managers.

The price of DaimlerChrysler shares collapse in 1999 and 2000 as the markets considered that the new company was unlikely to be able to find solutions to the problems of merging the two companies. By the beginning of 2000, the market valuation of DaimlerChrysler was less than the premerger values of Daimler-Benz and strong pressure was exerted on Jürgen Schrempp, the Chief Executive, to take radical action to cure the underlying problems. This resulted in the appointment of German managers (Dieter Zetsche and Wolfgang Bernhard) to run Chrysler operations in the USA and a clearer lead from German head-quarters on cost-cutting systems and on tactics for revamping the Chrysler marque.

The problems caused by cultural differences contributed to the poor performance of Daimler-Chrysler, but these differences were not the only problems that the company has faced. The ageing nature of Chrysler's marque and global pressures on the car industry to cut costs and develop new product lines face all major car companies. More-over, Chrysler had moved on from the freewheeling marketing approach that had developed under Lee Iacocca. In the early 1990s, Chrysler had recruited managers from General Motors who had set about rationalising production and procurement systems to reduce costs. Daimler-Benz was also not a standard engineering-based German company. Jür-gen Schrempp is regarded as a rather revolutionary manager in Germany where he had introduced many novel and American influenced management practices into Daimler-Benz.

The problems of integrating the two companies further increased when in March 2000 Daimler-Chrysler obtained a financial stake in Mitsubishi Motors of Japan. This company was in financial and operational difficulties and added a Japanese cultural dimension to the DaimlerChrysler venture. However, this venture is an attempt to grapple with the problems faced by all major car companies, that is, to cut costs by realising synergy benefits and to develop new markets and products in an industry that faces mature markets in the west and increasing problems connected to the environmental and congestion costs associated with the use of their products. These problems require global solutions to achieve synergy benefits in the design, produc-tion and distribution of products. Moreover, devel-oping new products and new markets in what is a mature industry with over-capacity is a difficult set of problems to solve. The cross-cultural problems simply add to these difficulties. However, to achieve synergy benefits will require many car companies to engage in significant cross-cultural ventures. The DaimlerChrysler case seems to illustrate the point about the relevance of the costs of dealing with cross-cultural ventures relative to the economic and strategic benefits of such ventures.

Economist (2000) 'Merger brief: the DaimlerChrysler emulsion', 29 July, pp. 81–2; *Economist* (2001) 'Schempp's repair job', 3 March, pp. 79–80

Case 7.2 Reforming South Korean chaebol

Chaebol refers to family clan in Korean culture and industrial chaebol are large groups composed of a variety of business interests that are controlled by family clans. Most famous South Korean firms are family-based chaebol – Hyundai (Chung family), Samsung (Lee family), LG (Koo family) and Daewoo (Kim family). Chaebol hold controlling interests in a large number of subsidiaries in a variety of fields. For example, Samsung has interests in trading companies, heavy engineering and construction and is best known in the west for electronic products. Chaebol have similarities to Japanese *keiretsu*, but whereas the top management in keiretsu are professional managers that have normally risen through the ranks of keiretsu companies, top management in chaebols are nearly always members of the founding family. The top person is either the leader of the founding family or his eldest son.

The origins of industrial chaebol were in the 1960s when South Korea underwent a major period of growth based on the development of export-orientated firms. The founding families established good relationships with the South Korean govern-ment and banks and financial institutions. Korean values of respect and deference to leading families and rigid hierarchical systems suited the develop-ment of chaebol. Chaebol also adopted paternalistic attitudes towards their workers that meshed well with Korean culture. Working practices were based on rigid codes of behaviour that focused power and respect on the hierarchy that controlled the chaebol. Entrepreneurial behaviour by junior or even middle managers was discouraged and control of strategic and even major tactical issues was lodged in the ruling family. From the 1960s until the Asian crisis in 1997, the chaebol system appeared to be in harmony with Korean cultural values and to work very effectively in the process of economic and business development.

The ability of chaebol to cooperate with govern-ment, banks and workers allowed them to marshal capital, labour and technical resources that led to remarkable growth in the South Korean economy and made the chaebol significant players in world markets for electronic products, shipbuilding and cars. The close network of leading families also permitted cooperation between the chaebol that helped with the gathering and processing of information necessary to adopt new technologies and enter new export markets. The main factor that binds chaebol together is not so much trust but more the respect for leading families and the close network of these families with government agencies and banks. Chaebol appeared to be remarkable success stories based on the blending of Korean cultural values into effective company structures that could create and develop competitive edge to meet the challenges of modern capitalism.

However, the chaebol began to experience problems from the mid-1990s when South Korea joined the World Trade Organisation (1995) and began to open markets to foreign competition. The wide spread of business interests of the chaebol led to a lack of strategic focus. This led to loss of competitive edge as in other parts of the world companies were focusing on core competencies and were developing competitive advantages in the areas in which they concentrated their operations. Moreover, the close links between the leading families, the government and banks led to a locking together of interests that encouraged over-investment in areas such as electronic products and car production. Korean cultural values stress the importance of not losing face, so failures were covered up and more investments were made in what were, in effect, lost causes in efforts to rectify poor performance. The close networks of government, banks and chaebol allowed over-investment and the continuance of ill-thought strategies because of the respect for hierarchical systems and the lack of independent scrutiny of the actions of the chaebol.

The Asian crisis in 1997/8 exposed many of the shortcomings of the chaebol, especially their large debts and very low or even negative return from many of their investments. Several of the chaebol effectively became bankrupt, including Daewoo and they were forced to sell off parts of their holdings and to close others. Major restructuring was begun to rationalise the holdings of the chaebol and to introduce more transparency into the management systems including bringing in outsiders into the top management positions. Policies to encourage a more entrepreneurial and less differential approach from middle managers have been introduced. Pressure from external agencies such as the

International Monetary Fund (IMF) persuaded the South Korean government to take a more arms' length approach to the chaebol and to encourage them to reform. Criticism from a new breed of young and entrepreneurial South Koreans of the stifling affect of the management of chaebol has also increased the pressures to reform the corporate governance of chaebol. However, the major pressures have come from external forces such as the IMF and the need to be more competitive and focused in export markets and to provide foreign investors with transparent information on performance.

It would seem that the chaebol are either going to reform and become very different types of company or disappear, to be replaced by company structures that are more similar to those that prevail in the west. Western multinational companies such as Ford and General Motors are acquiring interests in some of the subsidiaries of the chaebol and this will bring new thinking into the issue of corporate governance in South Korea. However, there is considerable opposition to these reforms from some of the leading families and from people in Korea who wish to retain traditional Korean values in their business systems. This cultural resistance is slowing the pace of reform but does not seem to be able to stop the process due to the very strong external pressures for change.

These developments reveal the limitations to the development of corporate governance systems based on national cultural values when countries become strongly linked to the global system of modern capitalism. Business systems based on national cultural values can prosper in a modern capitalist system providing that they confer competitive advantages. However, changing conditions, especially the opening up of domestic markets to foreign competition and integration into global capital markets, exert pressures to make national cultures conform to the requirements of modern capitalism.

Economist (2000) 'The chaebols spurn change', 22 July; Cho, D. (1999) 'Chaebols' in R. Tung (ed.) *The Handbook of International Business*, London, Thomson Learning.

8 Regional integration blocs

Learning objectives

By the end of this chapter, you should be able to:

- assess the conditions in which regional intergration blocs contribute to multilateral trade liberalism
- understand the different types of regional integration and the main implications that they have on international business transactions
- outline the main regional integration agencies and identify their main objectives
- outline the main economic effects of a customs union and a common market
- have knowledge on the effects of European Monetary Union on the strategies and operations of firms
- understand how regional integration blocs can develop into a single economic space
- highlight the important differences between various types of single economic spaces

Key terms

- economic integration • customs union • common market • monetary union • single economic space • multilateralism versus regionalism • European Union • NAFTA • Mercusor • APEC • FTTA

Introduction

Regional integration blocs are groups of countries that adopt programmes to link their economic, and in some cases political, systems by harmonising or coordinating laws, policies and institutional frameworks. The objectives for such integration vary, but economic integration by removing barriers to trade is always one of the key objectives. This process leads to growth in intra-bloc trade and an increase in direct foreign investment (DFI) flows. Some regional integration blocs have gone well beyond the removal of trade barriers by creating common or harmonised economic and political policies. These agencies are seeking to create the conditions between the members of the bloc such that their markets and the systems for governing economic activities are integrated into a single economic space. Regional integration blocs that successfully create a single economic space have in effect integrated the national economies of the members into one economy. This has implications for international business transactions because the economies of several countries become one economy.

In the post-World War II period, regional integration has been attempted by a large number of countries. The most successful bloc has been the European Union (EU). The EU began in 1951 when the Treaty of Paris established the European Coal and Steel Community among six countries (Belgium, France, Germany, Luxembourg, Italy and the Netherlands). In 1957 the original six countries signed the Treaty of Rome to form the European Economic Community (EEC). The UK, Denmark and Ireland joined the EEC in 1973 and Greece, Portugal and Spain joined in the 1980s. The objective of the EEC was to establish a common market and to move towards some type of economic union. The EEC evolved into the EU when in 1991 the Treaty of Maastricht committed the member states to form the Economic and Monetary Union (EMU) based on a single currency, the euro, a common monetary policy with a European Central Bank (ECB) and coordinated economic policies. The Maastricht Treaty also contains commitments to develop some type of political union. Austria, Finland and Sweden joined the EU in 1995 and most of the countries of central and eastern Europe and Turkey have applied to join the EU. Because of a number of preferential trading agreements, the EU has developed extensive economic relationships with many developing countries, most of the countries of central and eastern Europe and all the countries of the Mediterranean basin. The EU has developed a comprehensive institutional structure, including an intergovernmental decision-making body (European Council), an agency to draft EU laws and to administer policies (European Commission), a court to settle disputes about EU law (European Court of Justice), a directly elected parliament (European Parliament) and a central bank (European Central Bank). Examination of the economic effects of European integration is available in El-Agraa (2000) and McDonald and Dearden (1999) and the political effects in Nugent (1999).

Many other regional integration blocs have been established, for example, the North American Free Trade Agreement (NAFTA), Mercosur (Mercado Común Del Sur), Free Trade Area of the Americas (FTAA) and a proposed free trade area among the countries that are members of the Asia–Pacific Economic Cooperation (APEC). Analysis of the economic effects of these regional integration blocs is given in (El-Agraa, 1997; Frankel, 1997; Hufbauer and Schott, 1994). None of these has as ambitious objectives as the EU. However, NAFTA is currently 25 per cent larger in terms of output. Mercosur and NAFTA have made some progress in establishing free trade areas but FTAA and APEC have not gone much further than outlining rather vague commitments to begin the process of creating free trade areas.

This chapter outlines the various types of regional integration bloc and provides an economic assessment of the effects of removing trade barriers and of developing the conditions for the creation of a single economic space. The implications for international business transactions of these various types of trade liberalisation and policy harmonisation and coordination are considered.

Types of regional integration

The foundation of the analysis of regional integration was established by economists investigating the attempts by west European countries to create integrated markets in the post-World War II period (Balassa, 1961). Six major types of regional integration can be identified:

1 A free trade area is a group of countries where all tariffs, quotas and non-tariff barriers (NTBs) are removed.
2 A customs union is a free trade area with a common external trade policy including a common system for tariffs, quotas and NTBs imposed on imports into the customs union.
3 A common market is a customs union plus free movement of capital and labour, this is sometimes called a single market.
4 An economic union is a common market with harmonisation or coordination of economic and social policies to ensure effective free movement.
5 Economic and monetary union (EMU) is an economic union with a common or harmonised monetary policy.
6 Political union is the harmonisation or coordination of political systems to govern the EMU and in some cases includes common or harmonised foreign and security policies.

The EU is the only regional integration bloc that has made significant progress beyond the creation of a free trade area. The EU has established a monetary union between most of its members and has made progress toward EMU and a type of political union. Indeed, the EU together with the USA and Japan forms what has been called the Triad that dominates international trade and financial flows (Ohmae, 1990). However, regional integration blocs are also emerging in the Americas and are being discussed in Asia. Many developing countries, especially in Latin America are also seeking to establish regional integration blocs (see Exhibit 8.1)

Multilateralism versus regionalism

Regional integration blocs pose a threat to the attempts to promote multilateral trade liberalisation by the World Trade Organisation (WTO) because regional integration blocs only remove trade barriers among a subset of WTO members. Consequently, regional integration breaks the spirit of the multilateral approach to trade liberalisation adopted by the GATT agreement in 1947 (see Chapter 4). The main problem is that regional integration blocs do not grant all members of WTO most favoured nation (MFN) treatment. That is, they do not grant to countries that are not members of the regional integration bloc the same treatment in the application of tariffs, quotas and NTBs as they do to members of

---

Exhibit 8.1 Regional integration blocs

Major blocs

Bloc	Members	Objectives
EU	Austria, Belgium, Denmark, Finland, France, Germany, Greece, Luxembourg, Ireland, Italy, the Netherlands, Portugal, Spain, Sweden and the UK	Customs Union[1] Common Market[1] EMU[1] Political union[3]
NAFTA	Canada, Mexico and the USA	Free trade area[2]
Mercosur	Argentina, Brazil, Paraguay and Uruguay – Chile has a type of associated membership	Free trade area[2] Customs union[4] Common market[5]
APEC	Australia, Brunei, Canada, Chile, China (inc. Hong Kong), Indonesia, Japan, Malaysia, Mexico, New Zealand, Papua New Guinea, Singapore, South Korea, Taiwan, Thailand and the USA	Long-term aim to form a free trade area[5]
FTTA	All countries of North, Central and South America	Long-term aim to form a free trade area[5]

1. High level of integration achieved
2. Significant level of integration achieved
3. Low level of integration achieved

4. Very low level of integration achieved
5. No progress to institute practical measures to achieved objectives

Other regional integration blocs

Andean Common Market (ANCom) – Bolivia, Colombia, Ecuador and Peru

Central American Common Market (CACM) – Costa Rica, El Salvador, Guatemala, Honduras and Nicaragua

ASEAN Free Trade Agreement – members of the Association of Southeast Asian Nations (ASEAN) – Brunei, Indonesia, Malaysia, Philippines, Singapore, Thailand and Vietnam

None of these blocs has made any significant progress in establishing a free trade area.

Details on these and other regional integration blocs can be found in El-Agraa (2000), Frankel (1997), Hufbauer and Schott (1994), Schott (2001), Scollay and Gilbert (2001).

---

the bloc. GATT rules permit regional integration blocs to grant preferential treatment to its members providing that tariffs, quotas and NTBs applied to non-members do not increase because of the formation of the bloc (El-Agraa, 1997).

Some argue that regional trade blocs create significant trade diversion (see later) and thereby lead to welfare losses because of the failure to apply MFN treatment (Bhagwati, 1993). This harmful outcome is offset if regional blocs use trade liberalisation among their members as a route to extend the same trading privileges to non-members by the preferential trade agreements which they have with countries linked to the bloc and eventually to all WTO members (Bhagwati, 1991). The EU has a large number of such preferential trade agreements and NAFTA is moving towards such agreements with some countries in Latin America and Asia. Cooperation between the EU and NAFTA to extend their preferential trade arrangement to all countries linked to these blocs would encompass many of the members of the WTO. If the APEC free trade area makes progress and the EU develops links with the area, most of the WTO members would become involved in multilateral trade negotiations via a number of regional integration bloc agreements. This would be a very complex way to make progress towards multilateral trade liberalisation. Such a route is likely to lead to complex negotiations and therefore may prove to be an ineffective way to promote multilateral trade liberalisation.

Negotiations between the EU and the USA on trade liberalisation already exercise a strong influence on attempts at trade liberalisation in areas where the WTO struggles to reach multilateral agreements, for example, agricultural products, health and safety rules and regulation of international e-commerce (McDonald and Dearden, 1999). The large economic size of the EU and the USA (NAFTA) gives them considerable power in trade liberalisation programmes and agreement between these blocs appears to be prerequisite for progress at WTO negotiations. Given the power of these regional integration blocs, complex negotiations between these blocs may be the only feasible way to make progress in multilateral trade liberalisation. This route to multilateral trade liberalisation is fraught with problems because multilateral trade liberalisation allows trade to grow including trade with regional blocs.

Customs unions and common markets allow large regional integration blocs to develop concentrations of economic activity to serve the growth in trade resulting from multilateral and regional integration bloc trade liberalisation. This gives these large blocs market power and first mover advantages in industries that are subject to growth in trade resulting from trade liberalisation. The blocs therefore become reluctant to threaten these advantages by extending MFN treatment. Consequently, regional integration blocs may begin by helping multilateral trade liberalisation because the removal of trade barriers permits concentration to reap economies of scale. However, as the customs union and common market develops the advantages bestowed by them become a serious obstacle when the continuance of such liberalisation is considered to threaten competitive positions that have been established because of regional integration (Bagwell and Staiger, 1998; Either, 1998). Often the protection offered by regional integration blocs is lodged in non-tariff barriers (NTBs). Hence, regional integration blocs are often willing to remove tariff and quota barriers on a multilateral basis but removal of NTBs normally proves to be a more difficult objective to achieve.

The creation and development of large regional integration blocs that do not grant their most important trade liberalisation measures to non-members will have a significant affect on the development of international business activities. In particular, in those industries where economies of scale (minimum efficiency scale) can be reached by supplying the large economies of the bloc and where trade barriers remain against non-members the bulk of trade will be internal to the bloc. In this case, the global reach of firms will be restricted to those industries that require global markets to reap economies of scale and where multilateral trade liberalisation is successful. However, multinational corporations will engage in extensive DFI between the large integration blocs to gain access to their large markets, to provide sales and distribution routes for products that can be supplied from other parts of the world and to develop links to gather technology and other valuable assets. The strategic implications of this are examined in Chapter 10.

Trade effects of regional integration

Regional economic integration normally begins by removing tariffs, quotas and NTBs to establish either a free trade area or a customs union. A common market emerges when free movement of capital and labour is added to the customs union. Monetary union with a single currency further reduces the obstacles to trade by removing the costs of converting currencies and from exchange rate risk. The development of customs unions stimulates growth of export and imports between the members the bloc and direct foreign investment (DFI) flows. DFI flows are between the members (intra-DFI) and from countries outside the bloc (extra-DFI). The motive for intra-DFI flows is to take advantage of the new opportunities to produce and trade within the bloc. Extra-DFI inflows arises from firms located outside of the regional integration bloc that wish to have a presence in the markets of the bloc to take advantage of the new opportunities to produce and trade within the bloc. Progression towards a common market and monetary union strengthen these effects and the establishment of EMU with some type of a political union leads to the creation of a single economic space (SES). An SES is an EMU with a common political–economic system that governs economic activity that turns a regional integration bloc into an economy that is similar to a domestic economy. Therefore, in principle, the EU, which is developing into an SES, should become similar to a large domestic economy such as the USA.

Customs unions and common markets

The early attempts to assess the economic implications of the formation of customs unions (Lipsey, 1970; Viner, 1950) continue to influence the economic analysis of the effects of regional integration blocs. The main effects are split into two types – static and dynamic. Static effects arise when the stock of labour and capital is fixed and where technology and the competitive environment do not change. Dynamic effects emerge when these factors vary. The effects of a common market can also be analysed using the concepts of static and dynamic effects. The establishment of a common market is likely to stimulate more trade and DFI flows than a customs union because the free movement of capital and labour increases trading opportunities between the members of the regional integration bloc.

Static effects

Viner (1950) showed that the formation of a customs union was not necessarily advantageous to all members of a regional integration bloc or indeed to the world as a whole. The static effect of a customs union depends on the relative size of the trade creation and trade diversion effects of a customs union. Trade creation arises when the formation of a customs union leads to the movement of trade from high- to low-cost producers, whereas, trade diversion occurs when the reverse outcome emerges. The creation of a customs union leads to the elimination of trade barriers between members and the establishment of a common external tariff system against all non-members. The removal of trade barriers against members will increase imports from the lowest cost member of the customs union to members who have higher cost producers. If the exporting customs union member is the lowest cost producer in the world, trade creation exists because imports come from the least cost producer in the world. However, if the country with the lowest cost producers is not in the customs union and the imposition of the common external tariff results in an import price into the customs union that is higher than the price from the lowest cost producer in the customs union, trade diversion will result. Trade diversion arises because imports could be obtained at a lower cost if tariffs had been eliminated against all countries rather than just for the members of the customs union.

Therefore, in static terms, a customs union is beneficial if trade creation is greater than trade diversion. This outcome is more likely to occur if the customs union includes countries that have large numbers of low-cost producers and if the common external tariff is set at a low level. These conditions favour regional integration blocs that include large developed economies because they are more likely to include low-cost producers, at least for high value-added products. In these circumstances, trade diversion effects are likely to be low. This factor may explain why many regional integration blocs among small and less developed economies find it hard to make progress in establishing customs unions. In global terms, however, trade diversion can be avoided if trade liberalisation measures are offered on a most favoured nation basis, that is, the most preferential measures offered to any nation are made available to all nations. Therefore, the justification for a customs union rests on arguments that trade barrier reductions can be more substantial between groups of countries than if they are granted to all countries.

Dynamic effects

Two major dynamic effects arise from customs unions and common markets:

- stimulating a more competitive environment
- creating the conditions for economies of scale to be reaped.

The removal of barriers to trade can reduce monopoly power by increasing the possible sources of supply from other countries within the regional integration bloc. A reduction in monopoly power reduces prices and increases output thereby leading to net gains for consumers. Where production in national markets is characterised by large economies of scale the competitive environment may be monopolistic if national markets are big enough to sustain only a few plants. In these circumstances, the creation of a larger market by establishing a customs union may allow an expansion of suppliers to the new larger market and thereby lead to a reduction in price (Smith and Venables, 1988).

Increasing the competitive environment may also encourage producers to improve non-price competition factors such as the qualities of their products, thereby leading to benefits by increasing the demand for higher quality products. The increase in the competitive environment that should follow from the establishment of a customs union should reduce levels of x-inefficiency (i.e. overmanning, excessive inventories and other types of wasteful use of resources) and thereby boost the effectiveness of the use of capital and labour in production processes.

The emergence of these benefits depends on the existence of a competition policy that is able to stop firms from acquiring control over competing firms to prevent an increase in the competitive environment. However, firms may need to acquire competing firms or to forge alliances and joint ventures to gain access to new markets and to rationalise production to reap economies of scale. Clearly, a competition policy for regional integration blocs that assesses the benefits of concentration versus competition may be needed to create the conditions that will allow competition to increase and also for firms to have the ability to reap economies of scale and have effective access to new markets in the bloc. (See Case 8.1 for an example of the operation of the competition policy of the EU.)

The removal of trade barriers should lead to the integration of fragmented markets and thereby create a larger market for products. If transport costs are low, it becomes possible to serve the integrated market from existing or new plant allowing firms to reap internal economies of scale. The size of the benefits from economies of scale depends on the nature of the technical relationship between cost and output, in particular, the rate at which costs fall as output is increased and by the level of output at which average costs are minimised, that is, minimum efficiency scale (MES). Therefore, the magnitude of the benefits from internal economies of scale is determined by the degree of the integration of fragmented markets, the significance of transport costs and the technical relationship between cost and output. Consequently, customs unions will not necessarily lead to economies of scale benefits if most firms are operating at, or close to, MES and where transport costs are high. These factors are illustrated in Figure 8.1.

The integration of fragmented markets may also lead to geographical concentrations that generate external economies of scale. External economies of scale arise when firms cluster in a specific geographical area and form networks that result in reduced costs in conducting their business. These external economies of scale arise from such factors as the development of a pool of skilled labour, the creation of a network of suppliers and support services etc. Silicon Valley in California is the best-known example of a cluster. However, other examples exist: the City of London for international capital and money markets, Milan for high fashion and networks of SMEs that have formed clusters that confer international competitiveness (Porter, 1990). The establishment of customs unions and common markets may allow the market to become

Figure 8.1 Minimum efficiency scale and trade

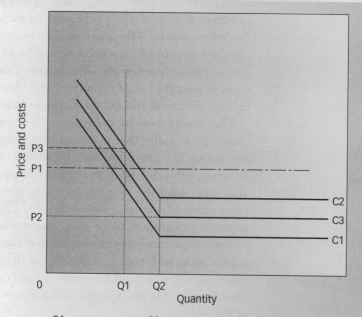

C1 = average cost without transport costs or tariff
C2 = average cost with transport costs plus tariff
C3 = average costs with transport costs and without tariff
Q1 = level of output in country X before removal of tariff
Q2 = minimum efficiency scale (MES)
P1 = price of good in country Y before removal of tariff
P2 = price of good in country Y after removal of tariff
P3 = price of good from country X with tariff and transport costs

Prior to removal of tariff, country X cannot supply country Y because price in country Y (P1) is lower than price of supplying from country X with tariff and transport cost, i.e. P3.

When the tariff is removed, country X is able to supply country Y and therefore move down, C3 reaping economies of scale. When the level of output reaches the MES at Q2, price in country Y could fall if the market is competitive (where P=AC) to P2. The price in country X would fall because the increased output to supply the market of country Y reduces the average cost of producing output for sale in both domestic and foreign markets. However, if transport costs lead to an average cost curve that lies above C3 the removal of the tariff would not stimulate supply to country Y and price would not fall. The size of the benefits from the removal of the tariff depends on the level of transport costs and the output level, that is MES compared to the pre-tariff level of output.

large enough to enable the development of existing clusters or for the emergence of new clusters. This issue is examined in more detail in Chapter 6.

The dynamic effects arising from the combination of a more competitive environment and the potential to reap economies of scale

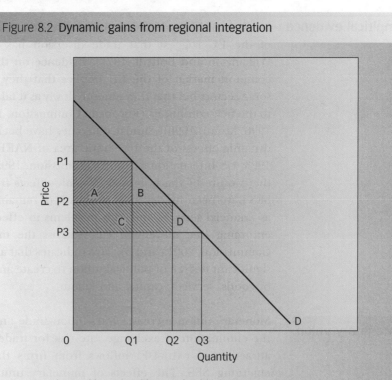

Figure 8.2 Dynamic gains from regional integration

D = demand in regional integration bloc
P1: Q1 = price and quantity before dynamic effects from customs union
P2: Q2 = price and quantity after increase in competition and reduction
         in x-inefficiency
P3: Q3 = price and quantity after economies of scale

A = gain to consumer from reduction in price due to increased competition
    and reduced x-inefficiency (from producer to consumer)
B = net gain to society from increase in quantity due to price decline to P2
C = gain to consumer from reduction in price due to economies of scale
    (from producer to consumer)
D = net gain to society from increase in quantity due to price decline to P3

Increase in efficiency flowing from these dynamic effects will boost growth of
incomes and thereby shift the demand curve to the right leading to higher gains to
society, as quantity bought would increase, thereby increasing net gains to
consumers.

leads to falling prices, higher output, more efficient production and
thereby higher growth. These effects bring benefits to consumers (see
Figure 8.2) and attract DFI flows to take advantage of new market
opportunities and expanding economies. Consequently, even if a customs
union or common market leads to trade diversion the dynamic effects
may mean it is still worthwhile engaging in regional integration.
Nevertheless, such integration may be harmful to the process of
multilateral trade liberalisation and could be classified as a second best
alternative to extending trade liberalisation to all trading partners.

Empirical evidence

Studies on the trade creation and diversion effects of the customs union of the EU suggest that trade diversion has been low (Mayes, 1978; Williamson and Bottrill, 1971). Evidence on the dynamic effects of the common market of the EU implies that they have been significant in some sectors but that they emerge slowly as it takes time for firms to adjust to the new conditions (European Commission, 1996; European Economy, 1996; Monti, 1996). Similar outcomes have been found in studies on the dynamic effects of the free trade area of NAFTA (Hufbauer and Schott, 1993; US International Trade Commission, 1995). In the case of the EU, the capture of the potential dynamic effects from the move towards an SES have been hindered by problems of remaining NTBs in sectors such as financial services and with problems in effectively implementing and enforcing free movement rules across the member states (European Commission, 2001a and b). This indicates that an SES probably requires a significant degree of political union to create and enforce free movement of goods, services, capital and labour.

Monetary union

Monetary union increases intra-union trade and DFI inflows because of the elimination of exchange rate risk for trade within the bloc and the attraction of extra-DFI inflows from firms that wish to locate in an emerging SES. The effects of monetary unions on the international monetary system and for exchange rate risk and monetary and financial conditions are examined in Chapter 5. In this section, the major implications for firms of European monetary union are considered. Analysis and discussion on the economic effects of European monetary union is available in (De Grauwe, 1997; Emerson et al., 1992; Gros and Thygesen, 2000).

The effects of the monetary union of the EU can be decomposed into direct and indirect effects (McDonald, 1997). The direct effects are the costs of changeover from national currencies to the euro and the transaction costs benefits of the single currency. The indirect effects are the changes to the macroeconomic and competitive environments. These factors are illustrated in Figure 8.3.

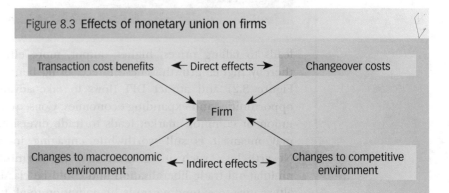

Figure 8.3 Effects of monetary union on firms

Direct effects Transaction cost benefits

- Elimination of currency conversion costs for intra-union trade.
- Elimination of hedging costs for intra-union trade.
- Reduced information-gathering costs arising from increased price transparency.
- Reduced treasury and financial control costs for intra-union transactions because of the use of a single currency.

Transaction costs benefits arise for all firms that engage in trade or financial transactions with other countries within the monetary union. Those firms with large trade in currencies and those with large-scale treasury and financial mangement systems connected to intra-union transactions will benefit most from the direct benefits of monetary union. However, large multinational corporations tend to have developed low costs means to cope with the problems of different and fluctuating currencies. Therefore, the most signficant gains are likely to be available for small and medium sized firms that engage in high levels of intra-union trade.

Changeover costs

- Alteration of contracts to denominate in euro.
- Alteration of money-handling systems.
- Alteration of recording systems – accounting, sales, tax, wages and payments systems.
- Staff training to implement changes.
- Dissemination of information to suppliers and buyers.

Changeover costs are likely to be large because they require firms to adjust their accounting, money-handling and pricing systems. This involves large expenditures to alter accounting and financial systems and to train staff and inform customers. Firms with large and complex money-handling systems and extensive intra-union trade and financial transactions will have significant costs. Those firms with limited money-handling systems and with no or very limited intra-union simple transactions will face minor costs. Therefore, banks, retailers and large multinationals will have significant changeover costs compared to most small and medium sized firms. Once changeover costs have been incurred, firms will reap the transaction costs benefits listed in following sections for as long as they trade within the monetary union. This means that eventually the changeover costs will be recovered and net benefits will be gained by firms from the direct effects of monetary union. However, all firms will incur changeover costs but not all firms will trade outside of their domestic economy. These firms will experience no net gain from the direct effects of monetary union.

Indirect effects Macroeconomic environment

- More stable prices and lower real interest rates.
- Changes to the growth/inflation path of members of the union.
- No exchange rate changes for intra-EU trade.
- New exchange rate regime for extra-EU trade.

Low and stable inflation delivers stable prices that do not distort the allocation of resources and lower real rates of interest because the risk premium to compensate for unexpected changes to inflation is low. Reductions in the real rate of interest contribute to a lower cost of capital. These benefits are available for firms in countries that have a poor potential to control inflation. They only arise if the central bank of the monetary union delivers conditions that are conducive to low and stable inflation. If the central bank delivers a worse inflation record than the best performing countries in the pre-union system, firms located in countries that had a good inflation performance will suffer from less stable prices and higher cost of capital. Consequently, the likelihood of reaping these benefits depends on the effectiveness of the anti-inflationary policy of the central bank and whether the countries in which firms are located had a good inflation record. The benefits of low and stable inflation only arise for firms that are located in countries that are unable to deliver a creditable anti-inflationary policy.

The growth path of an economy is determined in the long term by the growth of stocks of employed capital and labour, the level of technical change and institutional changes that influence productivity growth. However, the employment of capital and labour and the incentive to invest in technical change is affected by the ability to sell output. This in turn is influenced by the growth in aggregate demand, which can be altered by the monetary and fiscal policy stance of the monetary union. To control inflation, monetary policy has to be set such that aggregate demand does not expand beyond the ability of the economy to supply output without experiencing inflation. Therefore, there is a link between growth and inflation. Monetary policy has to tread the narrow path between controlling inflation while at the same time allowing aggregate demand to grow sufficiently to employ available capital and labour and to induce investment to improve productivity. Fiscal policy and 'supply-side' policies can contribute to the ability of economies to maximise growth, but the key policy is monetary policy, which seeks to restrain inflation.

Monetary union requires a common monetary policy for the union. Problems can emerge if the common monetary policy is suitable for the growth/inflation path of some countries but not for others. This problem has emerged in Euroland as monetary policy is determined largely by the need to keep the growth/inflation path in balance in the large economies of the union. Problems have arisen because Germany, the largest economy in Euroland, had a low growth to inflation path compared to smaller economies such as Ireland and Spain. However, monetary policy is dominated by the need to maintain overall balance between growth and inflation for the Union, which, is the major determinant of Euroland's monetary policy. Consequently, fiscal policy and 'supply-side' policies have to be used by countries experiencing 'inappropriate' monetary policy to enable them to maximise their growth/inflation path.

In Euroland, fiscal policy changes are restricted by a growth and stability pack, therefore, the main burden falls on 'supply-side' policies to make labour and capital markets more efficient to compensate for the 'inappropriate' monetary policy. This problem becomes serious if the 'one size fits all' monetary policy becomes acutely out of balance due to differences in economic conditions among the members of the union. Problems with 'one size fits all' monetary policy are potentially the most serious effects of European monetary union. This problem may affect firms located in countries with the potential to generate high non-inflationary growth because they may find that their ability to expand operations is constrained by monetary policy measures required to keep the growth/inflation path in balance in members with a lower growth to inflation path. This issue is also examined in Chapter 5.

Changes to the exchange rate regime affect all firms located in the monetary union that engage in intra- and extra-union trade. The elimination of exchange rate risk for intra-union transactions reduces costs and uncertainty and stimulates greater transactions between the members of the union. The effects of the new extra-union exchange rate regimes on firms depend on how much extra-union transaction they engage in and the stability of the exchange rate of the euro. If the euro is unstable, the fluctuating value of the currency will lead to significant exchange rate risk for extra-union transactions.

The macroeconomic effects of European monetary union depend on the efficacy of the anti-inflationary policy of the central bank, the effect of the common monetary policy on growth/inflation paths and the stability of the euro. The decision for firms on location either in or outside Euroland depends on the assessment of the effectiveness of the monetary policy of the central bank, the stability of the euro and the size of extra-union transactions. Location within Euroland will be attractive for firms planning substantial transactions within Euroland because they will face no exchange rate risk for these transactions. Firms that wish to engage on a more global basis could face significant exchange rate risk if the euro is not stable. However, if the euro is not stable it will be volatile against the US dollar. In these circumstances, firms that engage in extensive global transactions will face exchange rate uncertainty whether they are located inside or outside Euroland. Thus, European monetary union may encourage more emphasis on transactions within Euroland and thereby induce DFI flows to develop operations with this bloc. This will encourage a focus on regional bloc rather than global transactions, especially for products that are price sensitive. If Euroland does not provide a low and stable inflationary environment, this will also discourage DFI flows into

Euroland that are heavily orientated towards global transactions. If the common monetary policy results in a low growth to inflation path, Euroland could become less attractive as a destination for extra-DFI flows because other parts of the world may offer a greater potential for fast growth.

Competitive environment

- Increase in penetration of domestic markets by companies located in other member states.
- Increase in prospects for entering or expanding in the markets of other member states.
- Growth of relocation – possible development of geographical concentration.

The elimination of exchange rate risk and currency conversion costs, increased price transparency and increased DFI inflows to develop the markets of Euroland will stimulate competition. This will encourage relocation to take advantage of economies of scale and could stimulate geographical concentration to permit the reaping of agglomeration benefits (see Chapter 6). The increase in the competitive environment is also likely to stimulate greater competition in the qualities of products as well as in prices. This is likely to lead to concentration to enable economies of scale to be reaped and to develop new market opportunities (see Case 8.2). The key factors arising from the change in the competitive environment are illustrated in Figure 8.4.

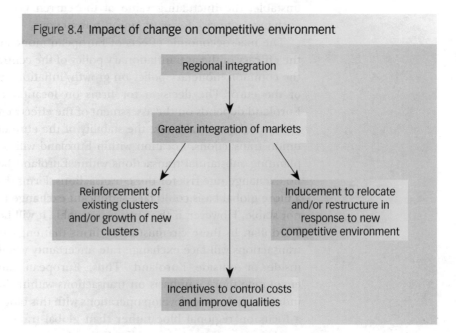

Figure 8.4 Impact of change on competitive environment

Regional integration

Greater integration of markets

Reinforcement of existing clusters and/or growth of new clusters

Inducement to relocate and/or restructure in response to new competitive environment

Incentives to control costs and improve qualities

Single economic space

An SES is an area that permits free movement of goods, services, capital and labour that is governed by a set of common or harmonised laws and policies. The existence of an SES does not mean that some markets within the area are not fragmented into specific geographic areas. Fragmentation of markets in a SES arise from economic, social and cultural differences that require different products and or marketing approaches for the various economic, social and cultural groupings within the SES. Many of these cultural groupings are geographically concentrated, therefore, fragmentation of markets can have a distinctive spatial character. These issues are examined in Chapters 6 and 11.

Most countries are SESs in the sense that they have frameworks that permit effective free movement of goods, services, capital and labour to take place. Regional integration blocs such as the EU are well advanced in the creation of an SES among its members. This implies that trade between the member states of the EU is becoming comparable to trade within a country and that trade between the SES of the EU and other countries is similar to trade between two countries. Regional integration blocs such as Mercosur, that are seeking to develop a common market, may also develop a type of an SES, thereby creating another large economic system similar to the EU. Regional integration blocs with lower level objectives, such as NAFTA or FTAA may also evolve into some type of an SES if they develop legal, taxation and policy frameworks to govern some aspects of intra-bloc trade. Development of SESs by regional integration blocs holds the prospects of a trading world dominated by a small number of SESs (EU, USA [NAFTA – APEC] and Mercosur).

The development of such a system of large SESs could lead to a reduction in the complexity caused by different political, economic and legal frameworks. This type of outcome from regional integration is prominent in the works of the gurus of the globalisation thesis (Giddens, 1999; Levitt, 1983; Ohmae, 1995). In the view of these gurus, the main problems of international business will be to overcome cultural obstacles that limited the growth and development of internationalisation. However, the operation of the international monetary system means that significant differences exist between SESs because of floating exchange rate regimes and currency and debt crises (see Chapter 5). Moreover, consideration of real world SESs highlights the very different characteristics that exist both between and within SESs. Consequently, the evolution of regional integration blocs into SESs will not necessarily lead to a less complex political–economic environment in which international business activities take place.

Existing SESs provide three main frameworks that effect the operations of markets:

1 Legal and taxation frameworks that create, develop and maintain the legal conditions that permit free movement to exist and that tax economic activities.

2 Macroeconomic policy frameworks that seek to secure a stable economic environment.

3 Political systems that introduce, implement, enforce and modify laws and policies that govern economic activities.

Legal and taxation systems

Legal barriers to free movement exist in some nation-states that would be regarded as SESs. For example, different laws govern the production and sale of goods and services in the states of the USA. State laws on technical regulations and environmental standards also vary between the states in the USA. Therefore, firms that wish to trade across state frontiers have to conform to the laws in the different states. Taxation systems are also different across the states of the USA. Federal laws in the USA are concerned with ensuring that there are no prohibitions or limitations applied to non-state suppliers simply because firms are not based in the state. Federal laws also ensure that markets (for inter-state trade) are not distorted by anti-competitive practices by companies. However, there are no federal laws on public procurement contracts issued by state agencies, thus states are free to limit their public procurement contracts to state-based companies. Furthermore, there are no federal laws that restrict the use of government aid by states which wish to subsidise the operations of companies located within their area of jurisdiction.

The EU uses a very different approach from the USA to remove barriers to free movement arising from such factors as different in taxation systems, technical regulations, public procurement and state aid policies. Differences in taxation treatment on the sale of goods and services and on income from savings are considered a serious distortion of free movement. Consequently, attempts are made to harmonise the differences in taxation on the sale of goods, services and savings. Selective harmonisation of technical regulations and environmental standards ensures a common framework exists for most aspects of environmental rules, health and public safety conditions and to ensure technical compatibility. In all other areas concerned with technical regulations and environmental standards, the member states accept the rules that prevail in the other member states by using the principle of mutual recognition. EU laws governing public procurement and government aid prohibit the use of preferential treatment of domestic firms by national governments.

The differences between the USA and the EU become more evident when regulatory frameworks concerned with the allocation of resources are considered. Some countries in the EU adopt an approach that tends towards a market-based approach while others take a more social market approach. The market-based approach focuses on limited interference by the state in the working of the market process. This approach has a strong emphasis on anti-trust policies to limit the ability of firms to acquire monopoly power and to use anti-competitive practices. Efficiency considerations are normally separated from equity issues. The market-based approach centres on creating an efficient economy as the best method of attaining high living standards. The social market approach regards the promotion of competitive markets as important, but links equity issues to efficiency concerns. Thus, policies to promote social cohesion and to help disadvantaged groups are seen as an important function of governments to help the economy deliver high living standards. The USA tends to a more market-based approach to regulating the market process than, for example, Germany or France. The UK occupies a position between that of most continental European countries and the USA.

The EU has developed a series of laws on employment and working conditions, for example, on working time, rights to consultation and equal opportunities that have created EU-wide minimum standards in this area. EU laws and policies on environmental and regional development issues also create a degree of uniformity across the member states in these areas. However, in many areas of regulation and policy the member states have rights to adopt higher standards and to adopt policies that complement and add to EU laws and policies. Thus, the EU does not have uniform regulatory and policy frameworks in these areas. In the USA, there are also differences across the states in these laws and policies, but in general, the federal government adopts a more market-based approach than does the EU. However, in the area of equal opportunities federal laws and policies are stronger than those that have emerged in the EU. The states within the USA tend to take a more market-based approach than do the member states of the EU in matters connected to social and economic regulation. These examples demonstrate that the approach to regulation of the market process varies considerably among and between existing SESs.

Macroeconomic policy frameworks

A remarkably standard condition in all existing single market systems is that they are also economic and monetary unions. Macroeconomic policies affect the operation of markets because monetary, fiscal and exchange rate policies determine the inflation and growth environment in which companies operate. All existing single market systems have common monetary and exchange rate policies. Fiscal policies are normally harmonised such that the central or federal governments have a strong influence on fiscal policy. However, the federal government of the USA has no power over the taxation and expenditure and borrowing decisions of the states. In contrast, in Euroland the growth and stability pack imposes a degree of control over the fiscal policies of the members of European Monetary Union.

Political frameworks

The EU has a very complex political system to make laws and policies and relies to a large extent on the governments in member states to implement, monitor and enforce these laws and policies (Nugent, 1999). This can lead to problems with different outcomes on firms due

Exhibit 8.2 Comparison of SESs in the EU and the USA

	EU	Implications for companies	USA	Implications for companies
Legal frameworks	1 Free movement of goods and services, but some limitations on the movement of some services, capital and labour 2 Mutual recognition of technical regulations with selective harmonisation 3 Member states use of state aids monitored and can be amended by commission 4 Most public procurement contracts are open to EU-wide competition, but not strategic defence equipment	1 Few limitations that restrict ability to supply EU markets from any location in the EU. However, some limitations on the movement of labour and some types of capital movements e.g. pension funds 2 Need to comply with EU technical regulations even if no EU trade 3 State aids can be modified by commission 4 Most large public procurement contracts open to EU-wide competition 5 Limited access to defence procurement contracts	1 Free movement of goods, services, capital and labour 2 Technical regulations vary across the states 3 States are free to use state aids without federal interference 4 States may restrict state procurement contracts to companies based in the state 5 Federal procurement contracts (including defence equipment) open to US-wide competition	1 No limitations on ability to supply US market from any location in the USA 2 Need to conform to the technical regulations that prevail in the states. Decisions have to made about which standard to adopt for major products e.g. emissions from cars 3 State aids free from federal government modification 4 State procurement contracts can be restricted to state-based companies 5 All federal procurement contracts open to US-based companies
Tax frameworks	1 Attempts to harmonise taxation of sales and savings 2 Systems to prevent taxation on sales from distorting trade	1 Prospects of significant changes to taxation systems across the member states 2 Companies must have systems to record EU exports and imports for tax purposes 3 No distortion of intra-EU trade because of tax differences – except for problem of personal cross-frontier shopping	1 States free to set taxes on sales and income and saving 2 No systems to prevent differences in sales taxes distorting trade	1 No prospect of changes to harmonise taxation systems across the states 2 No need to have systems to record intra-state trade for taxation purposes 3 Distortion of intra-state possible because of differences in state taxes and problem of personal cross-frontier shopping
Economic and social policies frameworks	1 EU economic and social policies that enhance the development of a social market approach in the member states 2 Member states permitted to have stronger social market-based policies than the minimum standards specified by the EU	1 Significant differences in the extent of the use of the social market approach across the member states 2 Employment and working conditions in the member states are significantly affected by EU laws and policies e.g. equal opportunities, working time and worker participation in the management process	1 States permitted to adopt their own approach to economic and social policies – a tendency for a market-based approach 2 Minimum federal standards in some areas that affect employment and working conditions	1 A variety of economic and social policies that affect employment and working conditions across the states 2 A limited influence by federal laws and policies that affect employment and working conditions e.g. minimum wage and equal opportunities

Exhibit 8.2 continued

	EU	Implications for companies	USA	Implications for companies
Macroeconomic policy frameworks	1 Single monetary policy and currency for members of European monetary union 2 Some controls on fiscal policy for members of European Monetary Union	1 For companies located in members of Monetary Union the general economic environment (inflation and growth) heavily influenced by common monetary and exchange rate policies 2 Significant differences in tax liability and rates because of fiscal policies of the member states 3 For companies located in those member states who are not members of monetary union the possibility of exchange rate fluctuations against the euro and dollar.	1 Single monetary policy and currency for all states 2 No controls on the fiscal policies of the governments of the states	1 All companies face the same general economic environment and exchange rate of the dollar 2 Differences in tax liability and growth rates arising from the fiscal policies of the states
Political frameworks	1 The implementation, monitoring and enforcing of EU laws and policies largely depends on the governments of the member states 2 The EU does not have its own agencies to enforce EU laws and policies 3 Lack of a well-defined EU-based political system to make and modify EU laws and policies	1 Companies face different implementation of EU laws and policies depending on the member state in which they are located 2 Companies face different monitoring and enforcement procedures for EU laws and policies and the effectiveness of these procedures varies across the member states 3 Companies seeking to influence the political system face a complex interrelationship between EU and national institutions	1 Monitoring and enforcing federal laws and policies are largely done by federal agencies 2 Well-defined political system constrained by a constitution to make and modify federal and state laws and policies	1 Companies face well-defined and uniform procedures governing the implementation, monitoring and enforcement of federal and state laws and policies 2 Companies seeking to influence the political system face a well-defined division of competencies between state and federal government. Moreover, political parties and other political institutions are well developed at both state and federal level

to the way that laws and policies are implemented, monitored and enforced in the member states (McDonald, 2000). In contrast, in the USA, there is a well-defined governmental system backed by federal political parties and frameworks to make, modify, implement and enforce federal laws and policies. Clearly, the political frameworks of the USA are very different from those of the EU. Consequently, although the EU is an SES with similarities to the USA it is governed by a very different system than that of the USA. Moreover, the SESs of the EU and the USA have differences within the states that compose the SESs, which affect the strategies and operations of firms located in these SESs. The major differences with indications of the main implications for firms are outlined in Exhibit 8.2.

Summary

This chapter has outlined the development of regional integration blocs in the post-World War II period. Clearly, the most significant regional integration bloc has been the EU, which has been enlarged to embrace nearly every west European country. In the near future, the EU could be extended to include many of the countries of central and eastern Europe. Moreover, with its many preferential trading agreements the EU has developed extensive economic relationships with many developing countries, with all of the countries of the Mediterranean basin and most of the countries of central and eastern Europe. The EU has developed a sophisticated institutional structure and has made considerable progress towards developing an SES. It has become, together with the USA and Japan, the heart of the world economy. Indeed, in terms of economic size, and volume of trade and investment it is considerably more important than Japan and is with the USA at the centre of international trade and financial flows. The introduction of the euro and the prospect of a larger EU are likely to lead to its having more influence in the world economy.

The EU is not the only regional integration bloc. NAFTA and Mercosur have made considerable progress in establishing free trade areas in North America and Mexico and in Latin America. Plans are also being made to establish free trade areas that encompass all the Americas and among many Asian countries. A Pacific free trade area is also planned by APEC countries. Many developing countries are also seeking to establish free trade areas. However, none of these regional integration blocs has the same objectives as the EU because they are seeking only to establish free trade areas or customs unions, whereas the EU is setting about to establish and develop an SES. NAFTA and Mercosur have developed some aspects of an SES because they have included arrangements for harmonising rules on environmental and labour issues connected to trade. Developments such as these could lead to the emergence of SESs among regional integration blocs. However, this process does not mean that the international business environment will become less complex because SESs tend to vary both between the members of the SES and across these systems.

The implications for multilateral trade liberalisation of the growth of regional integration blocs are not clear. It is possible that regional integration blocs could provide a means of spreading trade liberalisation across all the members of the WTO if the liberalisation programmes pioneered in blocs are extended to include all trading partners. However, if this does not happen regional trading blocs could lead to a world trading system in which the bulk of trade and investment operations occur within the blocs. In such a world, the major international business activities between the blocs could be DFI to allow multinationals access to the large markets of the blocs.

Undoubtedly, the development of regional integration blocs will exert considerable influence on the evolution of international business activities. It is likely that they will restrict the growth of global business operations because of the tendency for large blocs to generate centres of economic activity based on large markets and that generate economies of scale. If regional trade blocs extend trade liberalisation to non-members this tendency will be reduced, but even in these circumstances, large blocs will conduct the bulk of their economic activity within their own economy due to the advantages of economies of scale from supplying their own large markets. The global extent of firms in this kind of world will be in those industries that require global markets to reap economies of scale in cases where trade barriers are removed. The other global aspect of firms in this world reach will be DFI to gain access to the markets and technological advantages that are available in the large blocs.

Review questions

1 Outline the static and dynamic effects of a customs union and explain why regional integration blocs composed of small economies are unlikely to be economically beneficial.

2 Why are regional integration blocs likely to hamper the development of global supply systems?

3 Outline the main effects of European Monetary Union for firms and explain why the macroeconomic effects are likely to be most important.

4 Explain what an SES is and assess if the development of SESs by large regional integration blocs will reduce the complexity of the international business environment.

5 Why is it likely that the main international business activity between large regional integration blocs will be DFI flows?

Bibliography

Bagwell, K. and Staiger, R. (1998) 'Will preferential agreements undermine the multilateral trading system', *Economic Journal*, 108, pp. 1162–82.

Balassa, B. (1961) *The Theory of Economic Integration*, London, Allen and Unwin.

Bhagwati, J. (1993) 'Regionalism and multilateralism: an overview' in J. De Melo and A. Panagariya (eds) *New Dimensions in Regional Integration*, Cambridge, Cambridge University Press.

Bhagwati, J. (1991) *The World Trading System at Risk*, New York, Princeton University Press.

De Grauwe, P. (1997) *The Economics of Monetary Integration*, Oxford, Oxford University Press.

Either, W. (1998) 'The new regionalism', *Economic Journal*, 108, pp. 1149–61.

El-Agraa, M. (2000) *The European Union: Economics and Policies*, London, Financial Times Prentice Hall.

El-Agraa, M. (1997) *Economic Integration Worldwide*, London, Macmillan.

Emerson, M., Gros, D., Italianer, A., Pisani-Ferry, J. and Reichenbach, H. (1992) *One Market, One Money*, Oxford, Oxford University Press.

European Commission (2001a) *The Regulation of European Securities Markets: The Lamfalussy Report*, Brussels, European Commission.

European Commission (2001b) *2001 Review of the Internal Market*, Com (2001) 198 final, Brussels, European Commission.

European Commission (1996) *The Single Market Review, 38 Reports*, London, European Commission/Kogan Page.

European Economy (1996) 'Economic evaluation of the internal market, reports and studies no. 4', Luxembourg, Office for Official Publications of the EC.

Frankel, J. (1997) *Regional Trading Blocs in the World Economic System*, Washington, DC, Institute of International Economics.

Giddens, A. (1999) *Runaway World: How Globalization is Reshaping our Lives*, New York, Routledge.

Gros, D. and Thygesen, N. (2000) *European Monetary Integration*, London, Addison-Wesley Longman.

Hufbauer, C. and Schott, J. (1994) *Western Hemisphere Economic Integration*, Washington, DC, Institute of International Economics.

Hufbauer, C. and Schott, J. (1993) *NAFTA: An Assessment*, Washington, DC, Institute of International Economics.

Levitt, T. (1983) 'The globalization of markets', *Harvard Business Review*, 61, pp. 92–102.

Lipsey, R. (1970) *The Theory of Customs Unions: General Equilibrium Analysis*, London, Weidenfeld and Nicolson.

Mayes, D. (1978) 'The effects of economic integration on trade', *Journal of Common Market Studies*, 17, pp. 1–25.

McDonald, F. (2000) 'The European Union and employment relationships', *European Business Review*, 12, 4, pp. 208–15.

McDonald, F. (1997) 'European Monetary Union: some implications for companies', *Journal of General Management*, 23, 2, pp. 47–64.

McDonald, F. and Dearden, S. (1999) *European Economic Integration*, London, Addison-Wesley Longman.

Monti, M. (1996) *The Single Market and Tomorrow's Europe*, London, European Commission/Kogan Page.

Nugent, N. (1999) *The Government and Politics of the European Community*, London, Macmillan.

Ohmae, K. (1995) *The End of the Nation State: The Rise of Regional Economies*, New York, Harper Business.

Ohmae, K. (1990) *The Borderless World*, New York, Harper Business.

Porter, M. (1990) *The Competitive Advantage of Nations*, London, Macmillan.

Schott, J. (2001) *Prospects for Free Trade in the Americas*, Washington, DC, Institute of International Economics.

Scollay, R. and Gilbert, J. (2001) *Trading Arrangements in Asia Pacific*, Washington, DC, Institute of International Economics.

Smith, A. and Venables, A. (1988) *The Costs of Non-Europe: An Assessment Based on a Formal Model of Imperfect Competition and Economies of Scale*, research on the costs of non-Europe, Basic Findings, Vol. 2, Luxembourg, Office for Official Publications of the EC.

US International Trade Commission (1995) 'NAFTA update: early signs confirm benefits', *Industry Trade and Technology Review*, 2942, pp. 41–51.

Viner, J. (1950) *The Customs Union Issue*, New York, Carnegie Endowment for International Peace.

Williamson, J. and Bottrill, A. (1971) 'The impact of customs unions on trade in manufactures', *Oxford Economic Papers*, 23, pp. 323–51.

Useful websites

Sites of major regional integration blocs
www.europa.eu.int
  The site of the institutions of the EU
www.nafta-sec-alena.org
www.sice.oas.org/trade/nafta/naftatce.asp
  The sites for NAFTA
www.mercosur.org
  The site of Mercosur. Many of the links from this site are in Spanish
www.apec.org
  The site of APEC

Sites with reports and papers on regional integration blocs
www.iie.com
  Site of the Institute of International Economics that provides a large number of papers on regional integration

Case 8.1 European competition policy: the case of the GE–Honeywell merger

The EU has powers under the various treaties that established the EU to take action to prevent anti-competitive behaviour by firms. This has led to the development of a competition policy that is operated by the European Commission and allows the Commission to levy fines and to order changes in the behaviour of firms considered to be acting in an anti-competitive manner. Since 1990, under the provisions of the Merger Control Regulation the European Commission has the power to investigate large-scale acquisitions, mergers and strategic alliances. The power of the European Commission to take action against anti-competitive behaviour is not limited to European firms. Any firm that has significant sales, purchases or production within the frontiers of the EU is subject to the competition policy of the EU. This means that any large-scale merger or acquisition between US firms can be subject to the scrutiny of the European Commission because such US firms are likely to have considerable European operations. The competition policy provisions allow the EU to blocked consolidations that are deemed to be anti-competitive.

The proposed $40 billion takeover of Honeywell by GE became the most famous case of the power of the European Commission to block a takeover involving two non-European firms. The American regulators approved the deal in May 2001. Normally, when the US regulatory authorities approve a deal the European Commission does not oppose the proposed consolidation. However, in June 2000 the European Commission blocked the merger of MCI Worldcom with Sprint although the US regulator had approved this deal. The GE takeover of Honeywell had been referred for investigation by the European Commission in February 2001 and statement of concerns about the takeover was issued in May 2001. After the three week period allowed to respond to the report, the European Commissioner responsible for competition policy, Mario Monti, declared that he was not satisfied with the response of GE to his objections to the takeover.

At the heart of the objections of the European Commission was the link between aircraft engine manufacture by GE and avionics provision by Honeywell. The European Commission argued that it was possible that GE–Honeywell could put a package of engines and avionics together that would put engine-only manufactures (including the European joint venture between Rolls Royce and BMW) at a disadvantage. There was also concern that GE Capital (a subsidiary of GE) that provides aircraft-leasing services could be used to induce the purchase of GE–Honeywell engines and avionics packages in the large market for aircraft for leasing. Such a development would have serious implications for European engine and avionics producers. However, the threat was only a potential one and the European Commission has powers under Article 86 of the Treaty of Rome to prevent such abuse of market power. This potential anti-competitive act was deemed serious enough to require GE to provide a plan to satisfy the European Commission that such an outcome could not occur. GE responded by a promise to sell some of its avionics subsidiaries and to build 'Chinese walls' between GE Capital and GE–Honeywell. However, the European Commission decided that these measures were not sufficient and blocked the takeover.

This case illustrates the power of the EU to influence competition issues even among non-European firms and clearly demonstrates the power over the competitive environment that can develop in a large regional integration bloc that creates a strong institutional system to back up its programmes to integrate markets.

Economist (2001) 'GE/Honeywell: turbulence', 12 May, website of the European Commission – www.europa.eu.int and the website of GE – www.ge.com

Case 8.2 Integration of European bourses

In 2000, there were 30 stock exchanges or bourses in Europe. This means that they are small compared to large markets such as the New York Stock Exchange (NYSE) or NASDAQ (the US market for high tech stock). However, a large increase in initial public offers (IPOs) from privatisation programmes led to an increase in equity markets in Europe. The development of mutual funds (increased from 35% of the total in 1995 to 45% by 2000) and the development of pension funds also stimulated the growth of European equity markets. This growth has encouraged the search for deeper and wider markets to reduce spreads on buying and selling equity and to provide a wide range of added-value services, particularly when raising new equities. The national nature of bourses made it difficult to develop deep and wide markets, consequently European bourses tend to have larger spreads and fewer services than US markets.

The London Stock Exchange (LSE) is the largest European bourse. This is because, historically, the UK made more use of equity to fund investment compared to most European countries. The other European bourses are considerably smaller than the LSE.

Bourse	No. of companies listed	Turnover $ (trillion)
LSE	2,921	4.5
Euronex (Amsterdam, Brussels, Paris)	1,437	1.0
Deutsche Börse	988	2.0
Swiss Exchange	415	0.7
Milan Exchange	1,102	1.0
Data for 2000		

The benefits of large markets can be seen in the NYSE or the NASDAQ where most of the large multinational corporations issue equity. They do this because of the low commission costs of issuing equity in the USA compared to European bourses. The trade in equities also has low spreads compared to European bourses because of the depth of the US equity markets. This makes the US stock exchanges attractive compared to European bourses.

The main reasons for the fragmentation of European bourses has been exchange rate risk because of the denomination of prices in different currencies and the lack of common regulations governing equity markets and for financial reporting, transparency and takeover rules. However, European Monetary Union has reduced the exchange rate risk because equities are increasingly denominated in euro. Moreover, the EU has been developing harmonised rules for the regulation of securities markets and a report in 2001 (the Lamfalussy Report) proposed a plan to speed up the process of harmonisation and to devise regulatory systems that will permit the integration of European bourses. A directive on harmonised financial reporting has been agreed and is being implemented and a directive on takeover rules was proposed but it did not obtain approval from the European Parliament.

In response to these changes, several attempts have been made to consolidate European bourses. The bourses of Amsterdam, Brussels and Paris have formed a strategic alliance (Euronex) to become the third largest bourse in Europe in terms of turnover. The LSE and Deutsche Börse in Frankfurt sought to establish a merger but this fell through due to disputes about regulation, the use of the euro as the currency to denominate equities and over settlement and payments systems. Indeed, the latter problem appears to be one of the major stumbling blocks to consolidation of European bourses. Linking trading platforms in different countries with a common clearing and settlement system is one of the major obstacles to consolidation. Problems exist over the IT systems that should be used which will work. This problem is compounded by a lack of a common regulatory framework or even agreement as to the chief characteristics that such as framework should possess. This debate is over the degree to which bourses should self-regulate their operations and whether there should be one European regulatory or national regulators that cooperate with each other. Differences in financial reporting requirements, transparency rules and taxation systems also remain. Agreeing rules for takeovers is also a matter of heated debate. Although the EU has been working on the institutional and legal obstacles to integrating bourses for over ten years, significant problems are still limiting the consolidation of European bourses so that they can provide wide and deep markets that could rival the US exchanges. However, the forces for change in European bourses are large and determined attempts are being made to overcome the legal and regulatory obstacles. In this area, the EU is providing the forum to achieve regional integration of European bourses.

The benefits of economies of scale and scope that are possible from truly global exchanges based on linking trading platforms are pushing for trans-Atlantic cooperation with NASDAQ planning to link with the LSE and the Deutsche Börse to trade high tech equities. NYSE and the Tokyo Stock Exchange have already formed an alliance with Euronex, called GEM, to create a common clearing and settlement system. The major obstacles to these global exchanges are the problems of regulation and rules on financial reporting. Even in the regional integration bloc of the EU, these problems have thus far prevented significant consolidation of European bourses.

Economist (2001) 'Survey: global equity markets', 3 May; European Commission (2001a) *The Regulation of European Securities Markets: The Lamfalussy Report*, Brussels, European Commission

9

Market entry modes

Learning objectives

By the end of this chapter, you should be able to:

- understand the main methods used to penetrate foreign markets
- assess the benefits and costs of the respective market entry modes
- outline the various views on the internationalism process
- appreciate the nature of the debate about the motives for direct foreign investment
- be aware of the main trends in the process of internationalism

Key terms

- exporting • franchising • licensing • direct foreign investment
- internationalism • internationalism process • eclectic paradigm

Introduction

Foreign market entry modes differ in the degrees of risk they present, the control and commitment of resources they require and the return on investment they promise. One of the challenges of foreign market entry analysis is to identify the optimum entry mode that maximises returns and minimises risk – a tall order, which has yet to be satisfactorily resolved. In practice, optimisation is extremely difficult given the diversity that characterises entry mode choice and the bounded rationality (that is, limitations of time, resources and knowledge) that constrains management decisions.

Most analyses attempt to compare the advantages and potential disadvantages of a particular entry mode with supposedly superior or optimum modes, for example joint ventures or licensing versus wholly owned subsidiaries. Prevailing theories, for the most part, fail to consider the possibility that the entry mode choice of the firm is not predestined and therefore may not lend itself to prediction. For example, a firm may act intuitively when making an entry mode choice rather than make a thorough and rational evaluation of all contingencies or follow a predetermined path. Market entry analysis inevitably embraces market development also. Strictly speaking, therefore, analysis seeks to lay the foundations for understanding the firm's choice of conducting business abroad – whether through exporting, licensing, franchising, industrial countertrade (including buyback and turnkey projects), joint ventures, strategic alliances or wholly owned subsidiaries. Theoretical analysis has been particularly concerned with explaining the emergence, strength and resilience of multinational firms (MNEs) with wholly owned subsidiaries in a number of countries but whose activities can conceivably embrace the full range of modes for conducting foreign business.

This chapter will first discuss certain aspects of exporting – usually the first step, but often the only step in the internationalisation process of firms. This will be followed by an analysis of the *raison d' être* of foreign direct investment, licensing, franchising, joint ventures and strategic alliances. (See Chapter 3 for a discussion of industrial countertrade.)

Exporting

Despite the contribution trade theories have made to an understanding of the causes and consequences of international trade, none of them directly addresses aspects of trade at the level where most decisions are made, namely, at the level of the firm, simply because they address a different set of issues. Because theories make few behavioural assumptions concerning the motivation of firms and the environment in which they operate, they are incapable of explaining different attitudes towards exporting of firms with seemingly homogeneous characteristics with respect to product, managerial attitude and financial resources. Why, for example, should some firms become committed and successful exporters and others, within the same industry, appear unable or unwilling to respond to even the most promising opportunities? Most trade theories, by assuming that information is freely available, assume away a feature of international trade that is liable to deter potential exporters. A fundamental problem is how exporters acquire sufficient information about unfamiliar and distant markets, either geographically or psychically, to enable them to identify consumer tastes, competitors' strengths, gaps in the market, barriers to trade, and a host of other aspects that would allow them to assess whether their firm-specific competencies make them potentially successful exporters.

Most commonly, firms first become involved in international business through exporting and, even those that develop into fully fledged multinationals, continue to rely heavily on exporting to supply their various global markets and to maximise the allocation of resources throughout their business empires. Indeed, the largest proportion of world exports arise from intra-firm trade (UNCTAD, 1996), whether the supply of final product to subsidiaries or the supply of intermediate products, such as components and capital equipment. Since the first steps in the internationalisation process of most firms is through exporting, as the stages theory suggests, the analysis in this section will view exporting from the perspective of the fledgling exporter. From this perspective, relevant problems concern such issues as the perception firms have concerning the difficulties and obstacles that impede foreign market penetration, their response to export stimuli, the likely characteristics of successful exporters, and the expectations of firms about cost and price factors in export markets.

Export initiation
Many firms, especially in the services sector but also in manufacturing, are destined to remain as purely domestic enterprises either because their products or services are too standardised, uncompetitive, unsuited to foreign markets in other ways, too small and lacking in adequate managerial resources and skills, or production is located too far away from cost-effective transport routes. Conversely, many firms with export potential may have no clear idea of the costs involved or of the prospects for profit and growth. In many cases there may be no incentive to divert limited resources from other activities.

The majority of exporters are likely to have been drawn into exporting through *external stimuli*, of which the following are generally the most important:

- responding to invitations from domestic exporters and foreign firms to supply machinery, equipment or components
- responding to unsolicited orders from export agents and buyers for foreign firms (Amine and Cavusgil, 1986), such as large retailers seeking suitable additions to their product range
- following up potential opportunities drawn to firms' attention by trade associations, government agencies and chambers of commerce
- exhibiting at international trade fairs and exhibitions
- through merging with, or being taken over by, experienced exporters
- institutional changes, such as reductions in trade barriers.

Some firms may be inclined to react passively to exporting opportunities because of perceptions that they lack the skills to deal with documentation and shipping arrangements, because of language difficulties or because they are not prepared to make the necessary financial commitment, such as executive, clerical and administrative costs. Risk-averse firms, in particular, are likely to perceive that exporting is a relatively high-risk activity although, paradoxically, experienced exporters may regard market diversification to be a risk-minimising strategy.

At some point in its development a firm may decide as a deliberate matter of policy to seek out export opportunities, perhaps as an alternative to the allocation of funds to research and development, or the promotion of new products and processes, or the penetration of neglected segments of the home market. But until the feasibility of exporting has been fully explored, or a firm has acquired export experience, the contribution exporting may make to corporate objectives cannot be adequately assessed. Thus, a change of direction into exporting may be viewed as a corporate innovation rather than a natural development in a firm's growth process, but whether initiated by external or internal stimuli, partially at least, exporting is bound to be seen as an act of faith in the early stages.

Internal stimuli may be directly related to the firm's perceived competencies, which may be derived from one or more of the following:

- a differentiated product, protected by patent and with few close competitors
- technological advantages
- price and cost advantages
- non-price advantages
- location.

Internal export stimuli may also arise from competitive stress arising from a saturated or declining home market, excess capacity, recession, business pessimism about future prospects in the home economy or a failure to achieve objectives in the home market. Firms with a combination of high fixed costs and falling domestic sales may be attracted to foreign markets in the expectation that mainly direct (variable) costs will be incurred and that fixed costs can be spread over a larger output, thus reducing the ratio of fixed to variable costs. This is often a short-term strategy that gives rise to allegations of dumping.

Whether a firm will respond positively to different kinds of stimuli may depend on the international orientation of senior management. This may be based on a familiarity with foreign countries through birth, travel or education, knowledge of languages or simply an unwillingness to regard national boundaries as a constraint on market growth. The presence of these managerial characteristics is generally considered to be essential to persuade a firm to consider exporting as a serious option and to generate and maintain the initial impetus and commitment. In the absence of this orientation among existing staff, the arrival of new export-orientated executives in key positions may be the crucial change agent for firms with export potential.

Export motives

It is useful to distinguish between the motives of firms that are new to exporting and the motives of experienced exporters. For firms at the stage of export initiation, the preponderance of unsolicited orders and the practical difficulties of assessing the contribution exporting is capable of making to profits, suggests that profit cannot be regarded as a dominant export motive. At this stage of a firm's export development, exporting may best be regarded as an experimental innovation from which the firm gains the experience and knowledge of export processes and markets to allow it to form more rational expectations about the contribution exporting is capable of making, given time, to the firm's long-term objectives.

Since exporting cannot be regarded as an end in itself – except by firms and executives seeking the status of an international reputation – it is pertinent to consider the motives of experienced exporters. Some exporters, even of long standing, may regard exporting as an unimportant, uncommitted activity and have no clear motive other than to respond to any profit opportunity that promises low costs and low risk.

However, when the export commitment is a strong one, the primary motives are likely to be survival (security), profitability and growth.

Firms may regard survival as the dominant export motive when the home market is declining, seasonal, or under threat from import penetration. Sometimes, an export presence will allow a firm to switch its marketing effort between home and overseas markets, depending on the state of demand in the home market. Where there is a possibility of exploiting overseas markets in this way, the primary contribution of exporting is to maintain sales volume, albeit with lower profit margins, until such time as the domestic market revives. In the case of seasonal items, exporting to countries with peaks and troughs in demand that do not coincide with the domestic cycle enables firms to maintain sales volume and production levels. In these examples, excess capacity and surplus stocks are the stimulants and survival and stability are the motives for exporting.

In some industries, at any one time, home sales may be more profitable than foreign sales, whereas the experience may be reversed in other industries or product groups. Over time, in most industries, the ranking of profitability between home and foreign sales will fluctuate depending, inter alia, on exchange rate movements and market trends. Nevertheless, even for firms that are primarily motivated by profit, there will be little incentive to switch from one market to another if consumer loyalty requires a sustained marketing and sales effort and availability of supply.

It is reasonable to suppose that in the long term, however, a firm's export commitment will weaken if profitability fails to exceed anticipated targets. These targets may be determined by the typical export contribution to profits for the industry as a whole, or some other yardstick such as the perceived profitability of alternative activities (for example, new product development or overseas investment). Exporting need not necessarily be expected to make a greater contribution to profits per £1 of sales than domestic sales. Indeed, where comparisons with domestic markets are made, the appropriate measure is the expected profitability of *further* market penetration in the home market compared with the profit potential of foreign sales.

Whether growth aspirations are regarded as a profit strategy or as an independent goal subject to the realisation of satisfaction profits, exporting may be pursued in the belief that there is more growth potential abroad than in the home market. Oligopolists, especially, may nurture foreign markets to realise expansionist goals that are being constrained by small or stagnant home sales, or to react to the growth aspirations of rivals by pursuing them into overseas markets (Amine and Cavusgil, 1986).

Export motives, which may be categorised as aggressive or defensive, may fluctuate depending on the state of the domestic economy relative to trends abroad. Firms are apt to emphasise growth aspirations during periods of rising real gross national product and expanding markets and point to the need for survival in periods of recession.

Compared with firms that have never exported, current exporters are more likely to hold patents on their products, and domestically to serve national markets rather than regional ones. Among decision makers in exporting and non-exporting firms there are major variations in the perception of costs, profits and risk associated with exporting. Characteristically, in the pre-export period, firms that ultimately become exporters, compared with firms destined to remain as non-exporters, are inclined to perceive that there is greater profit potential in exporting and lower costs and risk involved. Exporters are likely to regard their products to be sufficiently differentiated and price competitive to succeed in foreign markets, and they have stronger growth aspirations than non-exporters. They are also more likely to be positioned in growth markets and to specialise in new products. Non-exporters are more likely to possess mature products and be positioned in low growth sectors of their market (see Table 9.1).

Table 9.1 Exporter and non-exporter profiles

Exporters

Patented products

New products in range

Perception of high profits from exporting

Perception of relatively low export risks and costs

Growth oriented

International orientation of management

Decentralised management decisions

High ratio of trained and formally qualified managers

Marketing orientated

Formal planning and budgets

Non-exporters

Non-patented products

No new products

Perception of low profits from exporting

Perception of high export risks and costs

Low growth experiences

Domestic orientation of management

Centralised decisions

Low ratios of trained and formally qualified managers

Production orientated

Informal controls

Burton and Schlegelmilch (1987)

Pricing in export markets

As we saw in Chapter 4, there are reasons to suggest that firms could and, in most circumstances, should charge different prices in different markets for the same product or service. In essence, all that is required is for there to be different price elasticities of demand in different markets, which the firm must be able to keep apart. That is to say, there must be no possibility of goods destined for the lower priced market being transferred, beyond the firm's control, back to the higher priced one. Although price discrimination may apply between any markets, the potential is greatest for firms selling both at home and abroad because of the likelihood that each market can be truly separated by time and distance. In practice, firms are certain to lack a detailed knowledge of demand conditions in all their markets to fine-tune their pricing decisions according to measurements of price elasticities of demand. Firms are more likely to set prices on the basis of intuition, past experience, competitors' prices, advice from their agents and by negotiation with customers. In other words, price will be based more on a mixture of hunch, guesswork and market intelligence than precise statistical analysis.

Where a discriminatory pricing policy is adopted, the price set by the firm will depend on a number of considerations. The strength of consumers' tastes for a product relative to the appeal of competitors' products and substitutes is clearly important. Consumer loyalty is something that can be sustained by advertising and promotion expenditure, which also allows a firm to enjoy higher prices. For a given product, demand is likely to be more price elastic the higher the level of income per capita. Price is inseparable from product quality and availability, marketing channels and credit terms offered to customers (a combination of characteristics described as the marketing mix if determined by a coherent and positive strategy) and the price and non-price strategies of competitors. The way in which the product is marketed is decisive and attention to design, service and delivery dates will allow more price flexibility. It will effectively create a price premium over competitors' prices, which provides a firm with a price 'spread' within which it may operate without weakening the demand for the product. Frequently, price is dictated by the volume of sales, which may depend above all on the channel of distribution. For example, discount stores and mail-order firms are extremely price conscious but offer the prospect of high volume. Higher price margins and lower volume usually prevail with traditional retailers.

Price is more decisive a factor in some markets than others because of the sophistication of the buyers in terms of their appreciation of the overall value of the product according to quality, performance, durability and reliability. In all probability, industrial buyers are more likely than domestic consumers to be trained or have enough knowledge of individual products to make an objective assessment of their attributes. Firms are price takers in highly competitive markets. They are required to accept an identifiable market price, and a basic decision for them is to decide whether sales and marketing effort in the market are worthwhile at that price. By the same token, when products are differentiated and non-price factors influence the buyers, so that price comparisons relative to overall value are difficult to make, firms may have considerable discretion in their price decisions. Between these extremes, firms may be required to negotiate prices with key-account customers. In industrial markets the seller's products may be only a small part of the buyers' total inputs, and service costs during the lifetime of the equipment may be some multiple of the initial purchase price. In these circumstances, price sensitivity would relate to service costs (that is, lifetime costs) rather than the basic purchase price.

Above all, that firm's price policy should be in harmony with its objectives. This implies, for example, relatively low prices if the immediate aim is to protect markets or to achieve growth through market penetration; a constant profit mark-up on unit costs to support target rates of return; and consideration of what the market will bear for short-term profit maximisation.

The concept of the product life cycle applied to individual products specifies clearly defined stages through which a product must pass – from the innovative stage to a period of market decline via stages of growth, maturity and market saturation. One of the purposes of life cycle analysis is to clarify the appropriate price strategy at each stage. Thus, it may be possible to apply higher prices in the new and innovative stage, but low prices may be appropriate in the mature and saturation stage.

Despite the arguments in favour of discriminatory pricing, many firms choose to charge the same price in markets at home and abroad. Why should this be so?

- Firms' behaviour may be irrational; they may ignore opportunities or wish to export with a minimum of fuss and effort.
- Price discrimination appears to increase with the size of the firm. Thus, small firms may simply lack the market knowledge necessary to set and adapt prices objectively according to changing circumstances.
- There may be a lack of confidence to deviate from uniform pricing.
- Agents or large key-account customers in different markets may be strong enough to insist on receiving the lowest market price.
- A firm may have a strategy that emphasises non-price features.
- Charging what the market will bear may antagonise customers and lose the firm its goodwill.

Allocation of costs

The interaction between sales revenue, sales volume, profit and costs is always of considerable importance to a firm, but the attractiveness of exporting relative to domestic sales will depend in particular on how costs are allocated between the various markets and also on the interpretation the firm places on a particular structure of costs.

The price of a product may be estimated by a cost-based pricing technique. This builds up from expected costs at some standard or forecast volume of sales according to the following kind of formula:

$$\text{Cost} + \frac{\text{costs x mark-up } (\%)}{100} = \text{price}$$

Although seemingly dominated by supply conditions (that is, the firm's cost structure), the formula is capable of taking demand facts into account by varying the profit mark-up from market to market. An alternative technique, preferred by firms which relate product prices directly to demand conditions, is to determine the price by reference to a market-based formula:

$$\text{Price} = \frac{\text{cost} \times 100}{100 - \text{mark-up } (\%)}$$

With cost-based pricing, an over-allocation of costs to exports will inflate the export price; with market-based prices the effect will be to underestimate profits. If export costs are under-absorbed, cost-based export prices will be deflated, and with market-based prices, profit will be exaggerated.

A conventional practice is to separate costs into fixed (or overhead) costs and variable (or direct) costs. Fixed costs remain unchanged over the planning period whatever the level of output. Variable costs, such as some labour costs, vary directly with the level of output. Quite typically, in a multiproduct firm, variable costs will be charged to each product as they are incurred, and fixed costs will be charged to each product in proportion to sales revenue or some approximate representative of sales volume, such as direct labour costs.

In assessing the merits of exporting, it is clearly important to allocate fixed costs as accurately as possible to either home or export sales, perhaps by splitting fixed costs between general overheads, which may be apportioned proportionately, and home or export overheads, which may be charged directly. However, for the many exporting firms that charge the same price abroad as at home, it is reasonable to assume either that fixed costs are allocated to each market according to sales revenue or that the same profit margin is desired in each market irrespective of different market conditions.

Usually, a firm's attitude to the profitability of exporting is inclined to harden over time. In the early years, when the firm may merely respond to fortuitous orders or when the domestic market is slack, only incremental costs and a nominal amount in contribution to overheads may be charged to exports. However realistic in the short term, this policy serves to exaggerate the profitability of exporting and therefore will require that fixed costs be fully allocated to exporting when the activity becomes established.

It is often the case that firms with similar experiences in export markets adopt quite different attitudes to the contribution that exports are making to overall corporate objectives, especially when exports appear be to be less profitable than home sales. Whether withdrawal from less profitable export markets is a sound decision will depend on the firm's ability to make up for lost sales in the home market and on the contribution being made by exports to the firm's fixed costs. Conversely, an increase in less profitable export sales, by allowing overheads to be spread over a larger sales volume, may actually contribute substantially to the firm's total profits. For firms with heavy fixed costs, sales volume is extremely important. When home markets are depressed or saturated, exporting is likely to offer a firm better opportunities to increase sales volume.

Trade channels

The channels of trade refer to the distributive routes taken by a firm's merchandise to the final customer. These can be categorised according to whether an intermediary, effectively performing the functions of a 'middleman', intercedes between the supplier and the overseas customer, in which case the distinction can be made between indirect exports and direct exports. A second useful classification distinguishes between domestic channels and foreign channels. By using a domestic channel, the exporter is spared the exposure to international trade risks.

The products of a firm may be exported by one of a variety of domestic channels, all of which imply an indirect route to the overseas customer. With domestic channels the export process takes place within the home country, allowing the exporter to avoid the risks, financial and otherwise, that are associated with the use of a foreign channel.

Domestic channels include the following:

- *Export houses*. These offer specialised knowledge of markets and regions.
- *Manufacturers' agents and specialist export managers* act on commission from the seller; confirming and indent houses act on commission from an overseas buyer.
- Export houses may also act on their own account or on commission (in which case, they can be classified as *agents*).
- *Selling directly* to local buying offices of large overseas companies, usually wholesalers of consumer goods and department stores.
- *In partnership with other exporters*, which incorporate the firm's products as parts or components in their own exports.
- *Piggybacking* – an arrangement where another, usually larger, firm exporting a complementary range of products markets the firm's products through its own trade channels.
- *Selling directly to a local procurement office* of a foreign government.

The usual overseas channels are as follows:

1 the firm's export sales force
2 sales to the firm's overseas sales offices or overseas production subsidiaries
3 sales to customers in response to orders secured by agents in the export market working for commission on the firm's behalf

4 via distributors in the export market, who acquire title to the exporter's goods. Routes 1 and 2, where its own staff represent the exporter, are direct (internalised) overseas routes. Routes 3 and 4 may be classified as indirect (external) overseas routes.

Choice of trade channel

Indirect exporting, in particular the role of export houses and specialist export agents, has declined with the emergence of intra-firm trade and the decline of arms' length trade and its future is threatened further by the advent of e-commerce. The role of these specialists can be predicted to decline further as e-commerce becomes established as a reliable and trustworthy channel to markets. In addition, there is a tendency for direct exporting (internalised transactions) to replace indirect exporting (externalised transactions) as a firm's commitment to exporting increases because of the need for closer ties between the producer and foreign customers. However, when an overseas subsidiary or sales office is substituted for indirect trade channels, a barrier can be raised against an effective and responsive relationship between the exporter and the overseas customer, depending on the degree of interest shown by the parent firm and the control it exercises over its foreign staff. It does not follow, therefore, that direct (internalised) exporting necessarily produces more efficient communications between producer and customer.

At any one time, of course, a mixture of experienced firms and new recruits will undertake exporting. Some firms will have formalised a strong commitment to export growth in their corporate objective, and home and export markets will have been integrated and subjected to rational analysis. Others may be inclined to regard exports as a mere sideline. Most indirect channels, domestic and foreign, are most heavily utilised by firms new to exporting; by firms which respond only spasmodically to export opportunities arising from unsolicited orders; and by those whose exporting effort depends on buoyancy of the home market and the expected profitability of a specific inquiry.

It is true, nevertheless, that indirect exporting might be the appropriate trade channel for firms wishing to sustain a substantial resource commitment to foreign sales but without the skills or financial resources to penetrate markets directly. Also, although indirect channels largely serve the needs of small firms and firms exporting in a small way, even the largest companies may rely on indirect routes (particularly agents) to supplement their direct export activities, especially in small or dispersed markets.

Whatever the reasons in favour of indirect trade channels, obvious managerial advantages accrue to firms using them, including a reduced need for specialist staff and more complicated organisation and control structures. In addition, domestic channels guarantee the virtual elimination of foreign trade credit and exchange rate problems.

Conversely, by relying on indirect channels, the firm, of necessity, becomes divorced from the customer and must trust to the market knowledge of its representatives and their willingness and ability to recognise and develop export opportunities. Perhaps the greatest potential weakness of indirect exporting is that the producer may be unable to dictate the pace of market penetration or influence the selection of markets and market segments or play an active part in the choice of product and marketing strategy, including the mix of price and non-price variables.

Because the choice of trade channel has clear implications for the ability of the firm to control its export operations and integrate home and export sales, the question arises as to the optimum or best-suited route to fit the circumstances of a particular firm. The appropriate choice is likely be a function of the firm's size, experience in exporting, commitment, and size and dispersion of its markets. In many circumstances, however, the choice might be strictly limited and dictated to by the structure of the market. For example, if the market is large and dominated by a handful of firms, the exporter might be compelled to deal with the customer directly and maintain close contact through an export sales staff. In small, geographically dispersed and standardised markets, the high costs to the firm of maintaining a direct marketing presence would indicate that market opportunities would be best exploited by the appointment of agents or export houses specialising in the promotion of a range of complementary goods. The exporter may also be required to respond to the power and preferences of the customer, for example, if a valued customer insists on trading through a particular distributor. The technical characteristics of the product will also play a part. If the technology behind the exported product, or the product itself, is advanced or complex or the product is purpose built to suit customer requirements, a close relationship with the exporter will be demanded by the customer. This will also be the situation if non-price characteristics are emphasised, such as pre-sales service, after-sales service and prompt delivery.

Theories of foreign direct investment

There are three major theoretical models that attempt to explain the internationalisation of the firm, that is the process of increasing involvement in cross-border operations – the *stages model, internalisation* or *transaction cost* analysis and *the eclectic paradigm*. Each one, interdisciplinary in nature, integrates social science disciplines, particularly economic and organisation theory and marketing. Although not the central focus of theories, entry mode choice is considered to be fundamental to an understanding of the internationalisation of firms. Each model, which in principle can be used to make predictions about foreign market entry decisions, shares a family resemblance in their assumptions and methodologies.

Exhibit 9.1 The Internet as a trade channel

The pace with which e-commerce has developed as a medium of commerce and international trade is the most significant business development in recent years. Any firm, whatever its size, can establish a site on the Internet, where there are no barriers to entry and access to commercial and marketing knowledge is virtually free and available to everyone, and automatically becomes a company with a global reach (Keegan, 1999: 486). In these early days of e-commerce, it is already apparent that many companies have established e-commerce activities with little regard for their ability to manage the new technology or to handle the legal implications surrounding e-commerce as a marketing and international trade channel. As with all technological breakthroughs in international trade, such as the advent of steam and railways in the 19th century, container traffic and air travel in the 20th, many firms will realise too late the effect a new technology will have on them and their markets, believing that their existing technologies and strengths will allow them to outperform it (Scarborough and Corbett, 1992: 152).

E-commerce trading offers a highly effective vehicle for a rapid entry into global markets, although the financial costs and risks are much higher than first envisaged in the early days. The management of export and finance of international trade functions, whereby the physical transfer of goods and the title to them are synchronised, remain the same as before, although the traditional trade channels and intermediaries, such as export houses, agents and distributors, can be expected to have their role reduced. The danger to both the supplier and the purchaser of goods and services is that e-commerce, which is difficult to control, unwittingly or otherwise may circumvent intellectual property rights and consumer and data protection laws.

Whether e-commerce, on balance, represents a threat or an opportunity is a key question for many industries, such as financial services, car dealerships, computer hardware and software, books and publishing, ticket agencies, educational services, and travel and estate agents.

Stages theory of international business expansion

The stages model has its theoretical base in the framework of bounded rationality (Simon, 1957), the behavioural theory of the firm (Aharoni, 1966; Cyert and March, 1963; March and Simon, 1958) and the theory of the growth of the firm (Penrose, 1959). In the original version the internationalisation of the firm is treated as a unilateral process in which the firm gradually and in orderly manner, first through exporting, increases its involvement in a foreign market (Vahlne, 1977, 1990; Johanson and Wiedersheim-Paul, 1975;). A direct relationship is postulated between the firm's current business activities, the knowledge it develops about a specific foreign market, the greater certainty that knowledge enhances and the increasing commitment of resources and decisions to that market.

Central to the model is the importance of cumulative market knowledge. Drawing explicitly on the work of Penrose (1959), the model identifies two kinds of knowledge: *objective knowledge*, which can be taught, and *experiential knowledge*, which can only be acquired through operational experience. On the assumption that experiential market knowledge generates business opportunities and simultaneously reduces uncertainty and risk, it is argued that commitment to a market will increase incrementally as the firm gains experiential knowledge from its current activities in the market. The model highlights the role of cumulative experiential knowledge as a trigger in the internationalisation process, the so-called 'establishment chain', that is, a step-by-step increase in a firm's involvement in a specific foreign market, moving from no regular export activities to exporting via independent representatives (agents and specialist distributors), to the establishment of a sales subsidiary and eventually to a local production unit. Entry into each stage signifies an increase in the commitment of time and resources to foreign market entry and development. This assertion offers grounds for predicting both the choice of market entry mode and the choice of foreign market. Going abroad exposes the firm to new experiences and to a combination of incentives and barriers to internationalisation. *Psychic distance*, signified by historical ties, and differences in language, culture and political and business systems, will have a bearing on the flow of information between the firm and the market and the time and resources needed to acquire the relevant information. Applying their cumulative knowledge in psychically close countries helps decision makers to stretch their bounded rationality to deal with the novelty of internationalisation. It is likely therefore that the specific foreign market chosen first is likely to be one that is 'psychically' close to the firm's home market.

The sequential, step-by-step approach is intuitively appealing in that it is a consequence of the presence of 'economies of scope in knowledge' (Casson, 1994), which refers to the ability to diagnose a market's potential. Economies of scope exist among markets that display uniform characteristics and find expression when a firm's knowledge of one market is used to diagnose other markets of the same type. The appropriate knowledge that gives rise to a process of international expansion is experiential knowledge and diagnostic know-how rather than factual knowledge.

In addition to the logic of a sequential and slow acquisition of know-how, the stages model also implies that firms with surplus resources but without sufficient experiential knowledge and diagnostic know-how can be expected to compensate for this by accessing these competencies through linkages with individuals and organisations outside the firm that possess such knowledge, whether export agents, or partners in licensing, franchising or joint venture arrangements, allowing them to make leaps in the establishment chain.

The relevance of the stages model has been the subject of some criticism, much of it based on the realisation that a firm's internationalisation process may start at any stage and may even reverse the sequence described in the stages model (for example, Anderson, 1993; Benito and Gripsrund, 1992; Forsgren, 1990; Turnbull, 1987). The model understates the tendency for various entry modes to be used simultaneously and in tandem, such as licensing and foreign direct investment, management contracts and turnkey projects, and some forms of countertrade. Also, the model ignores the influence on the internationalisation process of industry characteristics, such as maturity and technological levels, government policies, such as protectionist barriers, and the degree of internationalisation or globalisation that already exists in potential markets. However, the stages model continues to have some appeal as it undergoes continuous development following on from the attempt by

Johanson and Vahlne (1990) to incorporate industrial networks and multilateral commitments rather than just a unilateral commitment to market entry, as in the original model. Casson (1994), for example, revealed the implicit assumptions of the model to show that much more could be inferred about managerial behaviour than had been supposed. In sum, general criticism of the stages theory concerns the purity of the step-by-step establishment chain and the lack of precise differentiation between the various stages. More specifically, while the stages model and its more refined versions are persuasive in their treatment of the firm's decision making in the early exporting stages of internationalisation, they are unable to suggest which entry mode should be selected beyond the early stages. Also, although the accumulation of market knowledge is important as an explanation of a cautious and sequential entry into foreign markets in the early stages, when the firm becomes experienced and active in a number of foreign markets, a lack of market knowledge is no longer a problem and the firm should be in a position to make strategic choices from the diverse range of market entry and development modes.

The internalisation theory

The internalisation theory, based on the logic of *transaction cost economics*, offers another interdisciplinary approach for explaining the role and behaviour of international firms, specifically those firms that make commitments to foreign direct investment. First expounded by Knight (1921), Commons (1934) and Coase (1937), the analysis was developed by Hymer (1968, 1976) and Williamson (1971), and taken further by Buckley and Casson (1976) and Rugman (1980). In the context of international business, transaction cost analysis combines economic theory, organisation theory and contract law to explain the *raison d' être* of the firm's internal and external governance structures when serving foreign markets. Transaction cost analysis regards the firm as an alternative governance (hierarchy) to the market when impediments to market transactions between independent parties raise the transaction costs above the costs that would be incurred were the transactions to be managed within the firm.

Transaction costs are additional to the normal costs of production and arise because of the presence of various transactional impediments and uncertainties, which lead to added costs associated with the policing and enforcement of contracts. The behavioural characteristics of the independent parties in the market for a good or service are assumed to be *boundedly rational* and at least one party is opportunist and untrustworthy. There are other impediments to exchanges in the market. The first of these is *asset specificity* in production. If a specific asset is valuable in only a narrow range of uses so that its value is much lower in an alternative use, a costly bargaining process is likely to occur between the contracting parties. If the transaction is a recurring one, it will pay the firm, driven by the desire to minimise transaction costs, to manage (internalise) the transaction within the firm. Second, market transactions are subject to uncertainty, which give rise to frequent revision to contracts. Third, the quality of a product or service cannot be fully determined even in normal use. Fourth, where there are limited numbers of buyers and sellers to a transaction, small numbers bargaining raise the cost of using the market because the contract partner(s) may be hard to replace causing high 'switching' costs. Finally, information pertinent to a transaction may be unevenly distributed between the partners. With information asymmetry, a partner with lesser information, expecting to be exploited, will offer a lower price, one implication being that lower quality goods will be traded.

The interaction of these characteristics and transaction impediments in the market create market imperfections and market failure, giving rise to the information, negotiation and bargaining costs and the cost of enforcing contracts – the so-called market transaction costs. The assumption made is that, subject to bounded rationality, a firm will attempt to minimise the sum of transaction and production costs, choosing between a market (externalised) governance structure and a hierarchical (internalised) governance structure, in which parties conduct their transaction inside an organisational boundary. The transaction cost model (or *internalisation* theory) identify the drivers of efficiency-seeking operations. The firm will internalise those transactions that it can perform more efficiently than the market. The internationalisation of a firm's operations, especially through foreign direct investment, is possible if the firm can transfer its operations, including its competitive internalised transactions, across borders at minimal marginal cost and retain ownership and control.

Normally, the firm can only specialise within the internalised competencies encapsulated within its boundaries and managerial incentives to perform efficiently within the firm may be weaker than in the market. Because of this, switching between internally administered transactions and market transactions will always occur, but on balance internalisation will be favoured in transactions involving the movement of materials, organisational skills, R&D, marketing and finance. By internationalising its operations through foreign direct investment, the firm is able to gain access to the comparative advantages of other countries (whereas the exporter is confined to the comparative advantages on offer in the home economy).

The transaction (internalisation) models embrace the pioneering work of Hymer (1968). His starting position was to point out that a firm in a competitive market could never expect to set up cross-border operations and expect to compete against local firms because the additional transport, management and communication costs would eat into the 'normal' profit of the perfectly competitive firm. Therefore, foreign direct investment must be confined to firms in industries with monopolistic or oligopolistic market structures in which there are exploitable *market imperfections*, which can be commandeered by the firm and protected against predators, including firms in the targeted market. The advantages (competencies) firms may acquire in imperfect markets include differentiated products (protected by trade marks), proprietary technology (protected by patents), marketing and managerial skills, economies of scale and government intervention (such as protectionist barriers). In essence, the transactions cost model can readily incorporate market imperfections as firm-specific assets capable of being transferred profitably to foreign markets.

The basic conclusion of the efficiency-driven transaction cost analysis is that full ownership of foreign operations is likely to be preferred to alternative, collaborative modes, such as joint ventures and licensing since transaction costs will increase and the firm can lose its firm-specific advantages to an opportunistic partner. A less assertive conclusion might be that the analysis is useful, albeit in a narrow cost-based analysis to indicate circumstances when one market entry mode would be preferred to another (see following sections).

The eclectic paradigm

The eclectic paradigm, renamed from the original eclectic theory (Dunning, 1988), synthesises theories drawn from location and international trade theory, internalisation and industrial organisation. Dunning attempts to explain why firms should choose to serve foreign markets through overseas production rather than through domestic production and exporting. This is explained by the configuration of three sets of advantages – the O, I, L configuration.

Ownership-specific advantages

The firm must have ownership (proprietary) advantages over local firms in the foreign market. These may arise from proprietary technology and differentiated products (monopoly power) protected from imitation by patents and trade marks, economies of joint supply, access to resources, and specific advantages derived from the nature or nationality of the firm (such as government protection). The market power advantages bestowed on the firm by these market imperfections allow the firm to enjoy monopoly 'rents' on its assets and impede access by other firms to its markets. The firm acquires and nurtures these advantages prior to entering foreign markets. The possession and accumulation of ownership advantages gives the firm the incentive to coordinate its internalised markets with new activities and new assets in other countries.

Internalisation advantages

As discussed earlier (the *internalisation theory*), important elements of transaction imperfections include asset specificity, small numbers, product complexity, transaction uncertainty and information asymmetry and bounded rationality. The firm will transfer its ownership and transaction benefits across borders within its own hierarchy (wholly owned subsidiaries) if they can be transferred more efficiently relative to alternative arrangement such as selling or leasing to a licensee or engaging in a joint venture. The debt the O and I elements of the paradigm owe to the market imperfections and internalisation and transaction cost analyses should be obvious.

Location-specific advantages

In locating abroad, the firm is able to combine its domestically derived ownership-specific and internalisation advantages with factor endowments and other comparative advantages in the foreign market, such as low-cost labour net of productivity, the quality of the infrastructure, the availability of raw materials, natural resources and energy, and government policies (such as incentives and tax benefits). Note the debt to trade theories.

In the eclectic paradigm, imperfections present in imperfect market structures and transaction cost imperfections are complementary and combine with the location of comparative advantage to predict a firm's optimum foreign market entry mode. At the industry level, in its simplistic form, the eclectic paradigm can explain the likely direction of foreign trade and investment in particular industries. For example, if firms in an industry are typified by an abundance of ownership and internalisation advantages and there are location advantages in the home economy, the industry will tend be export oriented. In similar circumstances but for location disadvantages in the home economy, the industry will display a bias to servicing overseas markets through foreign direct investment. An industry would experience import penetration if foreign competitors had greater ownership and internalisation advantages plus location advantages. If foreign competitors had greater ownership and internalisation advantages but location disadvantages, an industry would experience inward foreign direct investment. In many instances, the O, I and L combination will be so finely balanced that industries will participate in intra-industry trade and intra-industry investment.

International joint ventures and strategic alliances

Joint ventures and wholly owned subsidiaries are the main forms of foreign direct investment. An international joint venture is a partnership of two or more independent firms which share resources when at least one partner's headquarters are located outside the venture's country of operation or when the venture operates outside all the partners' home countries. *Equity joint ventures* and *contractual joint ventures* are the basic forms of joint venture encountered in international business. In the former, the partners provide an agreed portion of the equity, which may take the form of funds or capital equipment, premises and management know-how. Contractual joint ventures, unlike equity joint ventures, have no separate legal entity. Rather, they involve the supply of technology, marketing and production know-how or management skills by one partner to the other on a contractual basis. This may turn contractual joint ventures into equity joint ventures if the long-term interests of the partners are best served and equity joint ventures commonly lead to mergers or acquisition by one of the partners.

The characteristics of the international joint venture have undergone major changes since the early 1980s. This is also true of the focus of analysis, which has seen a change from attempts to explain how value is added to *existing* activities, as in traditional international joint ventures, to how value is created from *new* activities and by a process of organisational learning, as in the more recent concept of international strategic alliances.

Traditional international joint ventures were typically alliances between western firms and firms or public sector entities in developing countries. From a western perspective, these ventures were set up to enable the western partner overcome entry barriers to national markets, often government imposed, such as trade barriers and legislation against foreign ownership. From the perspective of the developing country partner, joint ventures were the preferred means of acquiring foreign marketing and management skills and access to capital and technology, generating local export-orientated activities. Traditional ventures were usually to be found in mature industries, involving standardised products, and located in developing partner country's market. Responding to impediments of various kinds to unrestricted market access, these ventures were usually an alternative or substitute for exporting or wholly owned subsidiaries. Partners were rarely competitors. Economic analysis, such as transaction cost analysis, in most circumstances, reveals the joint venture as an inferior, second-best option for servicing foreign markets. Thus, firms should only contemplate joint ventures with foreign partners if exporting or wholly owned subsidiary options were impractical because of protection against imported goods, or restrictions on ownership, the use or resources, or the remittance home of profits and dividends.

Historically, traditional international joint ventures have demonstrated short lives and high failure rates – between 30 and 60 per cent, depending on the criteria used to measure success. Mortality rates are particularly high between western firms and public enterprises in developing countries. A synthesis of research on this phenomenon reveals the key reasons to be poor coordination between partners, conflicting or different goals, partner incompatibility, and an unequal division of control.

In recent years, although the traditional joint venture continues to dominate cooperative international agreements, many international alliances have begun to be formed that focus more on strategy and strategic intent. An international strategic alliance is a collaborative agreement in which partner firms of different nationalities have a presence in the same international or global markets and where at least one partner regards the alliance as a means to safeguard or enhance its competitive position (Burton and Saalens, 1994). These *strategic* alliances seek to create added value through exploiting the core competencies or comparative advantage of the respective partners. This strategic exchange of core competencies perceives the firm as being a portfolio of competencies rather than products. The main feature of these new, strategic alliances, in contrast to traditional international joint ventures, are their targeting of global industries and high technology industries; their domination by firms from the triad countries of North America, Western Europe and Japan; their strategic intent – each partner seeking capabilities it does not already possess. Often, partners are competitors in the other's markets but also in the alliance market. In traditional joint ventures partners seek to exploit their existing competencies in new markets. Partners in strategic alliances are seeking to gain new capabilities to be exploited on an international, even global, scale. Thus, technology transfer, R&D collaboration, production and market sharing agreements account for most strategic alliances.

Licensing

An international licensing agreement allows foreign firms either exclusive or non-exclusive rights (Brooke and Skilbeck, 1994) to manufacture a proprietor's product for a fixed term in specific markets. To monitor the use made of their licence agreements and to share in the profits, licensors frequently take an equity interest in the operations of their licensees. Patent protection against infringement grants the licensor an element of monopoly power, which is expressed in the quasi-rent that is earned when the patented product is licensed out. Such earnings usually take the form of lump-sum payments, technical fees and royalty payments as a percentage of sales revenue. In some cases, additional revenue can be earned from the supply of parts, components and managerial advice, although tie-ins such as these are not permitted in some countries (Cross, 2000: 163). The maximisation of earnings by transferring knowledge to countries through licensing rather than through exporting or direct investment will depend on the respect host governments show for intellectual property rights and on the ability of the licensor to prevent licensees from competing in each other's markets, which is not always possible because such arrangements are often illegal. Licence agreements are often linked to major turnkey projects in which training and managerial assistance is provided until such time as control passes to the licensees (Hood and Young, 1979: p. 8).

Despite the fact that licensing is a low-cost, low-risk means of entering a foreign market quickly, involves no exposure to the risk of asset expropriation, and provides a much shorter lead time for getting into a market than foreign direct investment, the market entry mode literature typically regards licensing as an inferior entry mode to exporting and foreign direct investment. In this view, licensing should only be indulged in when insurmountable impediments are imposed by foreign governments, such as high trade barriers and strict controls on foreign investment. Rugman (1982: 14) aptly sums up this perspective thus: 'Once we have a theory of the MNE we also have a theory of licensing. That which need not be internalised can be licensed.'

The debate over the optimality of licensing versus FDI or any other entry mode centres on issues of asymmetric information, the risks that proprietary information might become diffused and the possibility that partners may become competitors, issues of profitability, and cost and control. Information asymmetry between the licensor and the licensee makes it difficult for licensors to receive full value for their assets (and for the licensees to ascertain whether they are receiving full value from the licence). Even when both parties have the same information, according to Hymer (1976: 50): 'People read signals differently and so act differently even when their goals are identical.' Thus, neither party may be capable of evaluating correctly the value of the technology. Diffusion risks require the licensor to incur heavy policing costs, and where licensees, especially from less developed countries, lack the expertise to use the transferred technology efficiently, licensors may have to incur additional transfer costs to overcome the problem, thereby reducing the attractiveness of licensing. In addition, the licensor, without the ability to control prices and output, hands over a superior advantage and monopolistic power to the licensee, which prevents the licensor from achieving maximum profit (Hymer, 1976).

In an early comparison of the respective merits of licensing and foreign direct investment, Caves (1971: 273) made three observations. The first was that that licensing will be preferred if the licensor possesses a 'one-shot' technical or product innovation that can be transferred independently of managerial know-how. The second was that small firms would be predisposed to licensing if they face high fixed costs in securing the information necessary to undertake FDI. But Caves' central proposition was that barriers to entry force firms into choosing licensing as an alternative to exporting or FDI. This echoes a recurring theme in the literature, namely that all market entry alternatives to either exporting or foreign direct investment are suboptimal and take place because of the presence of market imperfections of one kind or another. In similar vein, Buckley and Davies (1981) contended that licensing is the favoured entry mode only when firms are faced with constraints, for example, on exporting or FDI. Small firms, for instance, faced with a shortage of capital and government restrictions on foreign direct investment may be forced to license their proprietary advantage.

A transaction cost perspective

Anderson and Gatignon (1986) attempted to develop a unified framework from a transactions cost perspective. They linked authority over decision making, that is, control over the foreign operations of a firm, to coordination strategies and the commitment of resources. In conditions of risk and uncertainty, each entry mode offers a trade-off between control and resource commitment. A high level of control is associated with FDI and dominant shareholder status. An exclusive and restrictive licensing contract, alongside franchising, contractual joint ventures and management contracts, is classified as a medium-control market entry mode. Low control is associated with non-exclusive and non-restrictive licensing.

The efficiency of an entry mode depends on the degree of control over decisions required by the firm relative to the actual control exercised. Thus, the optimum entry mode will be influenced by *transaction-specific assets, external uncertainty* (that is, the unpredictability of the entrant's external environment), *internal uncertainty* (the entrant's inability to determine the performance of its subsidiaries, partners or agents), and their *free riding* potential (their ability to benefit from an asset or transaction without bearing the cost).

Transaction-specific assets, which include working relationships and knowledge of the idiosyncrasies of a firm and its activities, are assets that have value only to a few users or uses. When transaction-specific assets are valuable, transaction cost analysis suggests that integration of activities and a high degree of control will be necessary, especially in the case of customised transactions and poorly understood or highly proprietary products and processes. Conversely, the more mature the product class, the less control will a firm require of a foreign business entity. The inference is that licensing, a medium or low control mode, will be best suited to standardised products and less sophisticated processes. Where there is *external uncertainty,* such as political instability and unstable economic conditions, licensing is favoured because of the need for a firm to accept lower levels of risk by avoiding the high levels of control that are associated with inflexibility and, therefore, high levels of risk. When *internal uncertainty* exists and the firm cannot objectively assess its performance, control becomes more desirable because it allows firms to monitor inputs and develop goal congruence and loyalty and so licensing is disfavoured. Socio-cultural differences between the entrant and the host nation, which affect internal uncertainty, can be dealt with by doing things the local way, for example, by licensing. *Free riding* arises when one party can benefit from the efforts of others without bearing any costs. Transaction cost analysis suggests that *ceteris paribus,* where the potential for free riding is high, entry modes offering high control are more efficient than medium and low modes, such as licensing.

Licensing will be a favourable option when mature technologies are being transferred, where licensees are technologically unsophisticated, thus making transfer costs low, and where technologies are peripheral or involve only parts of the overall manufacturing process, thereby giving only limited competitive advantage to the licensee. According to Contractor (1990), generally, where there is a mutual hostage situation, making contract provisions self-enforceable, and when the transparency of contracts is high, thus giving low monitoring costs, contractual modes, such as licensing, are likely to have an edge because of low transaction costs.

A strategic perspective

The transaction cost approach focuses on each entry mode in isolation and seeks out the optimal market entry mode, which is the one that maximises the long-term value of the firm. In practice, however, optimisation is extremely difficult due to the uncertainty of the future and the fact that decision makers are subject to bounded rationality. Thus, optimality must defer to a 'satisficing' solution. A strategic perspective appears to be more adept at identifying circumstances when licensing will be the preferred, rather than a second best, option. Hill et al. (1990) contend that the choice of entry mode depends on the firm's overall international strategy for its operations in different countries.

Licensing enhances a firm's strategic flexibility in comparison with wholly owned operations, because it involves less control, less potential risk of the loss of proprietary knowledge and lower resource commitment. A main *strategic* decision that the firm has to make is whether to adopt a global strategy or a multidomestic strategy. Where firms pursue a global strategy and the need for strategic coordination is high, such that national entities take instruction from the corporate centre, a high control entry mode will be favoured. In contrast, firms that pursue a multidomestic strategy will favour lower control entry modes, such as licensing.

The choice of entry mode is also influenced by *environmental* and *transaction* variables. Environmental variables include country risk, location familiarity and competitive conditions. Licensing, a low-resource commitment option, will be favoured when country risk is high; the cultural distance between host and home country is high; demand is uncertain or markets are declining; and competition in the host country is subject to rapid technological and regulatory change.

Transaction specific variables relate to the risk of dissipation of a firm's know-how through opportunistic behaviour. The greater the propensity of a partner to act opportunistically, the more likely it is that a high control mode will be favoured. Generally, the greater the stream of earnings generated by the proprietary knowledge, the greater the probability that an entry mode that minimises dissemination risk will be followed. This suggests that licensing will be the favourable option when the earnings stream is relatively low, as in the case of low tech know-how or when the technology is nearing the stage of standardisation. A high control entry mode will be favoured if the transferred knowledge is not easily packaged, whereas licensing will be favoured when the know-how is embedded in technical drawings and blueprints.

Hill et al. (1990) make the broad generalisation at the industry level that licensing will be a least favoured option in industries which are R&D intensive; when the industry globally is characterised by relatively homogeneous demand and competition conditions; when substantial scale economies are present in the manufacturing process; when the global industry is characterised by oligopolistic interdependence between a limited number of global players; and when the host market under consideration is the home base of global rivals of the MNE. Licensing is an increasingly least favoured entry mode in a global economy characterised by global markets, rapid technological change, deregulation and a breaking down of political cultural barriers.

Some general conclusions are that licensing is favoured:

- for standardised products and less sophisticated technological processes
- in unfavourable environmental conditions
- when mutual hostage situations make contract provisions self-enforceable
- when demand and environmental conditions are unstable.

International franchising

International franchising is undergoing a period of rapid growth in the global economy. It is a mode of expansion that offers large company advantages, such as economies of scale in marketing and production for the franchisor, and in the case of independent franchising a low-risk means of starting a business for the franchisee.

The term international franchising describes a diversity of business arrangements in which a parent company grants to others the right to use its products, technology, service or trademarks and brand names in a prescribed manner in return for a lump-sum payment and ongoing fees, usually calculated as some percentage of sales. In addition, the franchisor may allow an independent firm to operate their own franchised outlets. In some cases the franchisor may take an equity stake in affiliated subsidiaries and joint ventures and may hold significant shares in units run by managers directly employed by the franchisor (Burton and Cross, 1997). The franchise package can include the franchisor's intellectual property (trademarks, trade names and copyright), business know-how, operating manuals, marketing support, local exclusivity and training. In return the franchisee agrees to comply with the franchisor's standards and regulations.

Franchising, centuries old, was applied in the UK in the early 1800s when the 'tied house' system was introduced to control the sale of alcohol to innkeepers. In the mid-19th century, franchising began in the manufacturing sector when producers began to give exclusive rights to distributors. The Singer Sewing Machine Company, for example, established such a system in the USA in 1860. Franchising went into decline until exclusive distributorship entered the automobile industry in the 1900s. The main perceived advantage to the franchisors was that they were able to set up outlets without the need to finance them (Rudnick, 1984).

Organisational forms of franchising

When franchising began to boom in the 1950s, it became apparent that there were several types of franchising, including franchises between manufacturers and retailers (as in the motor industry), between manufacturers and wholesalers (as in soft drinks), between wholesalers and retailers (as when retailers form wholesaling companies), and trademark and trade name franchising, the commonest form (Mendelsohn, 1992; Vaughn, 1979). Supply dealerships, the first three types, are categorised as *first generation franchising*. In an international setting, first generation franchising can be regarded as a variant of the licences entry mode found in manufacturing. Trademark franchising is categorised as *second generation franchising* or *business franchising*. Most of the global growth in franchising since the 1950s is due to second generation franchising. This type, which can be broken down into job, investment, business, management, executive, retail shop and sales/distribution franchises (Chaplin, 1998), offers a far more comprehensive package than first generation franchising. However, the last has become increasingly sophisticated, so there is no longer a clear distinction between first and second generation franchising.

The business franchise concept, the most common form of agreement, is transferred abroad by one of a number of organisational forms. In *direct international franchising* the business package is transferred directly to independent units in the host country but serviced from the home country. The franchisor then proceeds to service these units directly from the home country. Direct international franchising will usually be a simple extension of the franchisor's domestic network and can be observed between partners from psychically similar countries (Hoffman and Preble, 1991). This is the characterisation of cross-border franchising commonly found in the literature and presumed to be the only organisational form, that is, an arms' length, contractual, and a non-equity form of international collaboration having much in common with international licensing in the manufacturing sector and which must therefore benefit the entrant in terms of low capital outlay and low risk, but, of course, low control (Anderson and Gatignon, 1986; Brooke, 1986; Contractor, 1990; Fladmoe-Lindquist and Jaque, 1995; Preble, 1992; Root 1988; Young et al. 1989). Table 9.2 shows the advantages and disadvantages of direct international franchising.

Because direct franchising is unsuited to markets with a different language and business culture, in such markets it is common for franchising companies to link up with intermediaries (subfranchisors), who purchase

Table 9.2 Advantages and disadvantages of direct international franchising

Advantages

Low risk, low cost entry mode

Offers the ability to develop new and unfamiliar markets relatively quickly and on a larger scale than otherwise possible

Use of highly motivated partners with local market knowledge and experience

Creates additional turnover with relatively low levels of investment in personnel, capital outlay, production and distribution

A way to test the market before committing to direct investment

A standardised, global company profile and brand image can be created, generating marketing economies of scale

Disadvantages

Lack of full control over operations, resulting in problems with cooperation, communications, quality control

Limits on franchisor's profits

Costs of creating and marketing the franchised package

Costs of protecting goodwill and brand names

Problems with local legislation, including transfers of fees and government restrictions on franchise agreements

Disclosure of trade secrets may create a future competitor

Risk to the franchisor's reputation if some franchisees underperform the right to develop their own network of units in the host market. These *master international subfranchisors* are granted the exclusive right by the franchisor to own and operate their own units and also to sell the format on to independent franchisees. In a variant of this, *area development franchising*, the subfranchisors are only permitted to operate their own units. The use of subfranchisors allows the parent firm to obtain closer control, reduce servicing costs, and use the local knowledge of their subfranchisors to adapt the franchise package to suit the local environment. Sometimes franchisors, at some stage, plan to buy out successful independent operations that have demonstrated growth and profit potential. In circumstances like these, since market penetration is effectively taking place by foreign investment, the characteristics of international franchising presumed by the traditional view, such as it being a low capital outlay, low-risk and a low-control market entry mode no longer applies.

Theoretical explanations for franchising

The managerial economics literature asserts that franchising is a hybrid organisational form and a hybrid capital instrument. As a hybrid organisational form, franchising lies between vertical integration and complete independence (Burton and Cross, 1997) – the parties are independent but the franchisee is encouraged to act in the interests of the franchisor, in the manner of intra-firm vertical integration. But the franchisor has full vertical control of its franchisees without the investment that vertical integration requires. A controversial issue concerns the rationale of decision by the firm to franchise through independent entities rather than through an intermediary (subfranchisor) or through company-owned units. Three arguments have dominated: resource scarcity explanations, market power explanations and the agency–principal relationship.

The *resource scarcity* explanation is that firms with limited access to capital will use franchisees to provide capital for expansion (Carney and Gedajlovic, 1991). As it matures, the franchisor will purchase the more successful entities. This argument has strictly limited validity, because franchisors are not only constrained by capital resources but by other factor's including time constraints on the franchising entrepreneur's ability to expand as rapidly as desired. Further, many large franchisors, which do not face such constraints to the same degree, own some of their outlets and franchise others. Rubin (1978) showed the capital constraint argument to be fallacious by arguing that since single franchisees would operate fewer units than the franchisor, the former carries more risk and therefore will require a higher rate of return on their investments, yielding less to the franchisor. An appealing argument is the *market power* explanation, which is derived from the fact that the contract between the franchising parties allows franchising to be viewed as a form of vertical organisation in which the franchisor has the ability to exercise monopoly power over downstream activities and control abuses.

The major emphasis in the literature has been on *agency theory* (e.g. Norton, 1998). Managers (agents), as employees, have a tendency to shirk if their remuneration is a fixed salary determined independently of their performance. In comparison, franchisees, working for themselves, will also work in the interests of the franchisor (the principal) because they are held 'hostage' to the agreement (which usually stipulate unilateral termination clauses), by the nature of their remuneration, and by their dependency on the franchisor for the services they need to function effectively.

Although franchising is commonly associated with small firms, it should be noted that franchising increases the supply of non-shirking managers, and is therefore a suitable vehicle for expansion for large firms and for physically dispersed franchised operations. Further, the high cost of monitoring manager–employees in wholly owned overseas subsidiaries also favours the use of franchised systems in international operations.

Franchising versus licensing

Franchising is often described as a form of licensing. In fact, the only commonality between the two modes is that they both involve the transfer of intellectual property rights. Even here, however, a licence agreement usually embraces a range of intellectual property embodied in patents, trademarks, trade secrets and know-how, whereas franchising is usually limited to trade marks. The licensee receives just a small part of the licensor's business format: the franchisee receives a complete business package, which includes all the elements the franchisee needs to operate successfully. Unlike the franchisor, the licensor has limited control over the way the licensee conducts business. Franchisees are usually selected by the franchisor; licensees tend to be self-selecting. Franchisees are start-up businesses that take on the 'image' of the franchisor: licensees are usually well-established businesses with their own identity. These and other difference are shown in Table 9.3.

Table 9.3 Differences between International franchising and licensing

Licensing	Franchising
Regarded as a low to zero-equity organisational form	Can involve substantial equity investment in the host country
Only part of a business package is transferred to the other party	Most of the entrant's business format is transferred
Usually concerns specific products	Franchisor passes on new elements of the business format
Simple direct relationship between the parties	Intermediaries can exist between the market entrant and local entities
Entrant has limited control over day-to-day activities of licensees	Entrant exerts considerable control over licensees' day-to-day activities
Licensees tend to be self-selecting	Franchisees are selected by the franchisor
Limited common characteristics between licensor and licensees	Established chains of commonly owned entities
Licensees are usually established businesses	Franchised outlets tend to be start-up operations
Substantial fee negotiations take place	Standard fee structure
Licensor's earnings based on royalties	Franchisor earns from royalties + fees + sale of inputs

Summary

In the spectrum of foreign market entry modes, the extreme modes are exporting, where the firm mostly utilises available resources in the home market, and foreign direct investment in wholly owned subsidiaries, where the firm mostly utilises resources located outside the home country. Intermediate modes include licensing, franchising, industrial countertrade, such as buyback and turnkey projects, joint ventures and strategic alliances.

Exporters face trade barriers (see Chapter 4), additional transport costs, and foreign exchange risks and the threat of non-payment – threats that may be deemed sufficient to deter potential exporters from taking the first steps into potentially lucrative markets. Many firms are destined to remain as purely domestic enterprises for these reasons; because their products or services are too standardised, uncompetitive or in other ways unsuited to foreign markets; they are too small or lack adequate managerial resources and skills; or their location is unsatisfactory in relation to cost-effective transport routes.

The majority of exporters are likely to have been drawn into exporting through external stimuli. For smaller firms, in particular, the initial entry into export markets usually stems from unsolicited orders and invitations to tender for specific orders. For such firms, this is the first step in the learning process leading to either decisions to withdraw from foreign markets or decisions to take a proactive stance and seek out further export opportunities as an alternative to expending further effort and expenditure on R&D or attempts to survive in mature home markets. The decision to enter export markets may be in response to internal stimuli, such as perceived competitive advantages or a failure to achieve objectives in the home market.

Foreign direct investment is growing more rapidly than world production and international trade, but is largely confined to investment flows within and between the triad countries. Multinational firms have traditionally preferred full ownership and control, as offered by wholly owned subsidiaries, to other forms of market entry, including equity stakes in joint ventures. The theoretical literature has stuck to the notion that either exporting or the wholly owned subsidiary, depending on where the comparative or competitive advantage lies for the firm, are the optimum entry modes, but this is increasingly being called into question. Theories of foreign direct investment attempt to explain 'how' and 'why' the firm should choose to leave its home base and set up operations abroad. To account for the strength and resilience of multinationals, the best-known theories are based on a combination of market imperfections in the home and host environments that give rise to exploitable ownership advantages, firm-specific advantages and location advantages. A forerunner to these theories, the sequential stages theory, is enjoying a revival of interest.

International joint ventures and strategic alliances offer major alternatives to exporting and foreign direct investment. The traditional joint venture between western partners and host government entities in developing countries has been considered in the literature as an inferior entry mode because the firm has to share some of its monopoly power, usually because the host market was regulated so that this was the only feasible way to enter the foreign market. This view still prevails, but there is growing recognition that the developing country partner may have 'competencies' to offer the venture based on local market knowledge. In traditional joint ventures, firms seek to exploit their existing strengths. In international strategic alliance, firms seek to acquire new strengths based on the 'leverage' of technological, marketing and/or organisational knowledge.

Although licensing and franchising offer low-cost, low-risk means of entering foreign markets and much shorter lead times, both modes are commonly regarded in the literature as inferior to exporting and foreign direct investment, only to be indulged in when there are punitive trade barriers or controls on foreign direct investment. In the case of licensing, in particular, the danger of creating a competitor is ever present. All too often, licensing and franchising are considered to have a strong family resemblance, identical twins almost, with 'licensing' being the appropriate term for goods and 'franchising' for services. However, because the differences far outweigh the similarities, this is a false premise, which can lead to faulty analysis.

Review questions

1 Demonstrate, with examples, the feasibility of a discriminatory pricing strategy for a firm with cross-border markets. Comment critically on attempts by the European Union, as in the motor industry, to eliminate prices discrimination from within its jurisdiction.

2 Evaluate the contribution the stages theory of internationalisation makes to an understanding of the internationalisation processes of firms. Consider the view that the theory is too deterministic.

3 Discuss whether transaction costs represent the most important parameters influencing a firm's choice of foreign market entry modes.

4 Compare and contrast the eclectic paradigm and transaction cost analysis for their explanations of the motives, strength and resilience of multinational firms.

5 Describe the characteristics and purpose of international strategic alliances. Outline the features of a strategic alliance that would seem to be necessary to justify the term 'strategic'.

6 Evaluate the advantages and disadvantages of the joint venture over licensing as a foreign market entry mode. Describe scenarios when licensing might be the preferable one of the two entry modes.

7 In what sense can licensing be described as a second best alternative to exporting? Under what circumstances would licensing be preferred to exporting?

8 International franchising is often regarded as a low-risk foreign market entry strategy. Does this view fully reflect the attraction of international franchising as a market entry mode?

Bibliography

Aharoni, Y. (1966) *The Foreign Investment Decision Process*, Boston, Harvard Business School Press.

Amine, L. S. and Cavusgil, S. T. (1986) 'Export marketing strategies in the British clothing industry', *European Journal of Marketing*, 24, 2, pp. 21–33.

Anderson, E. and Gatignon, H. (1986) 'Modes of foreign entry: a transactions cost analysis and propositions', *Journal of International Business Studies*, Fall, pp. 1–26.

Anderson, O. (1993) 'On the internationalisation process of firms: a critical analysis', *Journal of International Business Studies*, 24, 2, pp. 209–31.

Benito, G. R. G. and Gripsrund, G. (1992), 'The expansion of foreign direct investments: discrete rational location choices or a cultural learning process', *Journal of International Business Studies*, 23, 3, pp. 461–76.

Brooke, M. Z. (1986) *International Management: A Review of Strategies and Operations*, London, Hutchinson.

Brooke, M. Z. and Skilbeck, J. M. (1994) *Licensing: The International Sale of Patents and Technical Know-how*, Aldershot, Gower.

Buckley, P. J. and Casson, M. (1976), *The Future of the Multinational Enterprise*, London, Macmillan.

Buckley, P. J. and Davies, H. (1981) 'Foreign licensing in overseas operations: theory and evidence from the UK' in R. G. Hawkins and A. J. Prasad (eds) *Technology Transfer and Economic Development*, Connecticut: JAI Press.

Burton, F. N. and Cross, A. R. (1997) 'International franchising: market versus hierarchy' in G. Chryssochoidis, C. Millar and L. J. Clegg, *Internationalisation Strategies*, Basingstoke, Macmillan.

Burton, F. N. and Saalens, F. (1994) 'International alliances as a strategic tool of Japanese electronic companies' in N. Campbell and F. N. Burton (eds) *Japanese Multinationals: Strategies and Management in the Global Kaisha*, London, Routledge.

Burton, F. N. and Schlegelmilch, B. B. (1987), 'Profile analysis of non-exporters versus exporters grouped by export involvement', *Management International Review*, 27, 1, pp. 38–49.

Carney, M. and Gedajlovic, E. (1991) 'Vertical integration and franchise systems: agency theory and resource explanations', *Strategic Management Journal*, 12, 3, pp. 607–29.

Casson, M. (1994) 'Internationalisation as a learning process: a model of corporate growth and geographic diversification' in J. Stopford and N. Balasubramanyam (eds) *The Economics of International Investment*, London, Edward Elgar.

Caves, R. (1971) 'Direct investment and the theory of industrial organisation' in J. H. Dunning, *International Investment*, London, Penguin.

Chaplin, D. (1998) 'Franchise types' in *The United Kingdom Franchise Directory*, Norwich, Franchise Development Services.

Coase, R. H. (1937) 'the nature of the firm' in J. G. Stigler and K. E. Boulding (eds) *Readings in Price Theory*, Homewood, Richard D. Irwin.

Commons, J. R. (1934), *Institutional Economics*, Madison, University of Wisconsin Press.

Contractor, F. J. (1990) 'Contractual and cooperative forms of international business: towards a unified theory of modal choice,' *Management International Review*, 30, 1, pp. 31–54.

Cross, A. (2000) 'Modes of internationalisation' in M. Tayeb (ed.) *International Business: Theories, Policies and Practices*, Harlow, Pearson Education.

Cyert, R. D. and March, J. G. (1963) *A Behavioural Theory of the Firm*, Oxford, Blackwell.

Dunning, J. H. (1988) 'The eclectic paradigm of international production: a restatement and some possible extensions', *Journal of International Business Studies*, 19, 1.

Fladmoe-Lidquist, R. and Jaque, L. (1995) 'Control modes in international service operations: the propensity to franchise', *Management Science*, 41, 7, pp. 1238–49.

Forsgren, M. (1990) 'Managing the international multi-centre firm: case studies from Sweden', *European Management Journal*, 8, 2, pp. 261–7.

Hill, C. W. L., Hwang, P. and Kim, W. C. (1990) 'An eclectic theory of the choice of international entry mode', *Strategic Management Journal*, 11, pp. 117–28.

Hoffman, R.C. and Preble, J. F. (1991) 'Selecting a strategy for rapid growth', *Long-Range Planning*, 24, 4, pp. 74–85.

Hood, N. and Young, S. (1979) *The Economics of Multinational Enterprise*, London, Longman.

Hymer, S. H. (1976) *The International Operations of National Firms: A Study of Direct Foreign Investment*, Massachusetts, MIT Press.

Hymer, S. H. (1968) 'The large multinational corporation: an analysis of some motives for the international integration of business' in M. C. Casson (ed.) (1990) *Multinational Corporations*, Cheltenham, Edward Elgar.

Johanson, J. and Vahlne, J.-E. (1990) 'The mechanism of internationalisation', *International Marketing Review*,' 7, 2, pp. 11–24.

Johanson, J. and Vahlne, J.-E. (1977) 'The internationalization process of the firm: a model of knowledge development and increasing foreign market commitment', *Journal of International Business Studies*, 8, 1, pp. 23–32.

Johanson, J. and Wiedersheim-Paul, F. (1975) 'The internationalization process of the firm: four Swedish cases', *Journal of Management Studies*, 12, 3, pp. 305–22.

Keegan, W. (1999) *Global Marketing Management*, New Jersey, Prentice Hall.

Knight, F. H. (1921) *Risk, Uncertainty and Profit*, New York, Harper Row.

March, J. G. and Simon, H. A. (1958) *Organisations*, New York, Wiley.

Mendelsohn, M. (1992) *The Guide to Franchising*, London, Cassell.

Norton, S. W. (1998) 'An empirical look at franchising as an organisational form', *Journal of Business*, 61, 2, pp. 197–217.

Penrose, E. (1959) *The Theory of the Growth of the Firm*, London, Basil Blackwell.

Preble, J. (1992) 'Global expansion: the case of US fast food franchisers', *Journal of Global Marketing*, 6, 1/2, pp. 185–205.

Root, J. (1988) *Strategies for International Markets*, Lexington, MA, Lexington Books.

Rubin, H. (1978) 'The theory of the firm and the structure of the franchise contract', *Journal of Law and Economics*, 21, 3, pp. 223–33.

Rudnick, L.G. (1984) 'An introduction to franchising' in M. Mendelsohn (ed.) *International Franchising: An Overview*, Amsterdam, North Holland.

Rugman, A. (1982) *New Theories of the Multinational Enterprise*, New York, St. Martin's Press.

Rugman, A. (1980) 'A new theory of the multinational enterprise', *Columbia Journal of World Business*, 15, 2, pp. 23–9.

Scarborough, H. and Corbett, M. (1992) *Technology and Organisation: Power, Meaning and Design*, London, Routledge.

Simon, H. (1957) *Models of Man: Social and Rational*, London, Chapman and Hall.

Tordjman, A. (1994) 'Toys "Я" Us' in P. J. McGoldrick (ed.) *Cases in Retailing*, London, Pitman.

Turnbull, P. W. (1987) 'A challenge to the stages theory of the internationalization process' in S. R. Reid and P. J. Rossen (eds) *Managing Export Entry and Expansion*, London, Praeger.

UNCTAD (1996) *World Investment Report: Investment, Trade and International Policy Arrangements*, United Nations Conference on Trade and Development, Geneva, UNCTAD.

Vaughn, C. L. (1979) *Franchising*, Massachusetts, Lexington.

Williamson, O. E. (1971) 'The vertical integration of production: market failure considerations', *American Economic Review*, 61, 1, pp. 112–23.

Young, S., Hamill, J., Wheeler, C. and Davies, J. (1989) *International Market Entry and Development*, Hemel Hempstead, Harvester Wheatsheaf.

Case 9.1 International licensing – the experience of Apple Computers

Apple Computers Inc. sparked the computer revolution in the 1970s with Apple II and by the 1980s was the world's largest computer firm and a leader in design, research and technology (*Economist*, 10 December 1994). In 1984, Apple brought out an innovative new computer, the Apple Mac. IBM, the main competitor, manufactured its own hardware but licensed its operating system, Dos, from Microsoft. This system was also licensed to other computer manufacturers, whose own hardware mimicked IBM's. In 1988, IBN licensed out all its hardware patents in an attempt to set industry-wide standards. The strategy worked and IBM continued to dominate the market for Dos-based computers. Apple refused to license out its operating system, believing that it would lose proprietary advantage and create too many competitors. So Apple produced the Mac and all the rest produced PCs.

Microsoft next introduced a new operating system called Windows, which soon became the universal standard operating system for PCs. Since one software package could not be used on another operating system, the only customers buying Mac software were existing Mac users. The more PC software that came available, the more Apple's market declined.

Belatedly, Apple introduced an advanced chip to the market and decided in 1994 to license out their operating system – a reversal of its long-standing policy of protecting its proprietary knowledge – in the hope that software companies would design programmes for the Mac as manufacturers switched to their system. Problems of compatibility with IBM machines were eventually overcome in 1996 and the licensing of its operating system took off. However, Apple's expectations were disappointed because, instead of expanding the market, the licensees attracted mainly Apple's own customers. Fewer than 1% of cloners' sales were to customers new to Apple technology (*Economist*, 6 September 1997). The licence fees failed to cover Apple's R&D costs and lost sales, and Apple's sales shrank to 5% of the global market. Apple decided to revert to its policy of refusing to license its technologies.

IBM helped the personal computer industry to grow rapidly by licensing its hardware. Apple left it too late to collaborate with IBM and other competitors.

Economist (1994) 'Paradise lost', 10 December; *Economist* (1997) 'Powerless: Apple Computers shuns its clone makers', 6 September.

Case 9.2 PizzaExpress

The first PizzaExpress in the UK opened in London in 1965, the second in 1967. More branches were opened in 1968 and 1969. The first franchise was opened in 1972 as a means of keeping a manager who seemed set on going into competition with PizzaExpress by opening his own pizza restaurant. After becoming a public limited company in 1993 with a full listing on the London Stock Exchange, PizzaExpress began to grow outside the London area with a rapidly expanding portfolio of company-owned and franchised operations, quickly turning a regional business into a national one.

PizzaExpress offers a ten-year business format package to prospective franchisees, renewable for a further ten. Franchisees pay an initial lump sum and a 4% royalty on sales turnover in return for a package that includes operating manuals, recipes, administration, marketing and training. The agreement stipulates that franchisees have to stick to a standard menu, purchase all supplies through the parent and report sales figures weekly.

After becoming a public company, PizzaExpress changed its strategy in favour of company-owned outlets. A £25 million share issue funded the purchase of its franchised outlets. One reason for this total buyback strategy, it has been suggested, was to capture the full earnings potential of the outlets after allowing the franchisees to take on the risks of developing a new market.

Having seen a successful strategy implemented in the UK, PizzaExpress began to prepare a programme of international market entry in 1997 by opening two joint venture franchises in Los Angeles and an independent direct franchise in Cyprus. More franchises were set up later in the same year with a combination of direct and master franchising deals in France, Switzerland, Turkey, Egypt and the Gulf states. In 1998, further franchises were set up in Malta and Russia and a master franchise began

operations in India, with restaurants in New Delhi and Bombay, where recipes were changed to reflect local tastes.

The intentions of PizzaExpress are clear: the parent will buy up any franchise that generates growth and profitability. Although in the early stage of internationalisation, this strategy has proved to be an extremely successful market entry strategy, based on minimum risk and minimum resource commitment.

Case 9.3 The internationalisation of Toys 'Я' Us

As domestic markets become saturated and more competitive, many retailers, sufficiently large and powerful enough to devote resources to international operations and with experience of international business due to the growth of international sourcing, are expanding beyond the confines of their domestic market. With the capability of coordinating and controlling their international operations in consequence of the development of communications and IT, international retailers now derive a substantial proportion of their turnover from foreign markets. Despite this, there still remain substantial barriers to overcome if retailers, like manufacturers, are to become successful in their international operations, including exchange rates, tariffs and quotas, and social, legal and cultural differences. And they need to acquire detailed knowledge of shopping habits and consumer tastes, retailer regulations and the strength and style of competition in the targeted markets.

Toys 'Я' Us, founded in the USA during the 1950s, expanded rapidly in the 1980s both in the USA and abroad, to become the world's largest retailer of children's products with over 1,000 worldwide and sales of almost $10 billion in 1996 (www.toysrus.com). It also operates other specialist stores, such as 215 Kids 'Я' Us children's clothing stores, 98 Babies 'Я' Us stores and two Kids' World superstores.

Each store typically offers 30,000 different product lines, sold at 20% to 50% below prices in conventional toy stores. Toys 'Я' Us guarantees to match the price of any competitor and offers a money-back guarantee on returned goods. The first store outside the USA was opened in Canada in 1983, but the international expansion of Toys 'Я' Us began with the establishment of an international division in 1983. International expansion continued into the European Union and Japan. Because of similarities in language, culture, transportation infrastructure and population density between the UK and US markets, the UK was selected as the entry point for Toys 'Я' Us in European markets despite the fact the UK is only the third-largest toy market in Europe, behind France and Germany (Tordjman, 1994). Toys 'Я' Us now has stores in 13 European countries and has expanded into Southeast Asian markets.

The internationalisation of Toys 'Я' Us has combined direct franchising and master (joint venture) franchising, in around half its foreign stores, with wholly owned subsidiaries. Franchising allowed Toys 'Я' Us to expand rapidly and enter foreign markets that would otherwise have been difficult and expensive to penetrate and to reduce the risk in markets such as South Africa, Saudi Arabia, Indonesia and Turkey. Although the international retail concept is similar to the domestic retail concept and the focus remains on toys, 70% of the merchandise is adapted to suit local tastes in foreign markets. Toys 'Я' Us tapped into the experience of McDonald's via a joint venture franchise in the difficult Japanese market, where the traditional network of small Japanese retailers are protected by the Large Stores Law, which restricts the opening of large-format retailers and where Japanese suppliers are reluctant to upset their local customers by trading with foreign firms. Now Japan is the biggest Toys 'Я' Us market outside the USA.

10 International strategic management

Introduction

Strategy is the process of identifying, implementing, monitoring and controlling the means to satisfy the goals of the firm. These goals can be simple, such as profit maximisation or maximisation of rate of return to investments, to more complex goals that are a multifaceted parcel of objectives to satisfy the many stakeholders of the firm. Whatever the goals of the firm strategic decisions have to be taken on matters such as what products or services should be supplied, what should the firm produce itself and what should it buy in, where should it produce, how should it produce, where should it sell, how should it sell and how should it manage its operations. All firms, including those that only supply their domestic market, are involved in making these sorts of strategic decision. However, large multinational companies face a complex set of strategic choices because of their size and the international aspects of their operations. The large size of many multinational companies means that they are often involved in a number of different industries. For example, General Electric is involved in the markets for aircraft engines, financial services, e-business services, electrical machinery and electrical consumer durables, Such large companies have a number of strategic business units (SBUs) or subsidiaries that concentrate in the firms' activities in a particular industry, market or product line. Each of the SBUs faces the strategic questions of the type just listed. The company must also have a corporate strategy to decide which industries, markets and product lines to focus on, how to divide its many operations into SBUs, how to mesh all the SBUs into a coherent whole to meet the goals of the firm and how to manage the various SBUs. In addition to special issues connected to size, large multinational companies operate in a number of countries and therefore must adopt strategies to deal with the type of issues discussed in this book. The main issues are:

- how to manage cultural differences
- decisions on geographical location of the various operations of the firm
- managing international trade and investment issues
- international marketing issues
- international human resource issues
- policies to manage exchange rate risk and other matters connected to international financial issues
- assessing and developing strategies in response to actual or expected changes in the international business environment.

This chapter is focused on the international strategic management of large multinational companies. However, the strategic issues of small and medium sized enterprises (SMEs) that engage in international business are also considered. A section on strategic planning outlines the orthodox views on this topic. This is followed by an outline of alternative views that focus on the learning capabilities of firms as the major influence on strategic planning. Then comes a section on organisational strategy including strategic decisions on management systems for large multinational companies. The final section examines international strategic planning for SMEs.

Strategic planning

The orthodox view on the process of strategic planning requires multinational companies to make decisions on five basic elements that influence the strategic planning process:

1 Goals of strategic planning.
2 Cultural orientation of strategic planning.
3 Formulating strategic plans.
4 Implementing strategic plans.
5 Monitoring and controlling of strategic plans.

Goals of strategic planning

There are two main views on who should set the goals of firms – shareholders or stakeholders. Stakeholders include shareholders, suppliers of loans, labour, suppliers and consumers. Many multinational companies trade most of their shares in their home market, which can permit the pursuit of wider goals than maximising return to shareholders especially if the ratio of shares to debt is small and if shareholders are regarded as only one of the stakeholders rather than the major stakeholder. These factors mean that the goals of multinational companies can vary depending on their home base. For example, multinational companies that are listed in Anglo-Saxon stock markets face strong pressure to generate sufficient surplus to pay a level of return to shareholders that will be sufficient to prevent hostile takeover by managements that promise higher returns to shareholders. German or Japanese multinationals, in contrast, face less pressure to generate high surpluses to satisfy the short-term requirements of shareholders because they raise a higher proportion of their capital requirements from debt such as loans and the issue of bonds than from the issue of shares than do most multinational companies that are based in Anglo-Saxon countries. Some large German multinational companies are *Stiftungen* (foundations), for example, Bertelsmann the media company and Bosch the electrical engineering company. *Stiftungen* are required to run the firm to make profit but also to provide benefits to employees and for social causes. However, there are pressures on some of these to be listed on stock markets (see Case 10.1).

Multinational companies that are not publicly listed, or when they are listed only in national stock markets and have a low share of capital from shares, can adopt strategies that generate benefits to satisfy many of the non-financial goals of their stakeholders. Moreover, they may be able to pursue long-term strategies in the hope of generating high returns or large market share in the future (Hutton, 1997; Plender, 1997). However, the tendency is for large multinational companies to seek listing in the major stock markets of the world to access the liquidity necessary to finance their activities. This places a strong strategic imperative to generate sufficient surplus from operations to satisfy the requirements of shareholders (Martin, 2000). Therefore, the main goal of strategic planning among large multinational companies is to generate sufficient cash flow to settle debt and enough surplus from operations to provide funds to satisfy at least the minimum objectives of the stakeholders, with an increasing priority being given to the interests of shareholders.

<table>
<tr><td>

Cultural orientation of strategic planning

</td><td>

The parents in multinational companies have their own cultural values that lead them to take particular views on formulating goals and thereby the strategic direction of the firm. Four main types of cultural orientation have been identified (Chakravarthy and Perlmutter, 1985):

</td></tr>
</table>

- Ethnocentric predisposition where the values of the parent company guide strategic decisions.
- Polycentric predisposition leads to an emphasis to develop strategies that are tailored to the different national cultures and subcultural groups in which the firm operates.
- Regiocentric predisposition is a synthesis of the ethnocentric and polycentric predispositions leading to attempts to blend the values of the parent company with those of subsidiaries in the main regions where business activities take place.
- Geocentric predisposition results in global system approach that seeks to develop a strategic approach based on values that are held by all parts of the firm regardless of the location of the parent and the subsidiaries.

The cultural orientation of multinational companies influences the range of strategic approaches in areas such as governance systems, financial, human resource and marketing policies (see Exhibit 10.1).

This type of approach to examining the process of strategic planning highlights the importance of the cultural values of the parent company,

Exhibit 10.1 Cultural orientation and strategic planning

	Ethnocentric	Polycentric	Regiocentric	Geocentric
Governance	Controlled by parent company	Controlled by subsidiary companies	Controlled by combination of parent and main regional subsidiaries	Controlled by a combination of parent and all subsidiaries
Financial policies	Primarily organised to meet the needs of parent company	Primarily organised to meet the needs of subsidiaries	Primarily organised to meet the needs of subsidiaries in main regions	Primarily organised to meet the needs of all units of the firm
HRM policies	Key personnel from home country	Key personnel from host country	Key personnel from main regions	Key personnel from home or host or third countries according to ability
Marketing policies	Tendency to standardise products with minimum adaptation to local needs	Tendency to develop products for local market	Tendency to standardise across regions with significant differences between regions	Global products which are adapted to local needs

Chakravarthy, B. and Perlmutter, H. (1985) 'Strategic planning for a global business', *Columbia Journal of World Business*, 1, pp. 5–6.

but tends to downplay the importance of economic, political and cultural realities that constrain strategic planning. A multinational company that has a large proportion of its shares traded on Anglo-Saxon stock markets or the major international stock markets will face considerable pressure to deliver good returns to shareholders. This will focus strategic planning on the need to satisfy shareholders and will tend towards strong corporate governance and financial control systems by the parent company. Firms that have a strong presence in the European Union are likely to develop a regiocentric approach because of the emergence of a single economic space in Europe that is leading to harmonised laws and regulations that govern business activities (see Chapter 8). However, operations in Asia are less likely to be regiocentric because of the diversity of laws and regulations. Similarly, differences and similarities in cultural clusters (see Chapters 7 and 11) influence the efficacy of adopting national, regional or local approaches to marketing and HRM policies. The attractiveness of a polycentric and regiocentric approaches are undermined by economies of scale and scope, advantages from high levels of standardisation and the attractiveness of particular geographical locations for different types of operations (see Chapters 3 and 6).

Many of the economic, political and cultural realities that face multinational companies would seem to favour the development of a geocentric approach. Developing a truly global approach requires careful policies of regional, national and local adaptation to meet the diverse economic, political and cultural realities that multinational companies encounter. This requires a very capable and adaptable top management team. If the top management team is ethnocentric, they may fail to develop a sufficiently adaptable approach. However, a polycentric management team may fail to satisfy their shareholders leading to the appointing of an alternative management team. A geocentric predisposition will work only if the management is able to successfully balance the many trade-offs between conflicting goals, policies and strategies that are likely to emerge from this inclusive and wide-ranging approach to strategic planning. Consequently, a parent company that has an ethnocentric predisposition is unlikely to be able to develop a successful geocentric approach to strategic planning.

In many respects, a regiocentric approach is attractive for multinational companies that are centred in key regional areas such as the triad. The USA (or the North American region), the EU and Japan embrace most of the economic activity in the world. Furthermore, trading and financial relationships of the members of the Triad with third countries embraces most of the countries of the world. The growth of regional integration blocs such as the EU, NAFTA, Mercusor and the FTTA hold the prospects of the development of single economic spaces in these blocs that are amenable to a more regional approach to strategic planning. Many parent companies are likely to have an ethnocentric predisposition, consequently if economic, political and cultural realities encourage the development of different cultural approaches developing a regiocentric approach is more likely to be successful than the development of a polycentric or geocentric approach. Granting significant autonomy to regional headquarters that operate within a culturally homogenous bloc dilutes the harmful aspects of an ethnocentric predisposition by top management. Moreover, a firm that develops a sound regiocentric approach will be able to cover nearly all major trading opportunities in the world via the large size of members of the triad and their links to countries with which they have special economic and trading relations. In this type of approach, the need to adopt strategies to adjust to different economic and cultural clusters passes to headquarters in the large regional blocs who have better information and capabilities to deal with these differences. This type of approach is common, especially in the USA and the EU. For example, US multinationals such as Ford, General Motors and Kellogg's have European headquarters that are responsible for much of the strategic planning in Europe and North Africa. European multinationals such as Nestlé, Unilever and Volkswagen have US headquarters that cover many of the strategic planning processes for Canada, Mexico and the USA.

Formulating strategic plans

The goals of the firm and the cultural orientation provide the setting for the formation of strategy, but the practicalities of strategic planning require the carrying out of three activities:

1 external environmental assessment
2 internal environmental assessment
3 setting objectives to meet goals.

External environmental assessment

External environmental assessment requires firms to scan economic, political and cultural conditions followed by a more specific assessment of conditions in selected industries and markets. The scanning of macro factors such as economic, political, social and technical changes and expected developments is used to identify industries and markets that are expanding, contracting and in early stages of developments as well as the political risks associated with operations in different parts of the world. Use is often made of PEST (political, economic, social and technological factors) analysis to help to structure the assessment process. This is enables assessment of key issues such as good locations for production, R&D etc., so that advantages can be maximised or costs minimised. This leads to a focus on more micro issues such as the nature of the competition, detailed locational issues such as costs and benefits of particular location within a country or region. The latter issues involve gathering information on competitors, prices, sales, wage costs, taxes and institutional and cultural data on operating in different locations.

Assessing the external competitive environment is often based on Porter's five forces model and the application of these types of model to location in countries or regions to attain and maintain competitiveness (Porter, 1980, 1990). See Exhibit 10.2.

Exhibit 10.2 An adapted five forces model and location for competitiveness

The five forces of Porter's model are

- bargaining power of buyers
- bargaining power of suppliers
- potential entrants
- threat of substitutes
- rivalry among firms in industry.

By adding technical change, labour supply, provision of finance and the role of government to the Porter model, it is possible to assess the general factors that determine the competitive position of a firm in terms of particular locations.

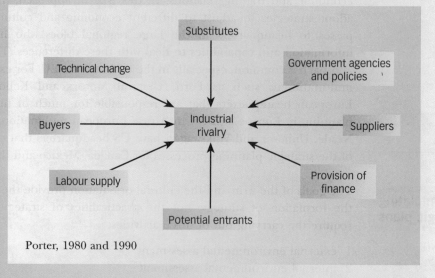

Porter, 1980 and 1990

In industries with buyers that have strong bargaining power and high-quality requirements firms will have to adopt strategies that keep costs under control and deliver high qualities. Firms located in countries where domestic buyers demand large quantities with high qualities, force domestic firms to produce at low cost (reaping any economies of scale that are available) and to deliver high-quality output. This leads to benefits in international markets as firms can enter this markets with low costs and high qualities.

If the suppliers to the industry are competitive, sources of supply will provide low-cost, high-quality inputs. Vertical integration or partnership agreements with suppliers will lead to advantages in cases where supply costs and quality can be improved because of economies of scope and lower transaction costs than buying on the market. In cases where suppliers can exercise monopoly power over buyers, vertical integration can also lead to competitive advantage.

Potential entrants can affect competitiveness if price competition would increase from entry and thereby threaten the ability of existing firms to make acceptable profits. However, potential entrants can provide incentives for existing firms to keep on top of costs and quality control procedures.

The threat of substitutes requires firms to develop their products and to set prices to deter entry by substitutes or to ensure that substitutes do not destroy their markets.

Rivalry among the members of the industry influences competitiveness by either very fierce price competition that makes it difficult to make adequate profits or low competition that breeds complacency that can result in firm failure with the arrival of new entrants or substitutes. Strategies to combat strong price competition can include a move to competition by qualities such a product differentiation or adding value by increasing the service input to the product or moving to niche markets.

Government agencies and policies affect competitiveness because of the effectiveness of support agencies that provide help with technical matters, for example, universities and other types of government R&D institutions. The system of regulations and policies in areas such as taxation, subsidies and bureaucratic rules also affects the competitiveness of firms. Firms located in countries where government agencies and policies are supportive of firms including creating and maintaining a competitive environment will prosper compared to those that face 'bad' government.

Exhibit 10.2 *continued*

The external environment is also influenced by the ability of the firm to adopt and adjust to technical change. Firms that are in locations that have agents involved in leading edge technical developments and that are networked with the agents involved in technical change will benefit from these links.

The characteristics of the supply of labour impact on competitiveness because providing sufficient quantities of suitable qualified labour at acceptable wages permits firms to make at least adequate profits. If national/local labour markets do not provide this, then the ease by which labour can migrate to areas of labour shortages is important.

The provision of finance services is important because difficult access to these services or when they are expensive hampers investment plans and the provision of working capital. Although firms can access international capital and financial services markets, this is expensive unless it involves large-scale operations such as raising bonds on the eurocurrency markets or hiring the services of international banks. Access to effective and price competitive financial services is important for many firms and

if this not available it adds to the costs of firms and undermines their competitiveness.

The Porter approach to assessing the external environment focuses attention on the many factors that affect the competitiveness of firms and illustrates many of the issues discussed in other chapters of this book, for example, the importance of geographical location, institutional frameworks, financial conditions etc. The approach also indicates the importance of adjustment to compensate for poor conditions by strengths elsewhere. For example, firms facing significant threat from new entrants or substitutes may be able to compensate by recourse to access to good sources of technical change or by vertical integration or partnership agreements with suppliers to secure cost and quality advantages. The approach clearly highlights the advantages that can arise from particular locations that grant access to desirable resources and the ability to reap agglomeration benefits. It is, therefore, not surprising that the work of Porter plays an important role in the examination of the benefits of geographical concentration of firms (see Chapter 6).

Internal environmental assessment

Internal environment assessment is the evaluation of the resources that are available or can be acquired by firms. These include the physical, knowledge and relationship assets of firms. Thus, a firm that has access to an ample supply of knowledge assets such as leading edge technologies and that has developed relationships assets (networks of people, firms and agencies) to make good use of these technologies is well placed to engage in high tech activities. Whereas a firm with good access to crude oil supplies and with refineries and chemical-processing plant in locations that have low costs will have competitive advantages in the petrochemical industry.

The work of Porter once again provides models for analysing these issues (Porter, 1985). At the heart of Porter's analysis is the concept of a value chain that traces the activities of the firm or for SBUs from inbound logistics (receiving inputs) through operations (making, testing and packaging products) to outbound logistics (distributing products to customers) into marketing and sales and after-sales services. The supporting activities of the firm such as management system, HRM functions and technical development are all included in the value chain. The objective of analysing the supply chain is to identify how to make improvements so that the value at the end of the chain is maximised. Multinational companies can use the concept of the value chain to decide how best to make use of its resources (see Case 10.2). Thus, if the best (in terms of maximising value) engineers and supporting services to develop products are located in Germany and the best scientists and supporting universities to conduct basic research are the USA, then R&D should be based in the USA and product development in Germany. If the lowest cost place to assembly the product is Poland for distribution to Europe and in Mexico to supply the Americas the location of inbound logistics, operations and outbound logistics should follow from these resource considerations thereby leading to a chain of activities that maximises value. This approach can embrace many of the aspects of the external environment assessment because it considers issues connected to location such as supporting industries and government agencies as well as the internal resources of firms.

Value chain analysis also allows incorporation of generic strategies to adapt to different competitive conditions. If the internal resources and locations of firm or an SBU lead to a value chain that does not confer competitiveness in the area of improving the qualities of products or in markets where products are standardised firms can concentrate on a *cost leadership strategy* by adopting policies to control costs that permits the firm to be price competitive. However, if the characteristics of the value chain and market conditions can provide the opportunity to develop products to make them distinct from competitors a *differentiation strategy* to build brand loyalty and/or expand value-added services leads to higher prices for products. If the value chain of an SBU or subsidiary confers advantages to specialise in a particular geographic or niche market a *focus strategy* that segments markets will permit the accumulation of benefits such as economies of scale and the capture of a larger market share. A firm that has value chains among its SBUs that differ would adopt a *mixed strategy* with cost leadership in some markets, differentiation and focus strategies in others.

Setting objectives to meet goals

After the goals are established and the completion of external and internal environmental assessments the next step is to set the objectives to meet the goals of the firm. Coordination of the various assessments is necessary to establish the best options that have emerged from the gathering and processing of information. This can involve techniques such as SWOT (strengths, weakness, opportunities and threats) analysis. The results of such analysis leads to selection of options that must be transposed into functional policies that embrace the distribution, financial, marketing, production and human resource management policies to allow the goals of the firm to be met. Firms that have SBUs or subsidiaries must break these objectives down into the component parts for each SBU and devise systems for coordinating the various activities of the firm.

The process of strategic planning is illustrated in Figure 10.1.

Figure 10.1 Process of formulating strategy

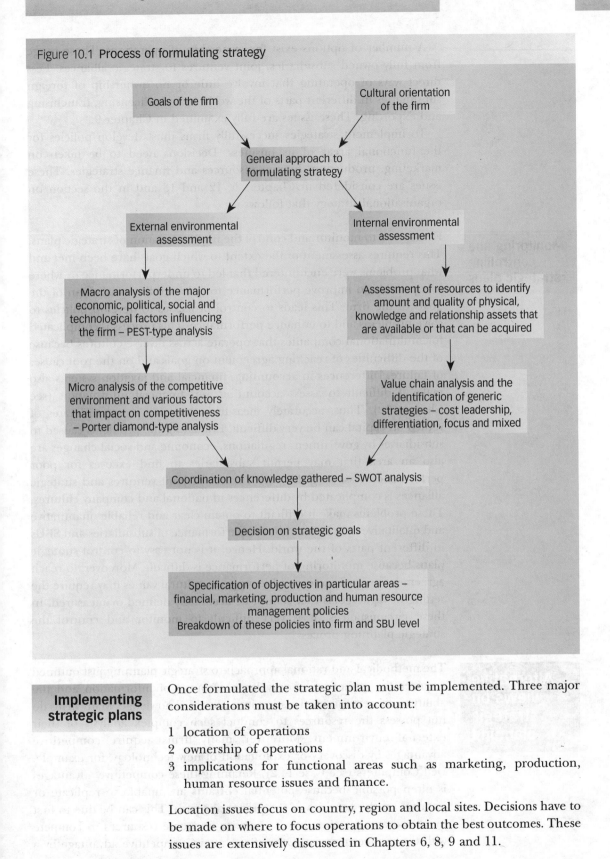

Implementing strategic plans

Once formulated the strategic plan must be implemented. Three major considerations must be taken into account:

1 location of operations
2 ownership of operations
3 implications for functional areas such as marketing, production, human resource issues and finance.

Location issues focus on country, region and local sites. Decisions have to be made on where to focus operations to obtain the best outcomes. These issues are extensively discussed in Chapters 6, 8, 9 and 11.

A number of options exist for ownership of operations. These range from fully owned subsidiaries, joint ventures to strategic alliances. Less direct ways of operating that involve little or no ownership of foreign subsidiaries in different parts of the world include, licensing, franchising and exporting. These issues are fully examined in Chapter 9.

To implement strategies successfully firms must develop policies for the functional areas of its business. Decisions need to be taken on marketing, production, human resources and finance strategies. These issues are considered in Chapters 5, 12 and 13 and in the section on organisational strategy that follows.

Monitoring and controlling strategic plans

Firms need to monitor and control the implementation of strategic plans. This requires assessment of the extent to which goals have been met and what problems were encountered that led to underperformance or where it is possible to improve performance to enhance the satisfaction of the goals of the firm. This leads to control processes to develop policies to solve problems and to enhance performance. This process is complicated for multinational companies that operate across diverse cultures because of the difficulties of reaching agreement on goals and on the root causes of failure. Differences in accounting, financial and taxation systems also make it difficult to assess accounting and financial information (see Chapter 12). Thus, accurately measuring revenues, costs and rates of return on capital can be very difficult. Evaluating the problems caused to subsidiaries by government regulations, economic and social changes are also an area that may permit subsidiaries to find excuses for poor performance. Assessing the performance of joint ventures and strategic alliances is complicated by differences in national and company cultures. These problems make it difficult to obtain clear and reliable quantitative and qualitative data to monitor the performance of subsidiaries and SBUs in different parts of the world. Hence, it is not easy to control strategic plans because monitoring of performance is difficult. Moreover, to reach agreement on goals across a wide range of cultural values may require the setting of vague goals that cannot be accurately defined or measured. In these circumstances, it is very difficult to monitor and control the strategic planning process.

Alternative views on strategic planning

The methodical and rational approach to strategic planning just outlined requires the gathering of very large amounts of information and the ability to convert this information into valuable knowledge. Many firms do not possess the resources to conduct such complex analysis of their external environment. Moreover, many firms acquire competitive advantages by discovery or exploitation of new technology, for example, Dell Computers (see Case 14.2). Retaining these competitive advantages is often possible because potential entrants are unable to replicate or improve on the activities of the pioneering firm. This can be due to first mover advantages or failure to acquire adequate resources to compete with the pioneering firm. Other firms attain competitive advantage by a process of clustering in areas that confer competitive advantages. These clusters are often the result not of rational calculation to locate in a particular area, but by historical accidents and a series of steps in response to events, for example, the firms that established themselves Silicon Valley or Route 128 (see Case 6.1). Firms that are not located in these clusters are unable to acquire the benefits that arise from being in these geographical concentrations (see Chapter 6).

Firms may also grow to become large multinational companies by a process of merger and acquisition in response to unexpected opportunities. Vodafone became a leading multinational mobile telephone firm by acquisition of firms such of Air Touch in the USA and Mannesmann in Germany. The strategy of Vodafone appears to be based largely on opportunistic acquisition as circumstances lead to mobile telephone firms becoming available for takeover. The main competitive advantage of Vodafone is its ability quickly to engineer the financial resources and management expertise to respond to opportunities to acquire firms. Vodafone has clearly demonstrated that it possesses considerable expertise in this area. The takeover of Mannesmann was the first large-scale hostile takeover in Germany and the first to involve a foreign company. However, Vodafone now faces the challenge of weaving its empire into a coherent whole and of meeting the competitive, technological and regulatory challenges and opportunities that await (*Economist*, 2000a). To meet this challenge Vodafone may have to develop the type of strategic planning approach outlined earlier.

Other firms gain and maintain competitive advantage not by careful strategic planning but by entrepreneurial skill backed by astute management of market conditions. For example, Microsoft established a dominant competitive advantage not by careful strategic planning that assessed and balanced the many factors just outlined, but primarily by developing a new technology that gave it monopoly power and, according to a federal US court, by protecting its monopoly by anti-competitive practices (*Economist*, 2001a).

Government policy can also provide the conditions that allow firms to establish themselves as major multinational companies. Thus, Electricité de France (EDF) the French electricity-generating company became a major multinational company not by careful strategic planning based on Porter-type analysis, but by taking advantage of the privatisation programmes that provided opportunities to buy foreign electricity generation and distribution companies. However, EDF is protected from takeover because it is a nationalised company and it has access to low-cost borrowing since its loans are guaranteed by the French government (*Economist*, 2000b).

Clearly, the route to the development of successful multinational companies does not necessarily depend on the type of detailed strategic planning shown in Figure 10.1. Indeed, detailed strategic planning may be more relevant for maintaining competitive advantages that have emerged from historical accidents (firms in Silicon Valley), or entrepreneurial behaviour (Bill Gates in the development of Microsoft or Michael Dell in Dell Computers), mergers and acquisitions (Vodafone) and the successful development of advantages arising from government policies (EDF). The main elements of this view of the strategic planning process are illustrated in Figure 10.2.

Strategic planning involves learning as implementing strategies leads to outcomes, some expected and other unexpected. New problems and opportunities also become evident as firms learn. The process of gathering information leads to attempts to convert the information into useful knowledge. Thus, as firms engage in the process of strategic planning and then implement it, they acquire information that is converted into knowledge. They seek to transfer this knowledge across their various activities to help them to satisfy their goals. However, transferring knowledge is difficult, particularly tacit knowledge (that which is personalised, non-routine and intuitive). Even the transfer of explicit knowledge (that which is codified, formal and specific) can be difficult if cultural understanding about the value and meaning of explicit knowledge is not shared. This leads to a rather slow and evolutionary strategic planning process that emerges as firms learn (Quinn et al., 1988).

The effectiveness of emergent strategies based on learning is connected to the development of relationship assets (membership of networks and access to resources that can help to transform information into useful knowledge) and the ability to transfer knowledge (especially tacit knowledge) across the various parts of the firm. The capability to monitor and control the strategic planning process is connected to the ability of the firm to learn, which is related to the characteristics of the organisational system. At the heart of this view of strategic planning is the ability of firms to accumulate relationship assets, sometimes called

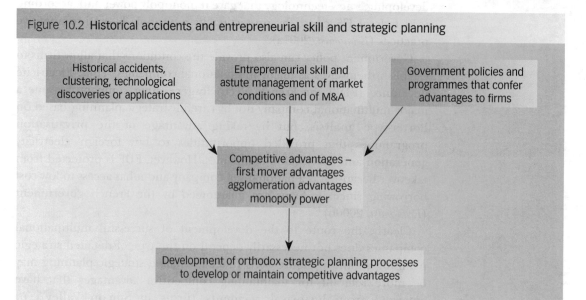

Figure 10.2 Historical accidents and entrepreneurial skill and strategic planning

relationship or social capital (Dasgupta and Serageldin, 2000). Thus, the strategic planning process can be viewed not as an exercise in rational measurement and calculation to gather and process information to design optimal strategies as illustrated in Figure 10.1, but as a process that evolves as firms learn better ways to achieve their goals (Gulati, 1999; Kale et al., 2000). This view of strategic planning implies that successful multinational companies will be those that develop their network of subsidiaries into effective learning machines. Techniques such as PEST and SWOT analysis and the use of conceptual frameworks of the Porter type are still useful in this approach to strategic planning as means to structure the strategic planning process. However, the process is more evolutionary and emergent as compared to the complicated exercise in optimisation outlined earlier. In this evolutionary view of strategic planning, mistakes are made, lessons are learned or there is failure to learn and firms often end up at very different positions than they first planned (see Case 10.3).

The main elements of the learning firm view on strategic planning are illustrated in Figure 10.3.

Figure 10.3 The learning firm and strategic planning

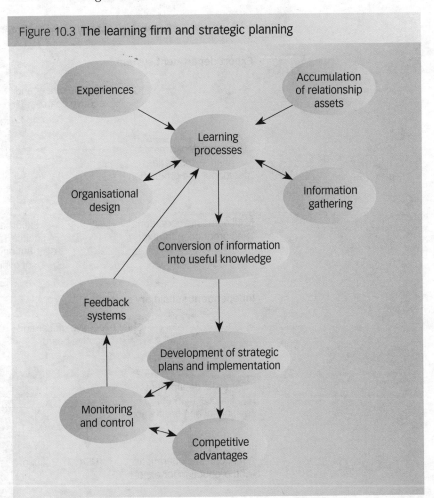

Organisational strategy

Managing international business operations requires the design and implementation of organisational systems. These organisational systems range from simple export systems to complex matrix structures that seek to weave a host of subsidiaries into a coherent transnational firm. Organisational strategy also seeks to create and develop relationships between parent companies and their subsidiaries.

Organisational systems

The simplest of organisational systems is to establish an export department to managing the process of exporting. This type of organisation is used by many small and medium sized enterprises (SMEs) where exporting is the primary means of conducting international business activities. Firms that expand exporting activity by developing significant production, distribution, sales, after-sales and marketing operations overseas may develop the simple export department system by establishing either a set of independent subsidiaries in its main areas of operations, or an international division system where overseas subsidiaries are managed by an international division at the parent company. Firms that develop an extensive network of subsidiaries that are involved in a multitude of

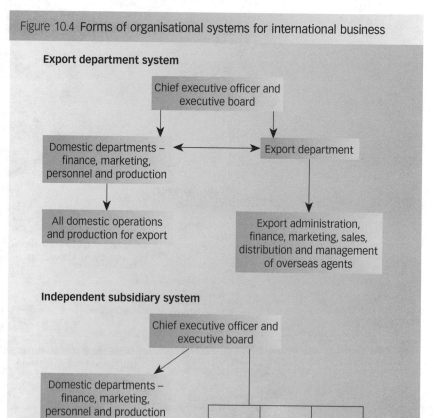

Figure 10.4 Forms of organisational systems for international business

Export department system

Chief executive officer and executive board

Domestic departments – finance, marketing, personnel and production ⟷ Export department

All domestic operations and production for export

Export administration, finance, marketing, sales, distribution and management of overseas agents

Independent subsidiary system

Chief executive officer and executive board

Domestic departments – finance, marketing, personnel and production

All domestic operations and production for export

USA   Japan   Brazil   China

operations often use matrix type of organisational systems that allow the various parts of the firm to interact with each other without the costly and time-consuming process of going through a hierarchical organisational system. Clearly, the more involved a firm is in international business activities the more complex is the organisational system necessary to manage these activities. These systems are illustrated in Figure 10.4.

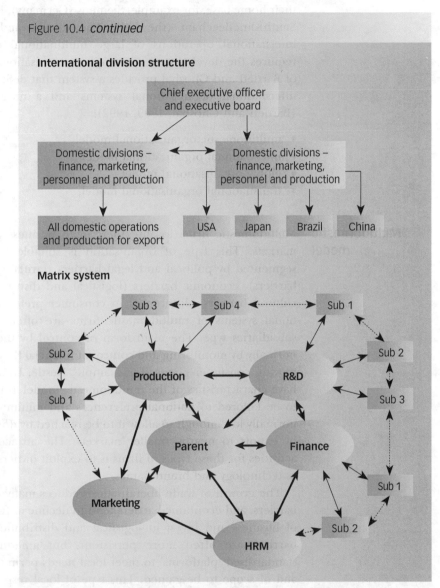

Figure 10.4 *continued*

International division structure

Matrix system

Centres (for production, marketing etc.) and subsidiaries (Sub) can communicate and arrange collaboration with any part of the system and need not go through the centres or the parent. Simpler matrix systems would restrict communications and collaboration to parent and centres with communication with subsidiaries via centres. Monitoring and control is exercised by the parent and the centres.

Large multinational companies often have extensive foreign operations. Indeed, many multinational companies that are based in small or medium sized economies conduct most of their business outside their home bases, for example Nestlé (Switzerland), Philips (the Netherlands) and Nokia (Finland). Some multinational companies based in large economies conduct a significant amount of business activities outside their home base, for example, Siemens (Germany), Renault (France) and SmithKlineBeecham (the UK). The volume and complexity of the international operations of large multinational companies normally requires the development of complex organisational systems. The work of Bartlett and Ghoshal provides a system that defines the main types of international organisational systems and a means to analyse them (Bartlett and Ghoshal, 1989, 1992):

- multidomestic organisational model
- international organisational model
- global organisational model
- transnational organisational model.

Multidomestic model

Multidomestic firms localise their main business activities in national markets. This type of organisation is suitable for markets that are segmented by political and legal barriers (tariffs, quotas and non-tariff barriers), economic barriers (logistical and distribution problems) and cultural barriers (differences in consumer preferences). The organisational systems of multidomestic firms are often of the independent subsidiaries type. The main form of control by the parent company is normally by monitoring and control of financial flows. Many firms in fast-moving consumer goods (for example, Nestlé, Unilever and Campbell) have characteristics of the multidomestic model as this enables products to be tailored to national preferences and minimum efficiency scale is normally low enough to allow it to be reached by domestic production or by export to nearby smaller markets. The attraction of international activities for these types of firms is to exploit ownership advantages such as technology and brand names.

The growth of trade liberalisation reduces many of political and legal barriers, and economic barriers tend to decline as firms expand the level of business and invest in logistical and distribution facilities. Cultural barriers are often more persistent, but amending products from standardised 'platforms' to meet local needs permits economies of scale and of scope to be gained. This type of local responsiveness is used by firms such as Coca-Cola and the meals provided by McDonald's. The basic product is the same everywhere but the 'platform' can be altered to suit local needs by increasing or reducing the amount of sugar and carbon dioxide in Coca-Cola and, for instance, offering a Big Mac meal with a veggie burger rather than a beef burger in countries such as India.

The multidomestic history of the car industry in Europe is reflected by the names of GM cars in Europe – Vauxhall in the UK and Ireland and

Opel in the rest of Europe, both of which were firms taken over by GM. However, the models are now the same and Vauxhall cars may be manufactured in Germany and Opel cars in the UK. Ford, which used to sell different models in the various European countries, sells the same models with slight variations across most of the world and uses the same names for their models in all countries. Car companies such as GM and Ford are no longer multidomestic firms, but in the post-World War II period until the 1970s, the European operations of GM and Ford had many of the characteristics of a multidomestic firm.

Firms such as Nestlé and Unilever continue to have some of the features of a multidomestic firm because of the persistence of cultural barriers to standardisation and the possibility to attain minimum efficiency scale at low levels of production. There is a case for a modern form of the multidomestic firm for industries that do not have strong economies of scale and where local responsiveness is important. However, to be successful such firms must devise organisational systems that enable them to learn from the spread of their international activities (Yetton et al., 1995).

International model
The post-World War II period of internationalisation was characterised by the development of direct foreign investment (DFI) by US firms to exploit new technologies such as electrical equipment. These firms expanded into foreign markets to take advantage of the new products that they have developed. The product life cycle theory of internationalisation explains the emergence of the international model based on observation of the process of exporting leading to DFI by US firms (Vernon, 1966). In the product life cycle model firms initially expand into foreign markets by exporting to reap economies of scale. However, as the product reaches maturity, DFI is used to locate production in countries with lower costs of production and to take advantage of the expansion phase in foreign markets. This induces an organisational model that manages subsidiaries to meet the needs of the parent. The independent subsidiary model with strong direction from headquarters or the international division system of organisation fits with the international model. Organisational systems based on the international model favour standardisation so that products can be exported to most parts of the world with local adaptation by subsidiaries. The R&D and product development activities of the firm are centred in the parent company, as are monitoring and control activities.

From the 1970s on the reduction in trade barriers from regional integration and GATT rounds and technical changes such as the introduction of electronic products such as computer-controlled machines and computer-aided design into production systems led, in many industries, to the potential to reap economies of scale and scope and the ability to supply from centralised production sites. This led to the rapid introduction of new products in all major markets, rather than a phased introduction as the product life cycle progressed. Hence, the stages of internationalisation ceased to be explained by reference to the life cycle of products. New stage theories based on learning explained the development of internationalisation by reference to the psychological barriers to internationalisation, in particular, learning to manage cross-cultural business activities (Johanson and Vahlne, 1977). In this era, the international model tended to give way to the evolution of global and transnational systems on the basis that firms learned how to manage cross-cultural activities and thereby seek to reap maximum benefit from their various resources, which induces shifts to new organisational systems.

However, the international model may not be dead, in that modern forms of this type of organisational system may exist, at least in Europe. There is evidence that the European subsidiaries of multinational companies based in large European countries are often little more than export outlets or low-cost production sites for parent companies (Chesnais et al., 2000). This outcome may arise when minimum efficiency scale requires large-scale operations and where transport costs are low, allowing supply by export to nearby countries. The low level of trade barriers and common or harmonised standards in Europe favours consolidation of production near large markets for industries with high minimum efficiency scale that can sell fairly standardised products (see Chapter 6). Firms located in large European economies are close to large markets and are well integrated into local networks and therefore do not need to establish local networks in their European subsidiaries to gain network advantages. However, DFI to locate activities in countries with low labour costs is attractive when large (but low-skilled) labour inputs are required. DFI to enhance exports in other large markets in the EU is also beneficial. In these circumstances, subsidiaries become outposts of the parent company often being little more than sales or distribution outlets or low-cost sources for intermediary products or for assembly of final products (McDonald et al., 2002). In these conditions, an organisational system not unlike the international model, where internationalisation is driven by the need to develop the operations of the parent company, may be attractive.

Global model

The global model is based on economies of scale and scope and the benefits of standardisation (Levitt, 1983). In this model firms operate internationally to exploit their ownership advantages and locational advantages such as lower labour costs. The organisational system is often of the international division type with strong control by the parent. Japanese multinational companies are traditionally identified with this model particularly with the international expansion of Japanese car and consumer electronic products companies. This process was driven by a desire to exploit their ownership advantages – new and efficient production systems based on just-in-time and total quality management systems (Womack et al., 1990). Foreign operations were necessary to reduce transport costs and to established operations within large markets that had significant trade barriers against Japanese exports (the USA and the European Union). The main role of subsidiaries is to act as export enhancers (sales and distribution or screwdriver plants) or in large markets to be assemblers of cars and consumer electronic products to supply, at low transport costs, within the free trade area. Technical change, increasing trade liberalisation and consumer resistance to standardisation undermines the global model (see following, section 'Transnational model').

However, this type of organisational system may continue to have life in subsidiaries located in small economies where the main attraction is to reap locational advantages such as low labour costs or to be channels of distribution. This type of organisational systems appears to be prevalent in DFI into central and eastern Europe to supply the larger and richer markets of Western Europe with standardised products that need little modification to meet local needs. Many investments in developing countries often have elements of the global model in that the main motivation is to secure low-cost production sites for which to supply richer markets with standardised products or to act as sales and distribution channels for standardised products. Parts of the international financial services industry such as international bond- and equity-issuing and trading, and foreign exchange trading also closely resemble the global model. This industry is involved with global products and can reap economies of scale and scope by developing deep and wide markets that are located in key regions from which they supply world or large regional markets (see Chapters 5 and 12).

Transnational model

The move towards standardisation is hampered by consumer resistance to uniform products and the growth of demand for products more tailored to customers requirements (*Economist*, 2001b). New IT-based technologies and the development of flexible production systems make it easier to reach minimum efficiency scale and thereby reduced the need for large standardised production runs. Regulatory requirements that require significant modification to products, especially in the service industries and in the legal requirements for after-sales service and product liability also contribute to the decline in the global model as an ideal type of organisational system. These factors led to a need for quick, efficient and flexible responses to changing regulatory, technical and consumer preferences developments. This focuses attention on the need for firms to be learning organisations that can make the best use of their network of subsidiaries (Birkinshaw, 2000). The adoption of this type of model leads to a matrix-type system of organisation with strategic planning that is emergent or evolutionary in character as firms learn how to be lean and flexible.

The main problem with this type of organisational system is controlling the learning process and ensuring that it leads to fulfilment of the goals of the firm. There is also the danger that the firm will not have well-defined goals but will embrace a host of goals from the wide variety of cultural values that are held across the organisation. Such firms may become little more than learning machines that are unable to transpose information into knowledge that is valuable for satisfying the goals of the firm. Many of the dot.com companies that crashed in 2000 fell into this category (*Economist*, 2000c). Moreover, as argued earlier, some multinational companies may still be able effectively to operate using new forms of the multidomestic, international or global model.

Relationship between parents and subsidiaries

Whatever the type of international organisation model used by multinational companies they have to establish and develop systems to govern relationships between headquarters and subsidiaries. Increasing competitive pressures are focusing attention on the need to achieve effective performance at every level of the operation of the firm leading to the creation of SBUs that are profit or cost centres (Porter, 1986). Moreover, incentives to make the best use of the network of subsidiaries and to create learning machines from the web of connections that firms create requires the cultivation of subsidiaries as key contributors to the process of value creation (Birkinshaw and Hood, 1998a and b). These pressures require the development of organisational systems that permit multinational companies to effectively communicate and negotiate with their subsidiaries to achieve the goals of the firms.

Two main approaches to these problems have been advanced:

1 The 'top-down' approach where the roles of subsidiaries are allocated by the parent (Bartlett and Ghoshal, 1986).
2 The 'bottom-up' approach where the level of integration within firms is primarily decided by the views of subsidiaries relative to the overall goals of the firm (Prahalad and Doz, 1987).

Both approaches focus on the benefits and costs of autonomy to subsidiaries as opposed to integration into the activities of the network of subsidiaries and the parent company. The difference in the approaches is mainly the method used to decide on the level of autonomy versus integration. The 'top-down' method is based on negotiations between the subsidiary and the parent with the latter in the driving seat. The framework for the negotiations comes from the strategic plans developed at headquarters. The 'bottom-up' approach is less centralised with subsidiaries having a large contribution to the development and implementation of strategic plans. The level of autonomy relative to integration is determined by the benefits from localised decisions (meeting the requirements of segmented markets, regulatory conditions and cultural values) compared to benefits of integrated and centralised decisions (economies of scale and scope and benefits from standardisation). These factors vary across industries, countries and markets; therefore, the best relationship between headquarters and subsidiaries will vary according to these factors. The main possibilities are illustrated in Figure 10.5.

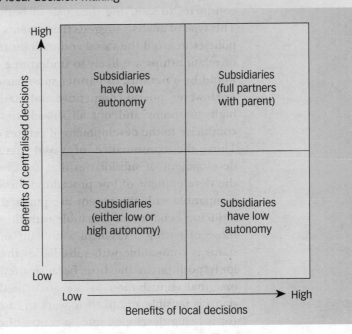

Figure 10.5 Headquarters' and subsidiaries' relationships – centralised versus local decision making

The allocation of autonomy to subsidiaries is problematic in the case of low benefits from centralisation and from local decisions (the bottom left-hand side in Figure 10.5). In this case, it is not clear which type of a relationship should be developed.

This approach to headquarters and subsidiary relationships does not consider the behavioural aspects of relationships between parents and subsidiaries. These issues have been investigated by reference to the concepts of autonomy (the extent to which management systems place power at the centre) and procedural justice (the extent to which management systems are based on concepts of trust and fairness in relationships between parents and subsidiaries). This work leads to a fourfold classification of subsidiaries (Taggart, 1996):

- Vassal – low procedural justice and autonomy.
- Partner – high procedural justice and autonomy.
- Militant – low procedural justice and high autonomy.
- Collaborator – high procedural justice and low autonomy.

Vassal subsidiaries are likely to be a problem for parent companies because of feelings of unfair treatment that undermine the performance of the subsidiary. Militant subsidiaries also pose problems because they feel aggrieved by what is considered unnecessary interference by the parent. This type of problem may arise when a firm is the subject of an unwanted takeover. Collaborator subsidiaries may be a successful relationship providing the low level of autonomy is accepted by the managers and workers in the subsidiaries. Partner-type relationships are ideal for subsidiaries that are centres of competence (Birkinshaw and Hood, 1998a) as they are likely to induce the type of behaviour that is conducive to satisfying the goals of both the parent and the subsidiary. This type of analysis suggests that parents and subsidiaries should develop policies to avoid the vassal and militant relationships because these types of relationships are likely to undermine performance. The ideal system would be a network of partner subsidiaries.

However, not all competitive and market conditions are conducive to high autonomy and not all subsidiaries are located in areas that are conducive to the development of centres of competence (see Chapter 6). Thus, the continuance of vassal status may be preferable to the development of subsidiaries that are given autonomy but then require the development of low procedural justice systems to ensure that goals compatible with the parent are pursued. In this case, the problems of inducing behaviour compatible with the goals of the parent move from those of having a vassal to a militant subsidiary. Granting collaborator status is compatible with subsidiaries that are content with their rather lowly position in the firm because they accept that they make only a marginal contribution to the goals of the firm. Developing a partner status is sensible and likely to work in cases where the subsidiary either is (or is being developed into) a centre of competence.

The problems and issues of developing the appropriate system for relationships between headquarters and subsidiaries highlights many of the recurrent problems with strategic planning – choosing the best system to managing across cultures, selecting the appropriate mix between standardisation and differentiation and locating activities in those places that yield the best competitive advantages. The decisions made on these types of problems largely determine what type of subsidiary relationship is best, or at least not harmful, for the satisfaction of the goals of the firm.

Strategic planning and small and medium sized enterprises

In principle, the limited resources available to SMEs restrict their ability to engage in international business activities. However, engaging in international business activities can permit SMEs to reap economies of scale and scope and to diversify to reduce the risks associated with concentration in domestic markets. Nevertheless, the transaction costs of gathering and processing the information necessary to engage in international business activities and the design and maintenance costs of systems to manage cross-cultural business, combined with the costs associated with exchange rate risk deters many, if not most, SMEs from engaging in such activities. Where they do engage in international business activities, traditional wisdom assumed that these operations are restricted to niche markets (Simon, 1996) and follow the stage theory of internationalisation by progressing from simple forms such as exporting to more complex entry modes as they accumulated knowledge of international business conditions (Johanson and Vahlne, 1977). Moreover, the costs associated with dealing with a large number of countries, especially those with substantially different cultural values, and of managing more complex modes of entry limits many SMEs to exporting to countries to which they are culturally close. The traditional view on the international business activities of SMEs was therefore that most would have little or no international activities and those that were involved would have limited international operations. Consequently, research on international strategic planning by SMEs of the type just outlined was considered to be of minor importance.

Government policy aimed at helping SMEs to cope with the demands of internationalisation is based on this view and has focused on reducing the transaction costs and uncertainty costs of international business operations by providing free or low-cost information on international conditions and markets and a variety of schemes to reduce risk such as export guarantee systems. One of the aims of European Monetary Union is to reduce the transaction and translation costs associated with intra-EU trade and thereby to stimulate increases in this trade especially among SMEs (see Chapter 8). This type of approach, based on reducing the costs associated with international business activities, dominates government policy towards the internationalisation of SMEs.

This traditional view of the internationalisation process has been challenged by observations of firms (some of them SMEs) that are heavily engaged in international business activities and that begin these activities at the point of foundation or soon after. These observations led to the development of the concept of the 'born global' firm (Knight and Cavusgil, 1996). These firms make extensive use of networks to simultaneously expand in several markets (Madsen and Servais, 1997). The use of networks permits SMEs to engage in rapid expansion into several foreign markets by concentrating in particular activities such as distribution and logistics in some markets and with sales and after-sales handled by partners in other markets (Oviatt and McDougal, 1994). The development of e-business systems offers the possibilities to expand networking by SMEs to further reduce the transaction costs of doing business (Kleindl, 2000). Most of the SMEs found to engage in 'born global' type of operations are in the high tech sector (Bell, 1995). The advantages to SMEs of geographical clustering highlight another type of networking that can aid internationalisation by SMEs (Brown and Bell, 2001).

Research into 'born globals' has identified the development of networks as the key strategic route to successful expansion of internationalisation by SMEs. Geographical concentration in clusters or industrial districts provides another networking route to internationalisation by SMEs. Many of the SMEs in successful industrial districts that are extensively involved in international business activities are not in high tech sectors; neither were they 'born global', rather they extended into rapid international operations because of historical developments (see Chapter 6). Many of the firms in the *Mittelstand* (the German SME sector) are not in the high tech sector and appear to have followed the traditional stage theory route to internationalisation (Simon, 1992). Clearly, understanding of the internationalisation strategies of SMEs is an underdeveloped topic in terms of both conceptual frameworks and empirical knowledge.

Summary

This chapter has investigated the process of strategic planning and the implications of strategic decisions for organisational strategy, including relationships between headquarters and subsidiaries. Strategic issues connected to the internationalisation of SMEs have also been considered. The many factors that influence international strategic planning make this a very complex and difficult process. Indeed, international strategic planning brings into focus the many and various factors that affect international business activities – economic, political, legal and technical factors as well as cultural and organisational factors and the competitive environment in which firms operate. The use of systematic and rational approaches to strategic planning appears to be an appropriate method to deal with his complexity. However, the information-gathering and processing requirements of this approach require substantial resources that are available only to large multinational companies. Moreover, changing circumstances arising from political, economic and technical changes lead to uncertainty as to the best way to plan international business activities. In these circumstances, a more emergent and evolutionary type of strategic planning based on learning can be more effective that the systematic approach.

Organisational strategy is influenced by historical developments such as trade liberalisation, technical change and government policies that shift thinking on ideal models organisation from multidomestic through to transnational. However, all the various types of organisational systems based on these models may make sense in contemporary settings depending on location of subsidiaries and the industries and markets in which multinational companies operate. Similarly, the question of the strategic development of the relationship between headquarters and subsidiaries is not settled and also appears to depend on factors such as location of subsidiaries and industries or markets in which the firm operates. Knowledge about appropriate international strategic planning for SMEs is in the early stages of development and our understanding of this topic is currently limited.

Review questions

1 How do the goals of a multinational company influence the strategic planning process?

2 Outline the major influences of the cultural predisposition of parent companies for strategic planning.

3 Assess the usefulness of a systematic and rational international strategic planning process.

4 Why might an emergent system of international strategic planning be preferable to a more systematic approach?

5 What are the main factors that affect the choice of organisational strategy?

6 Why is good networking essential for SMEs that adopt an international strategy of being 'born global'?

Bibliography

Bartlett, C. and Ghoshal, S. (1992) *Transnational Management: Text, Cases and Readings in Cross-Border Management*, New York, Irwin.

Bartlett, C. and Ghoshal, S. (1989) *Managing Across Borders: The Transnational Solution*, Boston, MA, Harvard Business School Press.

Bartlett, C. and Ghoshal, S. (1986) 'Tapping your subsidiaries for global reach', *Harvard Business Review*, 64, pp. 87–94.

Bell, J. (1995) 'The internationalization of small computer software firms: a further challenge to stage theories', *European Journal of Marketing*, 29, 8, pp. 60–75.

Birkinshaw, J. (2000) *Entrepreneurship in the Global Firm*, London, Sage.

Birkinshaw, J. and Hood, N. (eds) (1998a) *Multinational Corporate Evolution and Subsidiary Development*, London, Macmillan.

Birkinshaw, J. and Hood, S. (1998b) 'Multinational subsidiary evolution: capability and charter change in foreign-owned subsidiary companies', *Academy of Management Review*, 23, pp. 773–95.

Brown, P. and Bell, J. (2001) 'Industrial districts and small firm internationalisation' in S. Young and N. Hood (eds) *The Multinational in the Millennium: Companies and Countries, Changes and Choices*, London, Palgrave.

Chakravarthy, B. and Perlmutter, H. (1985) 'Strategic planning for a global business', *Columbia Journal of World Business*, 1, pp. 5–6.

Chesnais, F., Ietto-Gilles, G. and Simonette, R. (eds) (2000) *European Integration and Global Corporate Strategies*, London, Routledge.

Dasgupta, P. and Serageldin, I. (2000) *Social Capital: A Multifaceted Perspective*, New York, World Bank.

Economist (2001a) 'Microsoft trial: a loss of trust', 7 July, pp. 81–2.

Economist (2001b) 'Special report: mass customisation', 14 July, pp. 79–81.

Economist (2000a) 'Vodafone-Mannesmann: what next?', 10 February, pp. 88–9.

Economist (2000b) 'A giant awakes', 2 November, pp. 119–20.

Economist (2000c) 'Too few pennies from heaven', 1 July, pp. 107–10.

Gulati, R. (1999) 'Network location and learning: the influence of network resources and firm capabilities on alliance formation', *Strategic Management Journal*, 20, 3, pp. 397–420.

Hutton, W. (1997) *Stakeholding and its Critics*, London, Institute of Economic Affairs.

Johanson, J. and Vahlne, J. (1977) 'The internationalisation process of the firm – a model of knowledge development and increasing foreign market developments', *Journal of International Business Studies*, 8, pp. 23–32.

Kale, P., Singh, H. and Perlmutter, H. (2000) 'Learning and protection of proprietary assets in strategic alliances: building relational capital', *Strategic Management Journal*, 21, 2, pp. 217–37.

Kleindl, B. (2000) 'Competitive dynamics and new business models for SMEs in the virtual marketplace', *Journal of Developmental Entrepreneurship*, 5, 2, pp. 73–85.

Knight, G. and Cavusgil, S. (1996) 'The born global firm: a challenge to traditional internationalization theory', *Advances in International Marketing*, Greenwich, CT, JAI Press.

Levitt, T. (1983) 'The globalization of markets', *Harvard Business Review*, 61, pp. 92–102.

Madsen, T. and Servais, P. (1997) 'The internationalization of born globals: an evolutionary process', *International Business Review*, 6, 4, pp. 561–83.

Martin, J. (2000) *Value-based Management: The Corporate Response to the Shareholder Revolution*, Boston, MA, Harvard Business School Press.

McDonald, F., Tüselmann, H. and Heise, A. (2002) 'The development of pan-European industrial structures and the strategic development of subsidiaries' in F. McDonald, H. Tüselmann and C. Wheeler (eds) *International Business: Adjusting to New Challenges and Opportunities*, London, Palgrave.

Oviatt, B. and McDougall, P. (1994) 'Towards a theory of international new ventures', *Journal of International Business Studies*, 25, 1, pp. 45–64.

Plender, J. (1997) *A Stake in the Future: The Stakeholding Solution*, London, Nicholas Brealey.

Porter, M. (1990) *The Competitive Advantage of Nations*, New York, Free Press.

Porter, M. (1986) *Competition in Global Industries*, Boston, MA, Harvard Business School Press.

Porter, M. (1985) *Competitive Advantage*, New York, Free Press.

Porter, M. (1980) *Competitive Strategy*, New York, Free Press.

Prahalad, C. and Doz, Y. (1987) *The Multinational Mission: Balancing Local Demands and Global Vision*, New York, Free Press.

Quinn, J., Mintzberg, H. and James, R. (1988) *The Strategy Process*, Englewood Cliffs, NJ, Prentice Hall.

Segal-Horn, S. and Faulkner, D. (1999) *The Dynamics of International Strategy*, London, International Thompson Press.

Simon, H. (1996) *Hidden Champions: Lessons from 500 of the World's Best Unknown Companies*, Boston, MA, Harvard Business School Press.

Simon, H. (1992) 'Lessons from Germany's midsize giants', *Harvard Business Review*, 70, 2, pp. 115–23.

Taggart, J. (1996) 'Autonomy and procedural justice: a framework for evaluating subsidiary strategy', *Journal of International Business Studies*, 28, 1, pp. 51–76.

Vernon, R. (1966) 'International investment and international trade in the product cycle', *Quarterly Journal of Economics*, 10, 2, pp. 190–207.

Womack, J., Jones, D. and Roos, D. (1990) *The Machine that Changed the World*, New York, Rawson Associates.

Yetton, P., Davis, J. and Craig, J. (1995) 'Redefining the multidomestic: a new ideal type MNC', *Working Paper 95–016*, Sydney, NSW, Australian Graduate School of Management.

Case 10.1 Moving Bertelsmann to a public listing

Bertelsmann is a major international media company with interests in publishing, music and television. It ranks with companies such as Sony, EMI and Warner Music in the top echelon of companies supplying music CDs and is one of the major global media companies, although somewhat smaller than AOL TimeWarner, Viacom and Vivendi Universal. One of the reasons for this is that Bertelsmann is governed by a *Stiftung* (foundation) that 'owns' the company. The conditions of the foundation require Bertelsmann to seek to make profits but the interests of its employees and of community issues must also be taken into account in the strategic planning of the company.

Technological developments such as digital means of disseminating media products and the growth of computer-based systems for the distribution of media products (see Case 14.4) have induced strategic alliances, mergers and acquisitions in this industry. This led to the creation of giant multinational media companies such as AOL TimeWarner, Viacom, Vivendi Universal and the News Corporation. Bertelsmann's participation in this consolidation has been handicapped by its status as a *Stiftung*. One of the main problems is the difficulty of establishing alliances, mergers and acquisitions by issuing or swapping shares, as this would undermine the *Stiftung* basis of Bertelsmann. This means that the finance for these activities must be raised from cash holdings or loans. For many of the big deals taking place in the media and other industries this limits the room for strategic planning based on mergers and acquisitions. Attempts to expand in the US market have been hampered by the inability of Bertelsmann to issue and swap shares to finance alliances, mergers and takeovers.

The appointment of Thomas Middelhoff as chief executive of Bertelsmann in 1998 led to attempts to change the status of the company. To enable the acquisition of a controlling interest in RTL (a big European broadcaster) to go ahead, Bertelsmann swapped 25% of its voting shares for 30% of RTL's shares held by Groupe Bruxelles Lambert (a Belgian investment company). This was not large enough to give the Belgian company a controlling interest in Bertelsmann but it did indicate a change in direction. Middelhoff appears to be leading Bertelsmann into a new (more Anglo-Saxon) system of corporate governance to allow the company to develop strategic planning to prosper in the international media market.

Other German companies that are governed by a *Stiftung* are also moving away from this system of corporate governance and are becoming publicly listed companies, for example, Carl Zeiss in the optics industry and Fresenius in the field of medical equipment. This is deemed to be necessary to enable them to adopt international strategic plans based on alliances, mergers and acquisitions. However, the largest of the German multinational companies that is governed by a *Stiftung*, Bosch, has shown no interest in altering its system of corporate governance. This reluctance may be due to fears that a change in corporate governance would force the company to adopt a more Anglo-Saxon approach to strategic planning that might harm other stakeholders in the company, especially employees. There is also concern that a stronger focus of shareholder interests will lead to unwanted takeover bids and a focus on short-term strategies to boost profit at the expense of longer term goals such as growth. These concerns were raised when Vodafone took over Mannesmann and are at the root of the reluctance of the French government to privatise Electricité de France although this company is now a major multinational company in the energy field.

Economist (2001), 'Bertelsmann and other Stiftung', 'The man who would be cool: Thomas Middelhoff' 10 March; 'French investment abroad: behind the bluster', 26 May

Case 10.2 Siemens and the re-assessment of value chains

Siemens is a German multinational company with 14 strategic business units (SBUs) mostly connected to electrical/electronic engineering, but covering a wide variety of areas:

1 information and communication networks
2 information and communication mobile
3 business services
4 automation and drives
5 industrial solutions and services
6 production and logistical systems
7 building technologies
8 power generation
9 power transmission and distribution
10 transportation systems
11 automotive

12 medical solutions
13 Osram
14 Infineon.

The company operates in 190 countries and employs 470,000 people. The majority of its activities are based in Europe with the bulk of these operations in Germany, but with substantial undertakings in France, the UK and the Netherlands. It also has significant business units in North America. However, Siemens has production, sales, after-sales and distribution operations in all major areas of the world.

The company took advantage of the development of e-business systems to re-assess the value chains of its SBUs. The hope is that the reduction in search and transactions costs of gathering and processing information that are possible with e-business systems will provide a means of increasing value. Furthermore, the use of e-business systems for online buying and selling offers the prospect of reducing costs associated with these activities and of making them more effective (see Chapter 14). The strategy has four main elements:

- Development of a knowledge management system called 'sharenet'. This is a database of the technical knowledge of all Siemens SBUs. It includes technical specifications, details on project management methods and sources of supply of inputs and various types of technical help. This system can be used by any SBU to help overcome technical problems, construct tenders for contracts and find suppliers of key components.
- Development of a coordinated online purchasing system that is planned to boost online buying from 10% in 2001 to 50% by 2004. This, it is hoped, will reduce purchasing costs and improve the management of the supply chain by permitting easier tracking of orders, expediting of deliver dates and checking qualities.
- Creation and development of online selling from one website that is linked to Siemen's SBUs. Presently this system is restricted to 20 countries and is not linked to all the SBUs. However, it is planned to extend the online buying system to nearly all countries and to all SBUs by 2005. As most of Siemen's customers are other companies, the likelihood that online buying will be popular because companies are seeking to improve the management of their supply chains and e-business systems offers a good prospect of achieving improvements in this area.

- Reducing the administration and management costs of operating SBUs by standardising the IT systems that are used to develop compatible systems to allow operational activities to be shared to reap economies of scale and scope.

Siemens has taken the opportunity presented by new technology to re-assess the value chains of its SBUs to improve value added. This process requires the SBUs to standardise their IT systems and many of their administrative and management systems. This requires not only more standandardisation of physical assets (IT systems) but also of management systems. Moreover, to ensure that value chains are effectively linked to boost value added more centralised monitoring and control will be necessary. New centralised management systems will also be required to coordinate the mass of information generated by e-business systems. The problems of managing the disparate SBUs of Siemens will not necessarily be simplified by the use of e-business systems and the strategy to develop these systems may lead to the emergence of other strategies such as concentration on core businesses to reduce the transaction costs of managing the Siemens empire. Thus, the strategy may evolve as it raises new issues and problems.

Economist (2001) 'E-strategy brief: Siemens', 2 June; website of Siemens – www.siemens.com

Case 10.3 Bundling of business services

Bundling of products involves the combining of goods and services into a package that meets the needs of customers. Microsoft is a good example of bundling as it provides an operating system for PCs (Windows) complete with a bundle of software packages, for example, Microsoft Office, Internet Explorer and Outlook Express. This bundle often comes preloaded into a PC. A more mundane example of bundling is ready-made meals that need only to be reheated. Most firms are involved in bundling, for example, most people buy a car not the component parts for it. There is a sense in which all firms are searching for the level of bundling that should be undertaken. That is, to decide what to sell – the sum of the components of a package that customers assemble themselves or the complete package. Clearly, firms must make strategic deci-

sions about the level of bundling that it undertakes. This problem is akin to the diversification versus concentration on core products decision.

The advantages of bundling are that it reduces search costs for customers and distribution and transaction costs for producers. Moreover, it can help customers to reduce the costs of assessing the optimal bundling to achieve desired outcomes by paying a supplying firm to undertake this process. Imagine having to decide on the components needed for a car and arranging for them to be assembled. Bundling provides the potential for firms to gain competitive advantage by providing a bundle of goods and services that are attractive to customers and that allows premium prices to be charged because of the ability to provide higher value than the sum of the individual components in the package. The disadvantages of bundling are that it can confer market power to the firm that organises the bundling or that provides the key components in the bundle. Furthermore, bundling may lock customers into a package that is more expensive and less effective than a package composed of different components and systems. Microsoft is accused of practices that lead to this type of harmful effects from bundling. The decision by the European Union to oppose the proposed merger between General Electric and Honeywell was largely based on fears of anti-competitive practices from the bundling potential of the proposed company (see Case 8.1).

In the provision of business services such as auditing, financial advice, management consulting and legal services there exist incentives to bundle these services into one package. The consolidation of auditing firms into the 'Big Five' – Andersen, Deloitte & Touche, Ernst & Young, KPMG and PricewaterhouseCoopers – led to global dominance of accounting and auditing services by these firms. The 'Big Five' also provide consultancy, finance and legal services. The strategic objective of the 'Big Five' appeared to be to become full multidisciplinary practices (MDPs) that provided the complete range of professional business services. The attraction of MDPs is that they generate new business opportunities, achieve synergy benefits and they can lock customers into retaining the same firm because of the disruption costs involved in finding new providers of these services. Furthermore, network externalities (see Chapter 14) can be increased by extended network connections from auditing and accounting services to consultancy, finance and legal services.

Auditing firms set about a systematic strategic planning process to become multinational MDPs. The strategic planning process led to consolidation by merger and acquisition and the development of new services that resulted in the creation of the 'Big Five' as not only large auditing firms but also powerful players in the provision of consultancy and legal services.

This systematic strategic planning process ran into problems when regulators in the USA began to take action to prevent conflicts of interests between auditing and the provision of consultancy services to the same firms. This led Ernst & Young to sell their consultancy business to Cap Gemini. KPMG and Andersen Consulting (part of Andersen) floated their consultancy operations as separate companies – KPMG Consulting and Accenture. Resistance from the members of the legal profession in the USA, objecting to the auditing firms move into the provision of legal services, also hampered the implementation of the strategic plans of the 'Big Five'. As the 'Big Five' operate globally, they face myriad different regulatory authorities that take a variety of different views about the conflicts of interests and the effects on the competitive environment of the rise of MDPs. This led to a need to adjust the strategic plans. For example, the integration into MDPs in the UK faces fewer regulatory obstacles than is the case in France, Germany or the USA.

Resistance from large corporate clients to use the service of MDPs has also led to re-assessment of the strategic plans of the 'Big Five'. Large firms are well aware of the dangers of buying into 'bundled' provision of professional business services that might lead to conflict of interests that result in poor advice. They are also aware of the problems of locking into a poor level of service that could be improved by buying these services from a variety of different providers. Indeed, they are looking for firms that can provide a service similar to a 'prime contractor' for a large construction project, that is, a firm that would assemble from the best on offer, a bundle of professional business services. This bundle would not necessarily come from the same firm and would permit the creation of the most preferred bundle that is feasible. The 'Big Five' may evolve into these types of provider, or they may find themselves being replaced by firms that provide this service.

The 'Big Five' also face considerable competition in the area of consultancy services from large multinational companies such as McKinsey, Booz Allen and Hamilton, A. T. Kearney and Boston Consulting Group. In the area of IT consultancy, one of the fasting growing areas of consultancy, there is vigorous competition from the management consultancy firms and the consultancy arms of the large IT firms, for example, Hewlett-Packard, Intel, Cisco Systems and IBM. Competition from companies such as Goldman Sachs and Morgan Stanley Dean Witter means that there is fierce competition in professional services connected to finance. These consultancy companies are also involved in strategic planning processes involving mergers and acquisitions to consolidate their position and to extend their geographical and sector coverage.

These developments require strategic plans to be modified and in some cases for a change of direction to be implemented, For example, the setting up of independent consultancy companies such as Accenture or the disposal of consultancy businesses as in the case of Ernst & Young. In these cases, attempts to bundle professional services have been abandoned or significantly altered. The way in which the strategies of the 'Big Five' have evolved in response to unexpected problems from regulators, changes in the competitive environment and from customers indicates that strategic planning may begin as a coherent and systematic process, but events and what is learned from them often shift such strategic plans in other and sometimes quite different directions than those envisaged in the beginning.

Economist (2001) 'Special report: professional-service firms', 'Economic focus: a bundle of trouble', 'Microsoft trial: a loss of trust', 7 July; 'Management consultants: winners' curse', 21 July

International marketing

Introduction

International marketing is the process of exchanging products (goods, services and combinations of goods and services) across frontiers. This is usually paid for by money, however, it can involve exchange without the direct use of money, for example, barter or countertrade (see Chapter 3). The means of exchanging across frontiers include exporting, franchising, licensing and direct foreign investment (see Chapter 9). International marketing involves a range of activities such as market research, promotion, pricing, distribution and decisions on the characteristics of the products to be exchanged. The major difference between domestic and international marketing is that in international marketing products and the means of payment for exchange flow across frontiers. International marketing is concerned with the means by which international trade flows take place. Thus, international trade theories and studies examine the motives for and the economic effects of exporting, franchising, licensing and direct foreign investment (DFI), whereas, international marketing theories and studies investigate how these activities take place and how they could be accomplished more effectively. International marketing is closely linked to international strategic management (see Chapter 10) because it includes the process of deciding which markets to operate in, issues such as the mode of supply (for example, exporting or a joint venture), pricing of products and decisions on where to expand and contract selling operations.

This chapter begins with an overview of the key elements of the study of international marketing together with an assessment of how international marketing studies fit into the debates about internationalisation and on appropriate systems for international strategic management. This is followed by sections on the practical aspects of international marketing. The first of these sections investigates the main methods that are used to assess the various market environments in which international marketing takes place. The practicalities of deciding on the characteristics of products, pricing, promotion and distribution are then considered.

International marketing

The essence of what constitutes international marketing emerged in the literature in the 1980s and the early 1990s (Cavusgil and Nevin, 1980, 1981; Douglas and Craig, 1989, 1992; Håkansson, 1982; Johanson and Mattson, 1986; Turnbull and Valla, 1986) and two early works on the development of exporting (Bilkey and Teasar, 1977; Johanson and Wiedersheim-Paul, 1975). This work identifies the strategic and managerial issues connected to internationalisation as the major focus of research work in international marketing. A number of key issues emerged from this literature:

- stage theories of internationalisation and the link to international marketing
- networks in international marketing
- segmentation or standardisation.

Stage theories of internationalisation

The Uppsala internationalisation model suggests that internationalisation proceeds, by a process of learning, from exporting to the establishment of higher level activities including production sites and product development facilities (Johanson and Vahlne, 1977). A similar developmental process is postulated in innovation-related internationalisation models (Bilkey and Teasar, 1977). Stage models of internationalisation stress the importance of learning, often originating from exposure to similar but slightly different cultural environments, that induces the development of internationalisation strategies on a steady path towards more complex and deep involvement with foreign markets. However, these models are rather mechanistic and suggest that firms follow a rigid linear development of internationalisation that is often not verified by empirical work (Andersen, 1993). Theories based on the development of networks (Turnbull and Valla, 1986) have sought to clarify the complex factors that appear to determine the internationalisation path of firms. These theories adopt a less mechanical view of the process of internationalisation. The debate on how to best capture the many factors that influence the development of the internationalisation processes of firms notwithstanding, most of the theories and empirical evidence provides support for the view that internationalisation follows an evolutionary processes that develops over time. The time path and major characteristics of this evolutionary process seem to be influenced by a variety of factors, but it seems that firms normally follow a progression from simple to more complex activities. However, this is not a straightforward or a linear development and appears to be strongly influenced by sector and the characteristics of home and host countries.

The implications for international marketing of the view that the internationalisation process is a complex evolutionary process based on learning implies that marketing strategies and activities adjust in line with the acquisition of information and its conversion into useful knowledge. In these circumstances, marketing strategies may begin with simple exporting, alternatively more complex modes of entry such as DFI may begin early in the internationalisation process. The deciding factor is the knowledge that the firm possesses on matters such as market conditions and the means of producing, promoting and distributing products for foreign markets. In the complex evolutionary view of the internationalisation process firms may start with a small number of countries to which they are geographically and culturally close or with a wide range of countries that are geographically and culturally disparate from the host country. It is likely that most firms will begin with simple marketing strategies and objectives but may rapidly move to more complex plans that miss out many of the intervening stages suggested in the more traditional models of internationalisation. Therefore, the key to the development of the international marketing strategy is the ability of firms to acquire knowledge about foreign markets and the supply conditions to these markets and to rapidly adjust their plans based on the acquired knowledge and this need not follow a linear path of development from exporting to more complex entry modes.

Networks and international marketing

The increasing focus on the importance of networks for international business activities is reflected in the international marketing literature. Research by the IMP Group emphasised the importance of learning in uncertain and competitive environments that leads to sophisticated buying behaviour by firms rather than the mechanistic approach that is expounded in traditional views of international marketing (Håkansson, 1982). In the IMP view of international marketing the main drivers of strategy are the interactions between buyers and sellers as they seek to establish networks for production, promotion, distribution and after-sales service that deliver outcomes that are acceptable in an environment that is fast changing because of changes in the competitive and technology environments. This type of approach is also evident in the relationship approach to marketing where strategic alliances, partnerships and joint ventures are used to achieve desirable outcomes (Johanson and Mattson, 1986). The importance of networks for international marketing is also highlighted in the phenomenon of 'born global' firms and as a means to help small and medium sized enterprises (SMEs) internationalise (see Chapter 10). Clearly, networks and relationships within networks are important factors in international marketing for sales between firms and for arranging packages of products and distribution to final customers (see Case 11.1).

Segmentation or standardisation

The drive towards global standardisation was based on a view that the progressive removal of trade barriers plus the growth of global cultural values was creating an single economic system that could be supplied with global products and uniform marketing processes such as promotion and the use of common brand names (Levitt, 1983; Ohmae, 1995). The advantages of mass production in terms of economies of scale and scope could be realised in the sort of world painted by Levitt and Ohmae. However, the case that a single global economic system with very few economic, legal and cultural barriers is imminent has certainly been overstated (see Chapters 2, 4, 5, 6, 7 and 8). The persistence of economic, legal and especially, cultural barriers to mass production generated an approach from many marketers that markets should be segmented geographically according to cultural clusters and within countries by social and demographic groups (Czinkota et al., 1998; Halliburton and Hunerberg, 1993). The focus on segmentation led in some cases to fragmentation of markets that were broken down into ever more complex and overlapping segments. Moreover, the use of continuous improvement by product development resulted in layers of production, sales and distribution systems with a consequent generation of a multitude of organisational systems. These developments added to the production and transaction costs often with little benefit in terms of extra sales. A study by McKinsey estimated that the costs of product differentiation and continuous improvement in the car industry for cars with limited demand amounted to $80billion per year (Agrawal et al., 2001). Another example of the potential to waste resources by over-segmentation of markets is illustrated by Toyota when it reduced the product range by 25 per cent when it discovered that 20 per cent of its range accounted for 80 per cent of its sales (Pine et al., 1993).

The solution to this problem is sought in build-to-order (BTO) systems whereby using sophisticated information from the Internet, specifications from customers are matched to the supply chain to assemble the components to customers' exact requirements. This type of approach is being pursued by major car companies such as GM, Ford, Nissan and Volkswagen that are seeking to develop BTO systems that can deliver a car to the customers' specification in three days. White goods manufacturers in the US such as Whirlpool, General Electric and Maytag are also developing BTO systems to deliver products to customers' specifications (*Economist*, 2001). Operating BTO systems leads to lower production costs because of the reduced need for high levels of inventories of components, as BTO is a very lean and effective just-in-time system. Moreover, by customising the product, premium prices can be charged. BTO systems based on the use of the Internet also offer the prospects of customised promotion systems by use of common platforms for advertising and information dissemination that are tailored to the groups or even individuals that are targeted by e-business systems.

Financial services firms have been operating BTO packages in areas such as personal savings plans and financial packages for leasing systems for firms for many years. However, financial services do not require the assembling of physical components and they have zero or low logistical costs of assembling the components of a financial package. The pioneer of mass customisation using BTO for manufactured goods was Dell Computers. Dell's success was based on the use of standardised components that are slotted together according to customers' specification received via the Internet (see Case 14.2). The success of Dell Computers is largely due to the ability to use standardised components that can be assembled into different packages by fairly minor modifications to the basic platform of the PC. Furthermore, Dell is able to sell and promote online to people who are computer literate and therefore do not need sophisticated advice and after-sales services. Dell also does not face significant legal, economic or cultural differences that require significant changes to organisational systems to use the standard Dell marketing model across a variety of countries. Using standardised BTO organisational systems for more complex products (that can be significantly different rather than have only minor changes to the same basic package and where there are legal, economic and cultural barriers) will present an all together more challenging task. Moreover, some products can be successfully standardised to generate the ability to charge a price relative to cost of supply that leads to higher profit than a BTO system. This process of standardisation is well advanced in the commoditisation of components by using e-auctions by firms that sell to final customers (see Case 14.1).

BTO systems require the development of effective e-business and logistical systems that can deliver inputs and final products on very tight schedules. The problems of using such complex e-business systems for international business activities may hamper the use of this approach to mass customisation (see Chapter 14). Moreover, the cost of segmenting markets to this level, in terms of developing effective BTO organisational and logistical systems, may lead to similar results to the attempts to mass customise by producing and marketing myriad different models by the car industry. Economic, legal and cultural differences across countries may also limit the use of global BTO systems because technical regulations and differences in rules and what is culturally and legally acceptable as means of promotion will require adaptation of the basic BTO marketing model. This will further complicate the organisational complexity of effectively operating BTO systems.

Exhibit 11.1 Standardisation, segmentation and built to order

Conditions		Standardisation	Segmentation	BTO
High resistance to	Yes	Undesirable	Desirable	Desirable
uniform products	No	Desirable	Undesirable	Undesirable
High barriers	Yes	Undesirable	Desirable	Undesirable[2]
to trade[1]	No	Desirable	No effect	Desirable
Low costs of adjustment	Yes	Undesirable	Desirable	Desirable
relative to price[3]	No	Desirable	Undesirable	Undesirable
Minimum efficiency	High	Desirable	Undesirable	Undesirable
scale	Low	Undesirable	Desirable	Desirable
Ability to adapt basic product	High	Undesirable	Undesirable	Desirable
platform	Low	Desirable	Desirable	Undesirable

1 Legal, economic and cultural barriers
2 High barriers to trade requires BTO systems to be distinct in the different countries in which the systems are used thereby leading to high organisational costs due to dissimilar systems in the various countries

3 Costs are organisational and logistical resources to product differentiate or to BTO relative to the higher price that can be charged for non-standard products

Clearly, the differentiation to mass production debate has not yet been resolved and a judicious mix of standardisation to differentiation, including in some cases mass customisation appears to be the way forward, the selection of the appropriate approach being determined by the nature of the product, minimum efficiency scale, ability to easily adapt basic product platforms, the extent of legal, economic and cultural barriers and the ability to construct organisational systems that deliver the largest difference between price that can be charged and the costs of differentiation (see Exhibit 11.1).

Assessing market environments

The beginning of the practical process of international marketing is to assess market conditions in the various possible countries in which firms may choose to sell. The initial assessment involves screening foreign markets to discover the potential of different countries. This process includes consideration of rates of growth of economies, new developments such as opening up of markets in developing and emergent economies, technical changes that are creating new opportunities to sell and identification of long-term economic and demographic factors that are altering demand patterns. Thus, when China began the process of opening up its markets many firms identified it as a major new market because of its size, growth rate and new favourable climate to sell products. However, the experience of many multinational companies that entered Chinese markets was that it was not easy to take advantage of what look at first sight a good opportunity to expand sales. These experiences indicate the need for a deeper assessment of market environments. Four main types of assessment should be undertaken:

1 political and legal conditions
2 economic conditions
3 cultural conditions
4 competitive conditions.

**Political and
legal conditions**

Screening political and legal conditions requires examination of factors such as the level of trade barriers, taxation rates and restrictions on foreign ownership, including repatriation of profits and restrictions on capital movements. Legal frameworks governing the protection of intellectual property, labour laws and other aspects of business law should also be evaluated. The type of incentives available for DFI and the likelihood of being able to obtain exemptions from laws and policies that would hamper operations may also be considered. Risk assessment of the chances of political changes that could harm the firm must also be carried out. Most firms will be reluctant to enter countries that have high political risks unless the potential returns are high or when countries with high political risk are providers of raw material that are in short supply. The low level and main type of operations (exploitation of natural resources) of multinational company activities in sub-Saharan Africa is partly explained by high political risks. Assessment of these factors is often helped by specialist firms such as the Economic Intelligence Unit, which provides detailed assessment on these factors. However, many companies do not conduct a detailed assessment of the institutional system in other countries (see Chapter 7). Failure to carry out such investigations can lead to costly mistakes as was discovered by many of the firms that entered the Russian market in the belief that the fall of communism and the introduction of markets had led to political and legal conditions that were similar to those in developed countries (Shama and Merrell, 1997).

**Economic
conditions**

The economic health of countries is also assessed to determine whether the macroeconomic conditions are conducive to stable economic conditions. Thus, inflation rates, balance of payments, exchange rate stability, government budgets and the record of growth will be considered to evaluate the prospects for economic instability or crisis. Demographic factors will also be taken into account together with measures such as disposable income per head. These considerations enable appraisal of the strength of general demand. Microeconomic data, such as size and development of particular markets and price movements in these markets, are also needed. The levels of development of financial, physical and supporting human resources infrastructures are also scrutinised. This enables evaluation of the level and effectiveness of financial services and support that is available, the state of transport, energy, water supply and logistical systems and the support from educational and training agencies that can be expected. Data on these factors are often available from official agencies such as the IMF, OECD and various United Nations organisations. Private sector firms such as the Economic Intelligence Unit and Reuters also provide this kind of information. The State Department of the USA provides detailed information on some of these issues via its network of commercial sections in US embassies. Many large multinational companies have their own research departments that can assess these types of issues. However, smaller firms are less able to gather and assess this type of information. They are often dependent on official sources such as the OECD publications and the commercial sections of their government's embassies. Small firms also make use of networks of firms and agencies to help them with these types of assessment.

Cultural conditions

Screening to assess cultural conditions is perhaps the most difficult of the market assessments that should be carried out. The complex and path determined nature of cultural values (see Chapter 7) makes it very difficult for outsiders accurately to assess cultural values and how they affect norms for doing business. There is no shortage of airport lounge-type of books that give often rather trite advice on rules of social interaction in various countries, but more subtle understanding of how a culture operates and the impact on business behaviour is not easily learned other than by experience or the use of national partners that understand both home and host cultures. Failure to adequately screen for important cultural differences can lead to costly mistakes by using, for example, promotional techniques that are offensive or inappropriate to the home culture. Unfortunately, learning by making mistakes based on misunderstandings of cultural differences can be an expensive way to find out about the cultural values of countries. Making use of the commercial sections of embassies and experts in national cultures in universities may be a useful source of information for screening cultural factors. However, securing access to good sources of information is often difficult. The use of networks and collaboration with individuals, firms and agencies that have experience of operating in selected countries can help to overcome the lack of good information.

Competitive conditions

Evaluation of competitive conditions in foreign markets requires detailed knowledge about which firms are already in the market and which are likely to enter. Information on the types of product sold by competitors and other information such as prices, quality of after-sales and effectiveness of distribution systems of rivals helps to assess the prospects for capture of a sufficient share of the market to make entry worthwhile. Knowledge on technology used by main competitors and the effectiveness of their promotion, distribution and logistical systems provides a means to assess the prospects of successfully entering markets that are characterised by strong competition. In markets with low levels of competition, it is useful to know if potential competitors are planning to enter the market and to have some indications of their likely competitive advantages. However, gaining information of this type is very difficult because firms will seek to keep their plans and current operations secret. Information on these issues is normally obtained informally by observation of the activities of competitors. This can range from open observation to industrial espionage.

After the process of screening environments has been completed, firms analyse the information that has been gathered and processed. This can involve techniques such as PEST (political, economic, social and technological factors) and SWOT (strengths, weakness, opportunities and threats). A variety of models to formalise political risk assessment procedures may be used (Frank, 1999). Scenario building can also be used to assess how different policies of market entry and development might work out if political, economic, cultural and competitive conditions change. These models require significant resources and are therefore smaller firms are often unable to utilise them. However, some of the large consultancy firms offer these services. Nevertheless, the reliability of such work may be questionable if the work depends upon sophisticated techniques of assessment and pay less attention to the quality of the information that is used by these techniques. Clearly, even many of the large multinational companies that entered Russian markets in the early days of the transition to a market-based economic system did not gather good information on the environment in Russia, although some did make use of techniques such as PEST and SWOT. The problems that firms that entered the Chinese market encountered also indicates that prior assessment of new markets is often perfunctory (Osland and Cavusgil, 1996). Failure to undertake good-quality assessment of these environmental conditions often leads to learning by mistake and as many firms that entered China and Russia discovered this can be a very costly outcome.

Practical issues of international marketing

The 4Ps of marketing (product – standardised or differentiated, pricing, promotion and place) still have a place in international marketing but not as the cornerstones of marketing strategy, which, as indicated earlier, is centred on large issues such as the path of internationalisation, the importance of networks and debates about segmentation versus standardisation. However, practical decisions have to be taken on the 4Ps.

Product

Whatever decision is taken about the differentiation versus standardisation choice nearly all products require modification to fit in with legal, technical and cultural conditions in the host country. Some products need very little modification and commodities normally need none. Products sold to other firms normally require very little modification because items such as computers, or fax machine or the components for cars are fairly standard. Nevertheless, technical differences in areas such as electricity supply systems and health and safety rules differ across countries and thereby require firms to modify their products. Firms that sell famous brand name products may be faced with very limited need to modify their products. However, even some of the most famous brands are modified to satisfy local conditions. Thus McDonald's found it necessary to introduce more chicken-based products in its range in China because chicken is widely eaten in China, but beef is not.

Products sold to consumers often require more modification because of cultural differences. This is reflected in the extensive product differentiated undertaken by many of the firms involved in food products, for example, Campbell, Nestlé and Unilever. However, increasingly even food firms are standardising brand names, for instance, Mars, the chocolate bar manufacturer, uses the same brand name for most of its products everywhere in the world. Perhaps the most famous global brand name is Coca-Cola, used throughout the world. However, in the case of Coca-Cola there are slight variations in the amount of sugar and carbon dioxide to satisfy local tastes. Differences in income also influence product differentiation, as higher income countries often demand higher specifications and better level of after-sales service than poorer countries.

Strategic decisions on the level of standardisation strongly influence marketing choices on product modification, but legal, technical and cultural differences across countries continue to require modification of products. The most important strategic decision is on the level of differentiated that should be undertaken on top of essential legal, technical and cultural requirements

Pricing

Decisions on pricing are very important because of the effect on revenues and hence profits. Pricing decisions in foreign markets are complicated by exchange rate risk and the possibilities to engage in transfer pricing to avoid taxes (see Chapter 12). The price set for exports can also lead to problems if the government of the importing country considers that dumping is taking place. However, it often makes economic sense for firms to charge a lower price for exporters than for sales in the domestic market (see Chapter 4). Changes in the value of currencies also influence the price of exports (see Exhibit 11.2). Mark-up pricing (the system used by most firms) requires careful estimation of costs and assessment of the level of mark-up that foreign markets can sustain and whether the strategy of the firms is to penetrate or skim markets. The accuracy of cost estimates and the wisdom of mark-ups that are applied may be difficult for the exporting or parent company effectively to monitor if agents or employees in the host country are given autonomy to set prices. If the exporter or parent set prices, it may not have good information on costs and appropriate mark-ups. The policy of host governments towards price controls and to competition policy influences the pricing policy because skimming pricing may attract unwanted attention from government agencies.

Promotion

Promotion involves the creation and maintenance or increase of demand for products. The major decisions taken in promotion are whether to use the same promotion methods everywhere or to adapt the methods to different markets. Together with the decision on the standardisation of products, this leads to the following possible combinations of product and promotion packages:

Exhibit 11.2 Pricing and exchange rates

If a product costs €20.00 in Denmark and is exported to the USA at an exchange rate of €1 = $1.05 the product will sell to the US importer for $21.00. If the US importer's mark-up were 20% for the services of importing the product the price would become $25.2. Suppose the US distributor's mark up is 25%, the final selling price would be $31.50. At an exchange rate of €1= $1.00 the product would now be sold to the US importer for $20.00 leading to a final price (if US mark-ups remained constant) of $30.00. This reduction in price would stimulated increased demand for the product in the USA. If the Danish firm were faced with buoyant demand in its European market and had a capacity constraint a decision could be made to increase the price in euros to the US importer such that the dollar price remained at $21.00 (that is, a price of €21.00). Providing that US mark-ups remained constant the final price in the USA would stay at $31.50 and demand would not increase. However, the profitability of the Danish firm from exports would increase. Therefore, the change in the exchange rate leads to a need to make decisions about leaving domestic price unchanged and experiencing a change in demand, altering domestic price to keep demand constant or a domestic price change that both changes demand and the profitability of exporting. If US mark-ups alter in the light of the change in the exchange rate the decision process for the Danish firm is further complicated. Clearly, exchange rate changes have important implications for the pricing decisions of exporters and importers.

1 Same product and the same means of promotion.
2 Adapted product and the same means of promotion.
3 Same product and different means of promotion.
4 Adapted product and different means of promotion.

The first option, the global standardisation approach, is the least cost system and permits economies of scale and scope to be reaped. The fourth option has the highest cost and limits economies of scale and scope. The decision on which option to select will be influenced by strategic decisions on standardisation and on the need to adapt product and the means of promotion because of legal, cultural and technical factors. Legal conditions influence promotion policies because laws on advertising and promotion activities vary across countries. For example, what is permissible to state about the qualities of products and what is allowable in terms of social mores varies across countries. Thus, advertisements with scantily clad women are not permitted in many Islamic countries. Cultural differences often require different types of promotion, for example, advertisements that depict women in a predominantly domestic role are becoming culturally unacceptable in North America and much of Europe. Technical factors such as differences in the demographic and geographical coverage of newspapers and television and ownership of telephones and connection to the Internet also influence the ability to adopt the same promotion package.

The factors that affect the need to adapt products and promotion policies are likely to mean that hardly any products will be the same product and have the same means of promotion. Indeed, nearly all products will fall into the adapted product and different means of promotion category. However, depending on the marketing strategy selected and the extent of legal, cultural and technical barriers to standardisation the mix between product and promotion standardisation will edge towards one of the first three options. Industrial products are more likely to edge towards the global standardisation option than are consumer goods.

Distribution

The means of distribution are influenced by transport and logistical systems and in the case of consumer goods by wholesaling and retailing systems. These vary across countries for legal reasons, for example, transport laws and environmental rules on emissions and congestion and planning laws that restrict where production, distribution and retailing operations can take place. Technical factors also affect distribution as transport networks often have different characteristics because of geographical and historical factors. Thus in Europe railway systems are not technically compatible because of the use of different technical standards. Moreover, European transport networks are nationally based (often focused on national capitals) but economic considerations are pushing for European rather than national distribution systems (Cooper et al., 1994). Cultural differences also effect distribution because in some countries retailing outlets sell a wide range of products while in others retailers are more specialised. Some national distribution systems are close networks of producers, transport firms, wholesalers and retailers. This close network for distribution is one of the reasons why exporters have found it difficult to penetrate the Japanese market (European Commission, 2000). However, many national distribution systems are close networks. For example, access to UK supermarkets is a series of close networks controlled by the big supermarkets. To gain access to these networks foreign companies must gain access to these distribution systems.

Summary

This chapter has examined the current debates on international marketing strategy and some of the practical issues connected to selling in foreign markets. Contemporary debates on international marketing strategy are centred on the process of internationalisation, the balance between segmentation and standardisation and the role of networks. The literature suggests that international marketing strategy is not a rational measurement and calculation process but involves dynamic and evolutionary developments. Internationalisation does not always follow a linear path from exporting to more complex modes of entry such as DFI. Firms may miss sections of the linear path of internationalisation path or begin the process at different stages. Moreover, networks provide important means to overcome many of the problems of international marketing. Thus, international marketing strategy like international strategic management (see Chapter 10) is increasingly focused on firms as learning machines whose internationalisation policies evolve as firms learn and make new and hopefully more effective network connections. The debate on segmentation versus standardisation has not been settled and new developments such as BTO have added to the complexity of this issue.

Consideration of the practicalities of international marketing highlights the need for effective assessment of market environments to avoid the costly route of learning by making mistakes. However, obtaining and processing good information on political, legal, economic, cultural and competitive factors is difficult and probably beyond the reach of most small firms. Even large firms and consultancy companies are likely to find it difficult to obtain good information on these factors. Again, the use of networks of firms, agencies and individuals that have good knowledge on these issues holds the prospects of improving the flow of useful information.

Investigation of the 4Ps in international marketing reveals that strategic decisions on the mode of entry and segmentation versus standardisation have important implications for international marketing. However, differences in legal, economic, cultural and technical conditions affect selection of appropriate options for product, pricing, promotion and place.

Review questions

1 Outline the main ways that the internationalisation process of firms affects their international marketing strategy.
2 Why is the development of networks important for international marketing strategy?
3 Under what circumstances would a BTO system make sense as an international marketing strategy?
4 Why is good assessment of market environments important and why is it difficult to conduct such assessments?
5 Outline the conditions under which it would be possible to adopt a standardisation approach in product, promotion and place.
6 What issues are raised for pricing when exchange rates are volatile?

Bibliography

Agarwal, M., Kumaresh, T. and Mercer, G. (2001) 'The false promise of mass customization', *McKinsey Quarterly*, 3, pp. 12–22.

Andersen, O. (1993) 'On the internationalization process of firms: a critical analysis', *Journal of International Business Studies*, 24, 3, pp. 209–32.

Bilkey, W. and Tesar, T. (1977) 'The export behaviour of smaller Wisconsin manufacturing firms', *Journal of International Business Studies*, 9, 1, pp. 93–8.

Cavusgil, S. and Nevin, J. (1981) 'State of the art in international marketing' in B. Enis and K. Roering (eds) *Review of Marketing*, Chicago, IL, American Marketing Association.

Cavusgil, S. and Nevin, J. (1980) 'A conceptualisation of the initial involvement in international marketing' in C. Lamb and P. Dunne (eds) *Theoretical Developments in Marketing*, Chicago, IL, American Marketing Association.

Cooper, J., Brown, M. and Peters, M. (1994) *European Logistics: Markets, Management and Strategy*, Oxford, Oxford University Press.

Czinkota, M., Ronkainen, I. Moffett, M. and Moynihan, E. (1998) *Global Business*, London, Dryden Press.

Douglas, S. and Craig, C. (1992) 'Advances in international marketing', *International Journal of Research in Marketing*, 9, 3, pp. 291–318.

Douglas, S. and Craig, C. (1989) 'Evolution of global marketing strategy: scale, scope and synergy, *Columbia Journal of World Business*, 24, Fall, pp. 47–59.

Economist (2001) 'Special report: mass customisation', 14 July, pp. 79–81.

European Commission (2000) 'EU priority proposals for regulatory reform in Japan', *Directorate General for External Relations*, Brussels. Available on www.jpn.cec.eu.int

Frank, R. (1999) 'Political risk, assessment and management of' in Tung, R. (ed.) *The Handbook of International Business*, London, Thomson Learning.

Håkansson, H. (1982) *International Marketing and Purchasing of Industrial Goods: An Interaction Approach*, New York, Wiley.

Halliburton, C. and Hunerberg, R. (1993) *European Marketing: Readings and Cases*, New York, Addison-Wesley.

Johanson, J. and Mattson, L. (1986) 'International marketing and internationalization processes – a network approach' in Turnbull, P. and Paliwoda, S. (eds) *Research in International Marketing*, London, Croom-Helm.

Johanson, J. and Vahlne, J. (1977) 'The internationalisation process of the firm – a model of knowledge development and increasing foreign market developments', *Journal of International Business Studies*, 8, 1, pp. 23–32.

Johanson, J. and Wiedersheim-Paul, F. (1975) 'The internationalisation of the firm – four Swedish cases', *Journal of Management Studies*, 12, 3, pp. 305–22.

Levitt, T. (1983) 'The globalization of markets', *Harvard Business Review*, 61, pp. 92–102.

Ohmae, K. (1995) *The End of the Nation State: The Rise of Regional Economies*, New York, Harper Business.

Osland, G. and Cavusgil, S. (1996) 'Performance issues in US–China joint ventures', *California Management Review*, 38, 2, pp. 106–30.

Pine, B., Victor, B. and Boynton, A. (1993) 'Making mass customization work', *Harvard Business Review*, 71, September–October, pp. 108–22.

Shama, A. and Merrell, M. (1997) 'Russia's true business performance: inviting to international business?', *Journal of World Business*, 32, 3, pp. 320–32.

Turnbull, P. and Valla, J. (1986) *Strategies for International Industrial Marketing*, London, Croom-Helm.

Case 11.1 Networks and distribution by multinational media companies

The market for media products such as books, magazines, music CDs and cable and satellite television are dominated by large media multinational companies, for example, AOL Time Warner, Bertelsmann, Disney, News Corporation, Vivendi Universal and Viacom. These media companies face challenges from technical change such as cable, satellite and digital means of transmission that enlarge the quantity and type of media products that can be sold. The Internet also expands the volume and variety of media products that can be sold on a global basis. The response to these challenges has been to expand the possible number and means of selling media products by consolidating into large integrated companies that have access to a wide range of media products – films, music, television shows and news and other types of information. The multichannel media companies that supply television programmes operate from the USA, most are located in New York and provide another example of an internationally successful cluster. The headquarters of these firms take products, mainly from their US subsidiaries and sell them globally via their network of foreign subsidiaries. The revenues received from the large size of the US television and film market easily cover the high production costs of programmes and films and thereby provide a range of products for the world market that have normally already covered their costs of production. The marginal cost of supplying these products to world markets is therefore low, involving minor technical costs of transmission and dubbing or subtitling into other languages. If these companies get involved in the delivery systems for their products, they incur high costs associated with the provision of cable and satellite systems. Among the large media companies, only the News Corporation has gone down this route.

However, even given the costs advantages of using mainly US products and the dominance of American culture and the English language, multinational media companies face challenges in providing a sufficient range of products and of meeting the demands from customers for products tailored to cultural differences. In many markets domestic provision of media products still dominate the market. Even in the UK, where there are no language problems, domestic and terrestrial television companies dominate the British market. In response to these challenges, the large media companies have made arrangements, alliances and partnerships with companies to acquire a diverse range of products and to meet the demands for products that are more culturally attuned to the various markets that the media giants supply. For example, the BBC, in an alliance with the Discovery Channel, supplies most of the large media companies with television programmes on the natural world, science and history.

Alliances and partnerships are also made with companies in major markets to provide programmes and other input to adjust output to cultural values. Thus, MTV dilutes the American influence of its output by providing links to sources that deliver popular culture products such as music and film festivals in local markets. To provide large enough film libraries to feed the voracious appetite of multichannel television HBO (a provider of films by cable and sallellite television) operates a number of networks of providers. Hence, in Latin America, HBO library is comprised of films from Warner, Sony and Disney while in Asia, Sony, Paramount and Disney provide films. In Japan, the Star Movie channel (Warner, MGM, Paramount and Universal) competes with Sky Movie channel (Fox and Sony).

Although the media industry is dominated by large integrated multinational companies that have significant economies of scale and scope, they have had to develop networks (even with major competitors) to meet the needs of customers in the various markets in which they operate. These networks provide the range of products that they need and the ability to adapt to meet different cultural conditions. These network connections are stable but not static, as modification and the creation of new networks becomes necessary due to the acquisition of knowledge on how to better supply the various markets. Technical change, for example, the growth of the Internet as a means of distributing media products also requires the development of networks to allow effective supply of global markets. Change in the competitive environment brought about by technical change and mergers and acquisitions also stimulates the development of networks. Hence, the creation of AOL Time Warner linked a large media company (Time Warner) with a large Internet company (AOL) and this has stimulated a search for new or enhanced networks to adjust to the challenges presented by this new company. The growth of the use of the Internet as means of distributing music and audio-visual products also led to network connections between Internet and media companies (see Case 14.4).

Economist (1998) 'Survey technology and entertainment', 19 November.

12 International finance and accounting

Learning objectives

By the end of this chapter, you should be able to:

- understand the advantages and disadvantges of international financial listing
- assess the problems connected to managing foreign exchange risk
- outline the main factors involved in international taxation
- describe and assess the main differences in international accounting systems
- understand the problems of harmonising accounting systems
- assess the auditing and corporate governance problems connected to international business activities

Key terms

- international listings • foreign currency risk management • international transfer pricing • international budget and control procedures
- international financial accounting • auditing and corporate governance
- international accounting standards

Introduction

Viewed from one perspective, all a group's operations are managed in such a way as to lead to a satisfactory relationship between the group and the capital markets, and the capital markets' reactions to the group are the primary public index of management performance. Top managers are usually rewarded with share options and bonus arrangements so that their activity is addressed to the shareholders' prime interest: increasing the share price and maintaining a flow of dividends. Throughout the group, senior management's reaction to their subordinate managers' performance and ideas is conditioned by the overall market-induced requirement for regularly increasing profits.

We will, therefore, start this chapter by looking at the group and the international stock exchanges, and then go on to financial and tax management in general in an international context. Thereafter we will deal with accounting and control issues, looking at budgeting, risk assessment, and reporting performance both internally and externally. The focus is on the special aspects of the international company and it is assumed that the reader either has working management knowledge of finance and accounting at national level or can access a relevant national textbook if needed.

International listing

The primary purpose of being listed on a stock exchange is to raise equity finance for a company through an initial public offering (IPO). Large companies continue to raise fresh capital from the market throughout their lives to enable them to grow and to preserve a strategic equilibrium between the amount of equity financing and the amount of debt. Overall companies finance themselves from three sources:

1 internally generated funds – that is profits made by the company but not paid out by way of interest, tax or dividend and which are retained as additional equity (reserves)
2 the issue of shares onto the capital markets (also equity)
3 by borrowing money.

There is no golden rule about the best equilibrium between debt and equity. Each company has its own strategy in that area and has to consider the financial risk generated by high borrowings in the context of its other risks and its operational profile. In general the more risks a company carries, the higher the return the market will expect it to generate to compensate for investment, so a company with a high operational level of risk (e.g. software, Internet operators etc.) will tend to avoid a high financial risk.

For most companies there is a progression from being an owner-managed start-up, with enormous borrowing, through to being moderately successful and perhaps linking up with a venture capitalist or a company in a related field to provide development finance, through to an IPO and a listing. Many companies stop there, but international companies generally go further and at some point in their development start to be listed on one or more foreign stock exchanges. It is these companies which are our particular focus here and they have quite a variety of reasons for wanting an international listing, although the costs are also quite high.

Many countries in the world have their own stock exchange and indeed the creation of a national stock market is seen in developing countries and former communist countries as an essential part of their economic credentials. However, the reality is that most markets are relatively 'illiquid' – have few stocks quoted and attract very few investors and therefore are not very efficient at pricing a stock or at raising money. The most liquid exchanges are shown in Table 12.1. As can be seen, Europe, although dominated by the London Stock Exchange, has many important exchanges. These exchanges all compete with each other and are probably currently making the European market less efficient rather than

Table 12.1 Major stock markets

Exchange	€ million
New York Stock Exchange	12,708,441
NASDAQ	5,782,911
London	2,857,653
Paris	1,499,495
Deutsche Borse	1,428,873
Italy	726,565
Amsterdam	693,597
Spain	430,656

Market capitalisation of equity at the end of 1999

Figures adapted from website of Fédération Internationale des Bourses de Valeurs

more so. Europe would benefit from having a single large market like the USA, but none of the major European exchanges is willing to give way to any of the others (see Case 8.2). In practice the whole idea of a stock exchange is put in question by the Internet and it is far from impossible that there will develop a single worldwide market with no geographical base, but that is still some way off.

Advantages

There are, all the same, many reasons why an international company would want to be listed on a foreign exchange. Some of these are financial, some are strategic. The biggest and most efficient capital market in the world is the USA and many foreign companies go there because it is, as a consequence, cheaper to raise money there than elsewhere. The margin may be small, but if, like a bank, you raise a lot of money (either equity or debt) in the markets, the USA may be cheaper. Abbey National, the UK bank, is, for example, a big borrower in the USA. Major markets also attract foreign issuers whose domestic market is very small: so a number of South African companies are listed in London and the USA attracts particularly both South American and Israeli companies.

Another problem for the company is that it may consider it is undervalued in its home market. This was typically the case for high tech companies, although that is changing. In general they found that US investors would pay more for their shares than would European ones, so a US IPO and especially on the NASDAQ would be likely to yield more finance per share than would a European one. A related issue is that of the company with an unusual activity – investors on the home market may have difficulty valuing it because it is the only one of its kind on their market (for example British Airport Authority (BAA), the airport operator), so a listing on a foreign exchange where similar companies are listed may improve the price.

Despite the particular financial advantages, most international companies cite strategic reasons as the main motivation for a foreign listing. A listing on the national stock exchange gives both visibility and credibility to a foreign company. A company listed on the stock exchange is frequently the subject of reports in the financial pages of newspapers, which is in effect free publicity. Its presence on the market means that it is able to signal to the national government and to other businesses that it is making a serious commitment to a presence in that country. This in turn means that suppliers and customers are likely to take it more seriously. An example of this kind of listing would be Volvo's listing in Tokyo – Volvo has never raised money in Japan, but is listed in effect as part of a public relations campaign.

Some companies take the view that they are now players on an international stage and their competition is with similar companies on the world stage. To be taken seriously as a global player, an international company needs to be listed on all the main world stock exchanges where it can be measured against its competitors (Bay and Bruns, 1998).

There are other advantages, such as being able to offer senior managers incentive systems based on stock options. It is difficult to get a manager to value a share which he or she cannot easily sell, but a quite different matter when they can see its price every day in the newspaper and a phone call will turn it into cash. Equally, an ambitious company is much more likely to succeed in buying other businesses with its shares if they are listed on the local exchange. The obvious example of this is Daimler, which, amid much criticism from within Germany, became the first German company to be listed in the USA in 1993 – and then used its shares to acquire Chrysler in 1998.

Another phenomenon which occurs is that of the listed subsidiary. Sometimes international companies have some of their stock listed on foreign stock exchanges. Rupert Murdoch, chairman of News Corporation, is a past master of this, often buying large companies and then selling off a minority stake either onto a stock exchange or to an outside shareholder. Listed subsidiaries have advantages and disadvantages of their own. On the positive side, this is a good way to help finance an acquisition or to generate funds for the group when they are needed for expansion. Equally the share price helps establish the real value of a subsidiary, which may in turn boost the price of the parent company. For example, every time the share price of Cable & Wireless HKT (Hong Kong telephone operator) goes up, the price of Cable & Wireless, the UK-based major shareholder, also rises – the disadvantage, of course, is that the reverse is also true.

Sometimes a part-listing for a local subsidiary is also necessary for government approval or other purposes. Sometimes it is the result of a historical sequence of events, such as the acquisition by a multinational of a local listed company where a rump of shares is left on the market to provide value for shares issued to local staff or for other reasons. Such subsidiaries can be helpful, but may also stand in the way of some evolution. Cadbury Schweppes had a listed subsidiary in Australia for many years and had to go to a lot of trouble to buy out the shareholders when it wished to change its own structure.

Disadvantages

Not all companies would agree with the values of international listings. German and Swiss companies in particular have historically been reluctant to go to the US markets and one reason for this is the requirement in the USA to provide profit and some balance sheet figures calculated according to US accounting principles. This caused much embarrassment to Daimler when it was first listed in the USA (Bay and Bruns, 1998) but French and British companies have lived with this problem for years without anyone taking the slightest notice. Thus notwithstanding, the publication of two different figures for the group profits does leave a company feeling somewhat exposed. Figure 12.1 shows the published reconciliation between UK and US figures for SmithKline Beecham (before the merger with Glaxo). The question raised by these differences is which figure should the investor base their decision on?

The US market has other disadvantages. In particular, the prevailing culture is that the investor is protected by transparency in the financial

Figure 12.1 US GAAP reconciliation of income extracted from 1998 annual report SmithKline Beecham plc

	1998 £m	1997 £m	1996 £m
Net income per UK GAAP	606	1,044	999
US GAAP adjustments			
Purchase accounting and goodwill			
Amortisation of goodwill	(99)	(100)	(97)
Amortisation of intangible and other assets	(47)	(49)	(57)
Amortisation of diversified goodwill and loss on disposal	(84)	25	25
Intangible assets	(67)	(44)	(22)
Deferred taxation	(23)	42	17
Foreign currency hedging	6	(15)	25
Pension and other post-retirement benefits	(21)	(14)	(5)
Restructuring costs	3	(60)	(130)
Tax benefits of share option deductions	(50)	(40)	—
ESOT transactions	27	5	6
Stock compensation	(50)	(4)	(2)
Other, net	2	13	10
Deferred tax on US GAAP adjustments above	28	25	31
Net income per US GAAP	231	828	800

Source: www.sb.com

statements (in countries like Germany and Switzerland protection is thought to be best given by undervaluing the company in the balance sheet, while giving little information). The transparency approach leads to foreign companies being obliged to provide details of their activities, which they may not provide at home. This has the effect, ultimately, of causing the companies to reveal the information at home, leading to a view that they are at a disadvantage to their domestic competitors.

The USA is also an extremely litigious environment. Lawyers can be hired against a percentage of the damages awarded (generally about 20 per cent but sometimes much higher) with no fee if they lose the case and no liability for the other side's costs. Consequently, suing for damages is not a high-risk operation for the plaintiff. A non-US company, which lists in the USA, is in effect inviting claims and not only from people based in the USA.

Apart from this hidden cost, there is the visible cost of fees to lawyers, accountants and other advisers to make sure that every document issued in connection with the US listing is in compliance with the law and does not leave any loopholes for subsequent litigation. In addition, senior management must spend a lot of time in the USA answering questions from regulators and market participants. US investors expect regular 'roadshows' of senior executives and investor relations experts to visit major cities and provide regular updates on what the company is doing. It is difficult to have a clear idea of the marginal costs of listing in the USA but some companies cite these as around $2million a year in professional fees and related costs, before even thinking about senior executive time and travel costs tied up with supporting the operation on a continuing basis.

Another problem for a company listed on several stock exchanges is controlling the release of sensitive information. All major stock exchanges require that all information released by the company which might cause a movement in the share price (i.e. likely to influence investor decisions) should be released to all investors at the same time. This is obviously a sensible precaution to preserve confidence in the market, so that investors do not feel that insiders can benefit at their expense. This requirement is usually satisfied by either reporting information to the stock exchange's own investor information service or putting out a press release to major relevant media organisations – most companies do both. However, if the company is listed in (say) Hong Kong, Paris and New York, it means that press releases must go out simultaneously to all three places, irrespective of the time of day. This means that releases are often timed for the US market and arrive too late, therefore, for the French papers.

Another problem related to this requirement is that the company needs to control comment all over the world from its executives. A subsidiary company manager in Switzerland may innocently answer questions from the Swiss press about something which potentially affects worldwide investors and causes the stock exchanges in other countries to levy fines on the group.

A number of companies say these costs are just too high. They point out that all major investment funds are represented in both Europe and the Far East. Consequently if you want to sell to Nomura, Citibank or Deutsche Bank you can find them all at a regional centre near you – no need to go to Tokyo, New York or Frankfurt, they're all in London and Hong Kong and so on. And, just by way of a footnote, it would be a mistake to think that all major international companies are listed on stock exchanges. Some world companies such as Mars, Robert Bosch or BMW are controlled by families or trusts and are either not listed at all or only list debt or a small part of their equity.

Foreign currency management

The fact of having to work in many different currencies is the bane of the finance director's life in any multinational and, for example, one of the main economic reasons for creating the euro and a single currency zone in Europe is to remove the uncertainties caused by fluctuating exchange rates and thereby simplify trade within Europe. An analysis of currency flows and trade has been made in Chapters 5 and 8 (and see Jacque, 1999; Jain, 1999). This chapter will therefore not discuss the economic background further. We will concern ourselves only with how the finance function in an international company addresses the currency issue. The basic problem is illustrated in Exhibit 12.1.

Exhibit 12.1 Foreign exchange risk and the returns from a project

Suppose an American company invests $100m in a European project based in Italy. The project is expected to have a five-year life and to generate a return of 15% on the capital invested. The exchange rate at inception is $1 = €1.

Budgeted flows: The actual results of the investment will look like this:

	Depreciation		Profit			Depreciation		Profit	
	€m	$m	€m	$m		€m	$m	€m	$m
1	20.0	20.0	15.0	15.0	1	20.0	19.0	15.0	14.3
2	20.0	20.0	15.0	15.0	2	20.0	18.4	15.0	13.8
3	20.0	20.0	15.0	15.0	3	20.0	19.6	15.0	14.7
4	20.0	20.0	15.0	15.0	4	20.0	20.6	15.0	15.4
5	20.0	20.0	15.0	15.0	5	20.0	18.0	15.0	13.5
Totals	100.0	100.0	75.0	75.0	Totals	100.0	95.6	75.0	71.7

However, supposing that the actual results in Italy are exactly as budgeted, but the average rate of exchange in reality fluctuates as follows over the life of the project:

1	€1	= $0.95
2	€1	= $0.92
3	€1	= $0.98
4	€1	= $1.03
5	€1	= $0.90

While, from an Italian perspective, the project has come out exactly as expected, the US results, have hit the target only once in the five years. If, in addition, we suppose that a cash flow equal to the depreciation was repatriated to pay off the initial investment, there would be a shortfall of $4.4 million (only $95.6 million received in dollars) which would have to be offset against the profit flows, reducing the total from $71.7 million to $67.3 million or an average return of 13.5% instead of the target 15%.

Any multinational has to make a strategic decision about how it views itself and how it should formulate its currency risk management programme. Some companies take the view that they are an international business and that the shareholders should understand that in investing in such a business they are investing in a portfolio of investments in different currencies, and that each year the profit produced will vary both as a result of operational factors and of currency rate changes. They regard trying to manage currency fluctuations as an expensive and ultimately impossible task, which only Canute would attempt. How much the currency shifts affect reported profit depends in part also upon which currency you are using to report (Microsoft offers you the possibility of having its results in several different currencies on its website, www.msn.com).

The opposite view is that the company is based in one country and should be judged on its result in the national currency. So a French company like Peugeot, even though it is listed in the USA, might consider its French franc result as the key performance measure and the company should therefore be managed to reduce fluctuations against the French franc. There are many different positions which a group may take in relation to foreign currency risk and the degree to which they attempt to manage it or to delay the affects of long-term shifts in currency rates. Equally there are many different devices which may be used to moderate the affects of exchange rate changes.

Treasury management

The finance function in a multinational should include a treasury department whose tasks will include monitoring the worldwide cash flows of the group. In some companies the treasury department may be responsible for worldwide currency management for the group, but often coherent independent operating units within the group are left free to manage their own risk within centrally determined guidelines. Some companies, such as Philips or BP Amoco, operate a sort of internal bank, which handles all major borrowing and lending within the group and manages the foreign currencies. In this situation, the treasury function can offset flows in different currencies against each other and concentrate on managing only the difference.

Generally speaking, the basic approach to currency management is either to fix exchange rates in advance by one means or another or to 'hedge': to engage in opposite contracts so that two currency risks balance each other. If we take the euro project example (Exhibit 12.1), a simple hedge would have been for the US company to borrow €100 million to finance the project and repay the debt out of the euro cash flows from the project (the depreciation). This would not have affected the fluctuations of profit, but would have meant that there would have been no loss on the initial investment – in the example the company invested $100 million and only got $96.6 million back.

Alternatively the US company could have sold the future cash flows in euro onto the forward foreign exchange market. The forward market mostly operates for periods of less than a year but foreign exchange contracts can be booked with banks for virtually any period. The forward rate is calculated by adjusting the current exchange rate by the difference in interest rates between the two currencies. There is therefore a cost, but the advantage for the US company would have been that, in effect, it froze the exchange rate and therefore protected the project's dollar cash flows.

A variant on this is the use of options. The US company could have purchased an option from a bank to sell euros at a predetermined rate against the dollar. If the market rate moves against the company, it exercises the option, but if the rate moves favourably, the company simply exchanges the money on the current ('spot') market and drops the option. Here again, the option costs money, so it is very like buying an insurance policy against the currency risk – you have to pay a premium but you reduce the uncertainties.

Another device available is to enter into a 'swap'. The US company, through its bankers, could have lent $100 million to a European company wanting to invest in the USA, while borrowing €100 million from that company. At the end of the swap term, the US company pays back in euro from the project and the European company refunds $100 million from its American project. The swap allows both companies to avoid any exchange loss because they are lending their local currency and repaying out of project cash flows. The main risk here is the failure of the counterparty – the company at the other end of the swap might not meet its repayment commitments.

This illustration is framed in terms of a single project, but many companies, and particularly those with a single worldwide treasury unit, prefer to take positions based on aggregating the group's overall currency exposures. While the company may be involved in operations in as many as 50 or 60 currencies, the treasury function may borrow only in three or four major currencies to hedge the most important flows (e.g. US dollars, euro, perhaps UK pounds). The introduction of the euro has certainly simplified life for companies with major European cash flows.

We have not considered in detail where an international business would find large-scale loans in different currencies. In practice, this is relatively simple. There is a very large professional market for loans and most international companies go to this market. Usually they go to a single corporate banker who sets up a 'syndicate' of banks which agree to lend the money to the corporate and then themselves sell the debt to other financial institutions such as pension funds, investment trusts and insurance companies. There is a 'Eurocurrency' market, centred on London, which offers substantial loans in all major currencies. For details of transactions, you have only to look at advertisements in the *Financial Times* and similar papers which feature 'tombstone' adverts which say things like $1,000 million debt facility for XYZ Group arranged by 'dot dot dot' and then details of many banks. Equally, the borrower can go directly to national markets such as borrowing dollars in the USA, again on the professional market.

There is, of course, a public debt market run through the stock exchanges onto which companies issue bonds, which can be bought by anyone, but the sums involved tend to be smaller. In countries like France where there are limited opportunities for individual savers to put their money in interest-bearing bank accounts, there are unit trusts, which specialise in buying corporate bonds and in effect repackage the debt onto the private saver market. The pattern of corporate financing, particularly for medium sized companies but even for large ones, is influenced by national culture.

It is inherent in the arrangements for managing currency risk as just set out that the object of the exercise is to reduce or even neutralise currency risk. Under no circumstances should the treasury department set out to make profits from currency management. The recent history of multinationals is littered with stories of managers setting out to make a profit on the forward or futures markets and costing their company millions of dollars (see Case 12.1). Some of the most spectacular have not been in currency but in commodities or stocks, for example the collapse of Barings Bank – brought about by a single dealer in two months (but Leeson's strategy was based on the relative exchange rate of the yen to the dollar and the direction of its movement) and the dollar dealings of Mitsuomi Bank in New York. It is a fatal flaw: of course, large sums of money can be made in speculating in currency movements, and currency dealers can see this and sometimes get the idea that they could earn big bonuses by making such profits for their company and forget their brief simply to manage the risk. The result is that instead of reducing risk they bring further risk into the company, with often fatal results. You cannot beat the rule of the market – the higher the profit margin, the higher the risk to be taken.

Operating strategies

Managing foreign currency exposures is not limited to purely financial instruments, the operational side has also to be involved in this area. There are a number of operational issues such as pricing policy, sourcing of supplies, transfer pricing and choice of operating territories which need to be taken into account in the group's approach to exchange risk.

The group's price lists are a key source of exchange exposures. Usually a company fixes its prices for some period in advance and once it accepts an order, it is normal practice for the order to be honoured at the original price even if prices have moved in between times. Of course, a company can offer to make contracts only on the terms it wishes to, but frequently the company is in competition with others and cannot therefore afford to ask for more demanding contract terms. This means that once the price has been fixed for a particular territory, the supplier is bound to that price (and therefore potentially has an exchange exposure) from publication of the price list to satisfaction of the last order placed using that list.

If the company manufactures in (say) euros but sells in US dollars, it has an exposure to the $/€ exchange rate. Clearly, if it fixes the prices in euros, the exchange risk is passed to the customer. The manufacturer buys and sells in effect in the same currency and it is the customer who takes the risk. However, it is rarely the case that the competitive position is such that the supplier can pass on the exchange risk, so in this situation the price list would be fixed in dollars and the company has an exposure. Agents and other people in the selling chain find frequent price changes are bad for marketing, so the company is under some commercial pressure not to change prices too often.

It can, of course, use financial measures to hedge this exposure, but there are other possibilities. One of these is to source components from the same currency as that in which you are selling. For example, BMW complained that Rover cars do not sell well in Europe because all their components are manufactured in the UK and the low value of the euro against UK pounds means that a selling price in Europe, which covers costs, makes the Rover too expensive for the European car market. One way to avoid this would be for Rover to source more components from mainland Europe so that the currency in which it buys provides a currency hedge for continental sales.

A variant on this is to require component suppliers to quote supply prices in the currency of the market for the finished product. For example, aeroplanes and aeroengines are always priced in US dollars, so manufacturers can pass some risk back to their component suppliers by buying in dollars, irrespective of where their suppliers are located. At an extreme, the company can simply locate manufacturing plant in the country where the main market is. Some European car manufacturers have plant in South America, as well as North America and are exploring the Far East. Japanese manufacturers have plant in Europe and so on.

There are, at a micro level, some operational devices, which can do a little to help reduce currency risk. Where a company is manufacturing in one country but selling in another where the exchange rate is volatile, it may fix a very high transfer price into the selling country so that currency is moved out rapidly. The 'transfer price' is one of the complexities of international business. Where the same group manufactures in country A and sells in country B, it will have to fix a price at which the goods leave country A and enter country B – this is the transfer price and it is extremely significant in tax terms, which we shall come to. However, it can also be useful in managing exchange risk since payment of supplier invoices (from B to A) is usually done rapidly and on a continuing basis, so the risk period is short, whereas repatriation of profits is done much less frequently so the risk period is higher. The higher the transfer price between A and B, the more rapidly the currency shifts out of the risky area.

An operational pitfall is the existence of exchange controls in many countries. Typically, developing countries and former communist countries (but not necessarily only these) have problems about inflation and consequently currencies losing their value. As a consequence they try to limit imports by imposing exchange controls and the successful international company may find itself with vast amounts of cash, which it cannot convert into foreign currency and cannot usefully spend on buying raw materials or components. In such countries it is next to impossible to repatriate profits, and the only chance of getting money out is through high transfer prices, and even that can be next to impossible. Countries with exchange controls are better avoided, but this is not always possible and for that matter controls may be imposed many years after a company has established itself. Many stories abound about the lengths to which companies have been put to get their money out – for example, films being shot on location in some out of the way place to use up blocked funds belonging to an oil company or whatever.

International taxation

Not all companies have the same approach to taxation: some tend to regard it, like the weather, as something to be accepted as given, while others are more proactive. They consider that managing the group's international taxation is a significant part of maximising the performance of the company. Tax rules are constantly changing and are extremely complex, and so keeping track of them, avoiding being trapped into double taxation, and minimising charges are an extremely demanding exercise. Most large companies have an international tax management department and also use external advisers. In principle no investment decision should be taken by the company without referring it to the tax department, although in practice few companies are sufficiently well organised to provide this kind of internal consulting effectively.

One should be clear also that while financial statements focus on tax on profits, any company is involved in tax in other ways as well. In the EU all countries levy value-added tax (VAT), which is in effect an add-on to the price companies charge their customers. The tax is one on consumers and comes ultimately out of the pocket of the end consumer, but is collected through the different stages from raw material to retail. Companies collect VAT from customers, pay VAT to suppliers and give (or exceptionally reclaim) the difference to the government. VAT is not a tax on the company but the company has large costs (making sure staff know what the rules are, as well as accounting for it and documenting it) in collecting it for the government and fines if it gets the administration wrong. Other countries have sales taxes, which perform more or less the same function.

In addition, many countries levy large payroll-related costs on companies to pay for social security schemes. A recent survey showed that in some European countries 30 to 40 per cent of total staff cost is social security charges paid by the employer, quite apart from those paid by the employee. This means that there are hidden labour charges, which need to be taken into account when comparing costs in different locations.

As far as taxes on profits are concerned, over the years it has become established that taxation is due in the territory where a transaction takes place (we will leave aside the Internet for the moment). If that transaction is carried out by an entity which is not resident in that country, then the transaction may be taxable in the country of residence as well, although usually the country of residence will consider the foreign tax as a deduction. For international groups, then, tax is paid by subsidiaries on their operations in each country where they are based, and the parent is only directly concerned with the taxation of dividends paid by the subsidiaries to the parent. It is also the individual companies, which are liable for tax and not the 'group' as such, since the group is an economic and management entity rather than a judicial one. For legal purposes a group is a related network of individual companies and itself has no legal personality. The taxation of profits, which you see in group accounts, is the aggregate of the taxation in all the subsidiaries.

There are no international tax institutions or multilateral agreements, and even within the European Union, no harmonised tax rules anywhere in the world. Each territory is juridically independent and enters into bilateral agreements with other countries to cover tax arrangements for international transactions such as inward investment, payment of dividends, royalties, interest, withholding taxes etc. Switzerland is the taxman's nightmare (or tax adviser's dream?) – 26 different cantonal tax administrations with slightly different rules, all for a population of about 10 million people. Double tax treaties are the most significant instruments in the management of an international company's tax affairs and are mulled minutely by tax advisers. A multinational based in (say) the Netherlands will need to be familiar with all the treaties which the Netherlands has with other countries. Many of these treaties are similar in form – the OECD has published a model double tax treaty which is widely used – but of course the precise terms differ from treaty to treaty, even if the subject matter is the same.

Transfer pricing

While tax management in a multinational is extremely complex, the fact that tax is levied on a territorial basis (country by country) should, and to an extent does, provide opportunities for profits to fall down the cracks between countries, although you should appreciate that the one group of people who know as much about tax avoidance as the top tax consultants is government tax officials. In fact, there is a perpetual battle between consultants and regulators to test the law and find loopholes.

The most significant basic issue in this area is that of transfer pricing (OECD, 1979, 1994). As we said, many transactions between countries actually take place between fellow subsidiaries of multinationals. A pharmaceutical company for example, might be producing a number of basic chemicals in Italy, exporting these to Switzerland where they are used in manufacturing medicines, which are then sold in many other neighbouring countries. The price at which the Italian subsidiary sells to the Swiss one may well be artificial, as well as that at which the Swiss one sells to Germany. This problem is illustrated in Exhibit 12.2.

One should also make the point that when it comes to evaluating management performance, any special tax prices will distort performance

Exhibit 12.2 Transfer pricing

We can illustrate the problem with a hypothetical car. The gearbox and engine are manufactured in Germany, the vehicle is assembled in Spain and sold in France. The final selling price in France is €50,000. The materials and labour costs are:

Germany	€10,000
Spain	€15,000
France	€1,000
Total cost	€26,000
Sale	€50,000
Profit	€24,000

Let us say that the marginal tax rates on corporate profits are 50% in France, 55% in Germany and 30% in Spain, and that the profit is split equally between the subsidiaries, the results would look like this:

	Transfer within group	External transfer/costs	Gross sale	National profit	Tax	Net profit
Germany	0	10,000	18,000	8,000	4,400	3,600
Spain	18,000	15,000	41,000	8,000	2,400	5,600
France	41,000	1,000	50,000	8,000	4,000	4,000
Eliminate transfers between subsidiaries	−59,000		−59,000			
Group position	0	26,000	50,000	24,000	10,800	13,200

The overall after tax profit is €13,200 and the effective tax rate is 45%. However, if the transfer price was fixed differently, so that instead of splitting the profit equally between subsidiaries, the object was to minimise tax, this might be the result:

	Transfer within group	External transfer /costs	Gross sale	National profit	Tax	Net profit
Germany	0	10,000	11,000	1,000	550	450
Spain	11,000	15,000	48,000	22,000	6,600	15,400
France	48,000	1,000	50,000	1,000	500	500
Eliminate transfers between subsidiaries	−59,000		−59,000			
Group position	0	26,000	50,000	24,000	7,650	16,350

Profit after tax rises to €16,350 and the effective tax rate drops to 32%. This is tax management but, unfortunately, the tax authorities understand it well and there are extremely tough rules about how companies fix their transfer prices. Essentially the rules are that a group must charge a 'market' price when making transfers between subsidiaries (again there is authoritative OECD guidance). Of course there may well not be a proper market price available and there is obviously some room for manoeuvre. However, companies need to be very careful how they agree internal prices and document carefully in case of a subsequent tax investigation. There are regular infringements and heavy fines.

measures. In the example given in Exhibit 12.2, the internal accounts must agree with the prices invoiced between subsidiaries, so if an aggressive tax management policy was adopted as in the second set of figures, the managers in Germany and Spain would appear to be under-performing wildly as compared with their Spanish colleague. The group can hardly introduce a line into its internal accounts showing 'real' profits as opposed to 'tax' profits, since this would be evidence in the event of a prosecution that the transfer price was not remotely market based.

International payments

There are many payments which are made between a foreign subsidiary and its parent and these too need careful management. At an operational level there are issues such as transfers of technology, international advertising, accounting and other services, and at the financing level there are interest payments and dividends.

Transfers of costs between parent (or regional management office) and operating subsidiaries are often argued about within the company, but also may be the subject of tax disputes. Bearing in mind the territoriality issue, a host nation for a foreign operation will normally wish to maximise their tax taken from the subsidiary and are therefore likely to reject, for tax purposes, any charges levied from elsewhere in the group but outside the country where the subsidiary is established, such as contributions to the regional office costs or to international advertising campaigns, personnel, accounting or any other centrally provided service. At the same time, the parent or regional office which is actually paying these expenses and then trying to recover them may find that their national tax office refuses to accept as a deduction from their profits the proportion of charges considered to be incurred to benefit foreign subsidiaries. It is perfectly possible, therefore, for an international group to find that some of its expenses cannot be offset against tax anywhere and attention must therefore be given to that kind of question when looking at the supply of services between different countries.

This kind of problem may well occur when there is a transfer of technology. Supposing that the group's R&D unit in country A creates a new product and a system for manufacturing it, and then the product is manufactured in country B, the tax authorities in A may refuse to allow the research and development costs as a deduction from profits, because the product is actually being manufactured and revenue generated outside its territory. At the same time, country B tax authorities may refuse to accept the research and development charges because they were incurred outside its territory. Such arrangements have to be carefully structured and when a company is considering setting up a plant in a foreign country, it is normal to include the tax authorities in the negotiations to settle such details. Of course, another way to deal with that particular problem is for the subsidiary in country B to pay a royalty to the subsidiary in country A, which may well be covered in a double tax treaty.

It can also happen that income is taxed twice, because two jurisdictions believe that the transaction is part of their ambit. An actual example is where company A, based in the UK, set up a joint venture with company B, based in France. A provided finance while B managed the project, with the idea that profits would be split equally when the project was closed down (and so each venturer would pay tax – in this case capital gains tax – in their own country on their own half). No special legal vehicle was created and B carried out the transactions in its own name. In practice, the French tax authorities took the view that all the gains were attributable to *B* because *B* had signed all the contracts and the gains were therefore subject to French tax. When *A* received their share (after French tax) they had then to pay UK tax because the UK company was entitled to half the profit and had not been directly charged any French tax so could not show to the UK authorities that it had paid foreign tax on its share:

Overall gain	10,000
French tax	−2,300
Net gain	7,600
Half due to *A*	3,800
UK tax	
30% of 5,000	−1,500
Net after tax	2,300

In this case, although the rate of tax was relatively low, company *A* paid tax twice and therefore the deal which had in economic terms yielded a gain of 5,000 was not as profitable as it should have been after tax. Again, careful structuring of the deal in advance would have avoided this problem.

Receipts of tax and dividends from foreign subsidiaries are generally ruled by double tax treaties. These determine whether there is any tax withheld in the country where the payment originates and whether this may ultimately be reclaimed (another lengthy task for the tax department). These receipts are typically taxable in the hands of the recipient and sometimes it is tax efficient to flow such payments through an offshore subsidiary or something of that kind.

Tax havens have their uses in this context, but they are heavily circumscribed because often they do not have double tax treaties, and also many countries give themselves the right to levy taxes on profits which they believe are being sheltered in a tax haven by a company based in their territory. Sometimes groups use offshore companies to borrow on the international loan markets and also sometimes for captive insurance companies which insure group activities. A tax haven levies either no tax or a very low tax on offshore companies, but if a tax official in an industrialised country sees that a group has such offshore subsidiaries, this is taken as evidence that profits are being sheltered and the authorities may well start an investigation. A relatively new variant is the creation of special low tax trading zones where countries such as Botswana allow a reduced rate of tax for regional management centres. The tax rate is high enough to avoid the scheme being treated as a tax haven, but low enough to be attractive to international business.

Internet

Electronic commerce poses particular problems in international taxation: as we have seen, physical territoriality is the central issue in traditional taxation. Tax authorities are organised on individual countries or states and international transactions are typically covered by bilateral treaties.

The Internet does not recognise national boundaries and so taxation becomes very difficult (OECD, 1997). It is perfectly feasible to have an e-trader based in country A, using a service provider in country B, selling goods to a buyer in country C which are delivered from a warehouse in country D – where does the transaction take place? The Internet is the perfect tool to get round international tax problems. The trader is likely to pay profits tax in country A (unless the company moves regularly) but in theory profits tax should also be levied in country C. Supposing country C operates a value-added tax (VAT) or other sales tax, how is it to recover that from the seller in country A?

At the moment the tax authorities are generally taking a fairly relaxed view of the situation because e-commerce transactions are still a very small proportion of total retail sales. Even so, in the USA where some states rely upon sales tax for a significant part of their revenues, they are not happy about e-traders circumventing the sales tax and are suggesting that traders should pay a federal tax to compensate. Against that the federal government believes that e-commerce should not be attacked in this way.

Clearly, if a lot of retail business switched to the Internet, this would have a significant impact on both profits taxes and taxes related to sales, such as VAT. One could envisage a world where many traders would set up comfortable beachside establishments in pleasant tropical tax havens and conduct all their business in a tax-free ambiance. Legally, the imposition of taxes in e-commerce looks to be something of a nightmare, given the way existing tax structures work. The situation will certainly be changing but how quickly and in what direction no one would like to predict.

Budgeting and control

The literature (Buckley, 2001; Moffett and Yeung, 1999; Shapiro, 2001) on budgeting, measuring management performance, and control in large companies is extensive and it is well accepted that in practice budgets are capable of consuming unnecessarily large amounts of management time, diverting management attention from appropriate objectives, ossifying a company's approach to its business and stifling innovation. There is a growing though still small movement to do away with budgets and management reporting linked to budgets, but there is a basic problem that in a large multinational company, present in many different countries, there has to be a means available to coordinate management efforts, to evaluate the performance of operating units and to ensure that central management are aware of the risks being taken in all parts of the world.

Traditionally, the central platform in this system is the annual operating budget of the group. This provides the opportunity for discussing next year's performance and objectives, for identifying difficulties etc. and subsequently the gauge against which actual performance can be compared and controlled. In theory this system provides the targets, which will motivate and focus the very dispersed group in its activities, and many companies continue to refine and expand the way in which the budget works so that it takes in a wide range of data and can be operated flexibly.

Without revisiting the basic questions about budgets, we would simply observe that while the psychological problems about the 'gaming' nature of the budgetary process and its operation remain in a multinational, there are also cultural differences, which mean that management in different countries perceive the budget in different ways, and therefore react to it differently. Cultural issues are explored in Chapter 7, we would just note here that for some the budget is just a meaningless game to keep head office happy, and has no real relation to what is happening on the ground, whereas for others it is a question of honour to meet the budget commitment. Against such a background, the way in which the budget is negotiated will be approached by different subsidiaries in quite a different spirit.

Accounting differences

Budgeting systems are normally linked to the group's accounting systems. While the tendency is to widen the scope of the data used to guide management, the core of the system remains the accounting database. In an international context this brings in its train two issues, which do not occur in national systems. First, the question of how the accounting database is compiled. It is perfectly possible that individual subsidiaries use accounting policies different from those of the rest of the group, and as a consequence this will create false comparisons (Radebaugh, 1999).

Allocations are a key factor in accounting systems – costs have to be attributed to operating units or cost centres which are coherent in management terms, but just how the company splits costs and allocates them, and just how its management structure is organised may vary. For example, supposing a manufacturing unit has a distant depot for raw materials and operates its own transport for transfers between depot and factory and transfers from factory to the warehouse, which is near a motorway. Would you have one transport department to which all vehicle costs were allocated, and if so would these then be recovered through charges to other departments? If so, should the transfer to warehouse be considered a distribution cost or a manufacturing cost?

These decisions are based partly on size factors but also on cultural traditions. We will review national accounting differences later in the chapter, but these may well influence local accounting decisions, which mean that the data fed into the budgetary system and subsequently the budget/actual control may not be calculated the same way across the world. Groups may decide to live with this kind of problem, but the alternative is to insist on uniform accounting systems worldwide. Such systems are quite costly to operate because they require the preparation of manuals (these often run to many volumes and may have to be provided in more than one language) and training of new staff, as well as regular updates as systems evolve (any accounting system involves compromises between different objectives and constraints, and as the group's circumstances change or as key staff change, what is seen as an acceptable equilibrium is upset and the system is modified).

Exchange differences

The other basic problem in the budgetary process for an international operation is dealing with the foreign exchange differences. We illustrated in Exhibit 12.1 a US investment in an Italian project and you will recall that although the project turned out in line with forecast, exchange differences meant that the result in dollar terms was off-target. International groups have to be able to address this problem.

One policy is for regional management to review budget/actual comparisons with local management only in local currency. On this basis there are no exchange differences which intervene in the assessment of management and project performance at the front line. However, this does not deal with the problem when the regional office or the head office comes to review aggregate results for the region or the group. Obviously aggregate figures need to be in a common currency. Often this currency is that of the parent company, but not necessarily.

Even so, head office in particular is concerned with monitoring whether or not the group as a whole is going to be able to meet capital market expectations of profits. Therefore the budget/actual comparison month by month needs to build to an approximation of what the published group consolidated income statement will look like at the end of the year, which in turn means that the group's external reporting currency is likely to be linked to its internal reporting currency. Every group chief accountant fears having to explain to the chairman that, thanks to technical factors (which the chairman neither understands nor believes), what in monthly management report terms looks like beating the annual target will in annual income statement terms prove to be less profit than last year.

Generally, therefore, exchange differences have to be built into the monthly management reports at regional or head office level as a minimum. The technical issue is whether the reporting package is sophisticated enough to distinguish exchange differences from operating problems. There are a number of ways in which this can be done, principally using a form of flexible budgeting, which will involve either:

- restating the budget in actual exchange rate terms and throwing out an exchange rate budget difference
- showing the actual result calculated on the budget exchange rate, against actual result using the actual rate.

These issues are examined in Exhibit 12.3.

Financial accounting

We have already touched on the issue of local accounting practices versus group practices and the idea of using uniform practices throughout the group. Each country has its own regulations about financial accounting, primarily because of having a different history, a different economic framework and different ideas about regulation and how it should be carried out (Samuel et al., 1995; Walton et al., 1998). This means that local accounting staff will have been trained with different expectations about how accounting works and what it does. This does not mean that

Exhibit 12.3 Budgets and exchange rate risk

To take a simple example, suppose that a US company agreed the following budget for its French subsidiary:

	FF (000)	$ (000)
Sales	90,000	15,000
Cost of sales	36,000	6,000
Gross margin	54,000	9,000
Operating costs	21,000	3,500
Profit	33,000	5,500

The budget exchange rate was $1 = FF6.00. Supposing that the actual results were as follows:

	Figures used in France Actual FF (000)	Budget FF (000)	Figures used in USA Actual $ (000)	Budget $ (000)	Variance $ (000)
Sales	93,000	90,000	14,091	15,000	−909
Cost of sales	36,000	36,000	5,454	6,000	+546
Gross margin	57,000	54,000	8,637	9,000	−363
Operating costs	23,000	21,000	3,485	3,500	+15
Profit	34,000	33,000	5,152	5,500	−348

The actual exchange rate was $1 = FF6.60.

Looking at the dollar figures, the US management will see that sales (and unsurprisingly therefore cost of sales) are down, operating costs have been held level and profits are down. The French management, however, will be expecting congratulations on having increased sales and held the cost

of sales, with maybe some questions about why their operating costs have risen and eaten into the extra profit.

The exchange difference needs to be broken down so that US management can distinguish the different elements of performance. Using method (b) would give the following figures:

	Budget $ (000)	Actual at budget rate $ (000)	Management variance $ (000)	Actual at actual rate $ (000)	Exchange rate variance $ (000)
Sales	15,000	15,500	+500	14,091	−1,409
Cost of sales	6,000	6,000	0	5,454	+546
Gross margin	9,000	9,500	+500	8,637	−863
Operating costs	3,500	3,833	−333	3,485	+348
Profit	5,500	5,667	+167	5,152	−515

Use of this method retains the original dollar budget as the control figure, which is preferred practice, while permitting the differences to be broken out between management and the exchange rate effect. The actual

resulted is translated (as accountants say) at the budget rate, to provide a level comparison for performance, and then the French result is translated at the actual exchange rate to show the exchange difference.

what in France is seen as a sales transaction suddenly becomes an asset in Germany, the differences are more subtle than that but can lead to different profit measures and certainly different ways of allocating costs. We have already illustrated (see Figure 12.1) the effects of differences in the accounting measurements of SmithKline Beecham.

It may be helpful to recognise that the annual profit figure of a company or a group is always an estimate, not an ascertainable fact. The profit can only be measured irrefutably once the company has ceased to exist. At that point it is possible to calculate all the inputs and outputs, all the assets have been sold, all the liabilities paid off and the lifetime profit becomes a matter of fact. Before then, accountants are in the process of estimating what proportion of the lifetime profit has been generated in a particular period (month, half year, year). This is a matter of estimation because:

- some commercial transactions take place across two or more financial periods and have to be allocated between periods
- some assets are consumed over long periods and their actual life cannot be known until they are disposed of, therefore allocating their cost over accounting periods is open to error
- the outcomes of some transactions may not be known and have to be estimated
- there may be unforeseen consequences of past events, which arise later.

Making allocations and estimates is a key function in accounting measurement and the way in which these are done can be influenced by a number of factors. In some countries the tax system is intimately linked to accounting, and an accounting allocation for (say) depreciation fixes an upper limit on the expense, which the company can claim against tax. If you wish to claim the benefits of reduced tax as quickly as possible (enjoy them earlier rather than later – you cannot change the overall effect) you may be inclined to depreciate assets quickly, which will reduce profits this period and give higher profits later. Contrariwise, if your share price is going to be directly influenced by the size of the profits, you may prefer to defer cost allocations to future periods. The choice between a tax-oriented approach to accounting allocations and a stock exchange one is a key cultural variable which impacts upon profit measurement in different countries. There are many other relatively minor differences in approach on an array of allocation questions, all of which combine to give different annual profit figures based on the same information.

Accounting and its regulation are a phenomenon of developed economies. Accounting is a key prerequisite for large (or even fairly modest) business organisations and developing countries have to import accounting and accountants as part of the industrialisation process. Agriculture typically requires little accounting because it was historically done by individuals, not organisations. In the developed world the evolution of accounting has taken different tracks, which continue to impact on national accounting cultures.

Origins of commercial accounting

The French developed accounting rules in the 17th century. These were government mandated and they were introduced as a measure to combat bankruptcies. When a business goes bankrupt, it often brings down other businesses in its train and generally is bad for the economy because it diminishes confidence. The French initiative was designed to make all business people keep records of their transactions with third parties and to prepare an annual 'inventory' of their assets and their liabilities. The combination of these two measures meant that businesses should be aware of whether they were profitable or not, as well as the extent of the credit given to customers and credit taken by suppliers.

This engendered a tradition of state-controlled rules, which was widely taken up throughout continental Europe, partly because governments saw no need to reinvent the wheel and partly because Napoleon exported his Commercial Code (into which the earlier rules had evolved) in the baggage train of his armies. When tax on profits started to appear in the late 19th century in Germany and during World War I in many other countries, governments already had accounting rules so their tax rules simply built on these for profit measurement purposes.

This means that Europe has a tradition of government setting accounting rules and using them for tax, which is the prevailing culture in France, Germany, Belgium, Italy, Spain, Austria, Switzerland and so on (Walton, 1995). From this has developed the idea that accounting is primarily to do with tax assessment and that the accountant's job is to fix the figures so that tax is kept as low as possible. An accountant is therefore seen as a dry technician whose art consists of manipulating the figures and is at worst not far removed from that of the fraudster. There is no concept of accounting as an information system vital to understanding and managing the company or of the accountant as a key member of any management committee.

The Anglo-Saxon world, however, marches to a quite different beat. The evolution of accounting rules started in the 19th century as a consequence of the Industrial Revolution. The arrival of canals, railways and factories called for much larger and more risky investment (and when successful gave much higher rewards) than had previously been the norm and motivated a move towards risk sharing through companies with many shareholders. Anglo-Saxon accounting developed as a by-product of this, providing a means for shareholders to see what was happening with their money. The main object of this accounting was therefore reporting to the capital markets, and a corollary of this is that accounting rules apply only to limited companies, not to unincorporated business.

Taxation, however, has also followed a different path. First, in the UK taxes on profits were introduced in 1799 – a century before the rest of Europe. There was no framework of accounting rules and therefore statute law and jurisprudence were built up well before statutes started mentioning accounting (from 1844 onwards). Consequently, the British position has been that while the company's accounts are an indication of how management view a particular transaction, this is not necessarily how tax law views it. Taxes on profits arrived much later in the USA, but there the government decided that tax was too important to be left to accountants. No corporate accounting is free from a link to taxation, but at a formal level, continental European accounting makes a legal link, while Anglo-Saxon does not.

The second major difference between the two traditions is that continental European law is heavily influenced by Roman law. Statute law is presented as a series of codes such as the penal code, commercial code, civil code etc., which in theory represent a complete set of rules to cover every occasion. Jurisprudence also has a role but this is relatively minor. The Anglo-Saxon world, however, has a common law tradition, which based on government enacting statutes, which set out broad principles. The statutes are then left to the courts to interpret in the light of common practice. Jurisprudence plays a much more significant role and statutes deliberately leave room for judges to make judgements which relate to the circumstances of a particular case.

As far as accounting is concerned, this has meant that in the 19th century, statute law contained very few details about accounting, merely requiring companies to prepare a 'full and fair' balance sheet, at first. It was left to companies and their shareholders to sort out how this should be done, and ultimately professional advisers started to take a major role (the 'Big 5' audit firms can all trace the origins of some constituent firms to the mid-19th century in Britain). Over time this relationship has become modified with company law setting out more and more detail, but in Anglo-Saxon countries accounting regulation is still a sort of partnership between the state and the private sector, with the private sector playing a major role in setting detailed rules, or accounting standards as they are called.

International patterns

There are therefore two dominant traditions in international accounting that of the European code law countries, and that of the Anglo-Saxon world. The code law rules are primarily addressed to small and medium sized individual companies and are intimately permeated by tax considerations, while the Anglo-Saxon rules are primarily addressed to the needs of large groups to prepare consolidated accounts for the capital markets. That said, it should not be imagined that there are not significant variations between countries within each tradition (see Figure 12.1 for differences between the USA and UK). Accounting regulation moves along all the time and the pattern is constantly changing.

This leaves a question mark over the rest of the world. Essentially, the only other major tradition is that of communist accounting. The Russians developed their own accounting ideology, based upon German theories and this presents an interesting study for the professional, given that communism does not allow of the idea of profit or capital. However, it is of little practical use in the context of international business as such. What is important is to understand that communist accounting was based on the idea that a central elite in Moscow sent out detailed rules which were then applied by low grade staff in operating units. This means that there was no infrastructure of professional service firms, no accounting culture as we understand it, no idea of accounting as management information and, of course, no idea of profit measurement. This in turn means that former command economies in transition to a market economy are having to develop overnight professional bodies, accounting rules, audit etc. In effect they are obliged to install what has taken over

100 years to evolve in capitalist economies in a matter of a year or two with the inevitable problems that creates.

Outside the former communist world, most countries have patchworks of accounting regulation which have been built up over the years, largely reflecting their colonial heritage (Britain, France and Spain exported their domestic accounting to their colonies) and their trading links (e.g. Korea, the Philippines, Mexico and Canada are all influenced by US accounting, the Japanese system was originally based on the German model).

Harmonisation

Clearly this very fragmented pattern in accounting development creates problems both for international companies and for capital markets. How is a fund manager in one of the major financial institutions to compare the performance of a French multinational with that of its US competitor if the profit shown in their annual report is calculated on a different set of allocation rules?

Once internationalisation of business started to get seriously underway in the 1960s accountants and governments also started to become aware of the problem and this resulted in a number of initiatives. Within Europe the European Commission decided that harmonised accounting was necessary to make figures comparable and lead to a single European market (although that was not the rhetoric of the time). In the 1970s and 1980s a series of European company law directives was issued with a view to establishing common basic rules for individual company accounts (Fourth Directive), consolidated accounts (Seventh Directive) and professional auditors (Eighth Directive). These directives did much to remove old ways of presenting balance sheet and income statement information, but could not change the nature of the links to taxation. Indeed, both taxation and the capital market remain glaring omissions of European harmonisation, without which it is relatively difficult to think of harmonising accounting.

Apart from this regional initiative, there were three serious international attempts in the 1970s to do something about the need for harmonised accounting for international purposes. The United Nations set up an ad hoc working group on accounting, which immediately set to work on producing rules for publication of segment information. Ultimately the UN lacks the mechanisms to enforce rules in accounting as in other areas, and therefore its career as an accounting standard setter was short but its accounting initiative is still operating and remains the sole inter-governmental body which discusses regulation of accounting. It is now based in Geneva under the auspices of the UN Conference on Trade and Development (UNCTAD – an organisation, not an event, despite its title) and is called the ad hoc working group of experts on international standards of accounting and reporting (ISAR).

It has abandoned any idea of standard setting as such, but commissions research into current problems in accounting and issues position papers and guidance, which are debated by government representatives at an annual meeting. In recent years it has issued useful material about environmental accounting, the East Asian financial crisis, auditor liability and the accounting needs of small and medium sized companies in developing countries and economies in transition. The unit also manages accounting aid contracts in these countries.

The OECD set up an accounting standards group at much the same time as the UN and this also initially produced guidance on segment reporting. Thereafter the OECD mostly organised conferences for members to discuss current issues and largely abandoned activity in the accounting area in the 1990s. It is, however, active in supporting the development of accounting in former communist countries. It provides a secretariat for the Coordinating Committee on Accounting Methodology (CCAM) to which all members of the Commonwealth of Independent States belong. The CCAM is helping former Soviet countries work out new, but common, accounting regulations and develop audit professions and the necessary educational and cultural infrastructure. The OECD remains active in the taxation field, as discussed, and has started to be involved in corporate governance issues, which will be dealt with later.

The third and, as it turns out, most important, international harmonisation development was the creation of the International Accounting Standards Committee (IASC) which was set up in 1973. This was the initiative of Lord Benson, grandson of one of the four Cooper brothers who set up the eponymous accounting firm, now part of PricewaterhouseCoopers. Benson, with the help of the USA (American Institute of Certified Public Accountants – AICPA), set up a committee involving the professional accounting bodies of nine nations, with a secretariat in London. Benson became the first chairman and started issuing international accounting standards (IAS) with the idea of encouraging national rule makers to align their rules on his model rather than continue to diverge.

Over the years, the IASC has established itself as the only credible international rule maker in the area and its standards are in fact used in many countries as the basis of their own national rules, as well as being used by at least 700 international companies (outside the UK and USA) as the basis of their consolidated annual report (see www.iasc.org.uk). Currently, the IASC has gained endorsement of its standards by the International Organisation of Securities Commissions (IOSCO) as the basis for foreign listings. IOSCO, which represents national regulators of stock exchanges such as the SEC in the USA, wants to arrive at agreement on a single international 'passport' for companies which wish to be listed on exchanges outside their home country. While there is much more to this than accounting, accounting rules are central and IOSCO endorsement has been the crowning achievement in the IASC's rise to the peak of international regulation.

This rosy scenario is, however, threatened by the USA. First, US regulators believe that their accounting regulation is the best in the world and therefore (a) why should other countries not adopt that for stock exchange purposes and (b) why should the US capital markets admit companies with less than the best accounts? It seems unlikely therefore that the SEC will in the short term accept IAS-based accounts for foreign companies, and will continue to require reconciliations of account like that in Figure 12.1. However, IAS figures are not necessarily substantially different from US GAAP figures. IAS includes some options, which are not available to US companies (and US GAAP contain some options not available to IAS users). An IAS-user company can, by judicious choice of policies where choices *are* available, make their accounts very close to US GAAP and therefore reduce the differences shown in the reconciliation.

The IASC embarked on a major reorganisation in 2000 and has cut itself off from its direct links to the international accounting profession to become a free-standing non-governmental organisation. It has appointed a board of trustees, chaired by Paul Volcker (a former president of the US Federal Reserve Bank), whose function is to raise money and appoint a largely full-time board of standard setters called the International Accounting Standards Board (IASB) under the chairmanship of Sir David Tweedie (former chairman of the UK Accounting Standards Board). The new board will draw heavily on links with national regulators around the world.

In the meantime there has been a powerful move in Germany, France, Italy, Greece and Austria to introduce IAS into national regulation as the basis of consolidated accounts for companies based in those countries but listed on foreign exchanges. Currently, France and Germany also permit US GAAP as a basis, which does away with the need for companies such as DaimlerChrysler to produce reconciliations for the US market. Countries such as Australia and South Africa are aligning their national standards on IAS, and even the UK, which has long resisted the IASC rules, despite having been a major contributor both to the organisation and the creation of its standards, is starting to recognise that it needs a very strong reason if it wishes to issue a standard which differs from IAS.

Implications for international companies

This diversity clearly creates problems for international companies. Evidently the world is moving to a paradigm where the international group will prepare a single set of consolidated financial statements using accounting principles which are comparable with those used by all other international groups. For the moment these will follow either IAS or US GAAP and IAS statements will likely have a reconciliation to US GAAP which will become increasingly insignificant as companies align their accounting choices.

None of this, however, does away with the legal obligation to prepare local accounts according to local rules for all subsidiaries and to make tax returns. Multinationals, therefore, face the problem of still having to deal with a multiplicity of reporting frameworks. The situation of a British company with a German subsidiary is illustrated in Exhibit 12.4.

Exhibit 12.4 Reporting networks

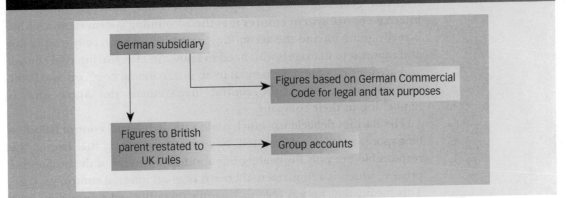

Group accounts

Any large multinational will have subsidiaries in many countries and will therefore be faced with reporting under many different sets of rules. We have already discussed this problem in relation to management accounting information and generally the solution adopted is to have a standard accounting system within the group, aligned on the same principles as are used for the published group financial statements. However, this is not the only solution and sometimes companies use hybrid measures, especially since some countries will be the site of much more complex operations than others.

It is possible for subsidiaries to use local rules and for adjustments to be made at head office. This can easily happen if a group takes over another major operation – for at least a lengthy transitional period the acquired operation will retain its own systems and rough adjustments will be made for management information purposes.

This still leaves the problem of local reporting to meet legal requirements and above all to resolve taxation issues. A large subsidiary is likely to have sufficiently well qualified in house staff to deal with the problem and restate the figures according to local rules. Alternatively, the local branch of the audit firm may be able to offer this service. In any event, the need to maintain official books on the basis of local rules but also to report internationally on group rules is a significant problem, which is unlikely to go away.

Internal control

Bound up with the reporting rules is the group's system of internal control. Any accounting system should be organised in a way which makes errors likely to be spotted and also discourages fraud. Equally the different participants in the control process need a clearly established set of rules about who is authorised to sign for what transactions and when higher authority should be sought. This is the system of internal control and is usually based on the idea called 'separation of functions' which means that a manager responsible for making a contract should not also be responsible for accounting for it or for making any payments or receiving any income associated with it.

The internal control system becomes more and more important as a company gets bigger and its operations become more far flung. The internal control system ensures that the accounting system captures what is really going on and the accounting system should correctly classify this and report it to managers who need to know. An effective internal control and accounting system is essential in an international company and is the only means by which the central management can know what is happening in their company.

The Barings debacle was much to do with an internal control failure in Singapore, as far as one can tell. Newspaper reports say that Leeson was responsible not only for dealing but also had oversight of the accounting process, which is a fundamental breach of good internal control practice. This meant that he was able to have his unauthorised transactions kept out of the normal reporting process. You may well argue that a company is always subject to individual human failings, which cannot be predicted, so there are going to be accidents. However, reporting systems should be able to signal problems effectively so that remedial action can be taken and internal control procedures are a necessary way of making sure that information is accurately reported.

Internal audit

International companies usually have an internal audit department whose functions may vary somewhat from one group to another. Historically, the internal audit unit consisted of company accountants who had oversight of the internal control systems and authority procedures. They were involved in preparing systems manuals and authority levels and also flew about the world making unannounced visits at subsidiaries to see whether group procedures were indeed being followed by local staff.

This part of the function still exists and a spell in internal audit is normally considered an essential training period for any accountant wishing to make a career in the group. However, the concept of internal audit has widened in the last 20 years so that it provides a much more thorough management service, dealing with risk assessment and decision evaluation. As general management attention has been drawn to the idea that a group involves many different activities with different levels of risk, it has become necessary to have systems for assessing and reporting risk to central management so that it may be addressed. This task has fallen to internal audit, as also has a wider role in assessing decision making.

A standard problem of accounting is that it gives you information about the consequences of the actions you have taken, but no information about the outcomes of actions you did not take. A manager facing a choice of whether to locate a plant in country A or country B makes his choice and the accounts show the results that flow from that. Internal audit may well be asked to model what the outcome would have been had the rejected alternative been chosen, this providing feedback to decision making and hopefully improving future decisions.

Auditing and corporate governance

The internal control system and internal audit service are also linked into the external audit. The external auditor will depend heavily on the effectiveness of the internal control system in reviewing the accounting systems and will usually work closely with internal audit in highlighting problem areas. This is, of course, normal at national level. However, there is an added dimension in international business in that the auditor who signs the audit report for the consolidated financial statements is legally responsible for any audit error in any of the financial statements of subsidiary companies on which the group accounts are based. The consolidated statements are also those widely published for investor use on stock exchanges and are therefore the accounts most exposed to litigation risk. Consequently, auditing rules allow for the auditor of the group statements to have oversight of and access to the working papers of the auditors of any subsidiary company.

Evidently, 'relying on the work of another auditor' as the jargon has it is potentially fraught when professional rules differ from country to country and this explains why the pattern of development of the audit profession has been for a small group of international auditors to emerge, the 'Big 5', which has offices all over the world. These firms can offer a worldwide service to international companies with theoretically uniform procedures and standards, thereby guaranteeing the quality of the audit. The Big 5 are:

- PricewaterhouseCoopers
- KPMG
- Ernst & Young
- Deloitte Touche Tohmatsu International
- Arthur Andersen.

These are not the only international firms – there are a number of highly respectable networks of large national firms, which are linked together – but these five are significantly larger than the others and their country coverage is much wider. These firms audit virtually all the major international companies and, in many cases, the audit firm is now better known than its client. It is certain that the international capital markets expect the reassurance of a Big 5 name on the financial statements of a major issuer.

Generally speaking, the audit is carried out according to the auditing standards of the country where the parent company is based. These standards are issued by the audit profession, not by government, and may vary from country to country, as also does the legal responsibility of auditors. Increasingly, international companies and international audit firms are instead starting to use international auditing standards as the basis of the audit, just as IAS are increasingly being used as the accounting base.

International auditing standards are issued by the International Auditing Practices Committee (IAPC) of the International Federation of Accountants (IFAC). IFAC, started in 1977, is the representative body of the accounting profession worldwide and its members are national accounting and auditing professional bodies. It is based in New York and deals with issues such as auditing, professional ethics, professional education, management accounting – and accounting standards for the public sector. It does not have as much public impact as the IASC (of which it has been a major supporter) but like the IASC is involved with IOSCO in supplying audit standards, which should be observed in the published accounts of internationally listed companies.

Corporate governance

In the 1990s public attention was increasingly drawn to the observation that large international companies have very great economic power and that their senior management are subject to relatively few constraints. In the largest companies listed on stock exchanges there are rarely any shareholders who individually have a major stake (say more than 10 per cent) in the company and might be in a position to influence a company. As a consequence, directors are only fired from outside the company either when it has been on the losing end of a takeover bid or there has been a major problem like consistently reducing profitability or some major scandal. Directors can therefore get away with many things without any criticism or reaction from shareholders.

This perception, fuelled by the occasional ecological disaster or overly generous remuneration package, has led to a number of initiatives designed to curb directors' powers, or at least make directors more accountable. At a practical level, institutional shareholders such as pension funds have started to issue codes of conduct, which they require companies to sign before the pension fund will invest. Sometimes institutional shareholders in a particular company have formed discreet action groups to put pressure on the board. Such shareholders are in general becoming much more proactive than they were and are increasingly seeing their own image as potentially tarnished if they invest in a company which behaves badly.

Governments and interested parties have started to commission reports and look at new ways of extending directors answerability. Britain had the Cadbury Report, France the Viénot Report, while Germany has even enacted legislation. The OECD formed an expert committee, which in its turn produced corporate governance guidelines (OECD, 1999). The broad thrust of these reports is that companies should recognise that they have a duty towards a wide range of 'stakeholders' and not just their shareholders. The stakeholders include the shareholders, of course, but also take in employees, suppliers, customers and the general public. It is not sufficient to consider the impact of corporate decisions on profits but one should consider all the other stakeholders as well.

International companies find themselves in the position that even if the rules in the country where the parent is based do not require it, there is an expectation in the international capital markets that they will provide additional disclosures and will set up mechanisms to monitor management behaviour. In this sense an international company typically is influenced by movements which are far from the parent's national culture. One of the key elements in corporate governance is that the executive directors of the company should share the board with non-executive, independent directors who are able to monitor the group's actions and speak out for the stakeholders.

In Germany there is a long-established tradition among very large companies to have a two-tier board system. An executive board, which runs the company and reports to a supervisory board, which represents shareholders, banks and employees. Outside this kind of arrangement, international companies are increasingly expected to appoint independent directors who have no involvement in the day-to-day running of the company but attend board meetings and sit on board committees.

One standard board committee under this system is the remuneration committee. This, as you might guess, is intended to fix the remuneration of the chief executive and other executive members of the board. This is supposed to increase the extent to which pay is related to external norms, but does not necessarily cause executives to be badly paid. Indeed, a flaw in this system is that independent directors are usually appointed by the chairman or chief executive, which may reduce their independence. Sometimes boards appoint what the SEC calls 'grey' directors – people who are executive directors in companies which are a major supplier or have some other commercial link to protect. Sometimes chief executives swap non-executive duties with each other.

Audit committee

A key committee of this type is the audit committee. Companies which are listed in the USA, must have such a committee (the stock exchanges require it, rather than the SEC) and it is becoming increasingly common even in companies with no US listing. The audit committee is intended to improve the quality of the company's financial reports. The idea is that the external auditors are normally appointed by the executive directors, and given that the annual audit fee for a major multinational will certainly run to several million dollars, without mentioning the value of ancillary consulting which may also be sold to the client, this puts the auditor's independence under pressure. However, if the appointment is taken out of the hands of the executive and given to independent directors, this provides some kind of firewall. Equally the internal audit department may have problems about reporting to executive directors whose work they are criticising and they too should have a direct line into the audit committee.

The idea of the audit committee is good but, like the remuneration committee, its effectiveness depends on the internal relationships within the board and the robustness of the independent directors, as well as their technical competence. In 1999 the New York Stock Exchange, NASDAQ, and the SEC took steps to make the process more robust by saying that in future the audit committee must have at least three independent directors on it, they must have some working knowledge of accounting and they must file an annual report, along with all the other financial statements, with the SEC. Other jurisdictions do not go so far and the role of the audit committee is still at an early stage of its evolution, even if such committees first started to appear 20 years ago.

Environmental and social reporting

It is also worth mentioning in this kind of area that international companies are also under some pressure to publish more information about their interaction with the environment and with society (Gray, 1996; Schaltegger, 1996). There is little or no regulation in this area so the information which is contained in annual financial statements is provided voluntarily and is usually not comparable with that provided by other companies.

As far as environmental reporting is concerned, companies tend to give data about gas emissions, water use and treatment and use of packaging materials. This information is typically to be found in the first (and unregulated) part of the annual report where companies discuss their activities. Sometimes a special report is issued independently and sometimes companies use special environmental auditors to carry out an assessment of their situation.

Evidently, part of the motivation for this is to show that the company is politically correct, but there are pressures from investors. Pension funds do not want to be found holding shares in gold-mining companies which release cyanide into the Danube or oil companies that pollute French beaches so they want reassurance that companies are managing their environmental risks in a positive way. This is not just a question of image, it is also a question of money. Totalfina announced a provision of $75 million in estimated results for 1999 and the share price of the Australian company managing the Romanian mine dropped out of sight when that leak occurred.

Summary

This chapter is intended to provide a rapid tour of the issues in accounting, finance and taxation which impact especially on international business. Probably the most significant factor in all this is the existence of in effect a global capital market where international companies are compared with each other, and whose strictures have done a great deal to harmonise approaches to financial reporting and corporate governance. This is a special environment which forces companies to change their management habits if they want to step onto the international stage.

Major companies are typically listed on several stock exchanges round the world, with a US listing seen as the final accolade to being considered a global company. International listing brings with it a need to report using accounting principles, which are more or less in line with Anglo-Saxon accounting and generally companies are using IASB rules or US rules. Corporate governance mechanisms are also an issue.

At an operational level an international company faces many problems associated with working in different currencies. It must try to balance its cash flows in different currencies to avoid making foreign exchange losses and at the same time have reporting systems which enable it to measure both underlying performance and exchange differences. In each country it will have to address local accounting and tax requirements, which differ from country to country, and it must install effective internal control and audit procedures so that, no matter how far away the group may reach, managers know what is going on all the time. You can see why there are a lot of accountants in the world.

Bibliography

Bay, W. and Bruns, H. (1998) 'Multinational companies and international capital markets' in P. Walton, A. Haller and B. Raffournier (eds) *International Accounting*, London, International Thompson Press.

Buckley, A. (2001) *Multinational Finance*, London, Financial Times Prentice Hall.

Gray, R. (1996) *Accounting and Accountability: Changes and Challenges in Corporate Social and Environmental Reporting*, London, Prentice Hall.

Jacque, L. (1999) 'Foreign exchange risk, management of' in R. Tung (ed.) *The Handbook of International Business*, London, Thomson Learning.

Jain, A. (1999) 'Foreign currency derivatives' in R. Tung (ed.) *The Handbook of International Business*, London, Thomson Learning.

Moffett, M. and Yeung, B. (1999) 'Financial management, international' in R. Tung (ed.) *The Handbook of International Business*, London, Thomson Learning.

OECD (1999) *Corporate Governance*, Paris, OECD.

OECD (1997) *Electronic Commerce: Opportunities and Challenges for Government – The Sacher Report*, DSTI/STI/IT (97), Paris, OECD.

OECD (1994) *Transfer Pricing and Multinational Enterprises*, Paris, OECD.

OECD (1992) *Taxing Profits in a Global Economy: Domestic and International Issues*, Paris, OECD.

OECD (1979) *Transfer Pricing Guidelines for Multinational Enterprises and Tax Administration*, Paris, OECD.

Radebaugh, L. (1999) 'Accounting, international' in R. Tung (ed.) *The Handbook of International Business*, London, Thomson Learning.

Samuel, J., Brayshaw, R. and Croner, J. (1995) *Financial Statement Analysis in Europe*, London, Chapman Hall.

Schaltegger, S. (1996) *Corporate Environmental Accounting*, Chichester, Wiley.

Shapiro, A. (2001) *Foundations of Multinational Financial Management*, Wiley, Chichester.

Walton, P. (1995) *European Financial Reporting: A History*, London, Academic Press.

Walton, P., Haller, A. and Raffournier, B. (1998) *International Accounting*, London, International Thomson Press.

Case 12.1 The humbling of Long-Term Capital Management

Two Nobel prizewinners, Robert Merton and Myron Scholes, and John Meriwether, a former head of bond arbitrage at Salomon Brothers, founded Long-Term Capital Management (LTCM). The approach of LTCM was based on the academic work of Merton and Scholes who developed a mathematical model based on the record of the price of financial assets such as government bonds that indicated how to hedge against deviations from trend prices.

LTCM would take a short position on a security such as a French government bond by selling bonds that it did not own in the hope of buying them back at a later date at a lower price in the derivatives market. To hedge against unfavourable movements in the price of the bonds LTCM would take a long position by buying low-risk assets such as US Treasury bonds. Profits were made if the price of the short position assets fell and the long position assets rose or stay the same. If this happened the spread between the two assets would increase and yield a profit for LTCM. The success of the model used to assess the level of hedging required to smooth out adverse price movements seemed to make this process a one-way bet as in the long run and on average the hedging process appeared to eliminate adverse price movements and allow profits to be made from the increase in spreads. For this process to work it was necessary to engage in large-scale hedging operations to average out unfavourable price movements. This required very large long positions on low-risk financial assets. This resulted in LTCM acquiring a very large debt to equity ratio to provide the funds necessary to take large long positions on low-risk assets. When LTCM ran into trouble in 1998 it had a debt to equity ratio of 50:1. However, in the late 1990s LTCM appeared to have found a near perfect way to make money out of changes in the prices of international financial assets and had little difficultly raising finance.

Problems emerged for LTCM when a series of currency and debt crises hit the financial markets. The Asian crisis in 1997 and the default on debt by Russia in 1998 led to a flight to quality assets, that is, to low-risk financial assets. This meant that many of the assets that LTCM had taken a short position on, betting that they would fall actually went up. Therefore the spread between short and long positions taken by LTCM fell by more than their model predicted because it was based on normal market conditions, but the Asian and Russian crises led to abnormal conditions, which the model could not deal with. LTCM found itself with insufficient hedges against the large-scale unfavourable price movements in high-risk assets.

The very high debt to equity ratio of LTCM made this a very serious problem because the company found itself short of funds to repay its loans. In attempts to rectify this shortfall LTCM liquidated assets to raise money to meet its commitments in its short positions. This dramatically reduced the capital base of the company and led to concern that the company would have to cease trading. The consequences of this would have been very serious as LTCM had liabilities of around $200 billion and these were held in all the major financial centres of the world. Failure of LTCM could have led to chaos in world financial markets. In order to prevent such an outcome the New York Federal Reserve organised a rescue plan by leading commercial banks. The loans from these banks prevented the collapse of LTCM but the company dramatically scaled back its operations and ceased to engage in large-scale hedging.

The problems that LTCM encountered clearly illustrate the problems of seeking to make money, in the long term, from hedging operations. The founders of LTCM included two Nobel prizewinners (awarded for contribution towards understanding of the working of financial markets!) and a world expert in international bond arbitrage. A sophisticated mathematical model based on the work of the Nobel prizewinners that should have enabled optimal hedging positions to be taken was also available to LTCM. However, this was to no avail when financial markets entered a period of crisis. Nevertheless, the experiences of LTCM have not prevented companies (including many non-financial services multinational corporations) seeking to beat the market by engaging in complex hedging operations. Fortunately, since the problems with LTCM no company has taken on such large liabilities and, consequently, the main risks are for the companies which seek to beat the market. In the case of LTCM the entire international financial system was put at risk.

Financial Times (1998) 'Emperor stripped bare: the collapse of John Meriwether's hedge fund is a defining moment for Wall Street', 25 September; 'LTCM had built up exposure of $200 billion', 26 September; 'Computer models were flawed', 28 September

13 International human resource management

Learning objectives

By the end of this chapter, you should be able to:

- discuss the meaning of international HRM
- have an understanding of the dimensions of international human resource activities
- be aware of the impact of internationalisation on the activities and policies of HRM
- understand the variables that moderate differences between domestic and international HRM
- understand the complexity involved in operating in different countries and employing different national categories of employees
- understand the role of strategic HRM in multinational enterprises

Key terms

• international HRM • domestic HRM • host country nationals • parent country nationals • third country nationals • emic-etic distinction • convergence hypothesis • divergence hypothesis • multidomestic industry • global industry • strategic HRM

Introduction

The globalisation of business is forcing managers to grapple with complex issues as they seek to gain or sustain a competitive advantage. Faced with unprecedented levels of foreign competition at home and abroad, firms are beginning to recognise not only that international business is high on the list of priorities for top management but also that finding and nurturing the human resources required to implement an international or global strategy is of critical importance. Effective human resource management (HRM) is essential, especially perhaps for small and medium firms, where international expansion places extra stress on limited resources, particularly people. As Duerr (1986) points out:

> Virtually any type of international problem, in the final analysis, is either created by people or must be solved by people. Hence, having

the right people in the right place at the right time emerges as the key to a company's international growth. If we are successful in solving that problem, I am confident we can cope with all others. (p. 43)

Writing in the mid-1980s on the state of the field of international human resource management (IHRM), Laurent (1986) concluded that 'the challenge faced by the infant field of international human resource management is to solve a multidimensional puzzle located at the crossroad of national and organizational cultures' (p. 101). The aim of this chapter[1] is to examine developments in the field of IHRM and to determine if any progress has been made towards completing the puzzle noted by Laurent. Specifically, three issues are examined: first, the various approaches which have been taken to the study of IHRM; second, the variables which moderate differences between domestic and international HRM; and third, recent work which examines the topic of strategic human resource management in multinational enterprises (MNEs).

Approaches to international HRM

The field of international HRM has been characterised by three broad approaches.[2] Early work in this field emphasised a cross-cultural management approach and examined human behaviour within organisations from an international perspective (Adler, 1997; Phatak, 1997). A second approach developed from the comparative industrial relations and HRM literature seeks to describe, compare and analyse HRM systems in various countries (see for example, Brewster and Hegewisch, 1994). A third approach seeks to focus on aspects of HRM in multinational enterprises (see for example, Dowling, et al., 1999).

The approach taken in this chapter reflects the third approach and our objective is to explore the implications that the process of internationalisation has for the activities and policies of HRM. In particular, we are interested in how HRM is practised in multinational enterprises (MNEs).

Each approach takes a somewhat different view of IHRM and it is the author's view that it is essential to identify the approach which a researcher is taking to the subject, as the approach taken influences what is *defined* as IHRM. One only has to look at the diversity in the programme at various international HRM conferences to see that there are multiple definitions of what constitutes international HRM.

Defining international HRM from the perspective of a multinational enterprise

Before offering a definition of international HRM, we should first define the general field of HRM. Typically, HRM refers to those activities undertaken by an organisation effectively to utilise its human resources. These activities would include at least the following:

- human resource planning
- staffing
- performance management
- training and development

- compensation and benefits
- labour relations.

We can now consider the question of which activities change when HRM goes international. A paper by Morgan (1986) on the development of international HRM is helpful in considering this question. He presents a model of international HRM (shown in Figure 13.1) that consists of three dimensions:

1 The three broad human resource activities of procurement, allocation and utilisation. (These three broad activities can be easily expanded into the six HR activities just listed.)

2 The three national or country categories involved in international HRM activities: the host country where a subsidiary may be located, the home country where the firm is headquartered and 'other' countries that may be the source of labour or finance.

3 The three types of employees of an international firm: *host country nationals* (HCNs), *parent country nationals* (PCNs) and *third country nationals* (TCNs). Thus, for example, IBM employs Australian citizens (HCNs) in its Australian operations, often sends US citizens (PCNs) to Asia–Pacific countries on assignment and may send some of its Singaporean employees on an assignment to its Japanese operations (as TCNs).

Morgan defines international HRM as the interplay among these three dimensions – human resource activities, types of employee and countries of operation. We can see that in broad terms international HRM involves

Figure 13.1 Model of international HRM in multinational enterprises

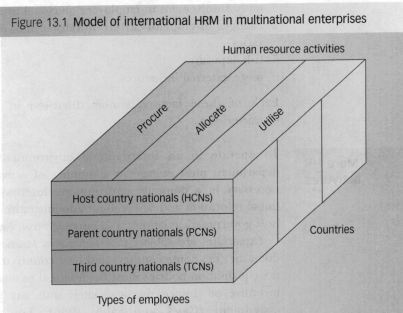

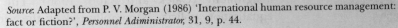

Source: Adapted from P. V. Morgan (1986) 'International human resource management: fact or fiction?', *Personnel Adiministrator,* 31, 9, p. 44.

the same activities as domestic HRM: (e.g. procurement refers to HR planning and staffing). However, domestic HRM is involved with employees within only *one national boundary.*

In this chapter it is argued that the *complexities of operating in different countries and employing different national categories of workers* is a key variable that differentiates domestic and international HRM, rather than any major differences between the HRM activities performed. Many firms underestimate the complexities involved in international operations and there is some evidence to suggest that business failures in the international arena may often be linked to poor management of human resources (Desatnick and Bennett 1978).

Increasingly, domestic HRM is taking on some of the flavour of international HRM as it deals more and more with a multicultural workforce. Thus, some of the current focus of domestic HRM on issues of managing workforce diversity may prove to be beneficial to the practice of international HRM. However, it must be remembered that management of diversity within a single national context may not necessarily transfer to a multinational context without some modification.

It is worthwhile examining in detail what is meant by the statement that international HRM is more complex than domestic HRM. Dowling (1988) has summarised the literature on similarities and differences between international and domestic HRM and argues that the complexity of international HR can be attributed to six factors, which differentiate international from domestic HRM. These factors are as follows:

1 more HR activities
2 need for a broader perspective
3 more involvement in employees' personal lives
4 changes in emphasis as the workforce mix of expatriates and locals varies
5 risk exposure
6 more external influences.

Each of these factors is now discussed in detail to illustrate its characteristics.

More HR activities

To operate in an international environment, a human resources department must engage in a number of activities that would not be necessary in a domestic environment: international taxation; international relocation and orientation; administrative services for expatriates; host government relations; and language translation services.

Expatriates are subject to *international taxation,* and often have both domestic (i.e. home country) and host country tax liabilities. Therefore, tax equalisation policies must be designed to ensure that there is no tax incentive or disincentive associated with any particular international assignment (Gajek and Sabo, 1986). The administration of tax equalisation policies is complicated by the wide variations in tax laws across host countries and by the possible time lag between the completion of an expatriate assignment and the settlement of domestic and international tax liabilities. In recognition of these difficulties, many multinational firms retain the services of a major accounting firm for international taxation advice.

International relocation and orientation involves arranging for pre-departure training; providing immigration and travel details; providing housing, shopping, medical care, recreation, and schooling information; and finalising compensation details such as delivery of salary overseas, determination of various overseas allowances and taxation treatment. Many of these factors may be a source of anxiety for the expatriate and require considerable time and attention successfully to resolve potential problems – certainly much more time than would be involved in a domestic transfer/relocation such as New York to Dallas, Sydney to Melbourne, London to Cardiff or Frankfurt to Munich.

A multinational firm also needs to provide *administrative services* for expatriates in the host countries in which it operates (Acuff, 1984). Providing administrative services can often be a time-consuming and complex activity because policies and procedures are not always clear-cut and may conflict with local conditions. For example, ethical questions can arise when a practice that is legal and accepted in the host country may be at best unethical and at worst illegal in the home country. For example, a situation may arise in which a host country requires an AIDS test for a work permit for an employee whose parent firm is headquartered in the USA, where employment-related AIDS testing remains a controversial issue. How does the corporate HR manager deal with the potential expatriate employee who refuses to meet this requirement for an AIDS test and the overseas affiliate which needs the services of a specialist expatriate from headquarters? These issues add to the complexity of providing administrative services to expatriates.

Host government relations represent an important activity for a HR department, particularly in developing countries where work permits and other important certificates are often more easily obtained when a personal relationship exists between the relevant government officials and multinational managers. Maintaining such relationships helps resolve potential problems that can be caused by ambiguous eligibility and/or compliance criteria for documentation such as work permits. US-based multinationals, however, must be careful in how they deal with relevant government officials, as payment or payment in kind such as dinners and gifts may violate the US Foreign Corrupt Practices Act.

Provision of *language translation services* for internal and external correspondence is an additional international activity for the HR department. Morgan (1986) notes that if the HR department is the major user of language translation services, the role of this translation group is often expanded to provide translation services to all foreign operation departments within the multinational.

Need for a broader perspective

HR managers working in a domestic environment generally administer programmes for a single national group of employees who are covered by a uniform compensation policy and taxed by one national government. Because HR managers working in an international environment face the problem of designing and administering programmes for more than one national group of employees (e.g. PCN, HCN and TCN employees who may work together in Zurich at the European regional headquarters of a US-based multinational), they need to take a broader view of issues. For example, a broader, more international perspective on expatriate benefits would endorse the view that all expatriate employees, regardless of nationality, should receive a foreign service or expatriate premium when working in a foreign location. Yet, some multinationals which routinely pay such premiums to their PCN employees on overseas assignment (even if the assignments are to desirable locations) are reluctant to pay premiums to foreign nationals assigned to the home country of the firm. Firms following such a policy often use the term 'inpatriate' to describe foreign nationals assigned to the home country of the firm.[3] Such a policy confirms the common perception of many HCN and TCN employees that PCN employees are given preferential treatment. Complex equity issues arise when employees of various nationalities work together and the resolution of these issues remains one of the major challenges in the international HRM field (see Case 13.1).

More involvement in employees' personal lives

A greater degree of involvement in employees' personal lives is necessary for the selection, training and effective management of both PCN and TCN employees. The HR department or professional needs to ensure that the expatriate employee understands housing arrangements, healthcare and all aspects of the compensation package provided for the assignment (cost of living allowances, premiums, taxes and so on). Many multinationals have an 'international HR services' section that coordinates administration of these programmes and provides services for PCNs and TCNs such as handling their banking, investments, home rental while on assignment, coordinating home visits and final repatriation.

In the domestic setting, the HR department's involvement with an employee's family is limited. The firm may, for example, provide employee insurance programmes. Alternatively, if a domestic transfer is involved, the HR department may provide some assistance in relocating the employee and family. In the international setting, however, the HR department must be much more involved in order to provide the level of support required and will need to know more about the employee's personal life. For example, some governments require the presentation of a marriage certificate before granting a visa to an accompanying spouse. Thus, marital status could become an aspect of the selection process, regardless of the best intentions of the firm to avoid using a potentially discriminatory selection criterion. In such a situation, the HR department should advise all candidates being considered for the position of the host country's visa requirements with regard to marital status and allow candidates to decide whether they wish to remain in the selection process. Apart from providing suitable housing and schooling in the assignment location, the HR department may also need to assist children left behind at boarding schools in the home country.[4] In more remote or less hospitable assignment locations, the HR department may be required to develop, and even run, recreational programmes. For a domestic assignment, most of these matters either would not arise or would be primarily the responsibility of the employee rather than the HR department.

Changes in emphasis as the workforce mix of PCNs and HCNs varies

As foreign operations mature, the emphases put on various human resource activities change. For example, as the need for PCNs and TCNs declines and more trained locals become available, resources previously allocated to areas such as expatriate taxation, relocation and orientation are transferred to activities such as local staff selection, training and management development. This last activity may require establishment of a programme to bring high-potential local staff to corporate headquarters for developmental assignments. The need to change emphasis in HR operations as a foreign subsidiary matures is clearly a factor that would broaden the responsibilities of local HR activities such as human resource planning, staffing, training and development and compensation.

Risk exposure

Frequently, the human and financial consequences of failure in the international arena are more severe than in domestic business. For example, expatriate failure (the premature return of an expatriate from an international assignment) is a potentially high-cost problem for international companies (Tung, 1981). Direct costs (salary, training costs, and travel and relocation expenses) per failure to the parent firm may be as high as three times the domestic salary plus relocation expenses, depending on currency exchange rates and location of assignments (Mendenhall and Oddou, 1985). Indirect costs such as loss of market share and damage to overseas customer relationships may be considerable (Zeira and Banai, 1984).

Another aspect of risk exposure that is relevant to international HRM is terrorism. Most major multinationals must now consider this factor when planning international meetings and assignments and it is estimated that they spend 1 to 2 per cent of their revenues on protection against terrorism. Terrorism has also clearly had an effect on the way in which employees assess potential international assignment locations (Gladwin and Walter, 1980; Harvey, 1993). The HR department may also need to devise emergency evacuation procedures for highly volatile assignment locations. The invasion of Kuwait and the ensuing Gulf War in 1991 is an example of a situation in which employees unexpectedly and very rapidly became at risk.

More external influences

The major external factors that influence international HRM are the type of government, the state of the economy and the generally accepted practices of doing business in each of the various host countries in which the multinational operates. A host government can, for example, dictate hiring procedures, as is the case in Malaysia. During the 1970s the government introduced a requirement that foreign firms comply with an extensive set of affirmative action rules designed to provide additional employment opportunities for the indigenous Malays who constitute the majority of the population but tend to be under-represented in business and professional employment groups relative to Chinese Malays and Indian Malays. Various statistics showing employment levels of indigenous Malays throughout the firm must be forwarded to the relevant government department.

In developed countries, labour is more expensive and better organised than in less developed countries and governments require compliance with guidelines on issues such as labour relations, taxation and health and safety. These factors shape the activities of the subsidiary HR manager to a considerable extent. In less developed countries, labour tends to be cheaper and less organised and government regulation is less pervasive, so these factors take less time. The subsidiary HR manager must spend more time, however, learning and interpreting the local ways of doing business and the general code of conduct regarding activities such as gift giving. It is also likely that the subsidiary HR manager may also become more involved in administering benefits either provided or financed by the multinational such as housing, education and other facilities not readily available in the local economy.

Variables that moderate differences between domestic and international HRM

In our discussion so far, we have argued that the complexity involved in operating in different countries and employing different national categories of employees is a key variable that differentiates domestic and international HRM, rather than any major differences between the HRM activities performed. In addition to complexity, there are four other variables that moderate (that is, either diminish or accentuate) differences between domestic and international HRM. These variables (shown in Figure 13.2) are the cultural environment; the industry (or industries) with which the multinational is primarily involved; the extent of reliance of the multinational on its home country domestic market; and the attitudes of senior management. These four additional variables are now discussed.

Cultural environment

There are many definitions of *culture*, but the term is usually used to describe a shaping process. That is, members of a group or society share a distinct way of life with common values, attitudes, and behaviors that are transmitted over time in a gradual, yet dynamic, process. As Phatak (1995) explains:

> A person is not born with a given culture: rather she or he acquires it through the socialisation process that begins at birth: an American is

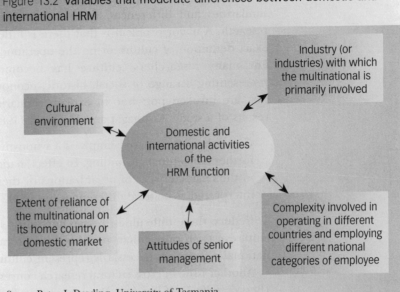

Figure 13.2 Variables that moderate differences between domestic and international HRM

Source: Peter J. Dowling, University of Tasmania.

not born with a liking for hot dogs, or a German with a natural preference for beer: these behavioral attributes are culturally transmitted. (p. 48)

An important characteristic of culture is that it is so subtle a process that one is not always conscious of its effect on values, attitudes and behaviours. One usually has to be confronted with a different culture in order fully to appreciate this effect. Anyone travelling abroad, as either a tourist or businessperson, experiences situations that demonstrate cultural differences in language, food, dress, hygiene and attitude to time. While the traveller can perceive these differences as novel, even enjoyable, for people required to live and work in a new country such differences can prove difficult. They experience *culture shock* – a phenomenon experienced by people who move across cultures. The new environment requires many adjustments in a relatively short period of time, challenging people's frames of reference to such an extent that their sense of self, especially in terms of nationality, comes into question. People, in effect, experience a shock reaction to new cultural experiences that cause psychological disorientation because they misunderstand or do not recognise important cues. Culture shock can lead to negative feelings about the host country and its people and a longing to return home (Harris and Moran, 1979).

Because international business involves the interaction and movement of people across national boundaries, an appreciation of cultural differences and when these differences are important is essential. Research into these aspects has assisted in furthering our understanding of the cultural environment as an important variable that moderates differences between domestic and international HRM. However, while cross-cultural and comparative research attempts to explore and explain similarities and differences, there are problems associated with such research. A major problem is that there is little agreement either on an exact definition of culture or on the operationalization of this concept. For many researchers, culture has become an omnibus variable, representing a range of social, historic, economic, and political factors that are invoked post hoc to explain similarity or dissimilarity in the results of a study. As Bhagat and McQuaid (1982) have noted:

> *Culture* has often served simply as a synonym for *nation* without any further conceptual grounding. In effect, national differences found in the characteristics of organizations or their members have been interpreted as cultural differences. (p. 653)

To reduce these difficulties, researchers must specify their definition of culture *a priori* rather than post hoc and be careful not to assume that national differences necessarily represent cultural differences.

Another issue in cross-cultural research concerns the *emic-etic* distinction (Berry, 1980; De Cieri and Dowling, 1995; Teagarden and Von Glinow, 1997). *Emic* refers to culture-specific aspects of concepts or behaviour, and *etic* refers to culture-common aspects. These terms have been borrowed from linguistics: a phon*emic* system documents meaningful sounds specific to a given language and a phon*etic* system organises all sounds that have meaning in any language (Triandis and Brislin, 1984). Both the emic and etic approaches are legitimate research orientations. A major problem may arise, however, if a researcher imposes an etic approach (that is, assumes universality across cultures) when there is little or no evidence for doing so. A well-known example of an imposed etic approach is the *convergence hypothesis* that dominated much of US and European management research in the 1950s and 1960s. This approach was based on two key assumptions (Hofstede, 1983). The first assumption was that there were principles of sound management that held regardless of national environments. Thus, the existence of local or national practices that deviated from these principles simply indicated a need to change these local practices. The second assumption was that the universality of sound management practices would lead to societies becoming increasingly alike in the future. Given that the USA was the leading industrial economy, the point of convergence would be toward the US model. Adoption of the convergence hypothesis has led to some rather poor predictions of future performance. For example, writing in the late 1950s, Harbison (1959) concluded the following with regard to the Japanese managerial system:

> Unless basic rather than trivial or technical changes in the broad philosophy of organization building are forthcoming, Japan is destined to fall behind in the ranks of modern industrialised nations. (p. 254)

To use Kuhn's (1962) terminology, the convergence hypothesis became an established paradigm that many researchers found difficult to give up, despite a growing body of evidence supporting a *divergence hypothesis*. In an important paper reviewing the convergence/divergence debate, Child (1981) made the point that there is evidence for both convergence and divergence. The majority of the convergence studies, however, focus on macro level variables (for example, structure and technology used by firms across cultures) and the majority of the divergence studies focus on micro level variables (for example, the behaviour of people within firms). His conclusion was that although firms in different countries are becoming more alike (an etic or convergence approach), the behaviour of *individuals within these firms* is maintaining its cultural specificity (an emic or divergence approach). As noted earlier, both emic and etic approaches are legitimate research orientations, but methodological difficulties may arise if the distinction between these two approaches is ignored or if unwarranted universality assumptions are made (Ricks, 1993). The debate on assumptions of universality is not limited to the literature in international management. Recently, this issue has become a topic of debate in the field of international relations and strategic studies where research from international management is cited (Huntington, 1996).

Importance of cultural awareness

Despite the methodological concerns about cross-cultural research, it is now generally recognised that culturally insensitive attitudes and behaviours stemming from ignorance or from misguided beliefs ('my way is best', or 'what works at home will work here') are not only inappropriate but also often cause international business failure. Therefore, an awareness of cultural differences is essential for the HR manager at corporate headquarters as well as in the host location (Tung, 1993). Activities such as hiring, promoting, rewarding and dismissal will be determined by the practices of the host country and often are based on a value system peculiar to that country's culture. A firm may decide to head up a new overseas operation with an expatriate general manager but appoint as the HR department manager a local, a person who is familiar with the host country's HR practices. This practice can cause problems for the expatriate general manager, however, as happened to an Australian who was in charge of a new mining venture in Indonesia. The local manager responsible for recruitment could not understand why the Australian was upset to find that he had hired most of his extended family rather than staff with the required technical competence. The Indonesian was simply ensuring that his duty to his family was fulfilled – since he was in a position to employ most of them, he was obligated to do so. The Australian, however, interpreted the Indonesian's actions as nepotism, a negative practice according to his own value system (Dowling, et al., 1989).

Wyatt (1989: 5) recounts a good example of the fallacy of assuming 'what works at home will work here' when dealing with work situations in another culture. HR department staff of a large firm in Papua New Guinea was concerned over a number of accidents involving operators of very large, expensive, earth-moving vehicles. The expatriate managers investigating the accidents found that local drivers involved in the accidents were chewing betel nut, a common habit for most of the coastal peoples of Papua New Guinea and other Pacific islands. Associating the betel nut with depressants such as alcohol, the expatriate managers banned the chewing of betel nut during work hours. In another move to reduce the number of accidents, free coffee was provided at loading points and drivers were required to alight from their vehicles at these locations. What the managers did not realise was that betel nut, like their culturally acceptable coffee, is, in fact, a stimulant, although some of the drivers were chewing it to cover up the fact that they drank beer before commencing work. As Wyatt points out, many indigenous workers used betel nut as a pick-me-up in much the same way as the expatriates used coffee.

Adjusting to a new cultural environment can cause problems for both the expatriate employee and the accompanying spouse and family members. Coping with cultural differences, and recognising how and when these differences are relevant, is a constant challenge for the expatriate employee. Helping to prepare expatriates and their families for the cultural environment has now become a key activity for HR departments in those multinationals that appreciate (or have been forced, through experience, to appreciate) the impact that the cultural environment can have on staff performance and well-being.

Industry type

Porter (1986) suggests that the industry (or industries if the firm is a conglomerate) in which a multinational enterprise is involved is of considerable importance because patterns of international competition vary widely from one industry to another. At one end of the continuum of international competition is the *multidomestic industry*, one in which competition in each country is essentially independent of competition in other countries. Traditional examples include retailing, distribution and insurance. At the other end of the continuum is the *global industry*, one in which a firm's competitive position in one country is significantly influenced by its position in other countries. Examples include commercial aircraft, semiconductors and copiers. It is important to note that this is a continuum and over time industries may move from one end towards the other – e.g. the world auto industry has moved from a largely multidomestic arrangement towards a more global position because of production integration and global sourcing of components.

The key distinction between a multidomestic industry and a global industry is described by Porter as follows:

> The global industry is not merely a collection of domestic industries but a series of linked domestic industries in which the rivals compete against each other on a truly worldwide basis. . . . In a multidomestic industry, then, international strategy collapses to a series of domestic strategies. The issues that are uniquely international revolve around how to do business abroad, how to select good countries in which to compete (or assess country risk), and mechanisms to achieve the one-

time transfer of know-how. These are questions that are relatively well developed in the literature. In a global industry, however, managing international activities like a portfolio will undermine the possibility of achieving competitive advantage. In a global industry, a firm must in some way integrate its activities on a worldwide basis to capture the linkages among countries.

(Porter, 1986: 23)

The role of the HRM function in multidomestic and global industries can be analysed using Porter's value chain model (Porter, 1985). In Porter's model, HRM is seen as one of four support activities for the five primary activities of the firm. Since human resources are involved in each of the primary and support activities, the HRM function is seen as cutting across the entire value chain of a firm. If the firm is in a multidomestic industry, the role of the HR department will most likely be more domestic in structure and orientation. At times there may be considerable demand for international services from the HRM function (for example, when a new plant or office is established in a foreign location and the need for expatriate employees arises), but these activities would not be pivotal – indeed, many of these services may be provided via consultants and/or temporary employees. The main role for the HRM function would be to support the primary activities of the firm in each domestic market to achieve a competitive advantage through either cost/efficiency or product/service differentiation (Schuler and MacMillan, 1984). If the multinational is in a global industry, however, the 'imperative for coordination' described by Porter would require a HRM function structured to deliver the international support required by the primary activities of the multinational enterprise.

The need to develop coordination raises complex problems for any MNE. As Laurent (1986) has noted:

In order to build, maintain, and develop their corporate identity, multinational organizations need to strive for consistency in their ways of managing people on a worldwide basis. Yet, and in order to be effective locally, they also need to adapt those ways to the specific cultural requirements of different societies. While the global nature of the business may call for increased consistency, the variety of cultural environments may be calling for differentiation. (p. 97)

Laurent proposes that a truly international conception of human resource management would require the following steps:

1 An explicit recognition by the parent organisation that its own peculiar ways of managing human resources reflect some assumptions and values of its home culture.
2 An explicit recognition by the parent organisation that its peculiar ways are neither universally better nor worse than others but are different and likely to exhibit strengths and weaknesses, particularly abroad.

3 An explicit recognition by the parent organisation that its foreign subsidiaries may have other preferred ways of managing people that are neither intrinsically better nor worse, but could possibly be more effective locally.

4 A willingness from headquarters not to only acknowledge cultural differences, but also to take active steps in order to make them discussable and therefore usable.

5 The building of a genuine belief by all parties involved that more creative and effective ways of managing people could be developed as a result of cross-cultural learning.

In offering this proposal, Laurent acknowledges that these are difficult steps that few firms have taken:

> They have more to do with states of mind and mindsets than with behaviors. As such, these processes can only be facilitated and this may represent a primary mission for executives in charge of international human resource management.

> (Laurent, 1986: 100)

Implicit in Laurent's analysis is the idea that by taking the steps he describes, a multinational attempting to implement a global strategy via coordination of activities would be better able to work through the difficulties and complex trade-offs inherent in such a strategy. Increasingly, MNEs are taking a more strategic approach to the role of HRM and are using staff transfers and training programmes to assist in coordination of activities.

Reliance of the multinational enterprise on its home country domestic market

A pervasive but often ignored factor, which influences the behaviour of MNEs and resultant HR practices is the extent of reliance of the multinational on its home country domestic market. When for example, we look through lists of very large firms (such as those that appear in *Fortune* and other business magazines), it is frequently assumed that a global market perspective would be dominant in the firm's culture and thinking. However, size is not the only key variable when looking at a multinational enterprise – the extent of reliance of the multinational on its home country domestic market is also very important. In fact, for many firms, a small home market is one of the major motives for 'going international'.

The United Nations Conference on Trade and Development (UN-CTAD) in its annual survey of foreign direct investment calculates what it refers to as an 'index of transnationality' which is an average of ratios of foreign assets to total assets; foreign sales to total sales; and foreign employment to total employment (*Economist*, 1997). Based on this index of transnationality, the most foreign-oriented multinational is Nestlé, with 87 per cent of assets, 98 per cent of sales and 97 per cent of employees located outside Switzerland. The 'top ten' multinationals are as follows:

1 Nestlé (Switzerland)
2 Thomson (Canada)
3 Holderbank Financière (Switzerland)
4 Seagram (Canada)
5 Solvay (Belgium)
6 Asea Brown Boveri (Sweden/Switzerland)
7 Electrolux (Sweden)
8 Unilever (Britain/Netherlands)
9 Philips (Netherlands)
10 Roche (Switzerland)

There is not a US firm in the first 15 multinationals listed and Coca-Cola and McDonald's are ranked 31st and 42nd respectively. The reason for this is as obvious as it is important – *the size of the domestic market for US firms.* A very large domestic market influences all aspects of how a multinational organises its activities.

For example, it will be more likely to use an international division as the way it organises its international activities and even if it uses a global product structure, the importance of the domestic market will be pervasive. A large domestic market will also influence the attitudes of senior managers (discussed in more detail in the next section) and will generate a large number of managers with an experience base of predominantly or even exclusively domestic market experience. Thus, multinationals from small advanced economies such as Switzerland (population 7 million), Belgium (10 million), Sweden (9 million) and the Netherlands (15 million) are in a quite different position from US multinationals based in the largest single national market in the world with over 280 million people. The demands of a large domestic market present a challenge to the globalisation efforts of many US firms. As Cavusgil (1993) has noted in an important book on internationalising business education, the task of internationalising business education in the USA is a large one. So too, is the task facing many US firms in terms of developing global managers.

Attitudes of senior management to international operations

The point made by Laurent that some of the changes required truly to internationalise the HR function 'have more to do with states of mind and mindsets than with behaviors' illustrates the importance of a final variable that may moderate differences between international and domestic HRM: the attitudes of senior management to international operations.

It is likely that if senior management does not have a strong international orientation, the importance of international operations may be underemphasised (or possibly even ignored) in terms of corporate goals and objectives. In such situations, managers may tend to focus on domestic issues and minimise differences between international and domestic environments. They may assume that there is a great deal of transferability between domestic and international HRM practices. This failure to recognise differences in managing human resources in foreign environments – regardless of whether it is because of ethnocentrism, inadequate information or a lack of international perspective – frequently results in major difficulties in international operations (Desatnick and Bennett, 1978). The challenge for the corporate HR manager is to work with top management in fostering the desired 'global mindset'. This goal requires, of course, an HR manager who is able to think globally and to formulate and implement HR policies that facilitate the development of globally oriented staff (Bartlett and Ghoshal, 1992; Pucik, 1997).

Theoretical developments: a framework of strategic HRM in multinational enterprises

An integrative framework of strategic international HRM has been presented by Schuler et al. (1993). Since the publication of these authors' framework, developments have brought the need to consider revision of the framework and De Cieri and Dowling (1999) have developed a revised framework of strategic HRM in multinational enterprises, which is shown in Figure 13.3.

As depicted in Figure 13.3, MNEs operate in the context of worldwide conditions, including the external contexts of industry, nation, region, and inter-organisational networks and alliances. For example, the removal of internal trade barriers and integration of national markets in the European Union has brought a new range of inter-organisational relationships. In addition, the introduction of the European Monetary Union in 1999 has

Figure 13.3 Model of strategic HRM in multinational enterprises

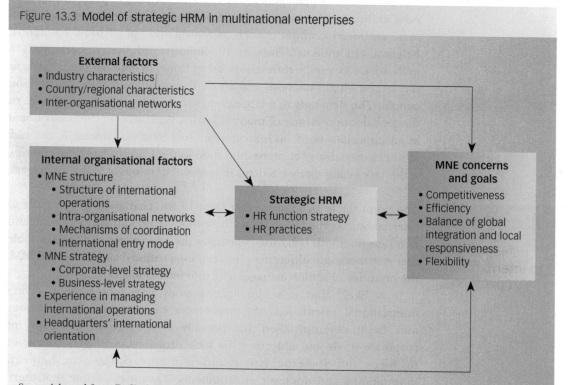

Source. Adapted from DeCieri, H. and Dowling, P. J. (1999) 'Strategic human resource management in multinational enterprises: theoretical and empirical developments', in P. M. Wright et al. (eds) *Research in Personnel and Human Resource Management: Strategic Human Resources in the 21st Century,* Supplement 4, Stamford, CT, JAI Press.

the potential to hold significant implications for inter-organisational relationships. External factors exert direct influence on internal organisational factors, HRM strategy and practices, and MNE concerns and goals. If we were to examine the impact of economic difficulties in the Asia–Pacific region since 1997, we would be likely to see examples of this influence where MNEs have had to reduce the scale of their operations due to more subdued demand for their products and services.

Internal organisational factors are shown in order of most 'tangible' to most 'intangible'. Multinational structure refers to both the structure of international operations and intra-organisational networks and mechanisms of coordination. The life cycle stage of the firm and the industry in which it operates are important influences on strategic HRM in MNEs as are international entry modes (e.g. international joint ventures or alliances) and levels of firm strategy. The most intangible internal organisational factors are experience in international business and the international orientation of the MNE headquarters. Following developments in the literature and integration of resource dependence and resource-based perspectives of Taylor et al. (1996), the model suggests that there are reciprocal relationships between internal organisational factors, strategic HRM and multinational concerns and goals.

With regard to HR strategy and practices, reciprocal relationships between strategic issues and HRM strategy and practices have been highlighted by research taking a resource-based perspective (Kamoche, 1997; Taylor et al., 1996). In addition, several studies have shown that HR activities such as expatriate management are influenced by both internal and external factors. Effective strategic HRM is expected to assist the firm in achieving its goals and objectives. This view is influenced by the emerging body of strategic HRM literature that examines the relationships between internal organisational characteristics, HRM strategy and practices and firm performance or competitive advantage (Becker and Gerhart, 1996; Dyer and Reeves, 1995). While some research has suggested that MNEs will gain by utilising and integrating appropriate HRM strategy and practices to enhance firm performance (Festing, 1997; Kobrin, 1994), there remains inconclusive evidence and important questions about the nature of this relationship (Caligiuri and Stroh, 1995; Peterson, 1996; Sparrow et al., 1994). The model offered by De Cieri and Dowling (1999) aims to assist in the cross-fertilisation of ideas to further develop theory and empirical research in strategic HRM in multinational enterprises.

Summary

This chapter has endeavoured to meet three objectives: first, to outline the various approaches which have been taken to the study of international HRM; second, to discuss the variables which moderate differences between domestic and international HRM; and third, briefly to outline recent work which examines the topic of strategic human resource management in multinational enterprises. Attention to these three points takes us some way to completing the 'puzzle of international HRM' which Laurent (1986) described some years ago.

Review questions

1 What are the main similarities and differences between domestic and international HRM?
2 Define these terms: PCN, HCN and TCN.
3 Discuss two HR activities in which a multinational firm must engage that would not be required in a domestic environment.
4 Why is a greater degree of involvement in employees' personal lives inevitable in many international HRM activities?
5 Discuss the variables that moderate differences between domestic and international HR practices.

Bibliography

Acuff, F. (1984) 'International and domestic human resources functions', *Innovations in International Compensation*, New York, Organization Resources Counselors.

Adler, N. (1997) *International Dimensions of Organizational Behavior*, 3rd edn, Cincinnatti, OH, South-Western.

Bartlett, C. and Ghoshal, S. (1992) *Transnational Management: Text, Cases, and Readings in Cross Border Management*, Boston, Irwin.

Becker, B. and Gerhart, B. (1996) 'The impact of human resource management on organizational performance: progress and prospects', *Academy of Management Journal*, 39, 4, pp. 779–801.

Berry, J. W. (1980) 'Introduction to methodology' in H. C. Triandis and J. W. Berry (eds) *Handbook of Cross-Cultural Psychology, Vol. 2: Methodology*, Boston, Allyn & Bacon.

Bhagat, R. S. and McQuaid, S. J. (1982) 'Role of subjective culture in organizations: a review and directions for future research', *Journal of Applied Psychology*, 67, pp. 653–85.

Brewster, C. and Hegewisch, A. (1994) *Policy and Practice in European Human Resource Management – The Price Waterhouse Cranfield Survey*, London, Routledge.

Caligiuri, P. M. and Stroh, L. K. (1995) 'Multinational corporate management strategies and international human resource practices: bringing IHRM to the bottom line', *International Journal of Human Resource Management*, 6, pp. 494–507.

Cavusgil, S. T. (1993) *Internationalizing Business Education: Meeting the Challenge*, East Lansing, MI, Michigan State University Press.

Child, J. D. (1981) 'Culture, contingency and capitalism in the cross-national study of organizations' in L. L. Cummings and B. M. Staw (eds) *Research in*

Organizational Behavior, vol. 3, Greenwich, CT, JAI Publishers.

De Cieri, H. and Dowling, P. J. (1999) 'Strategic human resource management in multinational enterprises: theoretical and empirical developments' in P. M. Wright, L. D. Dyer, J. W. Bordreau and G. T. Milkovich (eds) *Research in Personnel and Human Resource Management: Strategic Human Resources in the 21st Century*, Supplement 4, Stamford, CT, JAI Press.

De Cieri, H. and Dowling, P. J. (1995) Cross-cultural issues in organizational behavior' in C. L. Cooper and D. M. Rousseau (eds) *Trends in Organizational Behavior*, vol. 2, Chichester, UK, John Wiley and Sons.

De Cieri, H., McGaughey, S. L. and Dowling, P. J. (1996) 'Relocation' in M. Warner (ed.) *International Encyclopedia of Business and Management*, vol. 5, London, Routledge.

Delery, J. E. and Doty, D. H. (1996) 'Modes of theorizing in strategic human resource management: tests of universalistic, contingency, and configurational performance predictions', *Academy of Management Journal*, 39, pp. 802–35.

Desatnick, R. L. and Bennett, M. L. (1978) *Human Resource Management in the Multinational Company*, New York, Nichols.

Dowling, P. J. (1988) 'International and domestic personnel/human resource management: similarities and differences' in R. S. Schuler, S. A. Youngblood and V. L. Huber (eds) *Readings in Personnel and Human Resource Management*, 3rd edn, St Paul, MN, West Publishing.

Dowling, P. J., Welch, D. E. and De Cieri, H. (1989) 'International joint ventures: a new challenge for human resource management' in R. Luostarinen (ed.) *Proceedings of the Fifteenth Conference of the European International Business Association*, Helsinki, December.

Dowling, P. J., Welch, D. E. and Schuler, R. S. (1999) *International Human Resource Management: Managing People in a Multinational Context*, 3rd edn., Cincinnati, OH, South-Western.

Duerr, M. G. (1986) 'International business management: its four tasks', *Conference Board Record*, October, p. 43.

Dyer, L. and Reeves, T. (1995) 'Human resource strategies and firm performance: what to we know and where do we need to go?', *International Journal of Human Resource Management*, 6, pp. 656–70.

Economist (1997) 27 September, p. 119.

Festing, M. (1997) 'International human resource management strategies in multinational corporations: theoretical assumptions and empirical evidence from German firms', *Management International Review*, 37, 1, special issue, pp. 43–63.

Gajek, M. and Sabo, M. M. (1986) 'The bottom line: what HR managers need to know about the new expatriate regulations', *Personnel Administrator*, 31, 2, pp. 87–92.

Gladwin, T. M. and Walter, I. (1980) *Multinationals Under Fire: Lessons in the Management of Conflict*, New York, John Wiley.

Harbison, F. (1959) 'Management in Japan' in F. Harbison and C. A. Myers (eds) *Management in the Industrial World: An International Analysis*, New York, McGraw-Hill.

Harris, J. E. and Moran, R. T. (1979) *Managing Cultural Differences*, Houston, TX, Gulf.

Harvey, M. G. (1993) 'A survey of corporate programs for managing terrorist threats', *Journal of International Business Studies*, 24, 3, pp. 465–78.

Harvey, M. G. (1983) 'The multinational corporation's expatriate problem: an application of Murphy's law', *Business Horizons*, 26, 1, pp. 71–8.

Hofstede, G. (1983) 'The cultural relativity of organizational practices and theories', *Journal of International Business Studies*, 14, 2, pp. 75–89.

Huntington, S. P. (1996) 'The west: unique, not universal', *Foreign Affairs*, November–December, pp. 28–46.

International Human Resource Management Reference Guide 1997–1998, Alexandria, VA, Institute for International Human Resources, Society for Human Resource Management.

Kamoche, K. (1997) 'Knowledge creation and learning in international HRM', *International Journal of Human Resource Management*, 8, pp. 213–22.

Kirkbride, P. S. and Tang, S. F. Y. (1994) 'From Kyoto to Kowloon: cultural barriers to the transference of quality circles from Japan to Hong Kong', *Asia Pacific Journal of Human Resources*, 32, 2, pp. 100–11.

Kobrin, S. J. (1994) 'Is there a relationship between a geocentric mind-set and multinational strategy?', *Journal of International Business Studies*, 25, pp. 493–511.

Kuhn, T. S. (1962) *The Structure of Scientific Revolution*, 2nd edn, Chicago, University of Chicago Press.

Laurent, A. (1986) 'The cross-cultural puzzle of international human resource management', *Human Resource Management*, 25, pp. 91–102.

Mendenhall, M. and Oddou, G. (1985) 'The dimensions of expatriate acculturation: a review', *Academy of Management Review*, 10, pp. 39–47.

Morgan, P. (1986) 'International human resource management: fact or fiction?', *Personnel Administrator*, 31, 9, pp. 43–7.

Morishima, M. (1995) 'Embedding HRM in a social context', *British Journal of Industrial Relations*, 33, 4, pp. 617–43.

Peterson, R. B., Sargent, J., Napier, N. K. and Shim, W. S. (1996) 'Corporate expatriate HRM policies, internationalization, and performance in the world's largest MNC's, *Management International Review*, 36, pp. 215–30.

Phatak, A. V. (1997) *International Management: Concept and Cases*, Cincinnati, OH, South-Western.

Phatak, A. V. (1995) *International Dimensions of Management*, 4th edn, Cincinnati, OH, South-Western.

Pinney, D. L. (1982) 'Structuring an expatriate tax reimbursement program', *Personnel Administrator*, 27, 7, pp. 19–25.

Porter, M. E. (1986) 'Changing patterns of international competition', *California Management Review*, 28, 2, pp. 9–40.

Porter, M. E. (1985) *Competitive Advantage: Creating and Sustaining Superior Performance*, New York, Free Press.

Pucik, V. (1997) 'Human resources in the future: an obstacle or a champion of globalization?', *Human Resource Management*, 36, pp. 163–7.

Ricks, D. A. (1993) *Blunders in International Business*, Cambridge, MA, Blackwell.

Robinson, R. D. (1978) *International Business Management: A Guide to Decision Making*, 2nd edn, Hinsdale, IL, Dryden.

Schuler, R. S. and MacMillan, I. C. (1984) 'Gaining competitive advantage through human resource management practices', *Human Resource Management*, 23, 3, pp. 241–55.

Schuler, R. S., Dowling, P. J. and De Cieri, H. (1993) 'An integrative framework of strategic international human resource management', *Journal of Management*, 19, pp. 419–59.

Sparrow, P., Schuler, R. S. and Jackson, S. E. (1994) 'Convergence or divergence: human resource practices and policies for competitive advantage worldwide', *International Journal of Human Resource Management*, 5, 2, pp. 267–99.

Tayeb, M. (1994) 'Organizations and national culture: methodology considered', *Organization Studies*, 15, 3, pp. 429–46.

Taylor, S., Beechler, S. and Napier, N. (1996) 'Towards an integrative model of strategic international human resource management', *Academy of Management Review*, 21, pp. 959–85.

Teagarden, M. B. and Von Glinow, M. A. (1997) 'Human resource management in cross-cultural contexts: emic practices versus etic philosophies', *Management International Review*, 37, 1, special issue, pp. 7–20.

Triandis, H. and Brislin, R. (1984) 'Cross-cultural psychology', *American Psychologist*, 39, pp. 1006–16.

Tung, R. L. (1993) 'Managing cross-national and intra-national diversity', *Human Resource Management*, 32, 4, pp. 461–77.

Tung, R. L. (1981) 'Selection and training of personnel for overseas assignments', *Columbia Journal of World Business*, 16, 1, pp. 68–78.

Wyatt, T. (1989) 'Understanding unfamiliar personnel problems in cross-cultural work encounters', *Asia Pacific HRM*, 27, 4, pp. 5–18.

Zeira, Y. and Banai, M. (1984) 'Present and desired methods of selecting expatriate managers for international assignments', *Personnel Review*, 13, 3, pp. 29–35.

Notes

1 This chapter is based on Chapter 1 of P. J. Dowling, D. E. Welch and R. Schuler (1999) *International Human Resource Management: Managing People in a Multinational Context*, 3rd edn, Cincinnati, South-Western College Publishing, and is used with permission of the publisher.

2 This section is based on various presentations by the author and the following paper: H. De Cieri and P. Dowling (1999) 'Strategic human resource management in multinational enterprises: theoretical and empirical developments', in P. M. Wright, L. D. Dyer, J. W. Bordreau and G. T. Milkovich (eds) *Research in Personnel and Human Resource Management: Strategic Human Resources in the 21st Century*, Supplement 4, Stamford, CT, JAI Press.

3 The *International Human Resource Management Reference Guide 1997-1998* which is published by the Institute for International Human Resources (a division of the Society for Human Resource Management, Alexandria, VA) defines an *inpatriate* as a 'foreign manager in the U.S.' (page V-4). A 'foreign manager in the U.S.' is defined (on the same page) as 'an expatriate in the U.S. where the U.S. is the host-country and the manager's home-country is outside of the U.S.'. Curiously, the Reference Guide also states that the word inpatriate 'can also be used for U.S. expatriates returning to an assignment in the U.S.'. This is a contradiction of the first part of the definition of an inpatriate being a 'foreign manager in the U.S.' and is illogical. US expatriates returning to the USA are PCNs and cannot also be classed as 'foreign managers in the USA' – perhaps they are 'repatriates', but they are not inpatriates. As defined, this term is only of use in the USA.

4 Although less common in the USA, the use of private boarding schools is common in countries (particularly European countries) which have a colonial tradition where both colonial administrators and business people would often undertake long assignments overseas and expect to leave their children at a boarding school in their home country. This is especially true of Britain, which also has a strong cultural tradition of the middle and upper classes sending their children to private boarding schools (curiously described by the British as 'public' schools, even though they are all private institutions which charge fees) even if the parents were working in Britain.

Case 13.1 Sweden International – SWINT

Sweden International (SWINT) is a Swedish construction company established in 1982 to meet the needs of the construction boom in developing countries. Because of the need to adhere to local requirements in the construction industry, SWINT established subsidiaries in Singapore, Thailand and Saudi Arabia. The company's slogan is 'Quality for low price'.

Mats Larsson, a construction engineer, was selected in January 1988 as the manager responsible for SWINT's operations in Singapore. He had previously managed a project in South-East Asia for another Swedish firm. Larsson's wife, Anna, was an English teacher and she was enthusiastic about the move. She was able to obtain a visa that permitted her to work in Singapore. The couple felt rushed by the request to be in Singapore by February, but were impressed by the generous compensation package, based on the balance sheet approach.

Due to local shortages of skilled labour at that time, Larsson recruited Swedish engineers, technicians and skilled workers for numerous assignments. This met with the approval of top management and was in accord with corporate strategy. The company has developed two basic HRM strategies for the South-East Asian region:

1 differentiation based on recruiting Swedish employees to establish a reputation for reliability and quality

2 cost reduction by employing unskilled labour from local sources whenever possible.

However, Larsson noticed that it was necessary to employ host country and third country nationals. Top management at headquarters in Sweden allowed him some flexibility, provided that they were not employed in sensitive positions such as accounting. Top management deemed it necessary that these positions be filled by Swedish people or expatriates of Asian origin who had lived or studied in Sweden and thus knew the Swedish language and culture. When he needed assistant managers for the various departments of the Singapore project, headquarters placed advertisements in the Swedish newspapers for university graduates. Among those chosen was Andrew Wong, a Hong Kong business school graduate, and his Swedish wife, who had a degree in Cantonese and Mandarin from Stockholm University. Wong was employed in the administration department, Wong's wife was employed as a translator.

In mid-1991 SWINT won a contract to build a hospital in Shanghai, China. The contract required the company to train Chinese to install, operate and maintain the basic non-medical facilities such as elevators, electrical appliances and cooking and cleaning facilities. Larsson was transferred to Shanghai to be managing director of the project. His wife, Anna, was again happy about this transfer because she was very interested in Chinese culture.

Larsson requested that headquarters promote Andrew Wong to the rank of manager in charge of a new department in Shanghai devoted to recruitment, selection and employee development. He further recommended that Mrs Wong be trained for a market research position. He argued that they would be assets to the firm in its possible future operations within the entire Asian region. His request was rejected. Instead, a Swedish manager was appointed. Mr and Mrs Wong resigned from SWINT at this time. The Shanghai project was financially highly satisfactory for SWINT. The company was able to recruit the necessary Chinese engineers and technicians locally at reasonable salaries. Chinese wages were lower compared with those in the region and the fact that most employment contracts were for only one or two years helped lower the cost of the operation.

In the mid-1990s, SWINT was looking for new projects. Environmental analysis revealed that foreign direct investment in Malaysia was increasing, as Malaysia emerged as a viable option for investment as a result of changing government policy. SWINT targeted the Malaysian market and the chief executive officer visited Malaysia on several occasions, negotiating new projects. To show its commitment, the company established a branch office in Malaysia. Larsson was transferred to Malaysia. This time, his wife was not happy to move. She was pregnant with their first child and returned to Sweden for the birth. Larsson was not able to be at the birth of his child because there were major problems in the Malaysian office at the time. When baby Björn was four months old, Anna brought him to Malaysia. She was no longer working outside the home.

During the first weeks it became apparent to Larsson that there were difficulties in Malaysia which SWINT had not experienced before. Most of the projects available were large, requiring long implementation times and strict adherence to rules. Furthermore, competition for projects was fierce. Clear preference was given to firms employing local people. Larsson met many engineers and technicians who had worked for SWINT in Singapore but were now working for Japanese firms on long-term contracts. He also learned that the Wongs were working for another Swedish company operating in Malaysia. Both had managerial positions.

In 2001 the Malaysian market continues to present unforeseen difficulties for SWINT. The company found it difficult to develop strong performance in Malaysia and the return on investment was poor. In May Larsson flew back to Sweden to inform top management about the situation in Malaysia. One of the proposed projects was a joint venture with the Malaysian Organisation for Contracting and Construction to build an entire university campus. The project's duration was ten years at a total cost of $500 million Australian. SWINT's share was to be 49% and to include construction, training, and maintenance services. To Larsson's disappointment, headquarters' managers concentrated on the technical and financial aspects of the project. His requests to address SWINT's HRM policies were refused because top management saw the present policies as adequate. Some managers pointed to the success in Shanghai and saw no reason to change the management approach. In the meantime, Anna's parents, excited at seeing their grandson Björn, pressured them to stay. Larsson frustrated with headquarters, requested a transfer back to Sweden but was told that there were no plans for that. Larsson was told to return to Malaysia and improve his performance. He resigned.

International business and e-business

Learning objectives

By the end of this chapter, you should be able to:

- understand the main terms and concepts used in e-business
- appreciate the main types and methods of conducting business using e-business systems
- outline the main benefits and obstacles to the use of e-business systems for international business activities
- understand the empirical evidence on the benefits of and obstacles to the use of e-business systems
- discuss the role of global e-business systems for the internationalisation processes of firms
- assess the main issues and problems for the regulation of global e-business systems

Key terms

• definitions of e-business • impact of e-business on international business operations • potential and obstacles for global e-business systems • internationalism and e-business • regulation of global e-business systems

Introduction

The application of information and communications technologies (ICT) to business has been revolutionised by the ability to use the Internet and the World Wide Web (www) to gather, exchange and disseminate information. The Internet is a computer-based system of telecommunications equipment that allows agents to obtain and gather information. The www is an operating system that enables information to be displayed on computers via web pages that are transmitted by the Internet. This chapter uses the term Internet to include the www. Information flows freely across national borders on the Internet, hence conducting business activities by the creation and development of e-business systems has implications for the process of internationalisation by existing and potential traders. These systems normally do not require investment to build computer networks because e-business systems can be placed into the existing network of the Internet. This means that nearly any firm can gain access to e-business systems by connecting to the Internet. Consequently, both large and small firms can, in principle, use e-business systems for international business activities.

This chapter investigates the use of e-business systems as a means of conducting international business. The various types of e-business systems are outlined and the benefits of using these systems are explained. A review of the limited empirical evidence that is available is provided that suggests that e-business systems have not had the expected large-scale effects that have been predicted. An overview of the legal, economic, cultural and operational obstacles to the development of e-business are considered to explain the seemingly low impact of e-business on international business activities. This provides a basis for identifying the areas in international business that are most likely to be significantly influenced by the application of e-business systems.

E-commerce and e-business

The use of the Internet for business purposes is called e-business or e-commerce. An outline of the different types of e-business is given in Exhibit 14.1. E-commerce is the use of Internet based systems to provide an electronic marketplace to engage in exchanges of valuable information and products. E-business is a term increasingly used instead of e-commerce. It is possible to differentiate between these terms by defining e-business as e-commerce plus the use of Internet-based systems to improve business performance.

The use of electronic technologies to purchase products is not new. Systems such as electronic data interchange (EDI) have been use as a means of conducting business for many years. However, EDI systems are not electronic markets, rather they provide a means of directly linking stock control systems to purchasing, payment and delivery systems. The Internet allows interface between a large number of potential suppliers and customers thereby permitting the creation of a marketplace. These are real markets, albeit virtual marketplaces, because agents can trade information, goods and services.

E-business systems can extend beyond virtual marketplaces by using Internet-based systems to assemble and process information from customers, firms, organisations and governmental agencies to enhance the ability of firms more effectively to pursue their objectives. This includes the management of supply chains, assessing new market opportunities and adjusting to regulatory and technical changes. Internet-based systems can also be used to improve internal management systems. Such systems allow organisations to monitor, assess and communicate at low cost by using internal computer networks that can be accessed via the Internet. The information in these internal networks can be easily kept up to date and can be gathered, processed and disseminated at low cost. These systems allow for a virtual management system that enables much of the process of management to be conducted using Internet-based systems.

Exhibit 14.1 Outline of e-business

Definition of e-commerce

The application of information and communication technologies (ICT) to the production and distribution of goods and services on a global scale. (OECD, 1997: p. 20)

Definition of e-business

E-business is using electronic information to improve performance, create value and enable new relationships between business and customers. (www.PricewaterhouseCoopers.com, 2001)

Main types of e-business

Business to business (B2B)

Involves the use of ICT by firms to purchase supplies, distribute goods and services and to exchange information between firms and other types of organisation that provide information for firms. Electronic data interchange (EDI) systems enable firms to use ICT to issue purchasing orders, invoices and payments by electronic means. Traditional EDI systems are restricted to those firms that invest in the computer and linkage systems to allow EDI to operate. This limits the use of these types of EDI systems to large firms that can afford the large investment in computer-based ordering systems. Internet-based exchange can be provided by *extranets* – web-based platforms that can be accessed by any firm that has a web address or *intranets* – Internet-based systems that can only be accessed by authorised users. *Extranet* and *intranet* systems permit the creation of large networks of firms that can be used for purchasing goods and services and to manage supply chains.

Business to consumer (B2C)

Internet service providers (ISPs) such as AOL supplies access to the Internet for a large number of households and individuals. These ISPs not only provide a link to the Internet, they also connect potential customers to the web pages of firms that are offering to sell goods and services online. Potential customers that are searching for products can also access specialised search engines such as Lycos that enables searches to be made for desired products and information and links consumers to suppliers that provide online purchasing services. Online media companies such as Yahoo! provide a variety of free media services to customers and make revenue by selling advertising space on their web pages with hyperlinks to the web pages of firms wishing to sell products to consumers.

Consumer to business (C2B)

The Internet provides a low-cost and quick method for consumers to convey information to firms, for example, bids to purchase products, complaints about products, queries about payment, information on delivery times and methods. Consumers can also use the Internet to obtain information from firms, for example, information on prices, qualities and deliver dates for products. Firms may also use the Internet to gather opinions from existing or potential customers on such matters as the attractiveness of their products and the quality of their after-sales service.

Consumer to consumer (C2C)

Online auctions permit consumers to bid for second-hand products from other consumers. The Internet also provides a medium that consumers can use to exchange information about prices and qualities of products.

Peer to peer (P2P)

The Internet is used to transmit computer files, codes and other types of digital information. Indeed, this was the original use of the Internet when scientists, academics and computer enthusiasts swapped digital information by using the Internet. These P2P systems allow transmission of software, music, visual images, written text, indeed, anything that can be placed into digital codes. The most famous of these P2P operations is the transfer of music via the Internet. This type of activity has important implications for copyright and the protection of intellectual property (see Case 14.4).

Information exchange systems

Firms can establish intranet systems that provide access via the Internet to a network of computers within firms. These systems can contain sensitive information about suppliers, customers, prices and delivery dates that can be used by sales and purchasing staff to help them conduct their activities by providing current information on these matters from any place that has access to the Internet. These systems can also be used for internal management communications purposes. For example, parent companies can monitor and assess financial, sales, output and other data to convey instructions and advice to their subsidiaries. Extranet systems can also be used to exchange information across organisations to help to formulate strategies, overcome problems and to generate new business opportunities. These systems can involve firms, customers, governmental agencies, universities and other organisations that provide valuable information.

Benefits of e-business systems

At the heart of the benefits of using e-business systems is the ability to gain four benefits (Bradley et al., 1993; Palvia et al., 1996; Prakash, 1996; Speier et al., 1998):

- Removal of layers of intermediation involved in supplying markets leading to lower distribution costs to customers.
- The ability to reduce the time and effort associated with purchasing and selling, thereby generating lower search costs.
- Improved information-gathering, processing and dissemination systems providing low transaction cost systems for managing the contractual and administrative arrangements within and between organisations and with customers.
- Enhanced ability to develop markets and new business models because of access to a large pool of existing and potential customers, suppliers and other sources of information leading to network externalities because adding extra agents to a network leads to rising numbers of possible connections, hence increases the value of the network to users.

B2C systems

The reduction in layers of intermediation, lower search and transaction costs and to network externalities are at the heart of the benefits of B2C systems. Three main types of e-commerce B2C systems have emerged.

Bolt-on systems

Bolt-on systems are based on the addition of an e-business system as a value added service to existing supply chains (see Figure 14.1). These types of B2C systems are common among large retailers (e.g. www.tesco.com) and financial services providers (e.g. www.firstdirect.com). Some small and medium sized companies that supply niche markets such as wine, high-quality foodstuffs and clothing have also entered the world of online shopping by providing bolt-on systems to their supply chains. The more business that is generated by bolt-on e-business systems, the lower are intermediation and search costs. Moreover, the transaction costs of managing the supply chain reduces by use of standardised and effective information-gathering, processing and dissemination systems and network externalities generate more opportunities to expand and develop business. These benefits provide the attraction for established 'bricks and mortar' companies to develop online selling operations. Bolt-on systems can provide the basis for moving most or all selling operations to online systems. In cases where 'bricks and mortar' systems are necessary because of the need to satisfy customer requirements to see products, obtain human advice and to distribute products, bolt-on systems help to expand business to areas suitable for virtual selling. In these circumstances, bolt-on systems have similarities to mail or telephone ordering where there exists parallel 'bricks and mortar' retail outlet distribution.

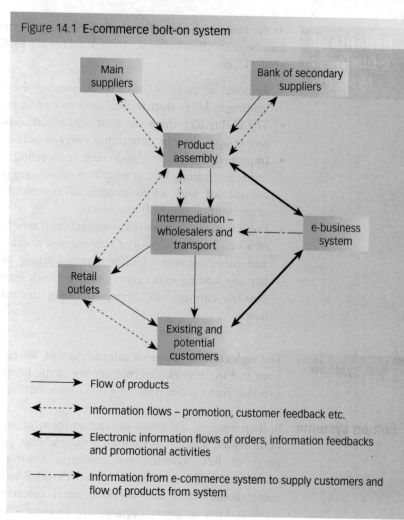

Figure 14.1 E-commerce bolt-on system

⟶ Flow of products

◀┄┄┄▶ Information flows – promotion, customer feedback etc.

◀━━▶ Electronic information flows of orders, information feedbacks and promotional activities

━┈─▶ Information from e-commerce system to supply customers and flow of products from system

Online provider systems

Online providers are firms that search the market and either provide the product to the customer from a variety of sources or direct customers to a list of possible suppliers. These online providers offer a type of service that is similar to a merchant as their main function is to act as middlemen linking suppliers with customers (see Figure 14.2). They do not necessarily remove all layers of intermediation because there are normally distribution systems associated with supplying final customers. However, some products such as financial services and software can be directly distributed online. Online provider systems reduce search costs by providing large amounts of information in a form that is conducive to customer requirements, thereby expanding the search area for products. The retailing layer of intermediation is removed and they also reduce uncertainty associated with shopping online because providers often shoulder most of the risks of ensuring that the products sold to customers conform to stated qualities and conditions. The costs to customers of lodging complaints and seeking redress for faulty or inappropriate products are reduced because customers deal directly with the online

Figure 14.2 Online provider systems

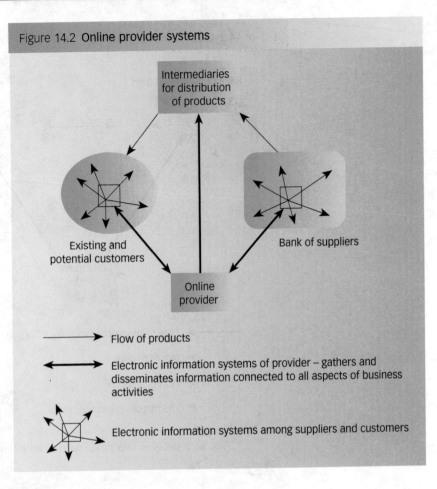

Intermediaries for distribution of products

Existing and potential customers

Bank of suppliers

Online provider

→ Flow of products

⟷ Electronic information systems of provider – gathers and disseminates information connected to all aspects of business activities

Electronic information systems among suppliers and customers

provider not with the many possible suppliers that the provider uses. Many of these online providers are well known, for example, Amazon.com and Jungle.com.

Smart search engines are another type of online provider. They scan the Internet for products and provide a list of suppliers and connect customers to the firms that are selected by customers. Some search engines cover a wide range of products, for example, Smartshop.com, Mysimon.com and Comparenet.com. Others search for particular products, for example, PriceSearch.com (computers), Bargainbot.com (books) and Giftfinder.com (gifts). The value of these search engines is that they provide a means of low-cost search for buyers, enlarge the potential size of the market for suppliers (network externalities) and reduce intermediation costs.

Online auction systems   The use of e-commerce systems for auctions (e-auctions) removes most of the layers of intermediation by facilating direct interaction between suppliers and final buyers (see Figure 14.3). Ebay.com and Qxl.com are examples of such web-based auction houses. Internet-based auction sites provide markets for a wide range of products including electronic and electrical equipment, holidays, hotel accommodation and air travel on an

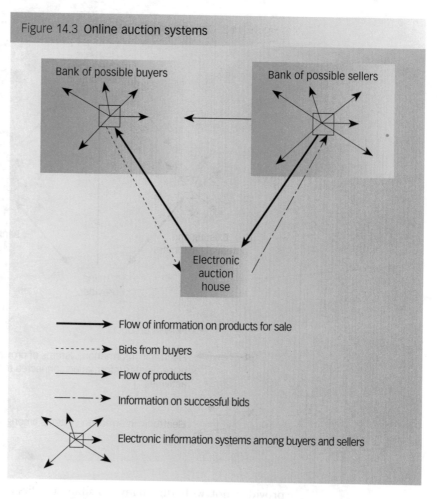

Figure 14.3 Online auction systems

auction basis. E-auctions create low-price markets for standard products and commodity-type items or where customers have a good understanding of the qualities of products they wish to purchase and therefore they do not have to inspect them before purchase. Online auction systems have low cost for the dissemination of information on products, low search costs and they also generate network externalities. However, buying at auction has high uncertainty for customers that are not knowledgeable about the qualities of products bought at auction.

B2B and intra-organisational systems

The ability to lower transactions, search and intermediation costs and to reap network externalities lead to the possibilty of benefiting from using e-business systems in B2B and intra-organisational systems. E-business systems can provide low-cost and effective systems for supply chain management, market intelligence gathering and processing and systems for improving inter-organisational management processes.

Virtual supply chains

Virtual supply chains based on B2B transactions use e-business systems to link potential buyers and sellers into large supplier networks (see Figure 14.4). These networks enable low-cost searches to be made to find, buy

Figure 14.4 Virtual supply chains and information-gathering networks

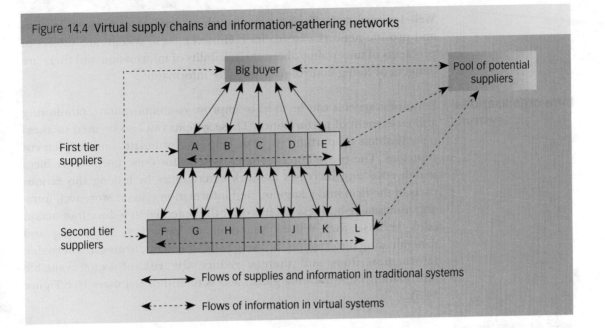

and arrange for delivery of goods and services needed for business operations. These virtual supply chains can be centred on a big purchaser that incorporate their suppliers into an e-business system. The best known example of such a B2B system is Global eXchange Services (GXS) a subsidiary of General Electric (see Case 14.1). Covisint a consortium of car makers (General Motors, Ford, DaimlerChrysler, Renault and Nissan) is another very large B2B network that is built on the purchasing systems of larger manufacturers. Significant network externalities are possible using such systems because suppliers can link with other suppliers and buyers in the network and new sources of supply and demand can be added to this virtual supply chain at very low marginal cost. These systems provide a measure of confidence in the network because contractual conditions, means of payment and logistical systems are normally based on rules set by the big buyer or the firm at the apex of the system. This reduces transaction costs by providing standardised and effective systems that can be modified to the needs of all the potential traders within the system. This process allows very large networks to be built up with the potential to deliver high network externalities with low transaction and search costs. However, as these networks grow the central firm may become peripheral or even unconnected to transactions that take place within the network. In this case, uncertainty over the reliability of suppliers and difficulties in using the standardised systems for transactions may limit the growth and usefulness of these virtual supply chains.

Market intelligence systems   E-business systems can also be used to expand and develop markets by gathering, processing and disseminating information on market, technical, regulatory and political conditions in a wide variety of markets.

Well-designed and effective systems reduce search and transaction costs and provide network externalities. However, these systems are subject to problems of uncertainty about the reliability of information and there are dangers of losing control over valuable information.

Intra-organisational systems

E-business systems can be used to improve communications, monitoring and assessment of performance. These systems can also be used to assess new business opportunities and help to formulate and implement strategies. The use of Internet-based systems for these purposes reduces search costs and increases network externalities by linking the various parts of the firm into a large unified information system. Moreover, intra-organisational e-business systems offer the potential to reduce transaction costs because they reduce the costs of gathering, processing and disseminating information. By using *intranet* systems, firms can internalise information flows and thereby reduce the risk of losing valuable information while allowing global access to authorised users (see Figure 14.5).

Summary of the benefits of using e-business systems

In principle, e-business systems offer the potential to obtain cost savings for purchasing and selling activities because of reducing intermediation, search and transaction costs and network externalities. They also open up new opportunites to enhance the effectiveness of business activities. Given this array of potential benefits it is hardly surprising that the application of e-business is often regarded by management and IT gurus as a means of securing a revolutionary transformation of business activities (Gates, 1995; Kelly, 1998; Wind and Mahajan, 2001).

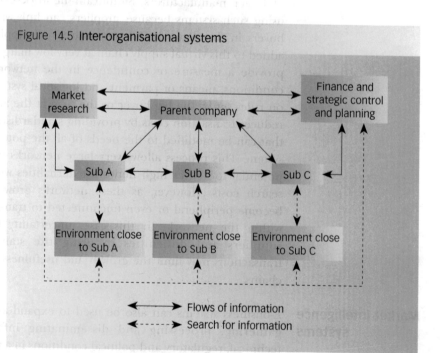

Figure 14.5 Inter-organisational systems

Benefits of e-business systems in international business activities

As the Internet is a global network, the cost-saving and business-creating opportunities of using e-business systems should increase the potential for firms to begin or to expand international business activities. These benefits should be available to both large and small firms because the Internet is accessible to any organisation, in any location, that has a portal to this global network. However, large firms are more likely to have access to the hard and soft computer technologies and human resources that are necessary to take full advantage of these benefits. Nevertheless, small and medium sized firms can also access these networks because the benefits of network externalities provide incentives to grant free access to large number of organisations. A variety of firms have also developed services to help small and medium sized firms to acquire the necessary technology and expertise effectively to use e-business systems.

The use of e-business systems in international business activities has focused on the prospects of expanding and speeding up the internationalisation process by both large and small and medium sized firms. Most attention has been focused on the use of the Internet for international marketing (Bennett, 1997; Hamill, 1997; Quelch and Klein, 1996) and in the development of global supply chains based on Internet-based buyer-supplier networks (Samli et al., 1997). The Internet is also thought to generate new and more effective relationship and communication systems for international selling and buying. These benefits flow from the provision of services such as search engines that link buyers and sellers; Internet-based agencies that provide verification of the bone fides of foreign agents, improved market intelligence gathering and processing, enhanced sales support by facilitating more extensive information gathering and processing connected to sales activities (Avlonitis and Karayanni, 2000; Sarkar et al., 1998). More effective strategic management of subsidiaries, joint ventures and strategic alliances is possible because of reduced search and transaction costs of monitoring, assessing and coordinating with partners (Bradley et al., 1993). Moreover, network externalities enhance the possibilites of multiplying the numbers of international partners thereby expanding the possibilties of increasing international business activities. A summary of these benefits and their effects is shown in Figure 14.6.

The lower costs of acquiring, processing and disseminating information can lead to increased ability to penetrate new markets by providing the means effectively to gather market intelligence, improved capabilties to manage international business activities and by providing low-cost access to international markets for purchasing and selling activities. These benefits can, in principle, allow firms rapidly to adopt internationalisation strategies without having to undertake slowly evolving expansion of international business activities. This may lead to growth of internationalisation strategies that are different from the views expounded by the various stage theories of the development of international business (see Chapter 11). These stage theories envisage internationalisation proceeding in a concentric manner that begins with simple operations, such as

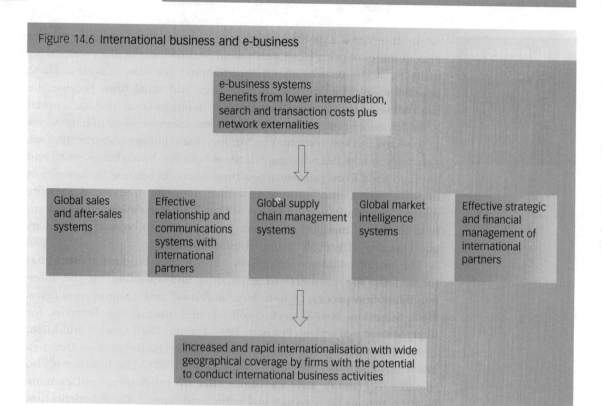

Figure 14.6 International business and e-business

indirect exporting to countries that are geographically and culturally close. This leads to expansion, as firms learn, to more complex operations such as DFI and also embraces countries that are geographically and culturally more distant. However, e-business systems may permit rapid moves to complex international business operations such as formation of global supply chains that include countries that are geographically and culturally distant. The benefits available from the use of e-business systems appear to offer the potential for radical change to the process of internationalisation.

Evidence on the benefits of e-business

There are only a limited number of studies on the impact of e-business on business activities. There are, however, a large number of case studies provided by management and IT gurus and consultancy firms (see, for example, www.ibm.com/e-business) that extol the virtues of e-business systems. The most notable example of the use of e-business systems to develop large scale B2B operations is GXS (see Case 14.1). Dell Computers have also shown that, at least in some markets, rapid growth with high profits is possible by using e-business systems (see Case 14.2).

The decline of dot.com companies' share prices in late 2000, the collapse in early 2001 and the slow-down in online buying led to criticism of the rosy picture outlined in such case studies (*Economist*, 2001a). These problems led some dot.com companies, such as Amazon and Yahoo to develop links to old economy 'bricks and mortar' firms for the purposes of distribution and obtaining products for their online customers

(*Economist*, 2000a & 2001b). These developments, referred to as 'clicks and mortar' systems are a cross between old economy firms and e-business-based firms. These developments suggest that many e-business systems are not so much a totally new way of doing business, but rather a tool that enhances performance by developing new business models that link e-business systems to traditional business operations.

The use of e-business systems to aid small and medium sized enterprises in developed countries seems to be primarily connected to improving communications and sales support by developing quick and low-cost information on export markets (Hamill and Gregory, 1997). A series of surveys on the use of e-business systems in small and medium sized firms in developing and transition countries found that very few used these systems to help them to develop new systems for exporting or for purchasing. The main obstacles that were identified were problems with payment systems and customs and taxation procedures (International Trade Forum, 2000). Cross-frontier online selling by small and medium sized firms seems to be hampered by problems of trust, coping with national taxation and regulatory systems and cultural differences (see Case 14.3).

There are few studies that seek to identify and measure the extent of the supposed benefits of e-business systems. Most of the studies that have been undertaken have focused on the US market and have considered the impact on prices of using e-commerce systems in the B2C sector. These studies focus on the effect of lower search and intermediation costs on prices. Theory predicts that these cost reductions should lead to lower prices and a smaller price dispersion with more frequent changes to menu prices. These predictions are based on an analysis that indicates that lower search and intermediation costs, as compared to traditional outlets, should stimulate competition thereby reducing prices. Electronic systems also make it easier and cheaper to alter the menu of prices in the light of changing market conditions. A study of the sale of CDs and books in the USA found that these predictions are supported by evidence (Brynjolfsson and Smith, 2000). However, this study found evidence of market power by some e-retailers such as Amazon.com and that this permitted substantial variations among online sellers. The wide range of prices may be connected to the power of brand names that conveys information to customers on such matters as reliability and quality that generates trust in the provider. The provision of value added services such as book reviews, provision of a simple returns policy, free samples (e.g. extracts of books) may also grant market power to some e-retailers. This study indicated that search costs for smaller providers were higher than for the famous brands because well-known e-retailers scored more hits on web-based searches because they were more heavily advertised in the Internet and had more hyperlinks to their web pages than smaller, less well-known e-retailers. The results of this study support similar studies that have been carried out on the US market (see Smith et al., 2000, for a review of these studies).

Very few studies have been carried out into international business operations in the B2C sector. A study on price competition in books between the USA and Canada found that the main Canadian online competitor to Amazon (Chapters) enjoyed considerable protection that was mainly due to shipping costs (Chakrabarti and Scholnick, 2002). However, although Chapters had a competitive advantage due to lower shipping costs to their Canadian customers they did not make full use of this to acquire the benefits by charging higher prices (net of shipping costs). The variation in the exchange rate between the US and Canadian dollar did not appear to make a signficant difference to prices. Price changes by Amazon tended to be the main determinant of prices in Canada rather than exchange rate changes. This indicates that Amazon has considerable influence on the level of prices in Canada, probably due to its market power. This study found that Internet-based international business opportunities between the USA and Canada were significantly effected by barriers to international trade especially shipping costs. In trade between countries that have more trade barriers than those between the USA and Canada, it is possible that e-business systems will encounter more regulatory and cultural obstacles to entering foreign markets.

Evidence on the impact of e-business on international business activities in the B2B sector is largely limited to case studies (OECD, 2001a). These indicate that there are significant savings to be had from using B2B systems based on the use of e-auctions to purchase supplies. Such systems also reduce costs by permitting very effective just-in-time systems and by reducing the transaction costs of managing supply chains (see Case 14.1). However, there are problems connected to establishing trust and protection of intellectual property. Processing the large amounts of information that are generated by e-business systems also presents challenges in terms of developing hardware and software systems and in acquiring and enlarging appropriate human resource assets to operate these systems (*Economist*, 2000b). The aggressive use of e-business systems by large buyers has also led to low prices for some suppliers and has raised issues about the monopoly power of big firms in networks based on e-business systems (*Economist*, 2000c). Problems have also been revealed with establishing workable B2B systems and in creating cooperative links between buyers and suppliers that are necessary to delivery supplies that conform to the required specifications and quality conditions while retaining control over intellectual property. These problems appear to be lessened if B2B systems are controlled by a large buyer and when the system is supplied by a large and well-known IT company. These conditions favour large multinational companies such as Ford, General Electric, Oracle and IBM (*Economist*, 2001c).

A study by A. T. Kearney in 2000 revealed that the use of B2B systems in the Internet economy was growing and was spreading from the USA to Europe and Asia. This study found that the focus of these systems were in clusters of high tech firms in areas such as Silcon Valley and other clusters that provided proximity benefits (see Chapter 6). These high tech clusters are increasingly using e-business systems to connect with one another thereby creating a network of firms that are embedded in a particular location such as Silcon Valley, but that are linked to other such clusters in different parts of the world. This study also found that barriers to international trade such as national taxation and regulatory systems were hampering the growth of these B2B systems. Difficulties of developing the required infrastructure systems and suitable quantities and qualities of labour were also holding back the development of B2B systems and were reinforcing the clustering effect of high tech firms (Joint Venture, 2000).

These studies indicate that e-commerce systems tend to lead to lower prices and reduced price dispersal and increase the frequency of menu changes. This indicates that e-commerce markets are more efficient than traditional markets. Electronic auction markets also hold the prospect of turning some products into commodities where competition is based mainly on price. These developments are mainly of benefit to consumers. This indicates that sellers will find it hard going to make high profits in such markets. Many dot.com firms have found it difficult to make money from their large networks of potential customers. This is the so-called problem of converting 'eyeballing' by Internet surfers into money-backed transactions. Transforming large Internet-based networks of potential customers into profitable businesses has proved to be difficult even for large dot.com firms such as Amazon and Yahoo (*Economist*, 2001b).

The view that the use of e-business systems will deliver a customer paradise where low search and intermediation costs plus network externalities lead to low-priced and high-quality markets perhaps underestimates the power of large multinationals to exercise a degree of control over e-markets. Brand names, access to essential assets (particularly intellectual property) and the ability to marshall large financial, legal and political influence grants some multinationals significant influence over developments in e-markets. The ability of firms providing music on CDs to prevent free access to music via the Internet demonstrates the power of large multinationals strongly to influence developments in e-markets (see Case 14.4). Studies have also revealed evidence that the power of Amazon's brand name and large Internet presence allow it to exercise power in B2C markets (see studies on the price of books and CDs examined earlier). The ability of larger buyers to use e-business systems to organise e-auctions for commodity-type items is bringing down prices and making more supplies amenable to this type of buying. However, the main beneficiaries of these e-auctions are large buyers such as GE, Ford and General Motors which have used these systems to force large price reductions from their suppliers.

The emerging evidence suggests that the use of e-business systems reduce prices and price dispersal, increases the number of commodity-type items and can lead to rapid growth of new types of business system.

However, these e-markets are not the friction and transaction cost-free models of perfect markets as outlined in economic theory. Market power can be exercised via brand names, restricted access to essential knowledge and assets and the ability to influence the institutional frameworks that govern e-business. Moreover, consolidation of firms, strategic alliances and the rise of new dominant firms is creating new and powerful firms that are able successfully to use the Internet for business purposes. These firms have many of the attributes of successful old economy firms in that they often have strong brand names, restricted access to essential assets, large size, extensive geographical coverage and significant economic and political power. The use of e-business systems is altering the nature of business models and is creating new and more price competitive markets for some types of product. New business models based on B2B systems are spreading from the USA to Europe and Asia. However, these are often based in high tech clusters and are dominated by large multinational companies that can provide proximity benefits and the infrastructure and labour supply conditions that are necessary for the development of effective B2B systems.

Obstacles to using e-business systems for international business activities

There are four major obstacles to the growth of e-business systems for international business activities:

1 Underdeveloped institutional systems for global Internet-based transactions.
2 Access to physical assets necessary to operate e-business systems.
3 Problems of converting information gathered from e-business systems into knowledge useful for expanding and developing internationalisation strategies.
4 Limitations to the value of network externalities.

Underdeveloped institutional systems

The growth of the Internet has revealed that existing institutional systems are not sufficiently developed to handle the challenges that arise from the use of global e-business systems. To enable global e-business systems effectively to operate requires the creation and development of institutional systems that can deal with a number of new problems created by the Internet (OECD, 2000; Office of the Presidency, 1998; UNCTAD, 1998 a and b).

- Agreed solutions to the problems of taxation for goods and services traded across frontiers on the Internet.
- Systems to ensure that technical and health and safety regulations are complied with in cross-border trade on the Internet.
- Protection of intellectual property for digitally transmitted information.
- Providing secure Internet transactions and ensuring rights to privacy in information exchanges.
- Creating effective consumer protection systems for products bought on the Internet.

- Regulation of telecommunication and computer systems to ensure effective and fair access to the Internet but that also allows for the appropriate development of these systems.
- Regulation of firms to prevent the exercise of monopoly power by firms using the Internet or providing Internet technologies and inter-mediation.
- Devising dispute-resolution systems for Internet-based international trade either within the WTO or some new institutional arrangements.

Finding solutions to these problems is hampered by the differing views on some of these issues that are held by governments and existing international institutions. The US government tends towards a self-regulation approach to the Internet while the Europeans and the Japanese are more inclined to favour the use of governmental regulations. Developing countries are concerned that they will have little or no influence on the evolution of institutional frameworks and that they will be forced to accept systems decided by the powerful Triad members.

The ability to use the Internet to avoid frontier controls also makes it difficult to devise systems to ensure that taxes are paid and that ensure compliance to national regulations and laws. Establishing effective means of monitoring and assessing international business activities on the Internet to ensure that e-business systems and telecommuncations and computer network providers are not being used by powerful firms to abuse market power also presents a great challenge. Agreement on procedures to regulate such monopoly behaviour is hampered by the problem of what constitutes abuse of market power. As many of the organisations that could exercise such power are likely to be American, European or Japanese based, the problems of reaching agreement with developing and transition countries are likely to be great. The possibilities that the Internet will significantly reduce the powers of national governments to tax and regulate their economies and societies causes concern in countries that fear that American liberal attitudes will prevail in the institutional frameworks that govern the Internet.

These institutional problems increase the risks associated with developing international business activities via the Internet. These risks will not be significantly reduced until there is clarification on the type of international institutional systems that are likely to be developed. These problems are similar to the difficulties raised in international trade caused by failure to agree on new systems to protect intellectual property and also to develop new regulatory frameworks for trade in financial and business services and for investments. The risks associated with these problems tends to restrict international trade in these sectors and to skew operations in these areas to large multinational companies that have the knowledge and assets to manage these risks (see Chapter 8). A similar outcome is possible for the use of global e-business systems.

**Access to
physical assets**

The use of e-business systems does not eliminate the need for physical assets. To permit large numbers of agents to use the Internet requires cheap and effective telecommuncations and computer networks and large-scale ownership of PCs or other means of accessing the Internet. Physical distribution systems must also be developed that permit fast and effective delivery of goods that are bought online (OECD, 1997 and 2001b; UNCTAD, 1998a and b).

In developed countries this is largely a problem of ensuring that technological developments in the area of telecommunications and computer equipment and software are developed and installed without the exercise of market power that restricts the development of e-business systems. Distribution systems for goods purchased online also need to be developed. To accomplish this, governments, particularly in Europe, have to complete liberalisation of telecommunications systems to ensure that they are efficient and competitive and thus deliver high quality at a low price. Access to the Internet for low-income as well as better-off households is also necessary if e-business systems are to encompass the majority of economic activities. Transport policies must also be geared towards effective physical distribution systems that take into account the demands for a cleaner environment. These are significant challenges for developed economies.

The problems that developing countries face in providing the required physical assets are formidable. Low-income levels result in small numbers of agents that have access to the Internet. Telecommunications and computer networks and transport systems suffer from under-investment and tend to be high priced and provide unreliable and poor-quality service. In many developing countries, the firms that provide these services are state owned or heavily regulated and do not have organsational cultures that are compatible with operations in competitive high-quality markets.

Governmental agencies in many developing countries lack experience and knowledge on the procedures and policies that are necessary to develop and maintain such markets (see Chapter 8). The results of these deficiencies in physical assets are that conducting large-scale international (or indeed domestic) business via e-business systems will be very difficult. These problems restrict firms from growing their conventional operations in developing countries and they are also likely to curtail the widespread use of e-business systems in these countries.

The time necessary to find solutions to the challenges of developing appropriate physical assets will hamper the growth of global e-business systems. In the case of some developing countries the obstacles presented by the lack of suitable physical resources are considerable. Providing appropriate infrastructures for effective traditional business transactions has eluded these countries for many years. It is hard to see why solving these problems for e-business systems will be any easier than it has been for traditional business activities.

Converting information into knowledge

Information that has value has to be transformed into knowledge. Transformation of information into knowledge requires action by agents who must evaluate and apply acquired information to the tasks and operations that they engage in (Stehr, 1994). The Internet can provide enormous amounts of information from a very large number of sources but the process of transforming this information into knowledge can be a daunting task. The provision of information on the Internet may lead to information overload that makes it difficult to transform information into knowledge. The problem has similarities to a student who collects large amounts of information from the Internet for an examination in international business but does not have time to read and assess the information to provide knowledge to answer the examination questions.

Information that is standardised and codified is relatively easy to transform into knowledge. For example, information on prices and delivery times for commodities can easily be converted into knowledge about the availabilty, price and quality of standardised products. Information that is acquired by experience and is tacit is more difficult to transform into knowledge. For example, information on the level of sales of products in different countries includes a wealth of (hidden) information on the economic, legal and cultural factors that influence these sales. Information on these factors can be gathered and processed, but this adds to the time and effort necessary to transform the information into knowledge. Moreover, agents must identify the type and volume of hidden information that they must gather and devise appropriate methods for processing this information.

Accurately converting information into knowledge can be very difficult in the virtual world of the Internet because it may present a misleading or difficult to understand view of the real world. This problem is rather like trying to understand what happened at a religious service by being told how long it lasted, how many people attended and what was done. Codifying and standardising the terms used to describe what happened to enable someone who had never been to such a service to understand this would require considerable effort and time. Even the use of audio-visual Internet-based systems would not convey the complexity of what happens in events such as religious services. The significance of language used, emotions expressed and the impact on the people present in the service could only be imperfectly conveyed by Internet-based systems. However, if the agent using the Internet system had experienced this type of service, the ability to transform the information into knowledge would be greatly enhanced.

There are also problems of verifying the validity and reliability of information gathered from the Internet. This problem can arise because of different cultural and institutional systems that present information in ways that are easily understood in their own system but are confusing or misleading to agents used to different systems. Some societies attach more importance to providing accurate and reliable data than others. There is also the possibility of deliberate attempts to mislead by providing false or exaggerated information.

The differences in economic, legal, political and cultural factors that make transforming information into knowledge for international business activities difficult, are not necessarily reduced by use of e-business systems. Indeed, they may be increased because of information overload. There is also an increased likelihood of encountering problems of adverse selection due to false or misunderstood information gathered in the virtual world. Fact-finding and familiarisation visits to countries being assessed for business opportunities or the use of people who are familiar with these countries may be just as important for effective e-business systems as they are in many traditional systems. In these circumstances e-business systems do not necessarily overcome many of the standard problems of internationalisation connected to lack of resources and inability to understand different cultural and institutional systems. Indeed, use of e-business systems may lead to a false confidence about the ability of firms to overcome these problems because of the ease of acquiring information.

These problems will be reduced as Internet-based systems are devised that provide verification of data and by increased standardisation and codification of Internet-based information. Expertise in transforming Internet information into knowledge should also develop as firms gain experience of using global e-business systems. These developments are most likely in organisations that have access to large pools of highly skilled human resources, the ability to marshall the necessary financial and technological assets to develop effective information-gathering and processing systems. Organisations that do not have access to these assets could make use of intermediaries that specialise in overcoming the problems connected to transforming Internet-based information into knowledge. Therefore, e-business systems will not necessarily remove layers of intermediation but will replace them with new types of intermediation. This line of reasoning suggests that international business activities will continue to be dominated by large multinational companies and that small and medium sized firms will operate largely in niche markets and will make significant use of new Internet-based intermediaries.

The movements to standardise information for international business purposes such as the use on international financial and accounting standards (see Chapter 13) and the development of standardised technical and health and safety rules or the use of mutual recognition of regulations will also help to reduce problems of converting information into knowledge. However, the growth of standardisation and codification runs the risk of hampering innovation and entrepreneurship and the use of mutual recognition is rendered difficult because of concerns about inadequate or inappropriate regulations especially for health and safety reasons (see Chapter 11). Organisations such as the WTO have struggled for many years to achieve such harmonisation for traditional business systems and even regional integration agencies among countries with similar cultural and institutional characteristics, such as the European Union, have made only slow progress in this area (see Chapter 9). It is not clear that finding solutions to these problems for e-business systems will be any easier. Moreover, the problems of converting information into knowledge for international business activities will be just as difficult in e-business systems as is the case for traditional systems. It is possible that the problems of information overload and adverse selection may be worse in the virtual world of e-business.

Limitations to the value of network externalities

Network externalities arise due to the fact that as the number of agents using a network increase the more valuable it becomes. Thus, because most people in developed economies have access to a telephone the value of owning or renting a telephone is large because it can be used to contact nearly everyone. Network externalities can expand at an increasing rate. For example, a telecommunications system that links two communities, composed of ten people in each community, leads to 100 possible two-way communications (10 x 10). Adding a third community of ten people leads to an extra 200 possible communications (10 x 20) and a fourth community adds an extra 300 possible communications (10 x 30). Therefore, adding more agents to a network leads to an increasing number of possible connections. This leads to increasing returns, that is, the benefits of expanding the number of agents using the networks increases at an increasing rate.

However, this rate of possible connection is only true if communities of equal size or of a larger size are added to the network. Suppose that the first connection is between two communities of ten people each and a third community of six people joins the network, this will add an extra 120 possible connections (6 x 20). If a fourth community of four people is connected this adds an extra 104 possible connections (4 x 26). Adding a fifth community of three people expands the connections by 90 (30 x 3). In this type of a world increasing returns from expanding networks are not attainable. Consequently, the benefits of expanding networks may not increase at an increasing rate.

Adding agents to global e-business systems may not lead to increasing returns if smaller and smaller communities are added as systems go global. This possibility could arise because of problems of recruiting communities that have different languages and cultures. Moreover, the physical asset restrictions (referred to earlier) may also limit the numbers of agents from developing countries that are able to join global networks. In some cases the most valuable connections to networks are made when they are first started. Adding increasing numbers of agents to networks generates more possible connections but does not necessary significantly contribute to the value of the network if later entrants bring information of limited value and small monetary-based transactions. Global networks may suffer for such diminishing value from network externalities because of the problems with physical assets and the difficulty of transforming information from culturally distant sources into knowledge.

Creating and developing networks results in high sunk costs because of the heavy investment in hardware and software and human resources necessary to establish the network. These costs must be sunk into the network before it is possible for agents to connect to the system. Agents connecting to networks incur costs because they must acquire the hardware, software and skills that are necessary to link to the networks. These costs inhibit the willingness of agents to join networks unless the benefits from network externalities exceed these costs. Network providers that can reap increasing returns may be able to induce agents to pay these costs to enable them to connect to networks because of the value of joining networks with large numbers of possible connections. However, network externalities may not be sufficient to cover connection charges for access to the network. Moreover, until these systems reach a capacity constraint, the marginal cost of allowing an agent to join these systems is zero. Therefore, in efficient markets, the cost of connecting to these networks should be zero. In these circumstances network providers will find it difficult to cover the sunk costs of creating and expanding the network. This problem has led to serious cash flow problems for many dot.com companies. In this situation network providers must be able to raise revenue or benefits in kind to cover sunk cost by some other means such as selling advertising on their web pages or charging commission for buyers and/or sellers that use the network to trade. Networks can also be used by providers to gain benefits by selling information/products themselves or obtaining low-cost information/low-priced products that are of value to the provider.

First movers who can build effective global networks that attract a large number of agents that provide revenue or benefits in kind sufficient to cover the sunk costs of creating and expanding the network are likely to dominate global networks. Second movers will find it difficult to find enough agents to raise revenue or benefits in kind that will cover the sunk costs. Consolidation of network providers, strategic alliances and anti-competitive practices may well be used to try and close the gap between sunk costs and revenue/benefits in kind. The name of the game is not only to have large networks but also to squeeze revenue/benefits in kind from these networks. These factors are likely to induce the development of multinationals and strategic alliances that control large global networks.

Summary of the obstacles to global e-business systems

The obstacles to the development of global e-business systems are likely to delay the acquiring of the benefits of lower, intermediation, search and transaction costs for international business activities, because it will take time for these obstacles to be reduced. Global e-business systems are unlikely to lead to frictionless and zero transaction costs exchanges due to the inability to create perfect institutional systems to govern global e-business, continuing problems with inadequate physical assets, difficulties in converting information into knowledge and finding ways to cover the sunk costs of establishing and developing global e-business networks. Effective solutions to the last two problems may require the emergence of large global network providers that can raise revenue/benefits in kind from their networks and that have the resources to overcome the problems of converting information from the virtual world of the Internet into knowledge. Such a development may lead to problems of anti-competitive behaviour. The extent of this possible problem will depend on the ability of regulators to control such behaviour. This problem may be reduced by technical changes that reduce the sunk costs of creating and developing networks thereby enabling more firms to provide global e-business systems and/or makes it easier to transform information into knowledge. These factors raise issues that are similar to the problems of providing efficient and competitive outcomes from any system that generates network externalities – such as gas and electricity networks (Shapiro and Varian, 1999).

Importance of size and sector

Clearly, the firms that gain most from global e-business systems are those that can reap high benefits relative to the costs associated with the obstacles to developing these systems. However, the ability to reap net benefits from global e-business systems is likely to be influenced by the size of firms and also by the sector in which they operate.

In the case of B2B operations, acquiring commodities and commodity-type items by using lean e-business global supply chain management systems offers the prospect of signficant cost savings that companies such as General Electric, Ford and General Motors have already begun to reap. The use of e-auction systems leads to low prices and very effective just-in-time purchasing systems with low inventories, even for non-commodity-type items. Search and transaction costs of managing global supply chains are considerably reduced by use of e-business systems. Marketing and selling operations are also affected by enhanced ability to gather market intelligence and to reduce intermediation, search and transactions costs connected to supplying foreign markets.

The firms most likely to be able to acquire such net benefits will be those capable of developing the hardware, software and human resources necessary to design, implement and develop successful global e-business systems. Firms that can create networks that have increasing returns and that recruit large numbers of agents that generate exchanges of valuable information and/or high levels of monetary transactions will benefit most. The ability to effectively transform information gathered from e-business systems into knowledge is also an important element for the ability of firms to derive net benefits from global e-business systems. Overcoming the cultural, institutional and physical asset problems associated with global e-busines systems is a further requirement to be able to reap high net benefits. These considerations suggest that large firms are more likely to be able to muster the necessary resources and wield the necessary market and political power successfully to use global e-business systems.

Analysis of the benefits and obstacles to the use of B2B systems suggest that large firms involved in purchasing commodities or commodity-type items and where it is possible to develop effective just-in-time systems for non-commodity items are most likely to benefit from global supply chains. The international marketing and selling operations of large firms will also benefit from the use of e-business systems. However, many of the problems that e-business operations face are similar to the problems that confront traditional international business operations. In particular, difficulties in operating across different cultures and institutional systems. The cultural and many of the economic barriers to selling products across frontiers will not necessarily be reduced by using e-business systems. Consequently, those firms that face low cultural and economic barriers are most likely to reap net benefits from using global e-business systems.

Small and medium sized firms may be able to find niche markets by developing knowledge that enable them to prosper in global e-business systems. For example, they may be able to supply information on matters such as verification of the bone fides of agents or on the reliability or meaning of Internet data. Some small and medium sized firms may be able to provide specialised products via B2B systems that large firms are unable or unwilling to supply. However, if these products and information are subject to economies of scale or scope such successful small and medium sized firms are likely to be taken over by large firms or they will grow to become large companies. Nonetheless, for those small and medium sized firms that have products, knowledge and resources to 'go global' e-business systems provide a potentially useful tool to help them to implement internationalistion strategies. However, it is probable that such firms would have gone global in the days before the advent of e-business. In other words, e-business systems may not increase the numbers of firms that 'go global' but they may be a crucial component in successful internationalisation strategies.

Global e-business systems will lower the costs of information gathering for small and medium sized firms engaged or seeking to be involved in international business B2B activities. However, the ability of these firms to convert the information into knowledge and to overcome the traditional cultural and institutional problems of conducting international business activities are unlikely to be reduced by using e-business systems.

The use of e-business systems for B2C face very similar benefits and obstacles as those of B2B systems. In B2C markets, the possession of well-known brand names provides significant benefits for B2C firms. International marketing and selling with an unknown brand name is not an easy task. Consequently, well-known brand names provide low-cost indications of quality and engender trust on matters such as reliability and safety. The brand name effect favours large firms that are able to create and sustain famous brand names. This reinforces the view that e-business systems do not necessarily reduce well-known and traditional obstacles to internationalisation. Online supply of customers often requires effective physical distribution systems that can require the development of appropriate 'clicks and mortar' operations. Thus, supplying international markets online does not necessarily lead to substantial lowering of intermediation costs. Furthermore, providing supplies of the correct type of products for a variety cultural and institutional systems may require sophisticated 'clicks and mortar' operations that can adapt products to local market conditions. This also favours large firms.

Firms that can directly supply online with few modifications to cater for different cultural and institutional requirements are the most likely to benefit from global B2C systems. Such firms might include suppliers of software, music and audio-visual products and information that is valuable to consumers. Small and medium sized firms may find niche markets that they can exploit. However, these firms are also likely to have gone global in the days before e-business. Successful small and medium sized firms that are involved in markets that are subject to economies of scale and scope are likely to follow the same path as their cousins in B2B markets (see preceding section).

It is probable that the use of global e-business sytems will not radically alter internationalisation strategies until the obstacles outlined earlier can be significantly reduced. The development of e-business systems and institutional and economic change will, over time, reduce some of these barriers. Nevertheless, some of these barriers, such as problems created by institutional systems and poor physical assets in developing and transition countries, are unlikely to be affected by the development of e-business. Cultural barriers, problems with transforming information into knowledge and balancing the costs of creating network externalities with revenue and/or benefits in kind affect developed, developing and transition countries. Developments in technology, organisational systems and in new Internet-based intermediaries may reduce these problems, but they are likely to remain significant problems. These factors indicate that international business activities will continue, at least in the medium term, to be dominated by large multinational firms, although some of them will be new giants created by the forces of the ICT revolution. Successful small and medium sized firms involved in international business will be successful niche market operators or they will become large by takeover or growth.

The speed and scope of internationalisation strategies will depend on the ability of firms to overcome the obstacles discussed earlier. In particular, the capacity to find solutions to the difficulties of converting information into knowledge, the network externality problem and to overcome cultural, physical asset and institutional complications. Those firms with assets to tackle these problems and that are supplying products or exchanging information that does not face large problems in these areas are most likely to benefit from using global e-business systems.

Summary

The chapter has outlined the potential for and obstacles to radical change in international business activities resulting from the use of e-business systems. The ability of e-business systems to reduce intermediation, search and transaction costs plus the benefits of network externalities has already led to significant changes. However, the limited evidence that is available suggests that these benefits have been, in some quarters, overstated. The problems experienced by dot.com companies that sought to become 'virtual companies' and the evolution of 'clicks and mortar' firms suggests that the main effect of e-business systems is to generate modified business models rather than to create completely new systems of doing business that are radically different from traditional systems. Many of the problems that traditional systems faced when conducting international business activities are also problems for e-business systems. Differences in economic, cultural and institutional systems are still a problem in e-business systems. Indeed, the growth of the Internet has created new problems such as the need for institutional systems that can effectively govern global e-business systems, problems with inadequate physical assets, devising systems and acquiring experience to enable effective transformation of information into knowledge and balancing network externalities with the ability to generate revenue or benefits in-kind to cover sunk costs.

These obstacles to the development of global e-business systems suggest that the pace and scope of internationalisation may not alter dramatically, at least until these obstacles are significantly reduced. Moreover, these obstacles are likely to restrict most small and meduim sized firms from rapid and extensive internationalisation by use of e-business systems. This view of the effects of e-business implies that it will not radically alter the process of internationalisation until the obstacles to establishment and development of global e-business systems are reduced.

Nevertheless, global e-business systems have already altered international business activities. Companies such as Amazon and Yahoo have created large international systems for e-retailing. Large B2B systems such as GXS have introduced global supply chain management systems and developed the use of e-auctions for procurement. Small and medium sized firms have access to new channels of distribution and new Internet-based intermediaries have emerged to help such firms to internationalise. Clearly, the growth of global e-business systems has already altered the conditions for conducting international business operations and this process is likely to grow and develop. E-business systems also offer the prospect of improved management of international business operations by providing low search and transaction costs systems to gather, process and disseminate information across national borders.

The idea that global e-business systems will usher in an age of frictionless and low transaction costs international markets is, however, unlikely to be true. Many problems connected to monopoly power, customer protection, adverse selection and the defence of national and regional cultures are likely to plague global e-business systems. The long-running debate about the need for and type of regulation of international business activities will probably increase as international business activities become ever more influenced by global e-business systems.

Review questions

1 Outline the main benefits of e-business systems for B2C and B2B operations. Assess the empirical evidence on the signficance of these benefits.

2 What are the main obstacles to the development of effective global e-business systems? Which types of firms are most likely to be able to overcome these problems?

3 Discuss the possible impact of the development of global e-business on the pace and scope of internationalisation. Consider the impact according to the size of firms and the industry or sector to which they belong.

4 Assess the main barriers to the development of frictionless and low transaction cost e-markets based on global e-business systems.

5 What problems have already emerged for the regulation of global e-business systems? What other problems are likely to emerge as global e-business systems spread?

Bibliography

Avlonitis, B. and Karayanni, D. (2000) 'The impact of internet use on business to business marketing', *Industrial Marketing Management*, 29, 2, pp. 441–59.

Bennett, R. (1997) 'Export marketing and the internet', *International Marketing Review*, 14, 5, pp. 324–44.

Bradley, S., Hausman, J. and Nolan, R. (1993) *Globalization, Technology and Competition: The Fusion of Computers and Telecommunications in the 1990s*, Boston, MA, Harvard Business School Press.

Brynjolfsson, E. and Smith, M. (2000) 'Frictionless commerce? A comparison of internet and conventional retailers', *Management Science*, 26, 4, pp. 563–85.

Chakrabarti, R. and Scholnick, B. (2002) 'International price competition on the internet: a clinical study of the online book industry' in F. McDonald, H. Tüselmann and C. Wheeler (eds) *International Business in the 21st Century: Change and Continuity – Strategies, Institutions, Regulations and Operations*, London, Palgrave.

Economist (2001a) 'We have lift-off', 3 February, pp. 91–3.

Economist (2001b) 'Time to rebuild', 19 May, pp. 79–80.

Economist (2001c) 'That falling feeling', 15 March, pp. 87–8.

Economist (2000a) 'Too few pennies from heaven', 1 July, pp. 107–110.

Economist (2000b) 'E-management: inside the machine', 9 November, pp. 1–52.

Economist (2000c) 'A market for monopoly', 17 June, pp. 85–6.

Gates, W. H. (1995) '*The Road Ahead*', London, Viking Penguin.

Hamill, J. (1997) 'The internet and international marketing', *International Marketing Review*, 14, 5, pp. 300–23.

Hamill, J. and Gregory, K. (1997) 'Internet marketing in the internationalisation of UK SMEs', *Journal of Marketing Management*, 13, pp. 9–28.

International Trade Forum (2000) 'Executive forum 2000', New York, ITF.

Joint Venture: Silicon Valley Network (2000*) Internet Cluster Analysis 2000*, San Jose, CA, Joint Venture. Available at www.jointventure.org

Kelly, K. (1998) *New Rules for the New Economy: 10 Ways the Network Economy is Changing Everything*, London, Fourth Estate.

OECD (2001a) *Business to Business E-Commerce*, Paris, OECD.

OECD (2001b) *Understanding the Digital Divide*, Paris, OECD.

OECD (2000) 'Dismantling the barriers to global electronic commerce', DSTI/STI/IT (00), Paris, OECD.

OECD (1997) 'Electronic commerce: opportunities and challenges for government – the Sacher Report', DSTI/STI/IT (97), Paris, OECD.

Office of the Presidency of the USA (1998) 'A Framework for Global Electronic Commerce', Washington, DC.

Palvia, P., Palvia, S. and Roche, E. (1996) *Global Information Technology and Systems Management: Key Issues and Trends*, Marietta, GA, Ivy League Publishing.

Prakash, A. (1996) 'The internet as a global IS tool', *Information Systems Management*, 13, 3, pp. 45–9.

Quelch, J. and Klein, L. (1996) 'The internet and international marketing', *Sloan Management Review*, 37, 3, pp. 60–75.

Samli, A., Wills, J. and Herbig, P. (1997) 'The information superhighway goes international: implications for industrial sales transactions', *Industrial Marketing Management*, 26, 2, pp. 51–8.

Sarkar, M., Butler, B. and Steinfield, C. (1998) 'Cybermediaries in electronic marketplace: towards theory building', *Journal of Business Research*, 41, 2, pp. 215–21.

Shapiro, C. and Varian, H. (1999) *Information Rules: A Strategic Guide to the Network Economy*, Boston, MA, Harvard Business School Press.

Smith, M., Bailey, J. and Brynjolfsson, E. (2000) 'Understanding digital markets' in E. Brynjolfsson and B. Kahin (eds) *Understanding the Digital Economy*, Cambridge, MA, MIT Press.

Speier, C., Harvey, M. and Palmer, J. (1998) 'Virtual management of global marketing relationships', *Journal of World Business*, 33, 3, pp. 263–76.

Stehr, N. (1994) *Knowledge Societies*, London, Sage.

UNCTAD (1998a) 'Policy issues relating to access to participation in electronic commerce', TD/B/Com.3/16, New York, UNCTAD.

UNCTAD (1998b) 'Implications for trade and development of recent proposals to set up a global framework for electronic commerce', TD/B/Com.3/17, New York, UNCTAD.

Wind, J. and Mahajan, V. (2001) *Digital Marketing: Global Strategies from the World's Leading Experts*, Pennsylvania, PA, The Wharton School.

Useful websites

Commercial sites with case studies, examples and data on the use of e-business
www.ibm.com/e-business
www.pricewaterhousecooper.com
www.cisco.com
www.forrester.com
www.bcg.com
www.oracle.com
www.sun.com
www.jointventure.org

Sites of institutions with reports on e-business
www.oecd.org
www.europa.eu.int
www.usic.org

Sites of publications with reports, reviews and case studies
www.economist.com
www.ft.com
www.infoworld.com

Case 14.1 General Electric – Global eXchange Services (GXS)

The origins of GXS stem from the 1960s when General Electric (GE) collaborated with Dartmouth College in the USA to develop BASIC, the first online interactive language. In the 1970s, the forerunner of GXS – GE Information Services – developed EDI systems for purchasing operations. In the 1980s Internet-based technologies were introduced to these EDI systems and by 2001, GXS had over 100,0000 trading partners in 58 countries, conducting one billion transactions per year with a value of $1 trillion. In 1998 GXS and Worldcom merged their data exchange systems thereby creating the world's largest Internet system for B2B transactions.

GXS provide software systems that permit secure information exchange for one-to-one, one-to-many and many-to-many B2B transactions. The system uses Internet data exchange (IDE) that can be used for purchasing, planning and managing supply chains and for logistics operations. IDE has been estimated by GXS to lead to cost savings of up to 30% on these activities.

The IDE system can be used to plan supply chains by searching for suppliers, subcontractors, transport and distribution services The system also allows information to be exchanged on technical specifications, project timetables, legal requirements to fulfil contracts, payment systems and drafting of contracts etc. Indeed, most of the planning, management and operational aspects of supply chains can be conducted by using GXS systems. IDE allows for purchasing operations to be linked to sophisticated just-in-time systems and for delivery and quality targets to be monitored and assessed. A large database of requests to tender for supply is available on the system and it is possible for 'virtual' companies to create a supply chain using the GXS system. These companies may only provide the service of constructing the components of the supply chain – suppliers, subcontractors, assemblers, logistical systems and installers. These virtual firms may have no physical contact with the products provided. An example of such a virtual firm is Nortel Networks, a subsidiary of Northern Telecom of Canada. Nortel Networks supplies telecommunications equipment by using B2B systems to construct a supply chain and often has no contact with the physical equipment that it supplies.

The most significant cost savings, up to 50%, have been acquired by GE using the IDE system of GXS to reduce prices and purchasing costs by using online auctions for commodity-type items. GE has also used the IDE system to help to codify specifications, delivery and quality data for several required supplies thus making them commodity-type items. This opens the way for expanding the use of online auctions and enlarging the cost savings possible by using IDE. GE has also used GXS to expand the size and scope of searches for supplies and has thereby achieved lower prices even for non-commodity items. GE plan to source 70% of supplies by using e-auctions and a large part of the supplies will involve international trade particularly from developing economies such as China.

The system used by GE for e-auctions is called trading processing network (TPN) and provides access to over two million items from 1,300 suppliers. TPN allows bids to be made for supplies and includes systems for settling payments, delivery arrangements and terms for contracts. In April 2001 GXS made TPN available to any member of its network of users.

Economist (2000) 'The shape of the new company', and 'Trying to connect you', 9 November; Infoworld (2001) www.infoworld, 14 April; 'Company profile on Nortel' in R. Tung (ed.) *The Handbook on International Business*, London, Thomson Learning, pp. 736–7, and website of GXS – www.geis.com

Case 14.2 Dell Computers

In 1984 Michael Dell founded Dell Computers to clone PCs based on IBM's design. The components for PCs rapidly became commodities that could be bought on global spot markets at low prices. Dell Computers pioneered the use of e-business systems to gather the components for PCs, assemble them and use the Internet to sell to customers. This system allowed Dell to operate with very low inventories, to have low intermediation costs and rapidly to build up a large network of potential customers. This allowed Dell to gain a large market share and to make high profits.

The crucial ingredients for the success of Dell were that PCs where highly standardised with a large and low-priced markets for the components that went into computers. Dell established a large market among customers who understood PCs and did not require sophisticated sales and after-sales service. Dell could therefore operate with low inventories and avoid the need for retail outlets. However, other computer companies have been unable to follow in

Dell's footsteps. Gateway, a PC supplier, was founded on the same lines as Dell but developed retail outlets as the demand for PCs has extended to people who require more help in making purchases and also need personal after sales advice and help. Other computer equipment firms such as Cisco Systems have not been able to go down the same path as Dell because they manufacture more complex computer equipment that requires a large number of non-standard components that cannot be bought on global spot markets. Hence Cisco Systems often have to keep large inventories because they have to order components well in advance of production. If demand for their computer equipment is not as forecasted they end up with stocks of components that cannot be sold on spot markets.

The Dell case indicates that the type of product sold and the characteristics of customers are important factors in the success or otherwise of e-business systems in terms of market share and profitability.

Economist (2001) 'A revolution of one', 14 April, p. 84

Case 14.3 International and European online retailing by UK- and Irish-based SMEs

To meet the expected demand from small and medium sized enterprises (SMEs) for software packages that provide the facilities to construct web pages, a number of companies have emerged to supply systems that enable companies to construct their own web page that is suitable for online selling. A study of 36 SMEs which had purchased a software package from two such companies (Intershop and RedWeb) revealed that 50% offered online buying services to their domestic customers. Only 40% offered online buying to customers in the EU and 35% provided this service to the rest of the world. Although the web facility included an effective online ordering system with a secure billing facility the majority of the firms with these systems did not use them to engage in international online selling. All the companies sold products that, in principal, could have been sold on international markets as they offered personal goods or services such as specialist clothing, holidays and travel services.

Distribution problems did not seem to cause many problems as most of the companies used their national postal systems to arrange delivery.

Many of the companies that did not sell online in international markets reported that they did not know how to deal with the problems of taxation, import duties and technical regulations. In the case of EU purchases, these issues are not a significant problem because there are no import duties and very few obstacles caused by technical regulations. Taxation issues for intra-EU transactions are also covered by well-known procedures. Nevertheless, few of the companies used their web page to sell in the EU market. All the UK SMEs provided information on prices only in their national currency. The Irish companies quoted their prices in Irish punts and euros. In all cases the information on the websites were written in English and no information was provided on taxation, import duties or regulations governing foreign purchasers. Moreover, the design of many of the websites were focused on the expectations and requirements of domestic buyers.

The main problems appear to be connected to taxation, import duties and technical regulations. None of the websites made any provision for economic, legal and cultural diversity that might affect demand for their products. Many of the problems that SMEs are experiencing with online selling in international markets seem to be similar to the problems they face with normal international selling. As well as the problems of providing suitable systems for online trading the SMEs also face problems convincing customers to buy online. These problems include consumer protection issues and providing sufficient after-sales and other value-added services. It seems that current web-based technologies and organisational systems prevent e-commerce systems from delivering SMEs from many of the traditional problems that make it difficult for them to engage in international selling.

Study by International Business Unit, Manchester Metropolitan University, 2000

Case 14.4 Napster and copyright on the Internet

Napster developed a software system that allowed music to be downloaded from the Internet. This system was provided free to anyone who had a PC capable of receiving codes for the music via Napster's web page. The technology pioneered by Napster can also be used to exchange digital information for other audio-visual products such as films and recorded television programmes. Not surprisingly, this free service caused audio-visual producers such as Sony, Warner Music, EMI and Bertelsmann Music Group some concern as their products were in danger of becoming free goods. Legal action to stop Napster was taken by the Recording Industry Association of America on behalf of the major music producers.

Courts in the USA supported the copyright privileges of music and other audio-visual producers by outlawing infringement of copyright by the digital exchange of audio-visual material. In response to these developments fee-paying online providers have emerged. These include a joint venture between Napster and Bertelsmann Music Group and MusicNet (an alliance between Warner Music, Bertelsmann Music Group and EMI). Software and computer manufacturers have also responded by creating software that prevents unauthorised copying of audio-visual material (e.g. Microsoft's Media Player) and a hardware system for preventing copying developed by Matsushita and Toshiba – Content Protection for Recordable Media.

The established providers of audio-visual material and software and hardware providers acted quickly to create systems that allow them to retain control of copyright in digital exchange systems. However, this does not mean the online provision will not take place, but it is unlikely to be free. Indeed, online provision has attractions for producers of audio-visual material because intermediation costs are reduced and access is provided to large networks of potential customers. The use of this technology is likely to lead to the creation of new business models that are likely to be dominated by large multinational corporations in the media industry. The creation of AOL Time Warner may be the forerunner of new multinational giants that are a fusion of media and Internet-based firms. These firms are likely to dominate e-business systems for the sale and distribution of audio-visual products.

Economist (2000) 'Napster and the rise of P2P', 4 November, pp. 109–10; *Economist* (2001) 'Napster loses another round', 17 February, pp. 86–91

Index